This handbook belongs to

_____
Name

_____
Address

_____
City/State/ZIP Code

_____
Telephone

_____
Trail Name (if any)

In case of emergency, contact

_____
Name

_____
Telephone

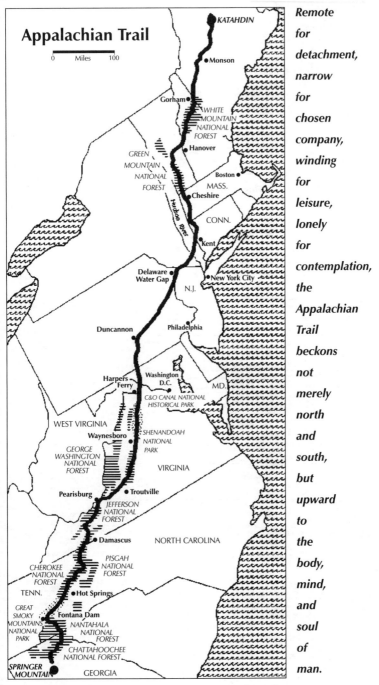

Appalachian Trail

0 Miles 100

KATAHDIN
• Monson
Gorham •
WHITE MOUNTAIN NATIONAL FOREST
GREEN MOUNTAIN NATIONAL FOREST
Hanover •
Boston •
MASS.
Cheshire •
CONN.
Kent •
Delaware Water Gap •
New York City •
N.J.
Duncannon •
Philadelphia •
Harpers Ferry •
Washington D.C.
MD.
C&O CANAL NATIONAL HISTORICAL PARK
WEST VIRGINIA
Waynesboro •
SHENANDOAH NATIONAL PARK
GEORGE WASHINGTON NATIONAL FOREST
VIRGINIA
Pearisburg •
• Troutville
JEFFERSON NATIONAL FOREST
• Damascus
NORTH CAROLINA
PISGAH NATIONAL FOREST
CHEROKEE NATIONAL FOREST
TENN.
• Hot Springs
GREAT SMOKY MOUNTAINS NATIONAL PARK
Fontana Dam
NANTAHALA NATIONAL FOREST
CHATTAHOOCHEE NATIONAL FOREST
SPRINGER MOUNTAIN
GEORGIA

Hudson River

Remote for detachment, narrow for chosen company, winding for leisure, lonely for contemplation, the Appalachian Trail beckons not merely north and south, but upward to the body, mind, and soul of man.

Often-quoted stanza above composed by PATC member Harold Allen in 1936

THE THRU-HIKER'S HANDBOOK

Bob "501" McCaw

2010 Edition

CENTER FOR APPALACHIAN TRAIL STUDIES

www.trailplace.com

The Thru-hiker's Handbook

Cover photo: *JERMM on top of the Priest, photo used with permission*

Center for Appalachian Trail Studies
17 South Meadow Drive
Sudbury, MA 01776-3391
781-752-6100

ISBN 978-0-9707916-6-5

Printed in the United States of America

2010 Edition

About this Handbook

The Thru-hiker's Handbook was first published in the spring of 1991 by the Appalachian Trail Conference. It replaced *The Philosopher's Guide,* ATC's original thru-hiker guide, which was retired by its author at the end of the 1990 thru-hiking season. *The Thru-hiker's Handbook* was published by ATC from 1991 through 1993, and by Dan "Wingfoot" Bruce from 1994 through 2007.

This is the third year of publication by the current author. Both the "trail" and the "town" sections of the book contain new information this year. I hope you find the *Handbook* complete and easy-to-use.

--Bob McCaw

How to Give Feedback

Users of this guide are requested to give feedback. Corrections, suggestions, comments, and information for improving the 2011 edition can be sent to "Handbook" c/o the Center at the address above, or e-mail feedback to <*webmaster@trailplace.com*>.

Contents

2010

JANUARY

S	M	T	W	T	F	S
					1	2
3	4	5	6	7	8	9
10	11	12	13	14	15	16
17	18	19	20	21	22	23
24	25	26	27	28	29	30
31						

FEBRUARY

S	M	T	W	T	F	S
	1	2	3	4	5	6
7	8	9	10	11	12	13
14	15	16	17	18	19	20
21	22	23	24	25	26	27
28						

MARCH

S	M	T	W	T	F	S
	1	2	3	4	5	6
7	8	9	10	11	12	13
14	15	16	17	18	19	20
21	22	23	24	25	26	27
28	29	30	31			

APRIL

S	M	T	W	T	F	S
				1	2	3
4	5	6	7	8	9	10
11	12	13	14	15	16	17
18	19	20	21	22	23	24
25	26	27	28	29	30	

MAY

S	M	T	W	T	F	S
						1
2	3	4	5	6	7	8
9	10	11	12	13	14	15
16	17	18	19	20	21	22
23	24	25	26	27	28	29
30	31					

JUNE

S	M	T	W	T	F	S
		1	2	3	4	5
6	7	8	9	10	11	12
13	14	15	16	17	18	19
20	21	22	23	24	25	26
27	28	29	30			

JULY

S	M	T	W	T	F	S
				1	2	3
4	5	6	7	8	9	10
11	12	13	14	15	16	17
18	19	20	21	22	23	24
25	26	27	28	29	30	31

AUGUST

S	M	T	W	T	F	S
1	2	3	4	5	6	7
8	9	10	11	12	13	14
15	16	17	18	19	20	21
22	23	24	25	26	27	28
29	30	31				

SEPTEMBER

S	M	T	W	T	F	S
			1	2	3	4
5	6	7	8	9	10	11
12	13	14	15	16	17	18
19	20	21	22	23	24	25
26	27	28	29	30		

OCTOBER

S	M	T	W	T	F	S
					1	2
3	4	5	6	7	8	9
10	11	12	13	14	15	16
17	18	19	20	21	22	23
24	25	26	27	28	29	30
31						

NOVEMBER

S	M	T	W	T	F	S
	1	2	3	4	5	6
7	8	9	10	11	12	13
14	15	16	17	18	19	20
21	22	23	24	25	26	27
28	29	30				

DECEMBER

S	M	T	W	T	F	S
			1	2	3	4
5	6	7	8	9	10	11
12	13	14	15	16	17	18
19	20	21	22	23	24	25
26	27	28	29	30	31	

Hiker Festivals along the A.T. in 2010

April 2-4 – April 1st Hiker Fool Bash, Franklin, North Carolina
TBA – White Blaze Day, Gatlinburg, Tennessee
May 13-16 – Trail Days, Damascus, Virginia
June 5 – Hiker Fest, Waynesboro, Virginia
August 1 – B-Town Chowdown, Bennington, Vermont
August 6-8 – Long Trail Festival, Rutland, Vermont
September 11-12 – Trail's End Festival, Millinocket, Maine
December 5 – Christmas Party, Franklin, North Carolina

Key to Symbols and Abbreviations

- 📖 – see cross reference
- S – shelter, lean-to
- ↺ – left off the A.T.
- ↻ – right off the A.T.
- ← – south on A.T.
- → – north on A.T.
- S,N – South, North
- m – mile or miles
- R – road crossing
- w – water source

- H – hostel or equivalent
- C – camping, campsite
- L – commercial lodging
- M – meals, place to eat
- G – grocery store, groceries
- O – outfitter store
- Lm – laundry facility
- f – stove fuel (any kind)
- ? – unreliable or limited
- ' – feet (with altitudes)

Introduction

The Thru-hiker's Handbook is a field guide designed for use by thru-hikers and long-distance section hikers on the Appalachian Trail. It is designed to help you know where you are and what is around you at any given point on the A.T., and to help you find goods and services when you leave the woods to rest and resupply in nearby towns.

The entire A.T. is described in this guide, which has two main sections. Section 1 is a "Mileage Index," which you will use primarily in the woods. It is a collection of tables listing Trail features together with each feature's distance in miles from Springer and Katahdin, with services available at each point revealed by coded abbreviations. Section 2 is a collection of "Thru-hiker Notes," primarily information about nearby towns and services. Both sections are arranged from Georgia to Maine as you read this guide front to back. The Section 1 mileage figures can be easily read by hikers traveling either northbound or southbound, with the off-Trail features cross-referenced to Section 2.

Information about a wide variety of features and facilities along the footpath and in nearby towns is provided. The information on nearby services is intended to be fairly complete and give enough detail that you can make an intelligent decision whether you want to go into town when you come to a road. In larger places, not every service is listed. It is important to note that this guide does not try to preview everything you can see or do on the A.T., though, nor does it try to provide every possible detail about any particular place or feature. It gives you basic information that will help you function efficiently and make good decisions during your hike, but leaves you plenty of leeway for scouting out things on your own. It assumes you will want to ask questions and explore.

This guide also assumes that you are the type of person who wants to form your own opinions about things, so it does not rate the various features on the footpath or businesses and services in towns for you, nor does it dictate to you the "best" or "approved" or "most popular" things to see and do on your hike. By not previewing everything, and by not rating or recommending one Trail feature, facility, or service over another, this guide leaves you free to be adventurous and spontaneous during your trek—to make your own decisions and pursue a personal journey of discovery as you hike your own hike.

As a way of keeping this guide compact and lightweight, some information useful for planning but not needed once a hike is underway is provided in the "Hiker Resources" section on our *Trailplace.com* website instead of being included here, as follows:

• ***Travel to Springer Mtn*** ... complete directions for traveling to Springer Mountain by personal vehicle or public conveyance (print out what you need).

• ***Travel to Mt. Katahdin*** ... complete directions for traveling to Mt. Katahdin by personal vehicle or public conveyance (print out what you need).

• ***Shuttles to Trailheads*** ... a searchable database of people or businesses who provide transportation to Springer Mountain or Mt. Katahdin, or to locations in between.

• ***A.T. Clubs, A.T.-related Websites*** ... links to the official websites of the local A.T. maintaining clubs, plus links to other important Trail-related websites.

In addition to this handbook, it is recommended that users carry a sectional map published by the Appalachian Trail Conservancy for each section that is being hiked. This guide provides elevation profiles corresponding to each "trail" page. These profiles will give you a general sense of the difficulty of a particular section the trail, but don't provide the detail a map would

Is this handbook totally accurate? Every effort has been to make it up-to-date, but the Trail and its surrounding communities are ever-changing. Reroutes will happen all year along the footpath and some businesses in Trail towns will undoubtedly close or change services, so expect a few surprises now and then. In general, though, the information in this guide should prove trustworthy.

If you find that things are not as described in the handbook, it will be greatly appreciated if you take notes about things that need to be changed and report them when you return home. Addresses for sending feedback are listed in this book, and you will be acknowledged as a contributor in the 2010 edition.

The following policies have been strictly observed since Dan Bruce began producing this handbook in 1990. No business or service ever pays to be listed. In addition, no one is paid for furnishing information. A conscious decision has been made to include as many establishments of use to hikers as possible. Because many hikers are on a tight budget, we have gone out of our way to list inexpensive places to stay.

A listing in this guide is not necessarily an endorsement or certification of quality of services offered. Some of the cheaper establishments may be a bit of an adventure! If you have problems, however, please let us know. Your feedback is very important.

Finally, as you begin your hike, a few words of advice are offered. Do not let yourself get focused only on the things listed in this handbook. It is merely a guide to features and services along the A.T., an aid to help your trip go a little smoother, with a tidbit of commentary thrown in here and there to give some perspective. Explore beyond the pages of this handbook each day and many wonderful things will happen during your hike that cannot be anticipated or described in any guidebook. The real story of your adventure is out there on the Appalachian Trail—waiting for you to live it.

HAVE A GREAT HIKE!

"There are only two ways to live life, as though nothing is a miracle, or as though everything is."—Albert Einstein

Always check for the latest updates to this guide before heading to the Trail; see the "Handbook Updates" section on our website <www.trailplace.com>.

Mileage Index

Features along the entire Appalachian Trail are listed in the mileage tables of this section, arranged geographically from Georgia to Maine in the order they would be encountered by a hiker traveling **northbound**. All directions off the Trail (either "right" or "left") are presented from the viewpoint of the northbounder as well. Each feature has mileage figures showing total distance from Springer and Katahdin. Distance between any two points on the A.T. can be calculated by subtracting miles for one point from the other. The symbol 📖 *p.142* indicates that additional information about a feature is available in the "Thru-hiker Notes" section, on the page indicated by the number that follows the little open-book symbol. The following meanings apply to symbols, abbreviations, and terms used in the mileage tables:

S – an official A.T. shelter; also called "lean-to" or "hut" in some areas. Shelters are listed with direction and distance off the Trail, type and location of water source, and distance to the next shelter south and north, the latter indicated in this way ←*S8.6m* | *N4.4m*→ on the line below the shelter's name.

R – a recognizable vehicle path, can be anything from an overgrown and/or unpaved woods road to an interstate highway.

H – a hiker hostel, or any place that offers basic hiker accommodations at substantially less cost than non-hikers are charged for overnight stay.

C – any place that has been regularly used for camping, including designated campsites and commercial campgrounds (but note that off-Trail camping is allowed anywhere along the A.T. except as noted herein as a "no camping" area).

L – any commercial lodging facility (usually means a hotel, motel, or B&B).

M – any place where prepared food or meals are sold (usually means a restaurant).

G – any place that sells grocery items (from convenience store to supermarket).

O – any place that sells basic backpacking gear (usually means an outfitter).

Lm – indicates laundry facilities available for use by the hiking public.

f – denotes that fuel for backpacking stoves is available by the ounce.

w – any source of water (but does not guarantee that the water is potable).

? – qualifies something as limited or unreliable (usually combined with one of the above abbreviations, e.g., "w?" indicates an unreliable water source).

Also note—The term "stream" denotes any kind of free-flowing water source, including brooks, creeks, and rivers. Towns are listed in bold print, with the most frequently used towns shown in all capital letters. Distance off the Trail to a town is usually from the A.T. to the post office, and all towns listed with ZIP codes have post offices. Some features shown as separated by one-tenth of a mile may actually be closer together.

Approach Trail

Miles from Springer	Features / Services	Miles from Amicalola
8.8	Amicalola Falls State Park 📖 p. 102 (1820') visitor center .... C,w	0.0
8.7	**Max Epperson Shelter** (1840') for thru-hikers only .... S	0.1
---	left 200ft, get water at visitor center, ←none|N7.2m→	---
8.3	Parking Lot (2050')..	0.5
8.0	Bottom of Amicalola Falls(2160') base of 600 step staircase....................	0.8
7.8	Top of Amicalola Falls (2520') parking lot.	1.0
7.6	Amicalola Lodge Road (2560') right 0.2m to lodge .... R,L,M,w	1.2
7.4	Trail to Len Foote Hike Inn (2570') right 5m to inn .... L,M	1.4
7.3	Stream (2560') footbridge .... w	1.5
7.2	USFS Road 46 (2585') steps on north side .... R	1.6
5.6	High Shoals Road (2760') .... R	3.2
4.0	Frosty Mtn (3384') spring right 0.2m, unreliable .... C,w?	4.8
3.7	Frosty Mtn Road, USFS Road 46 (3200') .... R	5.1
3.4	Trail to Len Foote Hike Inn (3250') right 1m to inn .... L,M	5.4
3.1	Woody Knob (3406')	5.7
2.8	Nimblewill Gap, USFS Road 28 (3100') .... R	6.0
2.6	Spring (3220') off trail to left, unreliable .... w?	6.2
1.5	**Black Gap Shelter** (3220') .... S,w	7.3
---	left 300ft, spring 200yds across trail, ←S7.2m|N1.7m→	---
0.0	Springer Mtn (3782') plaque, sign, register .... terminus	8.8

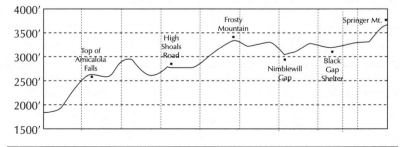

Georgia

Miles from Katahdin	Features / Services	Miles from Springer
2179.1	Springer Mtn 📖 p.103 (3782') plaque, sign, register .... terminus	0.0
2178.9	**Springer Mtn Shelter** (3730') sleeps 12, tent pads (1993) .... S,C,w	0.2
---	right 0.2m, water source is spring, ←S1.7m|N2.6m→	---
2178.8	Benton MacKaye Trail (3720') several crossings over next 5 miles.............	0.3
2178.1	Big Stamp Gap, USFS Road 42 (3350') parking area .... R	1.0
2177.5	Davis Creek (3380') .... w	1.6
2176.9	Stream (3100') several streams cross A.T. .... w	2.2
2176.3	**Stover Creek Shelter** (2870') sleeps 16, tent pads (2006) .... S,w	2.8
---	right 200ft, stream on A.T. before shelter, ←S2.6m|N5.0m→	---
2176.2	Stover Creek 📖 p.103 (2850') trail follows creek for about a mile................ w	2.9
2175.3	Stover Creek (2700') trail crosses on footbridge...................................... w	3.8
2174.9	Benton MacKaye/Duncan Ridge Trails (2580') both join A.T.	4.2
2174.9	Chester Creek (2545') unofficial campsites .... C,w	4.2
2174.8	Three Forks, USFS Road 58 (2530') trail goes straight ahead.................... R	4.3
2174.0	Trail to Long Creek Falls (2850') left 200ft to falls, BMT leaves to left............ w	5.1
2173.1	Logging road (3075') Hickory Flats, church pavilion 0.2m left................... R	6.0
2171.3	**Hawk Mtn Shelter** (3260') sleeps 12 (1993) .... S,w	7.8
---	left 0.2m, spring 350yds behind shelter, ←S5.0m|N7.3m→	---
2170.8	Hightower Gap, USFS Roads 42/69 (2854') .... R	8.3
2168.9	Horse Gap (2675')	10.2
2167.9	Sassafras Mtn (3340')	11.2
2167.3	Cooper Gap, USFS Roads 42/80 (2830') .... R	11.8
2166.7	Justus Mtn (3225')	12.4
2166.0	Phyllis Spur (3100')	13.1
2165.3	Justus Creek (2560') footbridge, unofficial campsites .... C,w	13.8
2164.0	**Gooch Mtn Shelter** (2730') sleeps 14, tent sites .... S,w	15.1
---	left 100yds, spring near shelter, ←S7.3m|N11.9m→	---
2162.9	Spring (2850') on A.T. to right .... w	16.2
2162.6	Gooch Gap, USFS Road 42 (2780') spring right 200yds .... R,w	16.5
---	left 2.7m to Suches (see Woody Gap below)	---
2160.4	Ramrock Mtn (3200') viewpoint, north of summit................................	18.7
2159.0	Woody Gap, GA60 📖 p.103 (3170') parking, picnic table, rest rooms........ R	20.1
---	left 1.9m–to **Suches, GA 30572** .... C,G,f?	---
---	right 6m–to private hostel .... H,L,Lm,f	---
2158.9	Spring (3200') 500ft left .... w	20.2
2158.0	Big Cedar Mtn (3740') AT skirts summit..	21.1
2156.8	Stream (3330') crosses A.T. .... w	22.3
2156.5	Granny Top Mtn (3395')	22.6

Georgia

Miles from Katahdin	Features / Services	Miles from Springer
2156.1	Dockery Lake Trail *(3025')* right 3m to lake	23.0
2155.8	Stream *(2880')* crosses A.T. .... C,w	23.3
2155.0	Side Trail to Henry Gap *(3120')* left 200ft to road	24.1
2153.5	Spring *(3400')* on A.T. to right, unreliable .... w?	25.6
2153.4	Jarrard Gap *(3260')* left 0.3m to stream, campsites .... C,w	25.7
2152.4	Turkey Stamp Mtn *(3770')*	26.7
2152.1	**Woods Hole Shelter** *(3620')* sleeps 7 *(1998)* .... S,w	27.0
---	*left 0.4m, spring on path to shelter, ←S11.9m	N1.3m→*	---
2152.0	Bird Gap *(3650')*	27.1
---	*Freeman Trail, to right, bypasses Blood Mt., leads 1.8m to Flatrock Gap*	---
2151.7	Slaughter Creek Trail *(3795')* descends to left, spring at intersection .... w	27.4
---	**Notice!** *no campfires permitted north from here to Neels Gap*	---
2151.6	Slaughter Creek Campsite *(3860')* to the right, tent platforms C	27.5
2151.5	Duncan Ridge Trail/Coosa Trail *(4150')* descends to the left	27.6
2150.8	**Blood Mtn Shelter** *(4461')* vistas (view of Springer Mtn), sleeps 8 *(1934)* .... S	28.3
---	*on A.T., no water, ←S1.3m	N8.6m→*	---
2149.4	Flatrock Gap *(3450')* spring left 0.2m, ... w	29.7
---	*Freeman Trail, right, bypasses Blood Mt., leads 1.8m to Bird Gap*	---
---	Balance Rock *(3440')* on A.T. to right	29.8
---	**Notice!** *no campfires permitted south from here to Slaughter Gap*	---
2148.4	Neels Gap, US19 📖 *p.103* *(3125')* .... R	30.7
---	*On A.T.–Walasi-Yi Center* .... H,G,O,Lm,f	---
---	*left 2m–to Vogel State Park* .... C,G?,Lm	---
---	*left 14m–to* **Blairsville, GA 30512** .... L,M,G,Lm	---
---	*right 17m–to* **Dahlonega, GA 30533** .... L,M,G,Lm	---
2147.3	Bull Gap *(3644')* spring left 200yds .... C,w	31.8
2146.9	Levelland Mtn *(3890')* AT skirts summit	32.2
2145.6	Rock Spring Top *(3520')* spring near A.T. to left, south of height of land.... C,w	33.5
2145.0	Wolf Laurel Top *(3766')* AT skirts summit	34.1
2144.2	Baggs Creek Gap *(3500')* spring 200ft left .... w	34.9
2143.7	Cowrock Mtn *(3842')* vistas	35.4
2142.9	Tesnatee Gap, GA348 📖 *p.104* *(3138')* parking area .... R	36.2
2142.4	Wildcat Mtn *(3700')*	36.7
2142.2	**Whitley Gap Shelter** *(3650')* sleeps 6 *(1974)* .... S,w	36.9
---	*right 1.2m, spring 0.3m beyond shelter, ←S8.6m	N4.6m→*	---
2142.0	Hogpen Gap, GA348 *(3450')* spring right 100ft, parking .... R,w	37.1
2141.1	White Oak Stamp *(3490')*	38.0
2140.4	Sapling Gap *(3450')*	38.7

Georgia

Miles from Katahdin	Features / Services	Miles from Springer
2140.1	Poor Mtn *(3650')*	39.0
2139.5	Wide Gap *(3150')*	39.6
2138.4	Sheep Rock Top *(3575')*	40.7
2137.6	**Low Gap Shelter** *(3040') sleeps 7 (1953)* .... S,w	41.5
---	*right 200ft, spring in front of shelter, ←S4.6m ｜ N7.2m→*	---
2137.2	Stream *(3180') crosses A.T.* w	41.9
2136.2	Poplar Stamp Gap *(3350') stream 300ft right* w	42.9
2135.7	Stream *(3570') several streams cross A.T.* w	43.4
2133.8	Cold Springs Gap *(3250')*	45.3
2132.6	Chattahoochee Gap *(3500') spring right 0.5m* w	46.5
---	*Jacks Knob Trail left following ridgeline 2.4m to GA180*	---
2132.0	Red Clay Gap *(3455') spring left 0.4m* w	47.1
2131.3	Rocky Knob *(3610') former shelter site* C	47.8
2131.1	Spring *(3540') left 50ft* w	48.0
2130.6	Spring *(3850') left 25ft* w	48.5
2130.4	**Blue Mtn Shelter** *(3890') sleeps 7 (1988)* .... S,w	48.7
---	*left 200ft, spring 300yds south on A.T., ←S7.2m ｜ N7.8m→*	---
2129.6	Blue Mtn *(4025')*	49.5
2128.2	Unicoi Gap, GA75 📖 *p.104 (2950') parking area, plaque* .... R	50.9
---	*left 11m*–to **HIAWASSEE, GA 30546** L,M,G,Lm	---
---	*right 10m*–to **Helen, GA 30545** L,M,G,Lm	---
2127.6	Stream *(3430') crosses A.T.* w	51.5
2127.2	Rocky Mt. Trail *(3700') to left*	51.9
2126.9	Rocky Mtn *(4020') campsites on side trail to right* C	52.2
2125.6	Indian Grave Gap, USFS Road 283 *(3115')* R	53.5
2124.9	Tray Mtn Road, USFS Road 79 *(3450')* R	54.2
2124.6	Cheese Factory Site *(3590') campsites, spring* C,w	54.5
2124.0	Cliff *(3820') on A.T. to right, vista*	55.1
2123.8	Tray Gap, Tray Mtn Road, USFS Road 79/698 *(3850')* R	55.3
2123.0	Tray Mtn *(4430')*	56.1
2122.6	**Tray Mtn Shelter** *(4200') grassy campsites, sleeps 7 (1971)* .... S,C,w	56.5
---	*left 0.2m, spring 250yds behind shelter, ←S7.8m ｜ N7.5m→*	---
2121.0	Steeltrap Gap *(3500') spring to right* w	58.1
2120.5	Young Lick Knob *(3800')*	58.6
2119.0	Swag of the Blue Ridge *(3400')*	60.1
2118.2	Round Top *(3780') A.T. does not cross summit*	60.9
2117.8	Sassafras Gap *(3500') spring right 150yds* w	61.3
2117.0	Addis Gap *(3310') stream right 0.5m at USFS 26* C,w	62.1

Georgia-North Carolina

Features / Services

Miles from Katahdin	Features / Services	Miles from Springer
2116.0	Kelly Knob *(4160')* A.T. skirts summit	63.1
2115.1	**Deep Gap Shelter** *(3550')* sleeps 12 (1983) .... S,w	64.0
---	*right 0.25m, spring on path to shelter, ←S7.5m	N8.0m→*	---
2114.2	Viewpoint *(3860')*	64.9
2114.0	McClure Gap *(3730')* campsite C	65.1
2112.8	Moreland Gap *(3050')* .... w	66.3
2111.6	Dicks Creek Gap, US76 📖 *p.105 (2660')* picnic area, parking .... R,w	67.5
---	*left 3.5m*–to private hostel .... H,C,M?,f	---
---	*left 11m*–to **HIAWASSEE, GA 30546** .... L,M,G,Lm	---
2110.5	Campsite *(3160')* stream 0.1m north on A.T. .... C,w	68.6
2109.8	Cowart Gap *(2900')*	69.3
2108.6	Buzzard Knob *(3680')* trail skirts summits of twin knobs	70.5
2108.3	Bull Gap *(3550')*	70.8
2107.1	**Plumorchard Gap Shelter** *(3100')* sleeps 14 (1993) .... S,w	72.0
---	*right 0.2m, spring 600ft across A.T., ←S8.0m	N7.3m→*	---
2106.4	As Knob *(3440')*	72.7
2105.8	Blue Ridge Gap *(3020')* USFS 72 (abandoned) .... R?	73.3
2104.8	Campsite *(3500')* on A.T. to left, spring unreliable .... C,w?	74.3
2104.6	Rich Cove Gap *(3400')*	74.5
2103.9	Viewpoint *(3670')* on A.T. to left	75.2
2102.7	Georgia-North Carolina border *(3820')*	76.4
2102.6	Spring *(3840')* to right and downhill 100ft .... C,w	76.5
2102.6	Bly Gap *(3850')* old road .... R?	76.5
2101.6	Courthouse Bald *(4520')* viewpoint left 30ft	77.5
2100.7	Sassafras Gap *(4220')*	78.4
2099.8	**Muskrat Creek Shelter** *(4600')* two streams cross A.T., sleeps 8 (1995) ... S,w	79.3
---	*right 100ft at second stream ←S7.3m	N4.9m→*	---
2099.2	Whiteoak Stamp *(4600')* spring right 400ft, unreliable .... w?	79.9
2099.0	Chunky Gal Trail *(4660')* left 5.5m to US64	80.1
2097.9	Wateroak Gap *(4490')*	81.2
2095.8	Deep Gap, USFS Road 71 *(4340')* parking, water 600ft right................. C,w	83.3
---	*Kimsey Creek Trail left 3.7m to Standing Indian Campground*	---
2094.9	**Standing Indian Shelter** *(4760')* sleeps 8 (1996) .... S,w	84.2
---	*right 100yds, water from stream, ←S4.9m	N7.6m→*	---
2093.4	Standing Indian Mtn *(5430')* summit right 600ft .... w	85.7
---	*Lower Trail Ridge Trail left 100ft to spring, 4.2m to Stand. Ind. CG*	---
2090.5	Beech Gap *(4480')* spring right 100ft, several streams cross A.T. to north.... w	88.6
---	*Beech Gap Trail left 2.8m to USFS Road 67*	---

North Carolina

Miles from Katahdin	Features / Services	Miles from Springer
2088.7	Coleman Gap *(4150')* rhododendron thicket	90.4
2087.7	Timber Ridge Trail *(4650')* left 2.3m to USFS Road 67	91.4
2087.3	**Carter Gap Shelter** *(4550') sleeps 8 (1998)* .... S,w	91.8
---	*right 300ft, piped spring across A.T. 400ft, ←S7.6m|N6.8m→*	---
2085.6	Viewpoint *(4720')* right 25ft	93.5
2083.6	Betty Creek Gap *(4320') spring right 100ft* .... C,w	95.5
2082.7	Mooney Gap, USFS Road 83 *(4480')* .... R	96.4
2082.5	Spring *(4510') on A.T. just south of steps, unreliable* .... w?	96.6
2082.4	Big Butt Mtn *(4600')* A.T. crosses steep slope	96.7
2081.4	Bear Pen Trail, USFS Road 67 *(4850')*	97.7
---	***Alternate!** go uphill on road to bypass Albert Mtn summit*	---
2081.1	Albert Mtn *(5220')* fire tower	98.0
2081.0	Road *(5050')* connects to Albert Mtn summit bypass .... R	98.1
2080.5	**Big Spring Shelter** *(4940') sleeps 8 (1959)* Pinnacle Trail right .... S,w	98.6
---	*left 300ft, spring 25yds behind shelter, ←S6.8m|N5.3m→*	---
2078.5	Stream *(4930')* crosses A.T. .... w	100.6
2077.7	Glassmine Gap *(4150')*	101.4
---	*Long Branch Trail left 2.1m to Standing Indian Campground*	---
2075.7	Spring *(4580') on A.T. to left, seasonal* .... w?	103.4
2075.2	**Rock Gap Shelter** *(3850') sleeps 8 (1965)* .... S,w	103.9
---	*left 250ft, piped springs at shelter, ←S5.3m|N7.5m→*	---
2075.1	Rock Gap, USFS Road 67 📖 *p.105 (3740')* .... R	104.0
---	*left 1.4m–to USFS Standing Indian Campground (fee)* .... C,w	---
---	*right 0.5m on blue-blazed side trail to Wasalik Poplar*	---
2074.5	Wallace Gap, Jct. of USFS Road 67 and Old US 64 *(3740')* .... R	104.6
2074.4	Stream *(3800')* crosses A.T. .... w	104.7
2073.9	Log steps *(4150')*	105.2
2072.1	Stream *(4250')* crosses A.T. .... w	107.0
2071.4	Winding Stair Gap, US 64 📖 *p.106 (3750') piped spring, parking* .... R,w	107.7
---	*right 10m–to **FRANKLIN, NC 28734** .... L,M,G,O,Lm,f*	---
2071.3	Gravel road *(3800') stream, footbridge* .... R,w	107.8
2071.1	Stream *(3850')* crosses A.T. .... w	108.0
2070.5	Campsite *(3980') where stream crosses A.T.* .... C,w	108.6
2070.3	Swinging Lick Gap *(4000')*	108.8
2069.4	Panther Gap *(4430')*	109.7
2067.7	**Siler Bald Shelter** *(4670') sleeps 8 (1959)* .... S,C,w	111.4
---	*right 0.5m on loop trail, spring on loop, ←S7.5m|N7.3m→*	---
2067.2	Siler Bald *(4940') shelter loop trail rejoins A.T.*	111.9
---	*left 0.2m to summit, right 0.6m on loop trail to Siler Bald Shelter*	---

North Carolina

Miles from Katahdin	Features / Services		Miles from Springer
2065.6	Wayah Crest Picnic Area *(4170') left 300ft, parking*	R	113.5
2065.5	Wayah Gap, NC1310 *(4150') paved*	R	113.6
2063.7	USFS Road 69 *(5000') piped spring right 40ft*	R,w	115.4
2063.3	Bartram Trail *(5290') joins A.T. for 2.5m, campsites to right*	C	115.8
2063.2	Wine Spring *(5290') on A.T. to left*	w	115.9
2061.6	USFS Road 69D *(5200') log steps*		117.5
2061.3	Wayah Bald *(5340') stone observation tower, rest rooms*		117.8
2061.1	USFS Road 69D *(5240')*	R	118.0
2060.8	Bartram trail *(4860') leaves A.T. to right*		118.3
2060.4	**Wayah Shelter** *(4600') sleeps 8 (2007), tent sites*	S,w	118.7
---	*right 170ft, water 200yd across A.T., ←S7.3m	N4.8m→*		---
2059.1	Licklog Gap *(4380') left 0.5m to stream*	w	120.0
2057.2	Stream *(4500') crosses A.T.*	w	121.9
2056.8	Burningtown Gap, NC1397 *(4240')*	R	122.3
2055.6	**Cold Spring Shelter** *(4920') sleeps 6 (1933), campsites above shelter.*	S,C,w	123.5
---	*on A.T., spring in front of shelter, ←S4.8m	N5.8m→*		---
2055.5	Balsam Ridge Trail *(4980')*		123.6
2054.9	Copper Ridge Bald *(5100') A.T. skirts summit*		124.2
2053.4	Spring/campsite *(4920') spring to left*	C,w	125.7
2052.0	Tellico Gap *(3850') power line, parking*	R	127.1
2050.6	Wesser Bald *(4630') right 120ft to fire tower*		128.5
2049.9	Spring *(4230')*	w	129.2
2049.8	**Wesser Bald Shelter** *(4115') sleeps 6 (1994)*	S	129.3
---	*left 250ft, spring 0.1m south on A.T., ←S5.8m	N4.9m→*		---
2048.2	The Jumpoff *(4000') views*		130.9
2044.9	**A. Rufus Morgan Shelter** *(2100') sleeps 6 (1989), no privy*	S,w	134.2
---	*right 200ft, stream across A.T., ←S4.9m	N7.7m→*		---
2044.1	US19 📖 *p.107 (1750') Nanatahala Outdoor Center*	R,H,C,L,M,G,O,Lm,f	135.0
---	*right 12m–to **Bryson City, NC 28713***	L,M,G,Lm	---
2044.0	Nantahala River *(1740') A.T. crosses on bridge*		135.1
2042.8	Power line *(2420')*		136.3
2042.5	Wright Gap *(2380')*	R	136.6
2041.6	Spring/campsite *(3040') rock formation to right, spring left 300ft*	C,w	137.5
2041.0	Grassy Gap *(3050') Grassy Gap Trail right*		138.1
2039.6	Stream *(3680') at switchback*	w	139.5
2039.2	The Jump-up *(3780') hairpin turn, views*		139.9
2038.1	Swim Bald *(4750') spring right 150ft, unreliable*	w?	141.0

Elevation profile showing 5000', 4000', 3000', 2000' with labels: Wayah Bald, Wayah Shelter, Wayah Gap, Cold Spring Shelter, Tellico Gap, Wesser Bald Shelter, Rufus Morgan Shelter, N.O.C.

North Carolina

Miles from Katahdin	Features / Services		Miles from Springer
2037.2	**Sassafras Gap Shelter** *(4330') sleeps 14 (2002)*	S,w	141.9
---	*left 300ft, spring beyond shelter, ←S7.7m | N9.1m→*		---
2036.0	Cheoah Bald *(5062') vistas*	C	143.1
2035.8	Bartram Trail *(4940') to left*		143.3
2033.6	Locust Cove Gap *(3670') seasonal spring left 150 yds*	w?	145.5
2032.6	Simp Gap *(3550')*	w	146.5
2030.5	Stecoah Gap, NC143 ▢*p.107 (3165') picnic table, spring 400ft left*	R,w	148.6
---	*left 10m–to* **Robbinsville, NC 28771**	L,M,G,Lm	---
2029.5	Sweetwater Gap *(3330')*		149.6
2028.3	Unnamed summit *(3980')*		150.8
2028.1	**Brown Fork Gap Shelter** *(3720') sleeps 6 (1996)*	S,w	151.0
---	*right 200ft, spring at shelter, ←S9.1m | N6.1m→*		---
2027.9	Brown Fork Gap *(3700') spring right 100ft*	w	151.2
2027.2	Unnamed knob *(3790')*		151.9
2026.1	Hogback Gap *(3500')*		153.0
2025.3	Cody Gap *(3650') spring left 100 yds*	w	153.8
2023.3	Stream *(3100') crosses A.T.*	w	155.8
2022.9	Yellow Creek Gap, Yellow Creek Mtn Road *(2980')*	R	156.2
2022.0	**Cable Gap Shelter** *(2880') sleeps 6 (1988)*	S,w	157.1
---	*on A.T., spring in front of shelter, ←S6.1m | N6.6m→*		---
2020.9	High Top *(3680')*		158.2
2020.6	Black Gum Gap *(3380')*		158.5
2019.8	Unnamed rocky summit *(3720') vista*		159.3
2019.2	Walker Gap *(3450')*		159.9
---	*Yellow Creek Mtn Trail left 2.7m to Fontana Village*		---
2019.0	Stream/campsite *(3200') crosses A.T.*	C,w	160.1
2018.9	Stream *(2950') crosses A.T.*	w	160.2
2016.5	NC28 ▢*p.108 (1820') park permits, spigot*	R,L,f,w	162.6
---	*left 2m–to* **FONTANA DAM, NC 28733**	L,M,G,O,Lm,f	---
2015.4	**Fontana Dam Shelter** *(1775') sleeps 24 (1982)*	S,w	163.7
---	*right 300yds, spigot and rest rooms, ←S6.6m | N11.3m→*		---
2015.1	Fontana Dam ▢ *p.109 (1710') visitor center, showers*	R,w	164.0
---	*Northbounders, pick up a park permit at information board in*		---
---	*the marina parking area just north of NC28 or at the registration*		---
---	*board on spillway side of the Fontana Dam visitor center*		---
2014.7	Great Smoky Mtns. Natl. Park ▢ *p.109 (1715')*		164.4
---	*southern boundary of Great Smoky Mtns. Natl. Park*		---

Great Smoky Mtns. Natl. Park

Miles from Katahdin	Features / Services		Miles from Springer
2014.0	End of paved road(1900')...		165.1
2010.7	Shuckstack (3900') right 0.1m to fire tower, vistas		168.4
2010.4	Sassafras Gap (3650')	R	168.7
---	Lost Cove Trail right 3.5m to Eagles Creek, left on road to NC28		---
2009.8	Red Ridge Gap (3500')		169.3
2009.5	Birch Spring Tent Site (3760') tent sites, spring left 100yds	C,w	169.6
2007.2	Doe Knob (4520')		171.9
---	Gregory Bald Trail left 3.1m to Gregory Bald		---
2006.8	Mud Gap (4260')		172.3
2005.8	Ekaneetlee Gap (3840') spring left 300ft	w	173.3
2004.1	**Mollies Ridge Shelter** (4570') sleeps 12 (2003), no privy	S,w	175.0
---	on A.T., spring near shelter, ←S11.3m | N2.5m→		---
2004.0	Devils Tater Patch (4775')		175.1
2002.4	Little Abrams Gap (4120')		176.7
2002.2	Big Abrams Gap (4080')		176.9
2001.6	**Russell Field Shelter** (4360') sleeps 14 (1971), no privy	S,w	177.5
---	on A.T., spring left 150yds, ←S2.5m | N2.9m→		---
---	Russell Field Trail left 4.8m to Cades Cove picnic area		---
2000.2	Little Bald (5040') vista		178.9
1998.7	**Spence Field Shelter** (4915') sleeps 12 (2005)	S,w	180.4
---	right 0.2m, spring beyond shelter, ←S2.9m | N6.3m→		---
---	Eagle Creek Trail right 8m to Fontana Lake		---
---	Bote Mtn Trail left 4.9m to Cades Cove		---
1998.3	Jenkins Ridge Trail (4920') right 6m to Pickens Gap		180.8
1997.5	Rocky Top (5441') vista		181.6
1996.9	Thunderhead (5527') vista		182.2
1996.6	Beechnut Gap (4780') spring left 200ft	w	182.5
1995.2	Overlook at ledge (5215') vista		183.9
1995.1	Brier Knob (5215')		184.0
1994.3	Starkey Gap (4500')		184.8
1993.5	Sugar Tree Gap (4435')		185.6
1992.7	Chestnut Bald (4950')		186.4
1992.4	**Derrick Knob Shelter** (4880') sleeps 12 (renovated 2007), no privy	S,w	186.7
---	on A.T., spring near shelter, ←S6.3m | N5.5m→		---
1992.2	Sams Gap (4760') spring left 100yds	w	186.9
---	Greenbrier Ridge Trail left 8.3m to Tremont		---
1990.4	Cold Spring Knob (5240')		188.7

Elevation profile with markers: Mount Shuckstack, Doe Knob, Mollie's Ridge Shelter, Russell Field Shelter, Spence Field Shelter, Thunderhead Mt., Brier Knob, Derrick Knob Shelter. Vertical axis: 2000', 3000', 4000', 5000', 6000'.

Great Smoky Mtns. Natl. Park

Miles from Katahdin	Features / Services	Miles from Springer
1989.8	Miry Ridge Trail *(4910')* left 9.2m to Elkmont	189.3
1989.6	Buckeye Trail *(4817')* spring right 200yds .... w	189.5
1986.9	**Silers Bald Shelter** *(5460')* sleeps 12 (2001), no privy .... S,w	192.2
---	on A.T., spring 300ft to west, ←S5.5m	N1.7m→	---
1986.7	Silers Bald *(5607')* vistas	192.4
1986.3	Welch Ridge Trail *(5450')* right 7.5m to High Rock	192.8
1985.7	Jenkins Knob *(5550')*	193.4
1985.2	**Double Spring Gap Shelter** *(5750')* sleeps 12 (renovated 2008) .... S,w	193.9
---	on A.T., spring in front of shelter, ←S1.7m	N6.3m→	---
1984.6	Goshen Prong Trail *(5750')* left 10m to Elkmont	194.5
1982.8	Mt. Buckley *(6582')* vista	196.3
1982.7	Clingmans Dome Bypass Trail *(6520')* right 0.5m to parking	196.4
1982.3	Clingmans Dome *(6643')* observation deck right 50yds, vistas	196.8
1980.0	Collins Gap *(5786')*	199.1
1979.4	Mt. Collins *(6188')*	199.7
1978.9	**Mt. Collins Shelter** *(5870')* sleeps 12 (1960) Sugarland Mt. Trail........... S,w	200.2
---	left 0.5m, water beyond shelter, ←S6.3m	N7.5m→	---
1976.1	Indian Gap *(5250')* interpretive sign, Road Prong Trail to left	203.0
1974.4	Newfound Gap, US441 📖 *p.110 (5045')* rest rooms .... R,w	204.7
---	left 15m–to **GATLINBURG, TN 37738** .... L,M,G,O,Lm,f	---
---	right 21m–to **Cherokee, NC 28719** .... L,M,G,O,Lm,f	---
1972.7	Sweat Heifer Creek Trail *(5890')* right 3.7m to Kephart Shelter	206.4
1971.7	Boulevard Trail *(6040')* left 5.3m to Mt. LeConte	207.4
1971.4	**Icewater Spring Shelter** *(5920')* sleeps 12 (1999) .... S,w	207.7
---	right 100ft, spring nearby on A.T., ←S7.5m	N7.4m→	---
1970.6	Charlie's Bunion Loop Trail *(5540')* bunion 0.1m left on loop....................	208.5
1970.2	Dry Sluice Gap Trail *(5380')* right 8.5m to Smokemont	208.9
1965.3	Bradleys View *(5483')* vistas	213.8
1964.0	**Pecks Corner Shelter** *(5570')* sleeps 12 (2000) .... S,w	215.1
---	right 0.5m on Hughes Ridge Trail, spring, ←S7.4m	N5.2m→	---
1963.0	Eagle Rocks *(5750')* views to left	216.1
1961.3	Mt. Sequoyah *(6000')*	217.8
1960.6	Chapman Gap *(5650')*	218.5
1959.8	Mt. Chapman *(6250')* A.T. does not cross summit....................................	219.3
1958.9	Big Cove Gap *(5825')*	220.2
1958.8	**Tri-Corner Knob Shelter** *(5920')* sleeps 12 (2004) .... S,w	220.3
---	right 300ft, spring in front of shelter, ←S5.2m	N7.7m→	---

Great Smoky Mtns. Natl. Park

Miles from Katahdin	Features / Services		Miles from Springer
1958.6	Balsam Mtn Trail *(6070')* *right 7m to Laurel Gap Shelter*		220.5
1957.6	Guyot Spur *(6360')*		221.5
1957.0	Guyot Spring *(6180')* *on A.T. to right*	w	222.1
1956.5	Old Black *(6320')* *A.T. does not cross summit*		222.6
1955.9	Deer Creek Gap *(6020')* *vistas*		223.2
1955.3	Yellow Creek Gap *(5940')*		223.8
1955.0	Snake Den Ridge Trail *(5810')* *spring left 0.8m*	w	224.1
1953.6	Camel Gap *(4645')*		225.5
---	*Camel Gap Trail right to Big Creek and Walnut Bottom*		---
1951.6	Cosby Knob *(5050')* *A.T. skirts summit*		227.5
1951.1	**Cosby Knob Shelter** *(4700')* *sleeps 12 (renovated 2006)*	S,w	228.0
---	*right 50yds, spring at shelter, ←S7.7m|N7.1m→*		---
1950.4	Low Gap *(4240')*		228.7
---	*Cosby Trail left 2.5m to Cosby Campground, ranger station*		---
---	*Walnut Bottom Trail right to Walnut Bottom*		---
1949.3	Sunup Knob *(5020')*		229.8
1948.3	Mt. Cammerer Trail *(4480')* *left 0.6m to tower, vistas*		230.8
1947.8	Spring *(4300')* *on A.T.*	w	231.3
1945.9	Lower Mt. Cammerer Trail *(3500')* *left 7.8m to Cosby Campground*		233.2
1945.0	Chestnut Branch Trail *(2900')* *right 2m to Big Creek Ranger Station*		234.1
1944.0	**Davenport Gap Shelter** *(2600')* *sleeps 12 (1998), no privy.*	S,w	235.1
---	*left 300ft, spring in front of shelter, ←S7.1m|N10.5m→*		---
1943.2	Davenport Gap, GSMNP boundary, TN32/NC284 📖 *p.111 (1985')*	R	235.9
---	*northern boundary of Great Smoky Mtns. Natl. Park* 📖 *p.109;*		---
---	*Southbounders, it is easiest to pick up a park permit at Bluff Mt.*		---
---	*Outfitters in Hot Springs, but it is possible to use ranger station*		---
1942.6	Powerline *(1930')*		236.5
1942.4	State Line Branch *(1800')* *crosses A.T. several times*	w	236.7
1941.9	Spring/campsite *(1650')*	C,w	237.2
1941.8	State Line Branch *(1550')* *crosses A.T. below cascades*	w	237.3
1941.7	Paved road *(1450')*	R	237.4
1941.6	Pigeon River *(1425')* *A.T. crosses on road bridge*	w?	237.5
1941.2	Interstate 40 *(1455')* *A.T. uses underpass, exits*		237.9
1941.1	Green Corner Road *(1470')* *aka Waterville School Road*	R	238.0

North Carolina-Tennessee

1940.7	Green Corner Road 📖*p.111 (1750') stream* .... R	238.4
---	*left 200 yds–to private hostel* .... H,C,L,M,G?,Lm,f	---
1938.4	Painter Branch *(3000') right 40yds to campsite, spring* .... C,w	240.7
1937.9	Stream *(3100')* .... w	241.2
1937.5	Spanish Oak Gap *(3720')*	241.6
1936.0	Snowbird Mtn *(4265') left 300ft to summit, FAA tower*	243.1
1935.5	Campsite/spring *(4100') right 250yds* .... C,w	243.6
1935.3	Wildcat Spring *(4050') left 25yds* .... w	243.8
1933.5	**Groundhog Creek Shelter** *(2920') sleeps 6 (1939) Deep Gap* .... S,w	245.6
---	*right 0.2m, spring 100yds beyond shelter, ←S10.5m│N7.4m→*	---
1931.2	Harmon Den Mtn *(3840') right to summit*	247.9
1931.1	Hawk's Roost *(3700') left 350ft to rock formation, campsite* C	248.0
1930.6	Brown Gap *(3500') left 300ft to spring* .... w	248.5
1930.0	Spring *(3900') left 100yds, in small ravine* .... w	249.1
1927.9	Max Patch Road, NC1182 *(4250') A.T. passes through stile* .... R	251.2
1927.8	Stream *(4175')* .... w	251.3
1927.1	Max Patch *(4629')* **Notice!** *no fires permitted on summit*	252.0
1926.6	Campsite *(4280') wet weather spring at old fence line* .... C,w?	252.5
1926.4	Logging road *(4050')* .... R	252.7
1926.1	**Roaring Fork Shelter** *(3950') sleeps 8 (2005)* .... S,w	253.0
---	*right 300ft, streams cross A.T. near shelter, ←S7.4m│N5.7m→*	---
1925.1	Stream *(3750') footbridge* .... w	254.0
1924.2	Stream *(3650') bridge, left on old roadbed to NC1182* .... w	254.9
1922.2	Spring *(3630') right 100ft* .... w	256.9
---	*old Roaring Fork Shelter location (no camping permitted)*	---
1922.0	Stream *(3500') footbridge, A.T. follows stream* .... w	257.1
1921.8	Lemon Gap, NC1182/TN107 *(3550') A.T. goes straight ahead* .... w	257.3
1921.1	Streams *(4000') two streams cross A.T.* .... w	258.0
1920.4	**Walnut Mtn Shelter** *(4260') sleeps 6 (1938)* .... S,w	258.7
---	*on A.T., spring 75yds to left in fenced area, ←S5.7m│N9.9m→*	---
1919.6	Kale Gap *(3700')*	259.5
1918.0	Bluff Mtn *(4686')*	261.1
1916.4	Big Rock Spring *(3700') log steps, spring to right in ravine* .... w	262.7
1914.8	Grassy road *(2720') campsite* .... R	264.3
1913.9	Garenflo Gap *(2510') power line, USFS road adjacent* .... R	265.2
1913.3	Streams *(2650') two small streams with footbridges* .... w	265.8
1911.8	Little Bottom Branch Gap *(2750') stream in deep gorge* .... w	267.3

North Carolina-Tennessee

Miles from Katahdin	Features / Services		Miles from Springer
1910.5	**Deer Park Mtn Shelter** *(2330') sleeps 5 (1938), graveyard nearby*	S,w	268.6
---	*right 300ft, stream 200yds across A.T., ←S9.9m|N14.2m→*		---
1907.5	USFS Parking Area *(1360') plaque, Jesuit Center adjacent*		271.6
1907.3	**HOT SPRINGS, NC 28743** 🏠 *p.112(1325')*	H,C,L,M,G,O,Lm,f	271.8
---	*Notice! Southbounders, get GSMNP permit at outfitter*		---
1907.1	French Broad River *(1290') A.T. crosses guardrail (north end)*	w	272.0
1905.9	Lovers Leap Rock *(1800')* overlook		273.2
1905.6	Viewpoint *(1820') right 40ft to overlook*		273.5
1903.3	Pump Gap *(2100')*		275.8
---	*blue-blazed trail left 0.9m to Silvermine Creek*		---
1902.4	Concrete dam and pond *(2400') spring feeds pond*	C,w	276.7
1902.2	Gravel road *(2450') follows Mill Ridge*		276.9
1902.1	Spring *(2450') 100yds beyond gate on USFS road to left*	w	277.0
1901.8	Mill Ridge *(2450') plaque and parking area*		277.3
1901.4	Tanyard Gap, US25/70 *(2280') A.T. crosses on overpass*	R	277.7
1899.5	Spring *(2900') footbridge, spring to right*	w	279.6
1899.0	Campsite/spring *(3550') in ravine 100ft to right*	C,w	280.1
---	*blue-blazed trail left 0.1m to Rich Mtn fire tower*		---
1898.6	Spring *(3400') on A.T. to left*	w	280.5
1898.2	USFS road *(3000') to Rich Mtn fire tower*	R	280.9
1898.0	Hurricane Gap *(2940')*	R	281.1
1896.3	**Spring Mtn Shelter** *(3550') sleeps 5 (1938)*	S,w	282.8
---	*on A.T., spring in front of shelter, ←S14.2m|N8.6m→*		---
1894.8	Spring *(3050') left 15ft in ravine*	w	284.3
1894.6	Deep Gap *(2950')*		284.5
1892.7	Logging road *(2300')*	w?	286.4
1892.6	Allen Gap, NC208/TN70 *(2235')*	R	286.5
1891.0	Log Cabin Road 🏠 *p.113 (2420') gravel*	R	288.1
---	*left 0.6m–to cabins, tent sites*	H,C,L,G,O,f	---
1887.7	**Little Laurel Shelter** *(3620') sleeps 5 (1967)*	S,w	291.4
---	*on A.T., spring 75yds across A.T., ←S8.6m|N6.8m→*		---
---	*Dixon Trail left 1.5m to Camp Creek Bald fire road/Paint Creek*		---
1886.4	Trail to Camp Creek Bald *(4720') left 0.2m to fire tower*		292.7
1885.7	Spring *(4300') on A.T. to left*	w	293.4
1884.7	Spring *(4350') on A.T. to right*	w	294.4
1884.6	White Rock Cliffs *(4450') right 50ft to overlook*		294.5
1884.4	Blackstack Cliffs *(4400') left 200ft to overlook*		294.7
1884.2	Firescald Ridge bypass trail *(4410') south end*		294.9

North Carolina-Tennessee

Miles from Katahdin	Features / Services		Miles from Springer
1882.7	Firescald Ridge bypass trail *(4180')* north end......................................		296.4
1882.3	Licklog Gap *(4140')* spring to left..,	w	296.8
1880.9	**Jerry Cabin Shelter** *(4150')* sleeps 6 *(1968)*	S,w	298.2
---	*on A.T., spring 300ft across A.T., ←S6.8m	N5.9m→*		---
1880.8	Chestnut Log Gap *(4160')*		298.3
1879.6	Sarvis Cove Trail *(4500')* to left, grassy area, views .... R		299.5
1879.5	Bassett Memorial *(4650')* honoring 1968 thru-hiker		299.6
1879.1	Boulder field/steps *(4700')* descends into ravine		300.0
1879.0	Big Butt *(4840')* left 100ft to overlook		300.1
1878.9	Unnamed woods road *(4800')* .... R		300.2
1877.7	Spring *(4500')* left 100yds in ravine .... w		301.4
1877.5	Spring *(4500')* right 125yds on dirt road .... w		301.6
1877.4	Shelton Graves *(4520')* headstones right 20ft		301.7
1875.8	Flint Gap *(3425')*		303.3
1875.0	**Flint Mtn Shelter** *(3570')* sleeps 8 *(1988)*...	S,w	304.1
---	*right 50ft, spring 300ft north on A.T. to left, ←S5.9m	N8.8m→*		---
1874.1	Campsite *(3400')* .... C,w		305.0
1872.2	Devil Fork Gap, NC212 *(3110')* A.T. crosses stiles .... R		306.9
1871.7	Rector Laurel Road *(2960')* aka Boone Cove Road .... R,w		307.4
1871.4	Stream *(3000')* crosses A.T. near barn, old cemetery .... w		307.7
1871.1	Stream *(3100')* crosses A.T., woods road adjacent .... R,w		308.0
1870.8	Stream *(3400')* crosses A.T. .... w		308.3
1870.3	Sugarloaf Gap *(4000')*		308.8
1868.9	Lick Rock *(4580')*		310.2
1868.3	Big Flat *(4200')*		310.8
1867.3	Rice Gap *(3800')* woods road, stone steps .... R		311.8
1866.2	**Hogback Ridge Shelter** *(4350')* sleeps 6 *(1986)*................................	S,w	312.9
---	*right 600ft, spring 400yds beyond shelter, ←S8.8m	N10.1m→*		---
1865.6	High Rock *(4460')* left 150ft to rocks		313.5
1863.8	Sam's Gap, I-26 📖 *p.113 (3800')* .... R,M		315.3
1862.6	Campsite *(4000')* on A.T., spring to left on old road .... w?		316.5
1862.1	Grassy area *(4440')* .... w?		317.0
1861.5	Street Gap *(4100')* right 0.6m to Puncheon Fork Road .... R		317.6
1860.3	Spring *(4320')* 20yds left .... w		318.8
1859.4	Spring *(4480')* on A.T. .... w		319.7
1858.1	Spring *(4900')* left 100yds .... w		321.0
1858.0	Trail junction/spring *(5000')* spring left 100yds .... w		321.1
---	*blue-blazed loop trail rejoins A.T. 0.9m north at Big Stamp*		---

North Carolina-Tennessee

1857.7	Streams *(5100') several small streams cross A.T.* .... w	321.4
1857.3	Big Bald *(5516') vista*	321.8
1857.0	Big Stamp *(5300') left 0.3m to campsite, spring* .... C,w	322.1
---	*blue-blazed loop trail rejoins A.T. 0.9m south*	---
1856.1	**Bald Mtn Shelter** *(5100') sleeps 10 (1988)* .... S,w	323.0
---	*left 0.1m, spring to left on way to shelter, ←S10.1m|N10.6m→*	---
---	**Notice!** *fragile zone, no tent camping permitted in shelter area*	---
1855.9	Stream/spring *(4900') on A.T., 200ft apart* .... w	323.2
1855.7	Campsite/spring *(5000') spring 800ft left* .... C,w	323.4
1854.7	Little Bald *(5185') wooded summit*	324.4
1854.0	Spring *(4500') on A.T. to left* .... w	325.1
1852.7	Whistling Gap *(3840') spring 500ft left* .... C,w	326.4
1852.0	Trail to High Rocks *(4180') loop rejoins A.T. 0.4m north*	327.1
1850.9	Stream *(3500') crosses A.T.* .... w	328.2
1850.5	Stone steps *(3160') left to campsites on stream* .... C,w	328.6
1850.4	Spivey Gap, US19W *(3180')* .... R	328.7
1849.6	Oglesby Branch *(3790') crosses A.T. twice, log footbridges* .... w	329.5
1849.1	Woods Road *(3700')* .... R	330.0
1846.6	Stream *(3350') crosses A.T.* .... w	332.5
1846.3	Stream *(3360') crosses A.T.* .... w	332.8
1845.7	Stream/spring *(3050') spring to left (in hemlocks)* .... w	333.4
1845.5	**No Business Knob Shelter** *(3180') sleeps 6 (1963)* .... S,w	333.6
---	*on A.T., water source 0.2m south on A.T., ←S10.6m|N10.5m→*	---
1845.4	Unblazed trail junction *(3180') left 1m to Unaka Springs, TN*	333.7
1843.1	Temple Hill Gap *(2850')*	336.0
1841.8	Temple Hill *(3240')*	337.3
1840.3	Viewpoint *(2300') cliffs to right*	338.8
1839.2	Nolichucky River 📖 *p.114 (1700')* .... R,H,C,L,M,G,O?,Lm,f	339.9
---	*left 3.8m–to* **ERWIN, TN 37650** .... H,L,M,G,Lm,f	---
1839.1	Railroad tracks *(1720')*	340.0
1837.9	Jones Branch 📖 *p.115 (1720')first of several crossings* .... w	341.2
---	*right 300ft–to hostel/campground on river* .... H,C,L,M?,Lm,f	---
1836.5	Jones Branch *(2250') northernmost crossing*	342.6
1835.0	**Curley Maple Gap Shelter** *(3070') sleeps 6 (1961) no privy*	344.1
---	*on A.T., spring 100ft in front of shelter, ←S10.5m|N12.9m→*	---
1834.9	Curley Maple Gap *(3130') abandoned USFS road*	344.2
1834.5	Spring *(3300') on A.T. to right* .... w	344.6
1834.0	Stream *(3250') crosses A.T.* .... w	345.1

North Carolina-Tennessee

| Miles from Katahdin | Features / Services | Miles from Springer |

1833.7	Spring *(3400')* on A.T. to right .... w	345.4
1830.9	Indian Grave Gap, TN395/NC197 *(3360')* .... R	348.2
---	*left 3.3m to Rock Creek Recreation Area, 6.6m to Erwin, TN*	---
---	*right 4.5m to Poplar, NC*	---
1830.2	Power line *(3700')*	348.9
1829.8	USFS Road 230 *(3780')* gravel surfaced .... R	349.3
1828.6	Beauty Spot *(4437')* vistas	350.5
1827.1	Deep Gap *(4100')* concrete boxed spring, campsite .... C,w	352.0
1825.5	Unaka Mtn *(5180')* wooded summit	353.6
1823.2	Low Gap *(3900')* right 200yds to spring .... w	355.9
1822.1	**Cherry Gap Shelter** *(3900')* sleeps 6 (1962), no privy .... S,w	357.0
---	*on A.T., spring 250ft on blue-blazed trail, ←S12.9m	N9.1m→*	---
1821.7	Cherry Gap *(3900')* left 100ft to seasonal spring .... R,w	357.4
1820.6	Little Bald Knob *(4320')* A.T. skirts summit	358.5
1820.3	Old logging road *(4050')* .... R	358.8
1819.0	Iron Mtn Gap, TN107/NC226 *(3725')* paved .... R	360.1
1817.6	Stream *(3900')* 500ft right .... w	361.5
1816.7	Rock overhang *(4300')*	362.4
1815.2	Campsite/spring *(4200')* left 200yds on blue-blazed trail .... C,w	363.9
1814.9	Greasy Creek Gap 📖*p.115 (4035')* left 300yds to spring .... R,C,w	364.2
---	*right 0.6m (on old roadbed)*–to private hostel .... H,C,M?,G?,Lm,f	---
1814.1	Campsite/spring *(4100')* left 100yds at old homestead .... C,w	365.0
1813.0	**Clyde Smith Shelter** *(4400')* sleeps 10 (1976), no privy .... S,w	366.1
---	*left 0.1m, spring 100yds beyond shelter, ←S9.1m	N6.4m→*	---
1812.1	Little Rock Knob *(4920')* vista	367.0
1811.4	Spring *(4280')* piped .... w	367.7
1810.8	Spring *(4080')* seasonal .... w?	368.3
1809.9	Hughes Gap *(4040')* left 700ft on road to seasonal spring .... w?	369.2
1808.6	Viewpoint *(5300')* right 30yds to overlook	370.5
1808.5	Beartown Mtn *(5480')*	370.6
1808.1	Ash Gap *(5340')* right 500ft to spring .... C,w	371.0
1807.3	Roan High Bluff 📖*p.115 (6150')* parking area .... R	371.8
---	*right 300ft to Cloudland Rhododendron Gardens*	---
1806.6	**Roan High Knob Shelter** *(6285')* sleeps 15 (1980), no privy .... S,w	372.5
---	*right 0.1m, spring 50ft on blue-blazed trail, ←S6.4m	N5.0m→*	---
1805.3	USFS Access Road *(5700')* to Roan High Knob .... R	373.8
1805.1	Carvers Gap, TN143/NC261 📖*p.115 (5512')* parking area, toilets ....w	374.0
---	*left 8.7m*–to Roan Mtn State Park .... C,L,M,Lm	---
1804.7	Round Bald *(5826')* vistas	374.4

North Carolina-Tennessee

Miles from Katahdin	Features / Services	Miles from Springer
1804.4	Engine Gap *(5600')*	374.7
1804.1	Jane Bald *(5826') vistas*	375.0
1803.2	Trail to Grassy Ridge Bald*(5900') right 0.4m to vista*	375.9
1802.8	Spring *(6000') on A.T. to right* .... w	376.3
1802.2	Old woods road *(5030')*	376.9
1801.6	**Stan Murray Shelter** *(5050') sleeps 6 (1977), no privy* .... S,w	377.5
---	*on A.T., spring 100yds on blue-blazed trail,* ←S5.0m	N1.7m→	---
1801.4	Elk Hollow Ridge *(5180')*	377.7
1800.9	Buckeye Gap *(4730') overgrown road*	378.2
1799.9	**Overmountain Shelter** *(4682') sleeps 20 (1983) Yellow Mtn Gap* .... S,w	379.2
---	*right 0.3m, spring between A.T. and shelter,* ←S1.7m	N8.7m→	---
1798.9	Spring *(4250') right 300ft* .... w	380.2
1798.3	Little Hump Mtn *(5459') vista*	380.8
1797.0	Bradley Gap *(4960') spring right 300ft* .... C,w	382.1
1796.1	Hump Mtn *(5587') vistas, plaque*	383.0
1795.2	Viewpoint *(5320') right 100yds to overlook*	383.9
1793.7	Doll Flats *(4560') vista to right*	385.4
1793.5	Campsite/spring*(4550') campsite in clearing near old road* .... C,w	385.6
---	*spring left 60yds on old road, then right 700ft in woods*	---
1793.1	Viewpoint *(4300') left 50ft at rock steps*	386.0
1792.9	Stream *(4000') 40ft left* .... w	386.2
1791.3	Spring *(3050') on A.T. to left, seasonal* .... w	387.8
1791.2	**Apple House Shelter** *(3000') sleeps 6 (1984), no privy* .... S,w	387.9
---	*on A.T., stream behind shelter,* ←S8.7m	N9.3m→	---
1791.0	Stream *(2820') A.T. crosses on bridge* .... w	388.1
1790.7	US19E 📖*p.115 (2880')* .... R,G,f	388.4
---	*left 0.3m*—to private hostel .... H,C,L,M?,Lm,f	---
---	*left 3.4m*—to **ROAN MOUNTAIN, TN 37687** .... M,G	---
---	*right 2.5m*—to **ELK PARK, NC 28622** .... G,f	---
1790.5	Bear Branch Road *(2950')* .... R	388.6
1790.4	Bear Branch *(2940') footbridge, power lines beyond* .... w	388.7
---	Spring *(3700') 10yds left, walled with stone* .... w	---
---	Woods road *(3600') cemetery adjacent* .... R?	---
1787.4	Buck Mtn Road *(3400')*	391.7
1787.2	Stream *(3385') crosses A.T., contaminated* .... w?	391.9
1787.1	Campbell Hollow Road *(3395')* .... R	392.0
1786.9	Stream *(3385') footbridge, wooden stairs* .... w	392.2
1786.4	Trail to Jones Falls*(3280') right 0.1m to waterfall* .... w	392.7

North Carolina-Tennessee

Miles from Katahdin	Features / Services	Miles from Springer
1784.7	Logging road *(3300')* borders Elk River .... R,w	394.4
1784.3	Campsite *(3300') left 100ft* C	394.8
1784.2	Stream *(3250')* .... w	394.9
1782.6	Log bridge *(3300')* crosses wetlands .... w?	396.5
1782.1	Mountaineer Waterfall *(3250')* .... w	397.0
1781.9	**Mountaineer Shelter** *(3470')* sleeps 14 *(2006)*, no privy .... S,w	397.2
---	*on A.T., stream above waterfall is water source, ←S9.3m│N9.6m→*	---
1781.4	Logging road *(3250')* .... R	397.7
1781.0	Campsite *(3300') right 150ft, in Slide Hollow* .... C,w?	398.1
1780.7	USFS road *(3500')* .... R	398.4
1780.6	Rock staircase *(3300')*	398.5
1780.3	Walnut Mtn Road *(3550')* .... R	398.8
1780.1	Campsite *(3400') stream* .... C,w	399.0
1778.1	Laurel Fork 📖*p.116 (3300')* log bridge, stream contaminated .... w?	401.0
---	*left (two trails, see note)*–to private hostel .... H,G,Lm,f	---
1777.6	Campsite *(3450') seasonal spring* .... C,w?	401.5
1777.4	Stream *(3450')* crosses A.T. .... w	401.7
1777.3	Stream/logging road *(3480')* .... R,w	401.8
1776.6	Stream *(3300')* crosses A.T. .... w	402.5
1776.4	Spring *(3400')* on A.T. to left .... w	402.7
1776.2	Bog *(3380')* remains of moonshine still 30ft left? .... w?	402.9
1775.9	Stream *(3300')* crosses A.T. .... w	403.2
1775.6	Hardcore Cascade *(3500')* rock bridge built by thru-hikers	403.5
1774.5	Stream *(3600')* crosses A.T. .... w	404.6
1774.2	Campsite *(3800') stream crosses A.T.* .... C,w	404.9
1772.3	**Moreland Gap Shelter** *(3815')* sleeps 6 *(1960)*, no privy .... S,w	406.8
---	*on A.T., spring 125ft in front of shelter, ←S9.6m│N7.9m→*	---
1771.2	White Rocks Mtn *(4206')* .... C,w	407.9
1768.2	Trail to Coon Den Falls *(4000') left 0.8m to falls*	410.9
1766.3	Dennis Cove, USFS Road 50 📖*p.116 (2500')* .... R	412.8
---	*left 0.2m*–to hostel (showers) .... H,C,f	---
---	*right 0.5m*–to campground, hostel .... H,C,L,G?,Lm,f	---
1765.2	Loop trail to Laurel Fork Shelter *(2200') right 0.5m to shelter*	413.9
1765.1	Laurel Falls, Laurel Fork Gorge *(2100')* campsites in gorge .... C,w	414.0
1764.4	**Laurel Fork Shelter** *(2200')* sleeps 8 *(1977)*, no privy .... S,w	414.7
---	*right 300ft (loop), stream 150ft on path, ←S7.9m│N8.8m→*	---
---	**Notice!** *use the blue-blazed shelter loop for high-water bypass*	---
1764.1	Spring *(1900')* on A.T. .... w	415.0

Tennessee

Miles from Katahdin	Features / Services		Miles from Springer
1764.0	Stream *(1900') crosses A.T., footbridge*	w	415.1
1763.8	Stream *(1900') crosses A.T., footbridge*	w	415.3
1763.6	Pine Tree Spring *(1900') below big tree at stream's edge*	w	415.5
---	📖 *p.116 left 1m (on blue-blazed trail)–to Hampton, TN*		---
1762.7	Woods road *(2400')*	R	416.4
1760.6	Pond Flats *(3700')*	C	418.5
1760.5	Spring *(3690') below rocky drainage area*	w	418.6
1757.6	Shook Branch Road *(2000') paved*	R	421.5
1757.4	US321 📖 *p.116 (1980')*	R	421.7
---	*left 2.6m–to* **HAMPTON, TN 37658**	H,L,M,G,f	---
---	*on A.T.–Shook Branch Picnic Area (water fountains, rest rooms)*		---
1756.9	Road *(2090') dirt surfaced, A.T. goes around gate*	R	422.2
1756.6	Beach/swimming area *(2080') 100yds right*	w	422.5
1756.1	Griffith Branch *(2100')*	C?,w	423.0
1755.6	**Watauga Lake Shelter** *(2130') sleeps 6 (1980), no privy*	S, w	423.5
---	*left 50yds, stream adjacent shelter, ←S8.8m	N7.1m→*		---
1755.4	Dam maintenance road *(2000')*	R	423.7
1754.5	Watauga Dam, north end *(1980')*	R	424.6
1753.2	Iron Mountain Gap, Watauga Dam Road *(2240') paved*	R	425.9
1750.2	Spring *(3300') on A.T.*	w	428.9
1748.8	Viewpoint *(3500') overlook to right*		430.3
1748.6	Spring *(3600') left 0.5m on blue-blazed trail*	w	430.5
1748.5	**Vandeventer Shelter** *(3620') sleeps 6 (1961), no privy*	S,w	430.6
---	*on A.T., trail to spring 0.1m south on A.T., ←S7.1m	N6.8m→*		---
1744.4	Campsite *(3600') piped spring 100yds. beyond*	C,w	434.7
1743.7	Campsite *(3500') grassy, level area*	C	435.4
1743.3	Turkeypen Gap *(3970')*		435.8
1743.1	Blue-blazed side trail *(3980') left 2.5m to Hurley Hollow Rd*		436.0
1742.5	Powerline *(3950')*		436.6
1741.9	Spring *(4000') right 100yds*	w	437.2
1741.7	**Iron Mtn Shelter** *(4125') sleeps 6 (1960), no privy*	S,w	437.4
---	*on A.T., spring 0.2m south on A.T., ←S6.8m	N7.6m→*		---
1740.5	Nick Grindstaff Monument *(4130') far side of chimney engraved*		438.6
1740.4	Spring *(4130') left 100yds*	w	438.7
1737.7	Logging road *(3600')*	R	441.4
1737.5	Spring *(3500') seasonal*	w?	441.6
1737.1	TN91 *(3450')*	R	442.0
1735.4	Double Springs Road *(3600')*	R	443.7
1735.0	Campsite/spring *(3900') 50ft right*	C,w	444.1

Tennessee-Southwest Virginia

Miles from Katahdin	Features / Services	Miles from Springer
1734.9	Spring *(4050')* .... w	444.2
1734.1	**Double Springs Shelter** *(4060') sleeps 6 (1960), no privy* .... S,w	445.0
---	*on A.T., springs 250ft below shelter, ←S7.6m	N8.3m→*	---
1734.0	Holston Mtn Trail *(4080') pre-1954 A.T. route*	445.1
1733.7	Locust Knob *(4020')*	445.4
1731.9	Campsite/spring *(3500') right (on far side of field)* .... C,w	447.2
1730.7	Campsite *(3360') level area on ridge* C	448.4
1730.6	Low Gap, US421 📖 *p.117 (3350') picnic table, boxed spring* .... R,w	448.5
---	*right 3m–to* **Shady Valley, TN 37688** .... M,G	---
1728.7	Double Spring Gap *(3750')* .... w?	450.4
1728.3	Spring *(3600') unreliable* .... w?	450.8
1727.3	McQueen's Knob *(3840')*	451.8
1726.9	McQueen's Gap, USFS Road 69 *(3653')* .... R	452.2
1725.8	**Abingdon Gap Shelter** *(3785') sleeps 5 (1959), no privy* .... S,w	453.3
---	*on A.T., spring 800ft behind shelter, ←S8.3m	N19.6m→*	---
1720.4	Backbone Rock Trail *(3300') right 2.3m to TN133*	458.7
1719.3	Tennessee-Virginia border *(3250') Mt. Rogers NRA sign*	459.8
1717.7	Spring *(2600') right 0.1m, site of old homestead* .... w	461.4
1715.6	**DAMASCUS, VA 24236** 📖 *p.117 (1928')* .... R,H,C,L,M,G,O,Lm,f	463.5
1714.5	Virginia Creeper Trail, US58 *(1930') wooden steps* .... R	464.6
1712.5	Feathercamp Ridge *(2500')*	466.6
1712.0	Iron Mtn Trail *(2850') rejoins A.T. 36.4m north at Chestnut Flats*	467.1
1711.2	Stream/logging road *(2800')* .... R,w	467.9
1710.0	Feathercamp Branch/US58/Straight Branch *(2200') picnic area* .... R,w	469.1
1708.7	Stream *(2500') footbridge* .... w	470.4
1708.0	Trail to Taylors Valley community *(2800') right 0.4m*	471.1
1706.5	Straight Mtn *(3500')*	472.6
1706.2	**Saunders Shelter** *(3100') sleeps 8 (1987)* .... S,w	472.9
---	*left 0.2m, spring 300ft beyond shelter, ←S19.6m	N6.4m→*	---
1705.1	Stream *(3100') footbridge* .... w	474.0
1704.3	Old logging road *(3000')* .... R	474.8
1703.9	Bear Tree Gap-Shaw Gap Trail *(3050') left to USFS campground*	475.2
1703.8	Pond/campsite *(3000') left 150ft to spring* .... C,w	475.3
1703.2	Streams *(2800') several streams cross A.T.* .... w?	475.9
---	**Notice!** *water from streams south of VA 728 not potable*	---
1702.0	VA728, Creek Junction Station *(2700') old railroad bed* .... R	477.1
1701.6	Luther Hassinger Mem. Bridge, Virginia Creeper Trail *(2700')*	477.5
1701.0	VA859, Whitetop Laurel Creek *(2980') gravel surfaced road* .... R,w	478.1

Southwest Virginia

Features / Services

Miles from Katahdin	Features / Services		Miles from Springer
1700.2	Lost Mtn *(3400')*		478.9
1699.8	**Lost Mtn Shelter** *(3100') sleeps 8 (1984)*	S,w	479.3
---	on A.T., spring 150yds behind shelter, ←S6.4m | N12.0m→		---
1698.7	US58, Summit Cut *(3260') stream adjacent*	R,w	480.4
1698.4	Streams/campsites *(3300') several streams cross A.T.*	C,w	480.7
1697.5	VA601 *(3450') A.T. crosses fence on stile*	R	481.6
1697.4	Stream *(3500') crosses A.T.*	w	481.7
1697.3	Campsite/spring *(3900') spring to left*	C,w	481.8
1696.9	Stream *(3950') crosses A.T.*	w	482.2
1695.0	Buzzard Rock, Whitetop Mtn *(5120')*		484.1
1694.5	Spring *(5250') on A.T., piped*	w	484.6
1694.3	Whitetop Mtn Road, USFS Road 89 *(5400') parking area*	R,C?	484.8
1693.3	Streams *(5100') several streams cross A.T.*	w	485.8
1691.8	VA600, Elk Garden 📖 *p.119 (4435') parking area, horse trail*	R	487.3
---	*left 3.5m–to Konnarock community*	G,M	---
---	*right 3.4m–to* **Whitetop, VA 24292**	G	---
1689.8	Deep Gap *(4960') spring 200ft right*	w	489.3
---	**Notice!** *fragile zone, no tent camping permitted in gap*		---
1689.5	Virginia Highlands Horse Trail, Mt. Rogers Trail *(5510')*		489.6
1688.8	Briar Ridge *(5500') vistas in meadow across fence*		490.3
1688.0	Trail to Mt. Rogers *(5540') left 0.5m to summit, no views*		491.1
1687.8	**Thomas Knob Shelter** *(5400') sleeps 16 (1991)*	S,w	491.3
---	*on A.T., spring in fenced area near shelter, ←S12.0m | N5.3m→*		---
1686.8	Rhododendron Gap *(5440')*		492.3
---	*blue-blazed trail to left rejoins A.T. north on Pine Mtn*		---
---	*blue-blazed trail right to Wilburn Ridge cliffs, rejoins A.T. north*		---
1686.2	Fatman Squeeze *(5300') natural rock tunnel*		492.9
1686.0	Grandview Peak *(5200') rock steps, A.T. passes below summit*		493.1
1685.8	Virginia Highlands Horse Trail *(5100') crosses A.T.*		493.3
1685.5	Trail to Wilburn Ridge *(4920') rejoins A.T. at Rhododendron Gap*		493.6
1685.3	Grayson Highlands St. Pk. 📖 *p.119 (4880') A.T. crosses fence*		493.8
1684.7	Trail to Massie Gap, US58 *(4850') 0.5m right to spring*	w?	494.4
1683.4	Quebec Branch *(4800') A.T. crosses adjacent fence on stile*	w	495.7
1683.3	Old logging road *(4780') fence, stream to right*	w	495.8
1682.5	**Wise Shelter** *(4460') sleeps 8 (1996)*	S,w	496.6
---	*on A.T., spring 100yds south on A.T., ←S5.3m | N5.9m→*		---
1682.4	Little Wilson Creek *(4450') A.T. crosses on bridge*	C,w	496.7
---	*northern boundary of Grayson Highlands State Park*		---

Miles from Katahdin	Features / Services	Miles from Springer
1682.2	East Fork of Big Wilson Creek *(4470')* .... C,w	496.9
1681.2	Campsite/spring *(4700') spring to right* .... C,w	497.9
1680.0	Stone Mtn *(4800')* vistas	499.1
1679.7	"The Scales" *(4625') rail-fence livestock corral, stiles*	499.4
1679.0	Stream *(4850') crosses A.T.* .... w	500.1
1678.3	Pine Mtn *(5000')*	500.8
---	*blue-blazed trail to left rejoins A.T. at Rhododendron Gap*	---
1676.6	**Old Orchard Shelter** *(4050') sleeps 6 (1970)* .... S,w	502.5
---	*on A.T., spring 100yds on blue-blazed trail,* ←*S5.9m*	*N5.0m*→	---
1676.3	Lewis Fork Horse Trail *(4040') crosses A.T.*	502.8
1675.8	Old Orchard Horse Trail *(4020') crosses A.T.*	503.3
1675.1	Stream *(3500') crosses A.T.* .... w	504.0
1674.9	VA603, Fox Creek *(3480') log footbridge* .... R,w	504.2
---	*left 2.5m to Grindstone Campground (showers, fee)* C	---
1672.6	Chestnut Flats, Iron Mtn Trail *(4320')*	506.5
---	*Iron Mtn Trail to left rejoins A.T. south near Damascus, VA*	---
1671.6	**Hurricane Mtn Shelter** *(4300') sleeps 8 (2004)* .... S,w	507.5
---	*left 100 yds., water from creek,* ←*S5.0m*	*N9.1m*→	---
1670.2	Stream *(3000') crosses A.T.* .... w	508.9
1669.7	Powerlines *(3000') creek to left*	509.4
1668.5	Trail to Hurricane Campground *(3150') left 0.5m (showers, fee)* C	510.6
1667.6	Comers Creek *(3100') cascade, not potable* .... w?	511.5
1666.4	Dickey Gap, VA650/VA16 📖 *p.119 (3313')* .... R	512.7
---	*right 2.6m–to* **TROUTDALE, VA 24378** .... H,C,M,G?,Lm,f	---
1665.6	Virginia Highlands Horse Trail *(3400') crosses A.T.*	513.5
1664.9	Raccoon Branch Campsite *(3570') right 0.2m, seasonal spring* .... w?	514.2
1664.3	High Point *(4040') left 600ft, view limited*	514.8
1662.5	**Trimpi Shelter** *(2900') sleeps 8 (1975)* .... S,w	516.6
---	*right 0.1m, spring in front of shelter,* ←*S9.1m*	*N10.6m*→	---
1661.8	Old woods road *(3000')* .... R	517.3
1661.0	VA672 *(2700') log steps* .... R	518.1
1659.9	Stream *(2500') crosses A.T., seasonal* .... w?	519.2
1659.8	Old ruins *(2480') on A.T. to right* .... C?	519.3
1659.7	VA670, South Fork of Holston River *(2450') bridge* .... R,w	519.4
1658.8	Stream *(2700') crosses A.T.* .... w	520.3
1658.6	Campsite *(2740') intermittent stream south on A.T.* .... C,w?	520.5
1658.2	Stream *(2800') crosses A.T., seasonal* .... w?	520.9
1657.3	Brushy Mtn *(3260')*	521.8

Southwest Virginia

1655.9	VA601 *(3250') gravel surfaced* .... R	523.2
1654.3	Power line *(3300')*...	524.8
1653.4	Stream *(3000') crosses A.T.* .... w	525.7
1653.2	Stream *(3050') crosses A.T.* .... w	525.9
1652.9	Stream *(3100') crosses A.T.* .... w	526.2
1652.0	Ponds *(3200') old manganese pit mines*	527.1
1651.9	**Partnership Shelter** *(3220') sleeps 16 (1998), no tenting* .... S,w	527.2
---	*on A.T., water from spigot,* ←*S10.6m* | *N7.1m*→	---
1651.8	VA16 📖*p.119 (3220') Mt. Rogers NRA Headquarters* .... R,w	527.3
---	*left 5.9m*–to **Marion, VA 24354** .... L,M,G,Lm	---
---	*right 3.2m*–to **Sugar Grove, VA 24375** .... M,G	---
1651.1	VA622 *(3250')* .... R	528.0
1650.6	Brushy Mtn *(3700')*	528.5
1648.1	Locust Mtn *(3700')*	531.0
1647.7	USFS Road 86 *(3540') boxed spring 100yds right* .... R,w	531.4
1646.8	Glade Mtn *(3900')*	532.3
1645.0	Stream *(3300') crosses A.T.* .... w	534.1
1644.8	**Chatfield Shelter** *(3150') sleeps 6 (1970s)* .... S,w	534.3
---	*on A.T., stream in front of shelter,* ←*S7.1m* | *N18.5m*→	---
1644.5	VA644 *(3050') gravel surfaced* .... R	534.6
1644.3	Vaught Branch *(3000') crosses A.T. several times* .... w	534.8
1643.3	Power lines *(2800')*	535.8
1643.0	VA615 *(2630') Settlers Museum living-history farm* .... R	536.1
1642.9	Phillips Branch *(2600') footbridge* .... w	536.2
1642.5	VA729 *(2600') gravel surfaced* .... R	536.6
1641.2	Middle Fork of Holston River *(2490')* .... w	537.9
1641.1	Railroad tracks *(2425')*	538.0
1640.3	US11/VA683 📖*Groseclose p.120 (2420')* .... R,L,M,G?,f	538.8
---	*left 3.5m*–to **ATKINS, VA 24311** .... G,Lm	---
1640.2	Interstate 81 *(2450') A.T. uses underpass* .... R	538.9
1639.3	Historical marker *(2500') Davis Fancy community*	539.8
1639.2	VA617 *(2520') stile* .... R	539.9
1638.6	Stream *(2500') intermittent* .... w?	540.5
1638.5	Spring *(2800') right 0.1m* .... w	540.6
1637.6	Former site of Davis Path Shelter *(2840')*	541.5
1635.1	Gullion Mtn *(3300') aka Little Brushy Mtn*	544.0
1634.0	Crawfish Valley, Reed Creek *(2600') campsite 0.3m right* .... C,w	545.1
1633.3	Stream *(3100') intermittent* .... w?	545.8

Southwest Virginia

Miles from Katahdin	Features / Services		Miles from Springer
1632.8	Spring (3300') seasonal	w?	546.3
1632.3	Tilson Gap, Big Walker Mtn (3500')		546.8
1631.8	Stream (3000') intermittent	w?	547.3
1630.9	VA610 (2700')	R,w	548.2
1629.5	North Fork of Holston River, VA742 (2500') bridge	R,w	549.6
---	*Alternate!* if bridge is underwater, northbounders can go right on		---
---	VA610 for 1.9m to VA42, then left 0.3m on VA42 to rejoin A.T. at		---
---	O'Lystery pavilion; southbounders go left on VA42, right on VA610		---
1629.1	Stream (2580')	w	550.0
1628.5	VA42 (2690') O'Lystery Pavilion (off-limits to hikers)	R	550.6
1626.3	**Knot Maul Branch Shelter** (2880') sleeps 8 (1980s)	S,w	552.8
---	on A.T., stream 0.2m north on A.T., ←S18.5m | N9.0m→		---
---	(also, intermittent spring located 300ft to left facing shelter)		---
1626.2	Stream (2620') footbridge	w	552.9
1625.2	Lynn Camp Creek (2400') footbridge, jeep road adjacent	R,w	553.9
1624.4	Lynn Camp Mtn (3000')		554.7
1623.4	Stream (2300') crosses A.T.	w	555.7
1623.2	Lick Creek (2250') footbridge	w	555.9
1623.1	Stream (2450') crosses A.T., rhododendron thicket	w	556.0
1621.0	USFS Road 222 (2300') Poor Valley	R	558.1
1620.6	Stream (2800') crosses A.T.	w	558.5
1619.1	Pond/spring (3800') 150ft left, spring on north side	w	560.0
---	*Notice!* northbounders, get water here for Chestnut Knob Shelter		---
1617.3	**Chestnut Knob Shelter** (4410') sleeps 8 (1994)	S,w	561.8
---	on A.T., no water, ←S9.0m | N10.0m→		---
1616.0	Walker Gap (3520') spring 300ft right, then left 60ft	R,w	563.1
---	*Notice!* southbounders, get water here for Chestnut Knob Shelter		---
1615.9	Stream (3700') seasonal	w?	563.2
1615.6	Unnamed knob (3800')		563.5
1615.4	Old stone wall (3850') remnants of wall to left		563.7
1611.3	Garden Mtn (4052') west 10yds to summit, vistas		567.8
1611.1	VA623 (3880')	R	568.0
1610.7	Viewpoint (4000') left to overlook		568.4
1610.3	Davis Farm Campsite (3600') left 0.5m, spring beyond	C,w	568.8
1608.7	Spring (2800') seasonal	w?	570.4
1608.2	Stream (2700') unreliable	w?	570.9
1607.3	**Jenkins Shelter** (2470') sleeps 8 (1960s)	S,w	571.8
---	left 200ft, stream 100yds beyond shelter, ←S10.0 | N14.0m→		---

Southwest Virginia

1607.2	Logging road/Hunting Camp Creek (2480') .... R,w	571.9
1603.1	Brushy Mtn (3080')	576.0
1602.5	VA615, Laurel Creek 📖 p.120 (2450') .... R,w	576.6
1602.4	Campsites (2460') picnic tables, stream nearby .... C,w	576.7
1600.4	Trail Boss Trail (3050') left 2m to VA615	578.7
1597.6	Power line (3000') double wire crosses A.T.	581.5
1596.1	USFS Road 282 (3000') .... R	583.0
1595.9	Power line (2950')	583.2
1595.6	US21/52 📖 p.120 (2920') do not disturb private residences .... R	583.5
---	right 2.5m–to **BLAND, VA 24315** .... H?,L,M,G,Lm?,f?	---
---	left 1.8m–to **Bastian, VA 24314** .... post office only	---
1595.5	VA612 (2800') .... R	583.6
1595.4	Interstate 77 (2750') A.T. crosses on bridge .... R	583.7
1594.8	Kimberling Creek (2700') .... w	584.3
1593.8	Unused woods road (2850') overgrown	585.3
1593.3	**Helveys Mill Shelter** (3090') sleeps 6 (1960s) .... S,w	585.8
---	right 0.3m, spring on blue-blazed trail, ←S14.0m	N9.8m→	---
1592.5	Spring (3050') right 0.5m on woods road, unreliable .... w?	586.6
1586.6	VA611 (2720') .... R	592.5
1585.2	Brushy Mtn (3100')	593.9
1583.5	**Jenny Knob Shelter** (2800') sleeps 6 (1960s) .... S,w	595.6
---	right 150ft, spring on blue-blazed trail, ←S9.8m	N14.2m→	---
1582.8	Stream (2300') A.T. crosses at culvert .... w	596.3
1582.4	Campsite (2300') small clearing on A.T., stream nearby .... C,w	596.7
1582.3	VA608 📖 p.120 (2200') Lickskillet Hollow, right 0.8m to store .... R,G?	596.8
1581.9	Log steps (2180')	597.2
1581.5	Log steps (2350')	597.6
1581.1	Power line (2500') log/rock steps	598.0
1579.9	Brushy Mtn (2700')	599.2
1579.6	Rock steps (2450')	599.5
1578.6	Log steps (2200')	600.5
1578.1	Log steps (2180')	601.0
1577.1	Kimberling Creek (2095') A.T. crosses on suspension bridge .... w	602.0
1577.0	VA606 📖 p.120 (2100') left 0.4m to store .... R,C,M,G,f,w	602.1
1575.1	Trail to Dismal Creek Falls (2300') left 0.3m to falls .... w	604.0
1570.9	Stream (2500') crosses A.T. .... w	608.2
1570.8	Stream (2500') crosses A.T. .... w	608.3
1570.7	Lions Den Road, dirt (2520') .... R	608.4

Southwest Virginia

Miles from Katahdin	Features / Services		Miles from Springer
1570.3	Streams *(2600')* two streams in rhododendron thicket	w	608.8
1570.1	Woods road *(2610')*	R	609.0
1569.9	Stream *(2620')* crosses A.T.	w	609.2
1569.6	Levee/pond *(2630')* levee to left, pond may lie beyond	w	609.5
1569.4	Branch of Dismal Creek *(2638')* crosses A.T.	w	609.7
1569.3	**Wapiti Shelter** *(2640')* sleeps 8 (1980)	S,w	609.8
---	*right 0.1m, water from Dismal Creek, ←S14.2m|N8.4m→*		---
1569.1	Branch of Dismal Creek *(2700')* crosses A.T.	w	610.0
1568.7	Branch of Dismal Creek *(3000')* crosses A.T.	w	610.4
1566.9	Viewpoint *(3800')* at rocky outcrop, vista		612.2
1566.6	Old jeep road *(3700')*	R	612.5
1564.8	Woods road *(3400')* Ribble Trail	R	614.3
---	*left on road 0.1m to Honey Spring Picnic Area*	w	---
1564.7	USFS Road 103, Big Horse Gap *(3860')*	R	614.4
1563.1	Sugar Run Gap, Sugar Run Road 🕮*p.120 (3382')*	R	616.0
---	*right 0.5m (take downhill fork)–to Woodshole Hostel*	H,C,f,w	---
1561.7	Viewpoint *(3800')* 50yds right to cliff		617.4
1561.0	Old woods road *(3560')*	R	618.1
1560.9	**Doc's Knob Shelter** *(3555')* sleeps 8 (1971)	S,w	618.2
---	*left 50ft, spring in front of shelter, ←S8.4m|N15.0m→*		---
1557.9	Pearis Mtn *(3440')* power lines		621.2
1555.7	Viewpoint *(3600')* at rock ledge		623.4
1555.6	Campsite/spring *(3600')* left 800ft to spring	C,w	623.5
1555.2	Angels Rest *(3550')* left 50yds to overlook		623.9
1554.2	Old logging road *(2700')*	R	624.9
1553.6	Spring *(2300')* left 300ft, seasonal	w?	625.5
1553.2	VA634 *(2000')* stile, alternate route to Pearisburg, 1m right	R	625.9
1552.7	**PEARISBURG, VA 24134** 🕮*p.121 (1620')*	R,H,L,M,G,Lm,f	626.4
---	*Center of town 1m right, hostel and Wal-Mart 2.4m right*		---
1552.2	New River, Senator Shumate Bridge *(1600')*		626.9
1551.9	Old roadbed *(1700')* borders field		627.2
1550.7	VA641, Clendenin Road *(1730')* Stillhouse Branch	R,w	628.4
1550.4	Power line *(1800')*		628.7
1550.3	Access road *(1820')* dirt surfaced	R	628.8
1549.8	Old woods road *(2500')*	R	629.3
1549.4	Stream *(2600')* crosses A.T.	w	629.7
1548.5	Campsite/spring *(3000')* left 100ft, spring	C,w	630.6
1546.8	Pipeline right-of-way *(3300')*		632.3

Central Virginia

Miles from Katahdin	Features / Services	Miles from Springer
1546.6	Pipeline right-of-way *(3300')*	632.5
1546.4	Power lines *(3300')*	632.7
1546.1	Rice Field *(3370')* vista	633.0
1545.9	**Rice Field Shelter** *(3375') sleeps 7 (1995)* .... S,w	633.2
---	*right 0.1m, spring 0.4m on blue-blazed trail,* ←S15.0m	N12.5m→	---
1545.1	Antenna *(3400') television tower*	634.0
1544.9	Power line *(3380')*	634.2
1544.3	Campsite/spring *(3300') right 50yds to spring* .... C,w	634.8
1540.8	Symms Gap Meadow *(3400')*	638.3
1540.5	Campsite *(3450') right at clearing under oak tree* C	638.6
1540.4	Symms Gap *(3300') old woods road* .... R	638.7
1539.8	Groundhog Trail *(3400') left to WV219/24*	639.3
1538.3	Dickinson Gap *(3300') stone historical marker*	640.8
1535.9	Allegheny Trail *(3500') yellow-blazed to Pennsylvania*	643.2
1534.5	Pine Swamp Branch *(3400') crosses A.T.* .... w	644.6
1533.4	**Pine Swamp Branch Shelter** *(2530') sleeps 8 (1980s)* .... S,w	645.7
---	*on A.T., stream in front of shelter,* ←S12.5m	N3.9m→	---
1533.1	VA635, Stony Creek Valley *(2400') USFS parking area* .... R,w	646.0
1532.0	Dismal Branch *(2420') log footbridge* .... w	647.1
1531.0	VA635, Stony Creek *(2450') bridge* .... R,w	648.1
1529.7	Spring *(3400') right 400ft* .... w	649.4
1529.5	**Bailey Gap Shelter** *(3535') sleeps 6 (1960s)* .... S,w?	649.6
---	*on A.T., seasonal spring across A.T.,* ←S3.9m	N8.8m→	---
1526.9	Overhanging rocks *(3700') on A.T. to left*	652.2
1525.8	VA613, Salt Sulphur Turnpike *(3900')* .... R	653.3
1525.6	Wind Rock *(4100') vista*	653.5
1524.8	Old woods road *(4000')* .... R	654.3
1524.4	Campsite/spring *(4000') spring to left* .... C,w	654.7
1523.8	Salt Pond Mtn *(4025') swampy area on top*	655.3
1523.2	Lone Pine Peak *(4054')*	655.9
1522.7	War Branch Trail *(3700') right 1.5m to Salt Sulphur Turnpike*	656.4
1522.4	Spring *(3600') on A.T. to left at rock field* .... w	656.7
1522.2	Spring *(3500') seasonal* .... w?	656.9
1520.7	**War Spur Shelter** *(2340') sleeps 6 (1960s)* .... S,w	658.4
---	*on A.T., water source is stream north on A.T.,* ←S8.8m	N5.8m→	---
1520.6	War Branch *(2335') water source for War Spur Shelter* .... w	658.5
1519.9	USFS Road 156, Johns Creek Valley *(2080')* .... R	659.2
1519.8	Johns Creek *(2080') bridge* .... w	659.3
1518.9	Stream *(2800') crosses A.T., seasonal* .... w?	660.2

Central Virginia

1517.9	VA601, Rocky Gap *(3264')* .... R	661.2
1517.4	Johns Creek Mtn Trail *(3750') left 3.5m to VA658*	661.7
1516.3	Big Pond *(3750') left 200yds to bog*	662.8
1516.1	White Rock *(3800') right 100yds to overlook*	663.0
1515.8	Kelly Knob *(3742')*	663.3
1514.9	**Laurel Creek Shelter** *(2720') sleeps 6 (1988)* .... S,w	664.2
---	*right 100ft, water from stream 0.1m north, ←S5.8m | N6.4m→*	---
1514.8	Laurel Creek *(2700') crosses A.T.* .... w	664.3
1514.4	Old woods road *(2600')* .... R	664.7
1513.9	Spring *(2300') right in rhododendron thicket* .... w	665.2
1513.1	Pastures *(2150') A.T. crosses several fences on stiles*	666.0
1512.5	VA42, Sinking Creek Valley 🕮*p.122 (2180') stile* .... R	666.6
---	*right 8m–to **Newport, VA 24128*** .... G	---
1511.6	VA630, Sinking Creek *(2100') bridge* .... R,w	667.5
1511.4	Stream *(2100') footbridge* .... w	667.7
1511.2	Keffer Oak 🕮*p.122 (2240') stile attached*	667.9
1510.9	Power line *(2300')*	668.2
1509.7	Power line *(3200')*	669.4
1508.5	**Sarver Hollow Shelter** *(3400') sleeps 6 (2001)* .... S,w	670.6
---	*right 0.3m, spring near shelter, ←S6.4m | N6.0m→*	---
1504.9	Sinking Creek Mtn *(3450')*	674.2
1503.2	Cabin Branch *(2450') 150yds right* .... C,w	675.9
1502.5	**Niday Shelter** *(1800') sleeps 6 (1980)* .... S,w	676.6
---	*right 60ft, stream 100yds across A.T., ←S6.0m | N10.1m→*	---
1502.0	Stream *(1700') borders A.T.* .... w	677.1
1501.2	VA621, Craig Creek Valley *(1540') hard-surfaced road* .... R	677.9
1501.0	Craig Creek *(1540') bridge* .... w	678.1
1500.7	Log steps/bridge *(1800')*	678.4
1500.1	Log steps *(2200')*	679.0
1499.0	Old woods road *(3000')* .... R	680.1
1497.4	Audie Murphy Memorial *(3080') left 200ft*	681.7
1495.3	Rock steps *(2500')*	683.8
1493.6	VA620, Trout Creek *(1500') register, footbridge* .... R,w	685.5
1493.2	Power line *(1750')*	685.9
1492.4	**Pickle Branch Shelter** *(1845') sleeps 6 (1980)* .... S,w	686.7
---	*right 0.5m, stream behind/below shelter, ←S10.1m | N13.6m→*	---
1490.2	Hemlock Point *(2600')*	688.9
1489.3	Cove Mtn *(3050')*	689.8

Elevation profile: 4000' — 3000' — 2000' — 1000', marking Laurel Creek Shelter, Sarver Hollow Shelter, Niday Shelter, Pickle Branch Shelter.

Central Virginia

1488.2	Dragon's Tooth *(3020')* right 200yds to vista	690.9
1487.2	Lost Spectacles Gap *(2500')* left 1.5m to VA311	691.9
1487.0	Devils Seat *(2650')* overlook	692.1
1486.9	Viewpoint Rock *(2400')* vista	692.2
1486.7	Rawies Rest *(2300')* knife-edge ridge	692.4
1486.1	Stream *(2200')* left 0.2m .... w	693.0
1485.7	VA624 📖*p.122 (1790')* North Mtn Trail left, rejoins A.T. north .... R	693.4
---	*left 0.4m*–to store .... G,w	---
1484.8	Stream *(1850')* footbridge .... w	694.3
1484.1	VA785, Blacksburg Road *(1800')* .... R	695.0
1484.0	Catawba Creek *(1800')* bridge .... w	695.1
1483.8	Stream *(1820')* unreliable .... w?	695.3
1480.1	Viewpoint *(2100')*	699.0
1479.8	VA311 📖*p.122 (1980')* .... R	699.3
---	*left 1m*–to **CATAWBA, VA 24070** .... M,G,f	---
1479.6	Old woods road *(2000')* .... R	699.5
1478.8	**Johns Spring Shelter** *(1980')* sleeps 6 *(2003)* .... S,w?	700.3
---	*right 50ft, seasonal spring in front of shelter, S13.6m	N1.0m→*	---
1477.9	Spring *(2140')* on A.T. to left, water source for shelter .... w	701.2
1477.8	**Catawba Mtn Shelter** *(2145')* sleeps 6 *(1984)* .... S,w	701.3
---	*on A.T., spring 0.1m south on A.T., ←S1.0m	N2.4m→*	---
1477.5	Campsite *(2160')* right 100ft C	701.6
1477.1	Road/power line *(2500')* .... R	702.0
1476.1	McAfee Knob *(3182')* left 100ft to overlook, vista	703.0
---	**Notice!** *no camping or fires at the overlook area*	---
1475.5	Pig Farm Campsite *(2650')* right 0.1m to spring .... C,w	703.6
1475.4	**Campbell Shelter** *(2580')* sleeps 6 *(1989)* .... S,w	703.7
---	*right 100ft, spring across road beyond shelter, ←S2.4m	N6.0m→*	---
1473.7	Snack Bar Rock *(2300')* A.T. passes between big rocks	705.4
1473.4	Rock Haven *(2300')* large rock overhang	705.7
1472.4	Old woods road *(2280')* .... R	706.7
1472.3	Brickey's Gap *(2200')*	706.8
---	*trail right 1.7m to Lamberts Meadow, reportedly difficult to find;*	---
---	*can be used as foul-weather bypass around Tinker Cliffs*	---
1471.0	Tinker Cliffs *(3000')* A.T. follows cliffs 0.5m north, vistas	708.1
1470.5	The Well *(3000')* natural rock hole	708.6
1470.4	Lunch Box Rock *(3000')* vistas	708.7
1470.0	Scorched Earth Gap *(2360')*	709.1

Central Virginia

Miles from Katahdin	Features / Services	Miles from Springer
---	*Andy Layne Trail left 3.1m to VA779, rejoins A.T. south at VA624*	---
1469.4	**Lamberts Meadow Shelter** *(2080') sleeps 6 (1974)* .... S,w	709.7
---	*right 200ft, stream 50yds beyond shelter, ←S6.0m|N14.4m→*	---
1469.3	Stream *(2070')* crosses A.T. .... w	709.8
1469.2	Blue-blazed trail *(2050')* rejoins A.T. south in Brickey's Gap	709.9
---	*trail can be used as foul-weather bypass around Tinker Cliffs*	---
1469.1	Lamberts Meadow Campsite, Sawmill Run *(2040')* left 100ft .... C,w	710.0
1465.4	Ruckers Knob *(2200')* power line	713.7
1465.1	Angel Gap *(1700')* pipeline right-of-way	714.0
1464.8	Power line *(1750')*	714.3
1464.0	Hay Rock *(1900')* large tilted sandstone upthrust, vistas	715.1
1462.8	Power line *(1900')*	716.3
1462.1	Power line *(1900')* vista at rock to left	717.0
1461.2	Power line *(1720')*	717.9
1461.1	Old woods road *(1700')* .... R	718.0
1460.6	Pipeline/railroad tracks *(1250')*	718.5
1460.5	Tinker Creek *(1250')* concrete bridge .... w?	718.6
---	**Notice!** *no camping permitted from US220 north to VA652*	---
1460.0	US220 📖 *p.123 (1300')* .... R,L,M,Lm,f	719.1
---	*right 0.8m–to I-81 interchange area* .... L,M,Lm	---
---	*left 0.3m–to shopping area* .... M,G,O,f	---
---	*left 1.3m–to* **DALEVILLE, VA 24083** .... post office only	---
1459.5	Power line *(1380')* A.T. crosses fence on stile	719.6
1459.1	Steps *(1350')* A.T. crosses footbridge	720.0
1458.8	Interstate 81/VA779 *(1450')* A.T. passes under I-81 on VA779 .... R	720.3
1458.6	Buffalo Creek *(1400')* bridge .... w?	720.5
1458.5	US11 📖 *p.124 (1410')* railroad tracks .... R	720.6
---	*left 0.8m–to* **TROUTVILLE, VA 24175** .... G	---
---	*right 2.2m–to I-81 interchange area* .... L,M,G,Lm	---
1458.0	Stream *(1500')* intermittent .... w?	721.1
1457.9	VA652 *(1520')* gate, stiles .... R	721.2
---	**Notice!** *no camping permitted from VA652 south to US220*	---
1457.0	Rock steps *(1800')*	722.1
1456.4	Tollhouse Gap *(1850')*	722.7
1455.6	Viewpoint *(2400')* right 250ft	723.5
1455.0	**Fullhardt Knob Shelter** *(2670') sleeps 6 (1960s)* .... S	724.1
---	*right 500ft, cistern (or spring 0.4m north), ←S14.4m|N6.2m→*	---
1454.6	Spring *(2600')* left 125yds, seasonal .... w?	724.5
1452.2	USFS Road 191, Salt Pond Road *(2250')* .... R	726.9

Central Virginia

1451.4	Curry Creek *(1700') crosses A.T.*	w	727.7
1449.7	Little Wilson Creek *(1700') crosses A.T.*	w	729.4
1449.5	Wilson Creek *(1700') crosses A.T., steps*	w	729.6
1448.8	**Wilson Creek Shelter** *(1830') sleeps 6 (1986)*	S,w	730.3
---	*left 100ft, stream 200yds across A.T., ←S6.2m|N7.3m→*		---
1446.4	USFS Road 186, Black Horse Gap *(2400') parkway 100ft right*	R,w	732.7
---	*USFS Rd 186 (aka Old Fincastle Road), spring 0.4m right*		---
1445.6	Blue Ridge Parkway - mile 97.0 *(2365') Taylors Mtn Overlook*	R	733.5
1444.5	Blue Ridge Parkway - mile 95.9 *(2430') Montvale Overlook*	R	734.6
1443.9	Blue Ridge Parkway - mile 95.3 *(2530') Harveys Knob Overlook*	R	735.2
1442.3	Hammond Hollow Trail *(2300') left 2m to VA634*		736.8
1441.5	**Bobblets Gap Shelter** *(1920') sleeps 6 (1961)*	S,w	737.6
---	*left 0.2m, spring adjacent to shelter, ←S7.3m|N6.4m→*		---
1441.1	Old woods road *(2330')*	R	738.0
1440.8	Blue Ridge Parkway - mile 92.5 *(2240') Sharp Top Overlook*	R	738.3
1440.1	Blue Ridge Parkway - mile 91.8 *(2435') Mills Gap Overlook*	R	739.0
1439.0	Rock steps *(2500')*		740.1
1438.4	Bearwallow Gap, VA43/Blue Ridge Parkway 📖*p.124 (2230')*	R	740.7
---	*left 5m–to* **Buchanan, VA 24066**	L,M,G,Lm	---
---	*right 5m (north on parkway)–to Peaks of Otter Rec. Area*	C,L,M	---
1436.8	Cove Mtn *(2720')*		742.3
1436.4	Little Cove Mtn Trail *(2560') right 2.8m to VA614*		742.7
1435.1	**Cove Mtn Shelter** *(1925') sleeps 6 (1981)*	S,w?	744.0
---	*right 200ft, no water at shelter, ←S6.4m|N7.1m→*		---
---	*(Cove Creek is located about 0.4m down blue-blazed trail beyond the*		---
---	*shelter, involves a steep 500ft drop in elevation)*		---
1433.3	Buchanan Trail *(1780')*		745.8
1433.0	Glenwood Horse Trail *(1630')*		746.1
1432.4	Stream *(1280') intermittent*	w?	746.7
1431.8	Jennings Creek *(950') bridge*	w	747.3
1431.7	VA614 📖*p.124 (950')*	R	747.4
---	*right 0.2m (then left 0.1m)–to Middle Creek Picnic Area*	w	---
1430.9	Rock outcropping *(1650')*		748.2
1430.2	Fork Mtn *(2040')*		748.9
1429.5	Trail to VA714 *(1500') right 0.8m to VA714 terminus*		749.6
1429.0	Stream *(1225') crosses A.T.*	w	750.1
1428.3	Hamps Branch *(1250') crosses A.T.*	w	750.8
1428.0	**Bryant Ridge Shelter** *(1320') sleeps 20 (1992)*	S,w	751.1
---	*on A.T., stream in front of shelter, ←S7.1m|N4.9m→*		---

Central Virginia

Miles from Katahdin	Features / Services		Miles from Springer
1427.9	Trail to Button Hill *(1360')* right 0.5m to VA714 terminus		751.2
1426.8	Old woods road *(2100')* .... R		752.3
1423.7	Floyd Mtn *(3560')*		755.4
1423.1	**Cornelius Creek Shelter** *(3145')* sleeps 6 *(1960)* .... S,w		756.0
---	*right 400ft, stream on way to shelter,* ←*S4.9m	N5.3m*→		---
1423.0	Cornelius Creek *(3100')* crosses A.T. .... w		756.1
1422.2	Black Rock *(3420')* left 200ft to overlook		756.9
1421.9	Stream *(3200')* footbridge, campsites .... C,w		757.2
1421.6	Cornelius Creek Trail *(3180')* left 3m to USFS Road 59		757.5
1421.0	Sugarland *(3280')* moss-covered rocky area		758.1
1420.5	Apple Orchard Trail *(3360')* left 300ft to spring .... w		758.6
---	*left 1m on blue-blazed trail to Apple Orchard Falls*		---
1420.4	Parkers Gap, USFS Road 812 *(3430')* steps .... R		758.7
1419.2	Coffee Table Rock *(4180')*		759.9
1419.0	Apple Orchard Mtn *(4225')* FAA radar dome, vistas		760.1
---	**Notice!** *no overnight camping or fires permitted on summit*		---
1418.7	The Guillotine *(4100')* boulder suspended over A.T.		760.4
1418.1	Blue Ridge Parkway - mile 76.3 *(3900')* .... R,w		761.0
---	*water right 0.2m on parkway to gate, then left 300ft to spring*		---
1418.0	Apple Orchard Spring *(3900')* seasonal .... w?		761.1
1417.8	**Thunder Hill Shelter** *(3960')* sleeps 6 *(1962)* .... S,w?		761.3
---	*on A.T., boxed spring (seasonal) on A.T.,* ←*S5.3m	N12.4m*→		---
1416.9	Hunting Creek Trail *(3600')* right 2m to USFS Road 45		762.2
1416.8	Blue Ridge Parkway - mile 74.9 *(3550')* .... R		762.3
1416.4	Thunder Hill Overlook *(3520')* parking area		762.7
1416.3	Viewpoint *(3500')* from raised rock on left		762.8
1416.2	Access road *(3550')* gravel surfaced, gate .... R		762.9
1415.2	Thunder Hill, Harrison Ground *(3685')* campsite to left C		763.9
1414.5	Harrison Ground Spring *(3220')* 100ft right .... w		764.6
1414.0	Springs *(2920')* on A.T. to right, also 150yds lower down .... w		765.1
1413.1	Petites Gap, USFS Road 35 *(2350')* parkway 100yds right .... R		766.0
1412.5	Archie's Notch *(2760')*		766.6
1411.9	Highcock Knob *(3070')*		767.2
1410.9	Marble Spring *(2300')* left 100yds to spring .... C,w		768.2
1410.4	Sulphur Spring Trail *(2515')* left 2.9m to USFS 35, rejoins A.T.		768.7
1408.6	Hickory Stand *(2650')* Belfast Trail		770.5
1408.1	Sulphur Spring Trail *(2590')* rejoins A.T. south		771.0
1407.3	Big Cove Branch *(1855')* crosses A.T. .... w		771.8

Central Virginia

Miles from Katahdin	Features / Services		Miles from Springer
1406.1	Campsite *(1500')*	C	773.0
1405.4	**Matts Creek Shelter** *(835') sleeps 6 (1961)*	S,w	773.7
---	*on A.T., stream in front of shelter,* ←*S12.4m* | *N3.9m*→		---
1415.4	Matts Creek Trail *(835') right 2.5m to US501*		763.7
1404.6	Campsite *(840') where Matts Creek enters James River*	C,w	774.5
1403.4	James River *(710') James River Foot Bridge (south end)*		775.7
1403.2	US501/VA130 🕮 *p.124 (735')*	R	775.9
---	*right 4.9m (on VA130)*–to private campground	C,L,G?,f	---
---	*left 5.9m*–to **GLASGOW, VA 24555**	L,M,G,Lm,f	---
---	*right 5.1m (on US501)*–to **BIG ISLAND, VA 24526**	M,G	---
1403.1	Lower Rocky Row Run *(740') bridge*	w	776.0
1403.1	Rocky Row Run *(760') bridge, campsites along creek*	C,w	776.0
1402.7	Powerline *(760')*		776.4
1402.5	Johns Creek *(790') crosses A.T.*	w	776.6
1402.1	VA812, USFS Road 36 *(830')*	R	777.0
1401.8	Johns Creek *(980') crosses A.T.*	w	777.3
1401.5	**Johns Hollow Shelter** *(1020') sleeps 6 (1961)*	S,w	777.6
---	*right 100yds, stream adjacent to shelter,* ←*S3.9m* | *N8.8m*→		---
1400.4	Old woods road *(1700')*	R	778.7
1399.5	Fullers Rocks *(2470') vistas*		779.6
1399.4	Little Rocky Row, Rocky Row Trail *(2430') left 2.8m to US501*		779.7
1398.8	Viewpoint *(2650') left 50ft to overlook*		780.3
1398.4	Big Rocky Row *(2992')*		780.7
1398.3	Viewpoint *(2905') left 40ft to overlook*		780.8
1396.9	Saddle Gap, Saddle Gap Trail *(2590') right 2.7m to VA812*		782.2
1395.8	Saltlog Gap *(2575') side trail overgrown*	w	783.3
1395.1	Pipeline *(2800')*		784.0
1394.3	Bluff Mtn *(3372') Ottie Cline Powell Memorial*		784.8
1393.4	Old woods road *(2750')*	R	785.7
1393.2	Punchbowl Mtn *(2870')*		785.9
1392.7	**Punchbowl Shelter** *(2500') sleeps 6 (1961)*	S,w	786.4
---	*left 0.2m, stream in front of shelter,* ←*S8.8m* | *N9.5m*→		---
1392.3	Blue Ridge Parkway - mile 51.7 *(2170')*	R	786.8
1392.2	Spring *(2160') right 100ft, piped*	w	786.9
1392.0	VA607, Robinson Gap Road *(2150') intersection USFS Rd 311*	R	787.1
1390.1	Rice Mtn *(2210')*		789.0
1389.4	Spring *(1700') on A.T. to left*	w	789.7
1389.0	Woods road *(1300') steps*	R	790.1

Central Virginia

Miles from Katahdin	Features / Services		Miles from Springer
1388.2	Pedlar River Bridge, USFS Road 39 *(1000') Little Irish Creek*	R,C,w	790.9
1385.4	Pedlar Lake Road, USFS Road 38 *(1320')*	R	793.7
1384.8	Spring *(1300') right 30ft, walled in stone*	w	794.3
1384.6	Old logging road *(1350')*	R	794.5
1384.2	Brown Mtn Creek *(1280') footbridge*	w	794.9
1384.1	Campsite *(1300')*	C,w	795.0
1383.5	Campsite *(1340')*	C,w	795.6
1383.2	**Brown Mtn Creek Shelter** *(1395') sleeps 6 (1961)*	S,w	795.9
---	*right 100ft, spring uphill from shelter, ←S9.5m | N5.6m→*		---
1383.0	Joseph Richeson Spring *(1400') right 50ft, boxed*	w	796.1
1381.4	US60 📖 *p.124 (2065') Long Mtn Wayside, parking*	R,G	797.7
---	*left 9.0m–to* **Buena Vista, VA 24416**	C,L,M,G,Lm	---
1380.5	USFS Road 507 *(2650') right 0.5m to spring*	R,w	798.6
1378.6	Bald Knob *(4059')*		800.5
1378.2	Viewpoint *(3800') 20ft right*		800.9
1377.6	**Cow Camp Gap Shelter** *(3160') sleeps 8 (1986) Old Hotel Trail right*	S,w	801.5
---	*right 0.6m, springs at shelter, ←S5.6m | N10.2m→*		---
1376.7	Stone wall *(3850') A.T. crosses wall*		802.4
1376.4	Cold Mtn *(4022')*		802.7
1375.5	Overhanging rock *(3680')*		803.6
1375.1	Hog Camp Gap, USFS Road 48 *(3420') spring 600yds to right*	R,w	804.0
1374.2	Tar Jacket Ridge *(3850')*		804.9
1372.9	VA634, USFS Road 63, Salt Log Gap *(3250')*	R	806.2
1372.4	Rock steps *(3250')*		806.7
1371.7	USFS Road 246 *(3500')*	R	807.4
1371.2	Greasy Spring Road *(3550') spring 0.2m left at double blazes*	R,w	807.9
1371.0	Spring *(3600') 60ft right*	w	808.1
1370.2	Wolf Rocks *(3895') vista*		808.9
1369.3	North Forks of Piney River *(3480') campsite south of streams*	C,w	809.8
1368.7	Spring *(3500') 200ft right*	w	810.4
1368.1	Elk Pond Branch *(3650') crosses A.T.*	w	811.0
1367.4	**Seeley-Woodworth Shelter** *(3770') sleeps 8 (1984)*	S,w	811.7
---	*right 300ft, springs 400ft beyond shelter, ←S10.2m | N6.9m→*		---
1366.3	Porters Field *(3550') left 100yds to spring*	C,w	812.8
1365.1	Fish Hatchery Road 📖 *p.125 (3455')*	R	814.0
---	*left 2.5m (left 1.6m on Fish Hatchery Road, then left 0.9m on paved*		---
---	*VA56)–to* **Montebello, VA 24464**	C,L,G?,Lm,f	---

Elevation profile: 4000' / 3000' / 2000' / 1000' — Brown Mt. Creek Shelter, US 60, Cow Camp Gap Shelter, Seeley-Woodworth Shelter

Central Virginia

Miles from Katahdin	Features / Services		Miles from Springer
1364.6	Spy Rock *(3860')* 400ft right to overlook	C	814.5
1364.3	Main Top Mtn *(4040')* on A.T. to right	C	814.8
1363.9	Overhanging rock *(3680')*		815.2
1363.5	Cash Hollow Rock *(3510')* Sentinel Pine, vistas		815.6
1362.2	Cash Hollow Road *(3270')*	R	816.9
1361.6	Campsites *(3400')* on A.T. to left	C	817.5
1361.4	VA826, Crabtree Farm Road *(3320')*	R,C,w	817.7
---	*left 0.5m to Crabtree Meadows CG, Crabtree Falls Trail*		---
1360.5	**The Priest Shelter** *(3840')* sleeps 8 *(1960)*	S,w	818.6
---	*right 0.1m, spring at shelter, ←S6.9m|N7.5m→*		---
1360.1	Viewpoint *(4000')* left 150ft to boulders, overlook		819.0
1360.0	The Priest *(4063')* wooded summit		819.1
1358.4	Viewpoint *(2890')* on A.T. to right		820.7
1357.0	Cripple Creek *(1780')*	w	822.1
1355.7	VA56, Tye River 📖 *p.125 (997')* suspension bridge	R,C,w	823.4
---	*left 4.1m–to campground*	C,L,G?	---
1353.9	Mau-Har Trail *(2000')* rejoins A.T. at Maupin Field Shelter		825.2
1353.1	Harpers Creek *(1800')* crosses A.T.	w	826.0
1353.0	**Harpers Creek Shelter** *(1800')* sleeps 6 *(1960)* tent sites	S,w	826.1
---	*left 100yds, stream next to shelter, ←S7.5m|N6.2m→*		---
1351.4	Viewpoint *(2800')* left to overlook		827.7
1351.0	Chimney Rocks *(3100')*		828.1
1350.9	Viewpoint *(3150')* 50ft left to overlook		828.2
1349.5	Viewpoint *(3800')* right 200ft to overlook		829.6
1349.3	Three Ridges *(3970')* wooded summit		829.8
1348.8	Hanging Rock *(3700')* vista		830.3
1348.3	Spring *(3500')* intermittent	w?	830.8
1347.2	Bee Mtn *(3035')*		831.9
1346.8	**Maupin Field Shelter** *(2720')* sleeps 6 *(1960)* tent sites	S,w	832.3
---	*left 300ft, spring behind shelter, ←S6.2m|N15.8m→*		---
---	*Mau-Har Trail rejoins A.T. south of Harpers Creek Shelter*		---
---	*left 2.5m–to Rusty's Hard Time Hollow 📖 p.125*	H,f	---
1345.5	Viewpoint *(3000')* left 20yds to overlook		833.6
1345.1	VA664, Reeds Gap *(2650')* left 300ft to parkway	R	834.0
1344.5	Blue Ridge Parkway - mile 13.1 *(2620')* Three Ridges Overlook	R	834.6
1342.4	Stream *(2500')* crosses A.T.	w	836.7
1341.8	Log steps *(2700')*		837.3
1341.5	Viewpoint *(2800')* left 150yds to overlook		837.6

Central Virginia

Miles from Katahdin	Features / Services	Miles from Springer
1340.7	Cedar Cliffs *(2850')* vista	838.4
1340.2	Blue Ridge Parkway - mile 9.6 *(2950')* Dripping Rock Parking Area .... R	838.9
1339.8	Laurel Springs *(2850')* seasonal .... w?	839.3
1337.5	Humpback Mtn *(3600')*	841.6
1336.5	Trail to Humpback Rocks *(3600')*	842.6
1335.0	Bear Spring *(2700')* on A.T. to left .... w	844.1
1332.8	Glass Hollow Overlook *(2300')*	846.3
1331.1	Mill Creek *(1690')* old road adjacent .... w	848.0
1331.0	**Paul C. Wolfe Shelter** *(1700')* sleeps 10 *(1991)* .... S,w	848.1
---	on A.T., stream next to shelter, ←S15.8m	N12.0m→	---
1330.1	Old cemetery *(1680')*	849.0
1329.4	Old cabin *(1800')* ruins to left	849.7
1329.2	Stream *(1820')* crosses A.T. in rocky area .... w	849.9
1327.9	Stream *(1780')* crosses A.T. .... w	851.2
---	*Notice!* Northbounders, go right on Blue Ridge Parkway where	---
---	A.T. leaves woods, then follow blazes across bridge over Interstate 64	---
---	and US250; directions reversed for Southbounders	---
1326.0	Rockfish Gap, Interstate 64/US250 📖 *p.126 (1900')* .... R,L,M	853.1
---	left 4.5m–to **WAYNESBORO, VA 22980** ......H,C,L,M,G,O,Lm,f	---
---	Northbounders, see information about backcountry permits for	---
---	Shenandoah National Park under Rockfish Gap on next page	---
1325.7	Skyline Drive - mile 105.2 *(1900')* concrete post with A.T. marker .... R	853.4
1325.2	Information Board 📖 *p.127 (2250')* left 0.2m to SNP Entrance Station	853.9
---	Northbounders, get backcountry permit at the Information Board on	---
---	A.T. here; if none available, get permit at Entrance Station	---
1322.3	McCormick Gap, Skyline Drive - mile 102.1 *(2435')* .... R	856.8
1321.0	Bear Den Mtn *(2885')* radio station, old tractor seats, vista	858.1
1320.5	Beagle Gap, Skyline Drive - mile 99.5 *(2530')* .... R	858.6
1319.6	Calf Mtn *(2975')* vista	859.5
1319.0	**Calf Mtn Shelter** *(2700')* sleeps 6 *(1984)* tent sites .... S,w	860.1
---	left 0.2m, spring on path to shelter, ←S12.0m	N13.0m→	---
1318.6	Power lines *(2350')*	860.5
1318.4	Spring *(2300')* on A.T. to right .... w	860.7
1318.0	Jarman Gap *(2175')* A.T. crosses fire road .... R	861.1
---	southern boundary of Shenandoah Natl. Park 📖 p.127 ; see info	---
---	about backcountry permits at Information Board above	---
1317.8	Spring *(2280')* on A.T. to right .... w	861.3
1316.2	Skyline Drive - mile 95.3 *(2200')* Sawmill Run Parking Area .... R	862.9
1314.8	Turk Mtn Trail *(2700')* left 0.9m to Turk Mtn	864.3

Elevation profile (4000' to 1000'): Humpback Mountain, Paul C. Wolfe Shelter, Rockfish Gap I-64/US250, Calf Mtn Shelter

Shenandoah National Park

1314.6	Turk Gap, Skyline Drive - mile 94.1 *(2625')* Turk Branch Trail .... R	864.5
1312.6	Skyline Drive - mile 92.4 *(3050')* .... R	866.5
1312.3	Wildcat Ridge Trail *(2950')* rejoins A.T. north	866.8
1309.5	Trail to Riprap Parking Area *(2800')* to the right	869.6
1309.2	Riprap Trail *(3000')* to the left	869.9
1308.5	Skyline Drive - mile 88.9 *(2650')* .... R	870.6
1306.7	Blackrock Gap, Skyline Drive - mile 87.4 *(2330')* fire road .... R	872.4
1306.5	Skyline Drive - mile 87.2 *(2400')* .... R	872.6
1306.0	**Blackrock Hut** *(2645')* sleeps 6 *(1941)* tent sites .... S,w	873.1
---	*right 0.2m, spring in front of shelter, ←S13.0m	N13.2m→*	---
1305.6	Trayfoot Mtn Trail *(3070')* to the left	873.5
1305.4	Blackrock *(3092')* open rocky summit	873.7
1304.4	Skyline Drive - mile 84.3 *(2800')* .... R	874.7
1304.2	Jones Run Trail *(2750')* left to Jones Run Parking Area	874.9
1303.7	Dundo Picnic Area *(2700')* left 0.1m, water pump .... w	875.4
1302.9	Browns Gap, Skyline Drive - mile 82.9 *(2600')* .... R	876.2
1302.4	Big Run Loop Trail *(2800')* left to Big Run Parling Area	876.7
1302.0	Skyline Drive - mile 82.2 *(2820')* vista .... R	877.1
1301.6	Skyline Drive - mile 81.9 *(2900')* Doyle River Overlook .... R	877.5
1300.7	Doyles River Trail *(2880')* right 0.3m to spring, cabin (locked) .... w	878.4
1299.8	Trail to Loft Mtn Amphitheater *(3300')* left at concrete marker	879.3
1298.6	Loft Mtn Campground 📖p.128 *(3200')* left 250ft (fee) .... C,G,Lm,f	880.5
1297.5	Frazier Discovery Trail *(3000')* left 0.1m to Skyline Drive	881.6
1296.8	Loft Mtn *(3320')*	882.3
1296.5	Trail to Ivy Creek Maintenance Hut *(3000')* left 200yds, spring .... w	882.6
1295.8	Ivy Creek *(2550')* crosses A.T. .... w	883.3
1294.4	Skyline Drive - mile 77.5 *(2900')* Ivy Creek Overlook .... R	884.7
1292.8	**Pinefield Hut** *(2430')* sleeps 6 *(1940)* tent sites .... S,w	886.3
---	*right 500ft, spring behind shelter, ←S13.2m	N8.2m→*	---
1292.6	Skyline Drive - mile 75.2 *(2600')* .... R	886.5
1291.8	Weaver Mtn *(2800')*	887.3
1290.7	Simmons Gap, Skyline Drive - mile 73.2 *(2250')* .... R,w	888.4
---	*right 400ft on road to Simmons Gap Ranger Station, water spigot*	---
1290.6	Power lines *(2300')*	888.5
1287.4	Powell Gap, Skyline Drive - mile 69.9 *(2295')* .... R	891.7
1287.0	Little Roundtop Mtn *(2700')*	892.1
1285.8	Smith Roach Gap, Skyline Drive - mile 68.6 *(2620')* .... R	893.3
1284.6	**Hightop Hut** *(3175')* sleeps 6 *(1939)* campsites .... S,w	894.5
---	*left 600ft, spring 125yds downhill, ←S8.2m	N12.4m→*	---

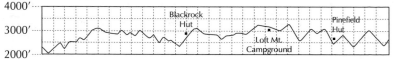

Shenandoah National Park

1284.1	Spring *(3500')* to the right under boulder	w	895.0
1284.0	Hightop Mtn *(3587')*		895.1
1282.5	Skyline Drive - mile 66.7 *(2635')*	R	896.6
1281.2	Swift Run Gap, US33/Skyline Drive - mile 65.5⌕*p.129 (2375') bridge*	R	897.9
---	*left 6.4m*–to **Elkton, VA 22827**	C,L,M,G	---
1281.0	Trail to old cemetery *(2400')* right 100yds		898.1
1280.9	Power line *(2500')*		898.2
1279.7	Saddleback Mtn Trail *(3000')* spring 1.1m right, rejoins A.T. north	w	899.4
1279.3	Saddleback Mtn *(3295')*		899.8
1278.7	Saddleback Mtn Trail *(2950')* spring 0.3m right, rejoins A.T. south	w	900.4
1278.2	South River Falls Trail *(3200')* right 1.5m to South River Falls	w	900.9
---	*left 0.1m to South River Picnic Area (rest rooms, water fountain)*		---
1277.6	South River Fire Road *(3400')*	R	901.5
1276.1	Baldface Mtn *(3600')*		903.0
1274.9	Spring *(3200')* on A.T. to left	w	904.2
1274.8	Trail to Pocosin Cabin (locked) *(3120')* right 250ft to spring	w	904.3
1274.7	Pocosin Fire Road *(3100')* right to spring at Pocosin Cabin	w	904.4
1273.0	Lewis Mtn East Trail *(3380')*		906.1
1272.9	Lewis Mtn Campground ⌕*p.129 (3380')* left 300ft (fee)	C,G,Lm,f	906.2
1272.2	**Bearfence Mtn Hut** *(3210')* sleeps 6 *(1940)* tent sites	S,w?	906.9
---	*right 400ft, seasonal spring at shelter, ←S12.4m	N11.5m→*		---
1272.0	Slaughter Trail *(3200')* to the right		907.1
1271.4	Bearfence Loop Trail *(3550')* rejoins A.T. north, vistas		907.7
1271.0	Trail to Bearfence Mtn *(3380')* right to rocks		908.1
1269.6	Bootens Gap *(3245')* A.T. crosses fire road	R	909.5
1269.2	Laurel Prong Trail *(3480')* right 2.8m to Camp Hoover		909.9
1268.7	Hazeltop *(3815')*		910.4
1266.8	Milam Gap, Skyline Drive - mile 52.8 *(3300')* parking area	R	912.3
---	*Mill Prong Trail right 1.8m to Rapidan Camp*		---
1265.9	Spring *(3300')* right 150ft	w	913.2
1265.7	Tanners Ridge Road *(3350')* cemetery to left	R	913.4
1265.1	Lewis Spring ⌕*p.129 (3380')* left to spring, 0.6m to Lewis Falls	w	914.0
---	*right 0.2m, then left 0.2m*–to Big Meadows Wayside	M,G,f	---
1264.6	Blackrock Viewpoint *(3600')* right 0.1m, vista		914.5
1264.2	Big Meadows ⌕*p.129 (3500')* right 0.3m (showers, fee)	C,L,M,Lm	914.9
1263.9	Monkey Head *(3500')* vista		915.2
1263.6	Davids Spring *(3450')* 50ft left	w	915.5
1262.6	Trail to Fishers Gap Overlook *(3100')* right 100ft to overlook		916.5
1262.5	Redgate Fire Road *(3050')*	R	916.6

Shenandoah National Park

Miles from Katahdin	Features / Services	Miles from Springer
1262.3	Franklin Cliffs *(3135')*	916.8
1260.7	**Rock Spring Hut** *(3465') sleeps 8 (1980)* .... S,w	918.4
---	*left 0.2m, spring at base of boulder,* ←*S11.5m* | *N10.9m*→	---
1260.4	Trail to Hawksbill *(3600') right 0.9m to Byrd's Nest # 2*	918.7
1259.4	Hawksbill Gap *(3350') left 0.1m to spring* .... w	919.7
1259.1	Cliffs *(3460') Crescent Rock*	920.0
1259.0	Trail to Crescent Rock Overlook *(3450') right 0.1m to overlook*	920.1
1257.9	Pollock Knob *(3560')*	921.2
1256.9	Skyland Road, south *(3550') horse stables to left* .... R	922.2
1256.1	Skyland Road, north 🕮 *p.129 (3700')* .... R	923.0
---	*left 0.3m–to Skyland* .... L,M	---
1256.0	Stony Man Nature Trail *(3700')*	923.1
1255.7	Trail to Stony Man *(3800') left 0.2m to summit*	923.4
1254.6	Little Stony Man Cliffs *(3600')*	924.5
1254.1	Hughes River Gap *(3097') Stony Man Parking Area 200ft right*	925.0
1253.7	Nicholson Hollow Trail *(3180') to the right*	925.4
1253.6	Crusher Ridge Trail *(3200') to the left*	925.5
1253.0	Spring *(3100') left 0.3m* .... w	926.1
1252.6	Power lines *(3220')*	926.5
1251.9	Pinnacles Picnic Area *(3400') restrooms, water fountain* .... w	927.2
1251.8	Trail to Jewell Hollow Overlook *(3300') right 100ft to overlook*	927.3
1251.5	Leading Ridge Trail *(3350') to the right*	927.6
1250.8	The Pinnacle *(3730')*	928.3
1249.8	**Byrds Nest #3 Shelter** *(3200') sleeps 8 (1964)* .... S,w?	929.3
---	*on A.T., no water at last report* ←*S10.9m* | *N4.4m*→	---
1249.1	Meadow Spring Trail *(3400') left 0.3m to spring* .... w	930.0
1248.5	Trail to Marys Rock *(3500') left 0.1m, vista*	930.6
1246.6	Thornton Gap, US211/Skyland Drive - mile 31.5 🕮 *p.130 (2310')* .... R	932.5
---	*right 0.1m–to rest rooms, phone* .... w	---
---	*left 6m–to* **Luray, VA 22835** .... C,L,M,G,O,Lm,f	---
1245.4	**Pass Mtn Hut** *(2690') sleeps 8 (1939)* .... S,w	933.7
---	*right 0.2m, spring at shelter,* ←*S4.4m* | *N13.1m*→	---
1244.6	Pass Mtn *(3050')*	934.5
1244.2	Skyline Drive - mile 28.5 *(2500') Beahms Gap Overlook* .... R	934.9
1243.1	Trail to Byrds Nest #4 Picnic Shelter *(2700') spring 100ft left* .... w	936.0
---	**Notice!** *no overnight camping or fires permitted at shelter*	---
1242.4	Neighbor Mtn Trail *(2400') to the left*	936.7
1240.8	Thornton River Trail *(2650') to the right*	938.3
1238.6	Stream *(2250') Jeremy's Run Trail left* .... w	940.5

Shenandoah National Park

Miles from Katahdin	Features / Services	Miles from Springer
1238.5	Spring *(2300')* right 100ft .... w	940.6
1238.4	Trail to Elkwallow Picnic Area *(2470')* right 200ft .... w	940.7
1238.0	Elkwallow Gap, Skyland Drive - mile 23.9 📖*p.130 (2480')* .... R	941.1
---	right 0.1m–to Elkwallow Wayside .... M,G	---
1237.2	Trail to Range View Cabin (locked) *(2900')* right 0.1m to spring .... w	941.9
1237.1	Power line *(2920')*	942.0
1236.8	Piney Branch Trail *(2950')* to the right	942.3
1236.5	Skyline Drive - mile 21.9 *(3105')* Rattlesnake Point Overlook .... R	942.6
1236.3	Trail to Sugarloaf *(3280')* left 50ft to summit	942.8
1235.9	Tuscarora Trail 📖*p.130 (3400')* to the left	943.2
1235.8	Trail to Hogback, fourth peak *(3440')* right 30ft to summit	943.3
1235.5	Skyline Drive - mile 21.1 *(3400')* .... R	943.6
1235.3	Trail to Hogback, third peak *(3440')*	943.8
1235.2	Skyline Drive - mile 20.8 *(3400')* Sugarloaf Trail right .... R	943.9
1235.0	Hogback, second peak *(3475')* radio antennae	944.1
1234.8	Spring *(3420')* right 0.2m, boxed .... w	944.3
1234.7	Hogback, first peak *(3420')* left 25ft to summit	944.4
1234.1	Trail to Little Hogback Overlook *(3050')* right 50ft to overlook	945.0
1233.9	Little Hogback *(3100')* vista	945.2
1233.4	Skyline Drive - mile 18.9 *(2850')* .... R	945.7
1232.3	**Gravel Spring Hut** *(2680')* sleeps 8 *(1940)* .... S,w	946.8
---	right 0.2m, spring at shelter, ←S13.1m | N10.5m→	---
1232.1	Skyline Drive - mile 17.7 *(2660')* Browntown Trail left .... R	947.0
1231.0	South Marshall Mt. *(3210')*	948.1
1230.5	Skyline Drive - mile 15.9 *(3090')* .... R	948.6
1229.8	North Marshall Mt. *(3370')*	949.3
1228.9	Hogwallow Spring *(2980')* right 30ft, piped .... w	950.2
1228.3	Hogwallow Gap, Skyline Drive - mile 14.2 *(2740')* .... R	950.8
1226.6	Jenkins Gap, Skyline Drive - mile 12.3 *(2400')* Jenkins Gap Trail .... R	952.5
1225.7	Compton Springs *(2550')* right 75ft .... w	953.4
1225.3	Trail to Compton Peak *(2910')* left 0.2m to overlook	953.8
1224.5	Compton Gap, Skyline Drive - mile 10.4 *(2415')* .... R	954.6
1224.3	Dickey Ridge Trail *(2500')* Indian Run Spring 0.3m right on road .... w	954.8
1222.7	Compton Gap Trail 📖*p.130 (2250')* overgrown fire road .... R?	956.4
---	right (straight ahead) 0.5m–to private hostel	---
1222.5	Shenandoah Natl. Park permit booth *(2300')* Possum Rest	956.6
---	northern boundary of Shenandoah Natl. Park 📖*p.127*; Southbounders,	---
---	get a backcountry permit for the park at registration board on the A.T. here	---
1221.8	**Tom Floyd Wayside** *(1900')* sleeps 6 *(1980s)* (not a SNP "Wayside") ...... S,w	957.3
---	left 200ft, spring 0.2m on blue-blaze, ←S10.5m | N8.1m→	---
1220.8	Trail to N. Virginia 4-H Center *(1300')* left 0.3m, swimming (fee) .... w	958.3

Northern Virginia

1220.3	VA602 *(1100')* .... R	958.8
1219.0	Sloan Creek *(1000') not potable, do not drink!* .... w?	960.1
1218.9	US522, Chester Gap 📖*p.131 (950')* .... R	960.2
---	*left 4m–*to **FRONT ROYAL, VA 22630** .... L,M,G,O,Lm,f	---
1218.8	Natl. Zoological Park, southern boundary 📖*p.131 (980')*	960.3
---	***Notice!*** *no camping or fires permitted for next 2.3 miles north*	---
1218.1	Bear Hollow Creek *(1200') crosses A.T.* .... w	961.0
1217.1	Old woods road *(1400')* .... R	962.0
1216.6	Natl. Zoological Park, northern boundary *(1800')*	962.5
---	***Notice!*** *no camping or fires permitted for next 2.3 miles south*	---
1216.1	Woods road *(1900')* .... R	963.0
1215.7	Fire Road 3460 *(1800')* .... R	963.4
1215.6	Stream *(1750') crosses A.T.* .... w	963.5
---	*right 400ft on blue-blazed trail to Tom Sealock Spring*	---
1214.8	Power line *(1700')*	964.3
1213.7	**Jim and Molly Denton Shelter** *(1310') sleeps 8 (1991)* .... S,w	965.4
---	*left 150ft, spring on A.T., ←S8.1m	N5.5m→*	---
1212.7	Stream *(1100') footbridge* .... w	966.4
1212.6	VA638 *(1120') paved* .... R	966.5
1210.8	Railroad tracks *(840') Goose Creek nearby*	968.3
1210.7	Manassas Gap, VA55/VA725 📖*p.132 (800') Discovery Monument* .... R	968.4
---	*left 1.2m (on VA55)–*to **LINDEN, VA 22642** .... G	---
---	*A.T. passes under Interstate 66 (no exits) on VA725*	---
1208.2	**Manassas Gap Shelter** *(1655') sleeps 6 (2002) Ted Lake Trail* .... S,w	970.9
---	*right 200ft, spring in front of shelter, ←S5.5m	N4.5m→*	---
1207.0	Stream *(1800') intermittent* .... w?	972.1
1206.3	Trico Trail *(2080') left 0.5m to Trico Fire tower, do not climb!*	972.8
1203.7	**Dick's Dome Shelter** *(1230') sleeps 4 (1985)* .... S,w	975.4
---	*right 0.2m, stream at shelter, ←S4.5m	N8.4m→*	---
1202.7	Spring *(1700') on A.T. to right* .... w	976.4
1201.5	Wooden park bench 📖*p.131 (1840')*	977.6
---	*right 1.7m on side trail–*to Sky Meadows State Park C	---
1198.9	Ashby Gap, US50 📖*p.132 (900')* .... R,M	980.2
1198.7	Stream *(1000') crosses A.T.* .... w	980.4
1197.4	Stream *(1250') crosses A.T.* .... w	981.7
1196.9	Stream *(1260') crosses A.T.* .... w	982.2
1196.6	Trail to Myron Glaser Cabin (locked) *(1000')*	982.5
1196.1	Stream *(1100') Duke Hollow* .... w	983.0

Miles from Katahdin	Features / Services	Miles from Springer
1195.7	Fishers Hill Loop Trail, south end *(1200') rejoins A.T. north*	983.4
1195.3	**Rod Hollow Shelter** *(840') sleeps 8 (1986)* .... S,w	983.8
---	*left 400ft, spring at shelter,* ←S8.4m | N6.9m→	---
1193.6	Stream *(845') Bolden Hollow* .... w	985.5
1192.1	Morgan Mill Stream *(825') Ashby Hollow, footbridge* .... w	987.0
1191.6	VA605 *(1100') power line* .... R	987.5
1190.8	Stream *(1000') Reservoir Hollow* .... w	988.3
1190.4	Spring *(1180') on A.T. to right, near old cabin ruins* .... w	988.7
1189.8	Buzzard Hill *(1300') left 150ft to summit*	989.3
1189.4	Streams *(800') Fent Wiley Hollow* .... w	989.7
1188.8	Tomblin Hill *(1250') ant mounds along A.T.*	990.3
1188.4	**Sam Moore Shelter** *(990') sleeps 6 (1990) Sawmill Spring* .... S,w	990.7
---	*right 0.1m, spring at shelter,* ←S6.9m | N14.1m→	---
1187.2	Spout Run *(700') steep ravine*	991.9
1186.0	Stream *(880') footbridge* .... w	993.1
1185.4	Bears Den Rocks ▢*p.132 (1300')*	993.7
---	*right 0.1m on side trail–to Bears Den Hostel* .... H,C,L,M?,G,Lm,f,w	---
1184.8	Snickers Gap, VA7/VA679 ▢*p.132 (1000')* .... R,M,G	994.3
1184.2	Viewpoint *(980') on A.T.*	994.9
1184.0	Stream *(800') Pigeon Hollow* .... w	995.1
1182.6	Stream/spring *(820') spring left 150ft* .... w	996.5
1182.3	Virginia-West Virginia border *(970') first or last crossing*	996.8
1182.2	Crescent Rock *(1300') vista*	996.9
1181.6	Sand Spring *(1150') left 200ft on River Trail* .... w	997.5
1181.5	Devils Racecourse *(1180') boulder field, stream beneath* .... w	997.6
---	*A.T. follows Virginia/W.Virginia border north to Loudoun Hgts Trail*	---
1178.7	Wilson Gap *(1380')*	1000.4
1178.1	The Lookout *(1600') boulder pile on right, no views*	1001.0
1177.5	Trail to Blackburn A.T. Center ▢*p.132 (1650') right 0.3m* .... H,f,w	1001.6
1177.3	Trail to campground *(1655') right 0.1m (keep left at fork)* C	1001.8
1177.1	Viewpoint *(1660') vista from cliffs to left*	1002.0
1176.5	Laurel Spring *(1480') left, unreliable* .... w?	1002.6
1175.9	Buzzard Rocks *(1500') left 0.1m, unofficial campsite* C	1003.2
1174.3	**David Lesser Memorial Shelter** *(1430') sleeps 6 (1994) tent sites* .... S,w	1004.8
---	*right 350ft, spring 0.2m downhill,* ←S14.1m | N15.6m→	---
1173.0	Old woods road *(1500')* .... R	1006.1
1171.3	Keys Gap, WV9 ▢*p.133 (830')* .... R,M,G	1007.8
1169.8	Power line *(900')*	1009.3

West Virginia-Maryland

Miles from Katahdin	Features / Services	Miles from Springer
1167.6	Old road *(1250')* stone Civil War redoubts .... R	1011.5
---	**Notice!** *no camping or fires permitted from here north to Potomac River*	---
1167.4	Loudoun Heights Trail *(1200')* right *(A.T. leaves ridge)*	1011.7
---	*A.T. follows Virginia/W.Virginia border south to Devils Racecourse*	---
1166.7	WV32, Chestnut Hill Road *(650')* paved .... R	1012.4
1166.4	Shenandoah River *(275')* A.T. crosses on bridge	1012.7
1166.0	US340 *(275')* see Harpers Ferry listing below .... R,C,L,M,G,Lm	1013.1
1165.7	Trail to ATC Offices *(425')* left 0.2m *(past Storer College campus)* .... f	1013.4
1165.1	**HARPERS FERRY, WV 25425** 📖 *p.133 (270')* .... L,M,G?,O,f	1014.0
---	*right on Shenandoah St to Harpers Ferry Natl. Hist. Park visitor center*	---
1165.0	Potomac River *(250')* Goodloe Byron Memorial Footbridge	1014.1
---	**Notice!** *no camping or fires permitted from here south to Loudoun Hgts*	---
---	*Trail; Potomac River is West Virginia-Maryland border*	---
1164.8	C&O Canal Towpath *(260')* A.T. north goes right at end of bridge	1014.3
1163.7	Sandy Hook Bridge, US340 *(260')* A.T. passes under bridge	1015.4
1163.5	Blue-blazed trail 📖 *p.134 (260')* left 0.2m *(across canal and railroad*	1015.6
---	*tracks)* then right 0.3m on paved road–to hostel .... H,C,L,M,Lm	---
1162.4	Weaverton Primitive Area *(260')* no camping, day use only	1016.7
---	**Notice!** *do not drink water from the Potomac River*	---
1162.2	C&O Canal Towpath *(260')* where A.T. leaves towpath	1016.9
1162.1	Railroad tracks/Keep Tryst Road *(260')* .... R	1017.0
1161.9	US340 Overpass *(280')* A.T. passes under highway	1017.2
1161.7	Weverton Road *(300')* .... R	1017.4
1160.8	Trail to Weverton Cliffs *(800')* right 500ft, vistas	1018.3
1158.7	**Ed Garvey Shelter** *(890')* sleeps 12 *(2001)* tent sites .... S,w	1020.4
---	*right 100ft, spring 0.4m downhill, ←S15.6m | N4.1m→*	---
1156.7	Dirt road *(1050')* Brownsville Gap .... R	1022.4
1156.4	Glenn R. Caveney plaque *(1120')* right 10ft	1022.7
1155.1	Gathland State Park 📖 *p.134 (930')* rest rooms on A.T. *(seasonal)* .... w	1024.0
---	**Notice!** *no camping or fires by A.T. hikers permitted in park*	---
1155.0	Crampton Gap, MD572/Gapland Road *(950')* war memorial .... R	1024.1
1154.9	Picnic pavilion *(920')* water spigot *(seasonal)* .... w	1024.2
1154.6	**Crampton Gap Shelter** *(1000')* sleeps 6 *(1941)* .... S,w?	1024.5
---	*right 0.3m, spring (intermittent), ←S4.1m | N5.0m→*	---
1152.0	Trail to Bear Spring Cabin (locked) *(1480')* right 0.5m to spring .... w	1027.1
1151.4	White Rocks *(1500')* cliffs to left	1027.7
1151.2	Lambs Knoll *(1600')* left 200ft, antenna tower	1027.9
1150.1	Tower Road *(1300')* paved .... R	1029.0
1149.6	**Rocky Run Shelters** *(970')* two shelters sleep 6 and 16 *(2008)* .... S,w	1029.5
---	*left 0.2m, spring at shelter, ←S5.0m | N7.5m→*	---

Maryland

Miles from Katahdin	Features / Services		Miles from Springer
1149.1	Power line *(850')*		1030.0
1148.6	Fox Gap, Reno Monument Road *(900') paved, plaque nearby*	R	1030.5
1147.8	Dahlgren Back Pack Campground 📖 *p.135 (990') hot shower*	C,w	1031.3
1147.6	Turners Gap, US40A 📖 *p.135 (1000')*	R,M	1031.5
---	*left 2m*–to **Boonsboro, MD 21713**	M,G,Lm	---
1147.4	Dahlgren Road *(1100')*	R	1031.7
1146.7	Stone fences *(1280') A.T. crosses two*		1032.4
1146.2	Monument Road *(1300')*	R	1032.9
1146.0	Washington Monument Road *(1400') public telephone 200ft left*	R	1033.1
1145.8	Washington Monument State Park *(1500') restrooms, spigot*	w	1033.3
1145.6	Washington Monument, circa 1827 *(1550') left 150ft, vista*		1033.5
1145.3	Power line *(1320')*		1033.8
1143.5	Boonsboro Mtn Road *(1300')*	R	1035.6
1143.2	Bartman Hill *(1380')*		1035.9
1142.8	Boonsboro Mtn Road *(1250')*	R	1036.3
1142.7	Interstate 70 📖 *p.135 (1225') A.T. crosses on footbridge*	R	1036.4
---	*blue-blazed trail at northern end of footbridge leads up to US40,*		---
---	*then left 0.4m*–to Greenbrier State Park	C,M	---
1142.2	Telephone line *(1320')*		1036.9
1142.1	**Pine Knob Shelter** *(1360') sleeps 5 (1939)*	S,w	1037.0
---	*left 0.1m, spring beyond shelter, ←S7.5m | N8.2m→*		---
1142.0	Trail to Pine Knob Shelter *(1370') left 0.1m to shelter (see above)*	w	1037.1
1140.5	Trail to Annapolis Rocks *(1730')*	C,w	1038.6
---	*at rocks, left 0.2m on blue-blazed trail to spring, tent sites*		---
1139.5	Black Rock Cliffs *(1800')*		1039.6
1139.0	Black Rock Creek *(1650') intermittent*	w?	1040.1
1138.8	Pogo Memorial Campsite *(1550')*	C,w	1040.3
---	*right 200ft to spring (off road to the right), also, spring left off A.T.*		---
1134.1	Wolfsville Road 📖 *p.135 (1400') paved*	R	1045.0
---	*left 0.3m*–to private hostel	H,M?,Lm	---
---	*left 2.4m*–to **Smithsburg, MD 21783**	M,G,Lm	---
1134.0	Stream/spring *(1400') right 40yds to boxed spring (water for shelter)*	w	1045.1
1133.9	**Ensign Cowall Shelter** *(1430') sleeps 8 (1999)*	S,w	1045.2
---	*left 150ft, spring just south, ←S8.2m | N4.9m→*		---
1133.6	Power lines *(1500')*		1045.5
1132.6	Foxville Road, MD77 *(1450') paved*	R	1046.5
1131.3	Power line *(1300')*		1047.8
1131.0	Spring *(1300') to the left behind hemlocks*	w	1048.1
1130.9	Stream *(1250') do not drink water!*	w?	1048.2
1130.8	Warner Gap Road *(1200') gravel surfaced*	R	1048.3

Elevation profile: Rocky Run Shelter — US 40A — I-70 — Pine Knob Shelter — Pogo Memorial Campsite — Ensign Cowall Shelter (2000' / 1000')

Maryland-Pennsylvania

Miles from Katahdin	Features / Services	Miles from Springer
1130.4	Stone wall *(1360')* A.T. crosses wall	1048.7
1130.1	Little Antietam Creek *(1200')* do not drink water! .... w?	1049.0
1130.0	MD491, Raven Rock Hollow *(1210')* .... R	1049.1
1129.8	Trail to Raven Rock Cliff *(1300')* right 150ft to cliff	1049.3
1129.0	**Devils Racecourse Shelter** *(1480')* sleeps 7 (1950s) .... S,w?	1050.1
---	*right 0.3m, spring (intermittent), ←S4.9m	N9.6m→*	---
---	*Devils Racecourse boulder field 0.1m beyond/below shelter*	---
1128.0	Quirauk Mtn *(1890')* A.T. bypasses summit	1051.1
1127.2	Trail to High Rock *(1800')* right 0.1m to vista	1051.9
1124.3	Pen-Mar Park 📖 *p.135 (1300')* picnic area, sunset pavilion .... M,G,w	1054.8
---	**Notice!** *no camping/overnight stay by hikers permitted in park*	---
1124.1	Maryland-Pennsylvania border *(1250')* railroad tracks .... R	1055.0
---	*Maryland-Pennsylvania border is the Mason-Dixon Line*	---
1124.0	Pen-Mar Road *(1250')* paved .... R	1055.1
1123.4	Falls Creek *(900')* bridge .... w	1055.7
1123.0	Buena Vista Road 📖 *p.135 (1300')* spring, 1.5m right to **Cascade, MD**... R,w	1056.1
1121.8	Old Route 16 📖 *p.136 (1300')* paved .... R	1057.3
1121.5	PA 16 📖 *p.136 (1200')* paved .... R	1057.6
---	*right 2.2m–to* **Blue Ridge Summit, PA 17214** .... M,G	---
---	*left 5m–to* **Waynesboro, PA 17268** .... L,M,G,Lm	---
1121.3	Mentzer Gap Road *(1250')* .... R	1057.8
1120.9	Rattlesnake Run Road *(1350')* .... R	1058.2
1120.7	Bailey Spring *(1300')* left 45ft, boxed .... w	1058.4
1119.4	**Deer Lick Shelters** *(1420')* two shelters sleep 4 each (1940s) ...... S,w	1059.7
---	*on A.T., spring 0.2m on blue-blazed trail, ←S9.6m	N2.4m→*	---
1118.5	Woods Road *(1300')* .... R	1060.6
1117.0	**Antietam Shelter** *(890')* sleeps 6 (1940) .... S,w?	1062.1
---	*on A.T., water (see Old Forge below), ←S2.4m	N1.2m→*	---
---	**Notice!** *do not drink water from Antietam Creek*	---
1116.9	Old Forge Picnic Ground *(900')* .... w	1062.2
---	*water available year-round from well house off A.T. to the left*	---
1116.6	Rattlesnake Run Road *(950')* .... R	1062.5
1116.0	Old Forge Road *(1000')* Tumbling Run .... R,w	1063.1
1115.8	**Tumbling Run Shelters** *(1120')* two shelters sleep 4 each (1940s) ...... S,w	1063.3
---	*left 100ft, spring 300ft across stream, ←S1.2m	N6.6m→*	---
---	*blue-blazed trail left 0.6m to Hermitage Cabin (locked)*	---
1114.6	Trail to Chimney Rocks *(1900')* right 400ft to vista	1064.5
1112.5	Power line *(2000')*	1066.6
1111.9	Snowy Mtn Road *(1750')* .... R	1067.2
1111.2	Swamp Road *(1600')* .... R	1067.9

Pennsylvania

Miles from Katahdin	Features / Services	Miles from Springer

1110.9	PA233 📖 *p.136 (1600') paved* .... R	1068.2
---	*right 1.2m–to **SOUTH MOUNTAIN, PA 17261** ....* M?,G?	---
1109.2	**Rocky Mtn Shelters** *(1520') two shelters sleep 4 each (1989)*................ S,w	1069.9
---	*right 0.2m, water (see note below),* ←S6.6m	N5.6m→	---
---	*follow dirt road in front of the shelter about 80yds, then go left*	---
---	*on blue-blazed trail to spring (on the right where blazes end)*	---
1106.2	US30 📖 *p.136 (960')* .... R	1072.9
---	*left 3.5m–to **Fayetteville, PA 17222** ....* L,M,Lm	---
1105.8	Caledonia State Park 📖*p.137(950') rest rooms, pool* .... C,w	1073.3
---	***Notice!** no overnight camping permitted along A.T. inside park*	---
1104.5	Three Valley Trail *(1300') to the left*	1074.6
1104.3	Locust Gap Trail *(1380') Quarry Gap Road*	1074.8
1104.0	Spring *(1300') on A.T. to the right* .... w	1075.1
1103.6	**Quarry Gap Shelters** *(1455') two shelters, each sleeps 4 (1935)*........... S,w	1075.5
---	*on A.T., spring/stream in front of shelter,* ←S5.6m	N7.4m→	---
1103.4	Stream *(1460')*	1075.7
1102.8	Hosack Run Trail *(1750') to the right*	1076.3
1102.2	Ridge Road *(2000')* .... R	1076.9
1102.1	Stillhouse Road *(1980') Sandy Sod Junction* .... R	1077.0
1101.3	Powerline *(1800')*	1077.8
1100.9	Old woods road *(1950')* .... R	1078.2
1099.5	Middle Ridge Road *(2050')* .... R	1079.6
1099.0	Means Hollow/Canada Hollow/Ridge Roads *(1900') intersection* .... R	1080.1
1098.6	Milesburn Cabin (locked) *(1635') spring 100yds left* .... R,w	1080.5
1098.2	Ridge Road *(1800')* .... R	1080.9
1097.5	Rocky Knob Trail *(1850') nature loop*	1081.6
1096.8	Power line *(1900')*	1082.3
1096.2	**Birch Run Shelter** *(1795') sleeps 8 (2003)*... S,w	1082.9
---	*on A.T., spring in front of shelter,* ←S7.4m	N6.2m→	---
1094.9	Shippensburg Road *(2050') Big Flat Fire Tower* .... R	1084.2
1093.0	Trail to Michener Cabin (locked) *(1820') right 0.2m, spring*..................... w	1086.1
1092.4	Tumbling Run Game Preserve *(1850') extends 0.7m north*	1086.7
---	***Notice!** no camping or fires permitted in game preserve*	---
1091.7	Tumbling Run Game Preserve, entrance road *(1820')* .... R	1087.4
1090.9	Woodrow Road *(1800')* .... R	1088.2
1090.1	Sunset Rocks Trail *(1350') to the right, rejoins A.T. north*	1089.0
1090.0	**Toms Run Shelters** *(1300') two shelters, each sleeps 4 (1936)*............... S,w	1089.1
---	*on A.T., spring behind old chimney,* ←S6.2m	N10.9m→	---
---	***Midpoint of A.T. for "Class of 2009" @ mile point 1089.6***	---

Pennsylvania

Miles from Katahdin	Features / Services		Miles from Springer
1088.9	Michaux Road *(1300')*	R	1090.2
1088.2	Halfway Spring *(1100') right 150ft*	w	1090.9
1087.9	Sunset Rocks Trail *(1000') to the right, rejoins A.T. south*		1091.2
1087.7	Stream *(950') crosses A.T.*	w	1091.4
1086.6	PA233 *(900')*	R	1092.5
1086.3	Pine Grove Furnace State Park 🕮 *p.137 (820')*	C,w	1092.8
---	on A.T.–Ironmaster's Mansion, camp store	H,G,Lm,f	---
---	*Notice! camping only at designated areas, pets on leash in park*		---
1086.1	Fuller Lake *(820') beach, swimming, concession stand*	w	1093.0
1085.3	Midpoint marker 🕮 *p.137 (1100')*		1093.8
1083.8	Trail to Pole Steeple *(1300') left 0.5m to cliff, vista*		1095.3
1080.5	Limekiln Road *(1080')*	R	1098.6
1080.3	Trail to Pine Grove Rd 🕮 *p.137 (980') left 0.7m to campground*	C,G,Lm,f	1098.8
1079.3	Tagg Run *(805') water not potable*	w?	1099.8
1079.1	**James Frye Shelter at Tagg Run** *(800') sleeps 9 (1998) tent sites*	S,w	1100.0
---	*right 0.2m, spring 0.4m on blue-blazed trail, ←S10.9m│N8.1m→*		---
1078.6	Pine Grove Road 🕮 *p.137 (640') left 0.3m to campground*	R,C,M	1100.5
1077.8	Railroad tracks *(680')*		1101.3
1077.7	Hunters Run Road, PA34 🕮 *p.137 (980') right 0.2m to store*	R,G,f,w	1101.4
1075.9	PA94 🕮 *p.137 (880')*	R	1103.2
---	*left 2.5m–to* **Mt. Holly Springs, PA 17065**	M,G,Lm	---
1075.8	Power line *(900')*		1103.3
1075.7	Sheet Iron Road *(780')*	R	1103.4
1075.2	Stream *(700') crosses A.T.*	w	1103.9
1074.9	Stream *(650') telephone line nearby*	w	1104.2
1074.5	Old Town Road *(750') dirt surfaced*	R	1104.6
1073.1	Whiskey Spring Road *(800') Whiskey Spring on A.T. to right*	R,w	1106.0
1072.4	Viewpoint *(1200')*		1106.7
1071.9	Pipeline right-of-way *(1000')*		1107.2
1071.1	Little Dogwood Run *(800') stream*	w	1108.0
---	*right 1.7m on orange-blazed trail to BSA Camp Tuckahoe*		---
1071.0	**Alec Kennedy Shelter** *(950') sleeps 7 (1991)*	S,w	1108.1
---	*right 800ft, spring on blue-blazed trail, ←S8.1m│N18.2m→*		---
---	*Notice! no camping permitted from Alec Kennedy Shelter north*		---
---	*to Darlington Shelter, except at official Backpacker's Campsite*		---
1070.1	Center Point Knob *(1060')*		1109.0
---	*right to White Rocks Ridge Trail; White Rocks formation marks the*		---
---	*northern end of the Blue Ridge Mountains*		---

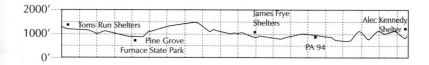

Pennsylvania

Pennsylvania

Miles from Katahdin	Features / Services		Miles from Springer
1045.5	**Cove Mtn Shelter** *(1200') sleeps 8 (2000)*	S,w	1133.6
---	*right 0.2m, spring 400ft downhill,* ←S7.3m	N8.6m→		---
1043.6	Hawk Rock *(1225')* on A.T. to left, vista		1135.5
1043.3	Rock slide *(800')*		1135.8
1042.3	Sherman Creek *(385')* A.T. crosses on bridge	w?	1136.8
1041.9	PA274 *(390')* left 0.7m to supermarket	R,G	1137.2
1041.4	**DUNCANNON, PA 17020** 📖 p.139 *(385')*	R,L,M,Lm,f	1137.7
1040.4	PA849, Newport Rd *(380')* campground	R,C	1138.7
1040.2	US22/322 *(380')* Juniata River, left 0.2m to truck stop	R,M	1138.9
1040.1	Susquehanna River 📖 p.140 *(380')* Clarks Ferry Bridge	R	1139.0
1039.6	US22/322/railroad tracks *(380')*	R	1139.5
1039.2	Susquehanna Trail *(680')* to the left, rejoins A.T. north		1139.9
1038.9	Stream *(650')* intermittent	w?	1140.2
1038.8	Woods road *(1200')*	R	1140.3
1038.6	Spring *(1200')* left 200ft	w	1140.5
1038.2	Susquehanna Trail *(1250')* to the left, rejoins A.T. south		1140.9
1036.9	**Clarks Ferry Shelter** *(1180') sleeps 8 (1993)*	S,w	1142.2
---	*right 300ft, spring at shelter,* ←S8.6m	N6.7m→		---
1036.6	Power line *(1380')*		1142.5
1035.7	Pipeline right-of-way *(1400')*		1143.4
1033.8	Pipeline right-of-way *(1390')* microwave tower nearby		1145.3
1033.4	Tower access road *(1300')*	R	1145.7
1033.0	PA225 *(1280')* parking area	R	1146.1
1032.8	Radio antenna *(1320')*		1146.3
1032.4	Power lines *(1300')*		1146.7
1031.3	Fumitory Rocks *(1360')*		1147.8
1031.1	Table Rock *(1380')* right 50ft, vista		1148.0
1030.8	Trail to Camp Hebron *(1250')* left 1.5m to church camp		1148.3
1030.2	**Peters Mtn Shelter** *(1180') sleeps 20 (1994)*	S,w	1148.9
---	*on A.T., spring 800ft down blue-blazed trail,* ←S6.7m	N18.0m→		---
1029.3	Victoria Trail *(1200')* right 1.5m to PA325		1149.8
1027.4	Viewpoint *(1380')* right 200ft to overlook		1151.7
1026.8	Shikellimy Rocks *(1320')* on A.T.		1152.3
1026.1	Shikellimy Trail *(1220')* right 0.9m to PA325		1153.0
1023.9	Spring *(840')* right 300ft	w	1155.2
1023.5	PA325 *(550')* parking area	R	1155.6
1023.4	Clarks Creek *(560')* Water Tank Trail to right	w	1155.7
1023.2	Spring *(650')* on A.T. to the right	w	1155.9
---	*Henry Knauber Trail right 1.6m to Horseshoe Trail*		---
1020.2	Horseshoe Trail *(1600')* to the right at stone marker		1158.9

Pennsylvania

Miles from Katahdin	Features / Services		Miles from Springer
1020.1	Stony Mtn *(1650')*		1159.0
1019.5	Rattling Run *(1500') crosses A.T.*	w	1159.6
1019.4	Old woods road *(1500')*	R	1159.7
1017.1	Yellow Springs Trail *(1380') crosses A.T.*		1162.0
1016.8	Yellow Springs Village *(1420') just a clearing, no buildings*		1162.3
1014.7	Sand Spring Trail *(1390') to the left*		1164.4
1014.5	Cold Spring Trail *(1400') to the right*		1164.6
1012.3	Rausch Creek *(1000')*	w	1166.8
1012.2	**Rausch Gap Shelter** *(980') sleeps 12 (1972) no tenting*	S,w	1166.9
---	*right 0.3m, spring in front of shelter,* ←*S18.0m* | *N13.4m*→		---
1011.8	Woods road *(880') old railroad bed, cinder surfaced*	R	1167.3
1011.6	Rausch Creek *(870') A.T. crosses on stone bridge (under repair)*	w	1167.5
1011.5	Rausch Gap Village *(880') ruins, water from well*	w	1167.6
---	**Notice!** *no overnight camping permitted at village site*		---
1011.3	Haystack Creek *(860') footbridge*	w	1167.8
1010.5	Second Mtn *(1350')*		1168.6
1010.1	Spring *(650') on dirt road to the left, unreliable*	w?	1169.0
1009.9	Old woods road *(550')*	R	1169.2
1009.5	Stream *(500') dirt road adjacent*	w	1169.6
1008.1	PA443 *(600')*		1171.0
1007.5	Junction PA443/PA72 *(500') parking*	R	1171.6
1006.1	Swatara Gap, PA72 *(450')*	R	1173.0
1006.0	Swatara Creek *(435') Waterville Iron Bridge*	w	1173.1
1005.7	Old State Road 📖 *p.140 (450') right 2.4m–to* **Lickdale, PA**	R	1173.4
---	*A.T. passes under Interstate 81 on road, no exits*		---
999.8	Woods road *(1500')*	R	1179.3
998.8	**William Penn Shelter** *(1380') sleeps 16 (1996) spring 700ft left*	S,w	1180.3
---	*right 400ft, spring across A.T.,* ←*S13.4m* | *N4.0m*→		---
996.6	PA645 *(1250') tower nearby*	R	1182.5
995.0	Dick Kimmel Lookout *(1400') vista*		1184.1
994.9	PA501 📖 *p.140 (1440')*	R, H	1184.2
---	*left 3.6m–to* **Pine Grove, PA 17963**	L,M,G,Lm	---
994.8	**501 Shelter** *(1460') sleeps 12 (1980s) caretaker (no fee)*	S,w	1184.3
---	*left 800ft, water from spigot at house,* ←*S4.0m* | *N15.1m*→		---
994.3	Trail to Pilger Ruh *(1465') right 0.2m to spring, historical marker*	w	1184.8
994.2	Trail to Applebee Campsite *(1460') left 50 yds to campsites*	C	1184.9
993.1	Kessel Trail *(1380') to the right*		1186.0
992.9	Viewpoint *(1520') right 100ft to overlook*		1186.2
991.8	Round Head/Shanaman marker *(1600')*		1187.3
991.7	Trail to Showers Steps *(1450') right 500ft to spring*	w	1187.4

Pennsylvania

Miles from Katahdin	Features / Services		Miles from Springer
989.6	Shikellimy Overlook *(1350')* vista		1189.5
989.2	Hertlein Campsite *(1220') spring, register on tree* .... C,w		1189.9
---	*tent platforms 0.1m north on A.T., dam and pond nearby*		---
988.4	Pipeline right-of-way *(1510')*		1190.7
985.8	Fort Dietrich Snyder marker *(1420') left 0.1m to spring* .... R,w		1193.3
985.5	PA 183 *(1440') Rentschler marker 50ft to left north of road* .... R		1193.6
984.2	Black Swatara Spring *(1580') right 500ft to spring* .... w		1194.9
983.1	Stream *(1600') crosses A.T.* .... w?		1196.0
981.5	Eagles Nest Trail *(1580') to the right*		1197.6
980.4	Trail to Sand Spring *(1500') right 300yds to walled spring* .... w		1198.7
---	**Notice!** *no overnight camping or fires permitted at spring area*		---
979.9	Game lands road *(1580')* .... R		1199.2
979.7	**Eagles Nest Shelter** *(1510') sleeps 8 (1994)* .... S,w		1199.4
---	*left 0.3m, spring on path to shelter, ←S15.1m	N14.7m→*		---
977.8	Shartlesville-Cross Mtn Road 📖 *p.141 (1300')* .... R		1201.3
---	*right 3.6m–to* **Shartlesville, PA 19554** .... L,M,G		---
976.8	Rock steps *(1280')*		1202.3
976.3	Game lands road *(1490')* .... R		1202.8
975.1	Phillips Canyon Spring *(1500') right 400ft, seasonal* .... w		1204.0
974.2	Marshalls Path *(1380') trail crosses A.T.*		1204.9
973.5	Auburn Lookout *(1400') on A.T. to left, vista*		1205.6
973.4	Game lands road *(1400') A.T. borders, does not cross road* .... R		1205.7
973.1	Game lands road *(1395')* .... R		1206.0
972.6	Dynamite Road *(1390')* .... R		1206.5
972.5	Pipeline right-of-way *(1390')*		1206.6
972.1	Pipeline right-of-way *(1380')*		1207.0
971.3	Railroad tracks *(430')*		1207.8
971.2	Schuylkill River *(410') A.T. crosses on railway bridge*		1207.9
971.1	**PORT CLINTON, PA 19549** 📖 *p.141 (400')* .... R,H,L,M		1208.0
---	*left 0.4m on Penn St–to pavilion (free overnight stay)* .... w		---
970.4	PA 61 Overpass *(430') A.T. goes underneath* .... R		1208.7
970.3	Blue Mountain Road 📖 *p.142 (430') paved two-lane side road* .... R		1208.8
---	*right 3m–to* **Hamburg, PA 19526** .... L,M,G,O,Lm,f		---
968.0	Pocahontas Spring *(1200')* .... C,w		1211.1
967.8	Minnehaha Spring *(1350') unreliable* .... w?		1211.3
965.2	Windsor Furnace *(800') Hamburg Watershed*		1213.9
---	*right 0.5m on blue-blazed trail to campsite, water* .... C,w		---
---	**Notice!** *no overnight camping in watershed except at campsite above*		---
965.0	**Windsor Furnace Shelter** *(940') sleeps 8 (1970s)* .... S,w		1214.1
---	*left 0.1m, stream near shelter, ←S14.7m	N9.1m→*		---

Pennsylvania

Miles from Katahdin	Features / Services	Miles from Springer
963.4	Pulpit Rock *(1582')* vista	1215.7
---	**Notice!** no overnight camping or fires permitted in area	---
961.6	Blue Rocks Trail 📖 *p.142 (1600') right 1.3m to Blue Rocks*	1217.5
---	right 1.5m–to campground .... C,L,M,G?,Lm	---
961.2	Trail to The Pinnacle *(1635') right 200ft to overlook*	1217.9
---	**Notice!** no overnight camping or fires permitted at overlook	---
959.2	Gold Spring *(1585')* .... w	1219.9
---	**Notice!** no overnight camping or fires permitted at spring	---
957.5	Spring *(1080') on A.T. to left* .... w	1221.6
955.9	Hawk Mtn Road 📖*p.142 (635') paved* .... R	1223.2
---	left 1.4m–to Hawk Mountain Sanctuary .... w	---
---	**Eckville Shelter** *(535') sleeps 6, shower and toilet, caretaker, no fee* .... S,w	---
---	right 0.2m on Hawk Mtn Rd, spigot on porch, ←S9.1m | N7.4m→	---
955.7	Old logging road *(550')* .... R	1223.4
955.5	Stream *(550') footbridge, walkway over swampy area* .... w	1223.6
954.1	Trail to Hawk Mtn Lookout *(1350') to the left*	1225.0
953.0	Dan's Pulpit *(1650')* vista	1226.1
952.3	Unnamed trail *(1600') right 0.7m to spring* .... w	1226.8
951.7	Dan's Spring *(1520') right 400ft, seasonal* .... w?	1227.4
948.5	**Allentown Hiking Club Shelter** *(1450') sleeps 8 (1997)* .... S,w	1230.6
---	right 100ft, spring 0.5m on blue-blazed trail, ←S7.4m | N10.0m→	---
---	(if dry, continue on yellow-blazed trail to year-round spring)	---
947.2	Tri-County Corner *(1560')*	1231.9
946.6	Fort Franklin Road *(1400')* .... R	1232.5
946.2	Old woods road *(1400')* .... R	1232.9
944.4	PA309, Blue Mtn Summit 📖*p.142 (1360')* .... R,C?,L,M,w	1234.7
944.2	Old woods road *(1380')* .... R	1234.9
942.7	Power line *(1390')*	1236.4
942.6	Trail to New Tripoli Campsite *(1400') left 0.2m, spring 100ft beyond* ..... C,w	1236.5
941.6	The Cliffs *(1550')* vista	1237.5
940.9	Bear Rocks *(1530')* .... R	1238.2
939.5	Bake Oven Knob Road *(1400') gravel surfaced, parking area* .... R	1239.6
939.1	Bake Oven Knob *(1560')* vista	1240.0
938.5	**Bake Oven Knob Shelter** *(1380') sleeps 6 (1940s)* .... S,w	1240.6
---	right 100ft, spring 500ft beyond shelter, ←S10.0m | N6.8m→	---
936.1	Ashfield Road, Lehigh Furnace Gap *(1320') power line adjacent* .... R	1243.0
934.2	Pennsylvania Turnpike *(1580') in a tunnel 800ft beneath A.T.*	1244.9
933.1	North Trail *(1550') to the left, rejoins A.T. north*	1246.0
931.7	**George W. Outerbridge Shelter** *(1000') sleeps 6 (1965), no privy* .... S,w	1247.4
---	on A.T., spring 300ft north on A.T., ←S6.8m | N16.8m→	---

Pennsylvania

Miles from Katahdin	Features / Services	Miles from Springer
931.3	Power line *(500')*	1247.8
931.1	Lehigh Gap, PA873 📖*p.142(380')* .... R,M	1248.0
---	*right 2.4m*–to **Slatington, PA 18080** .... L,M,Lm,f	---
---	*right 2.5m*–to **Walnutport, PA 18088** .... M,G	---
931.0	Lehigh River *(380')* A.T. crosses on bridge .... R	1248.1
930.8	Lehigh Gap, PA248/PA145 📖*p.143 (380')* .... R	1248.3
---	*left 2m on PA248*–to **PALMERTON, PA 18071** .... H,L,M,G,Lm,f?	---
930.7	Old railroad bed *(500')*	1248.4
930.6	Winter Trail, south end *(500')* to the left, rejoins A.T. north	1248.5
---	**Alternate!** *Winter Trail follows railroad bed north, bypasses rocks*	---
929.8	Winter Trail, north end *(1420')* to the left, rejoins A.T. south	1249.3
928.1	"Metallica" Spring *(1450')* left 200ft on blue-blazed trail .... w	1251.0
926.9	Power line *(1400')*	1252.2
925.9	Old road *(1380')* information board, pipeline .... R	1253.2
925.7	Little Gap 📖*p.144 (1100')* paved road .... R	1253.4
---	*right 1.5m*–to **Danielsville, PA 18038** .... L,M,G	---
925.4	Tower Access Road *(1390')* trail avoids top of knob...............................	1253.7
922.4	Viewpoint *(1500')* right 400ft to overlook, vista	1256.7
---	**Notice!** *no overnight camping or fires permitted at overlook*	---
922.0	Power line *(1520')*	1257.1
920.9	Delp's Spring *(1580')* right 0.3m, unreliable .... w?	1258.2
919.0	Trail to Stempa Spring *(1520')* right 0.5m on bbt .... w	1260.1
918.9	Campsites *(1520')* two sites 0.1m apart on A.T. C	1260.2
918.4	Smith Gap Road 📖*p.144 (1550')* left 1m to water source .... R,w	1260.7
914.9	**Leroy A. Smith Shelter** *(1410')* sleeps 8 *(1972)*................................... S,w	1264.2
---	*right 700ft, spring downhill 0.2m on road, ←S16.8m|N13.8m→*	---
---	*(if upper spring dry, try lower springs downhill 0.4m and 0.5m)*	---
914.7	Power line *(1500')*	1264.4
913.0	Pipeline right-of-way *(1450')*	1266.1
911.3	Hahn's Lookout *(1500')* vista	1267.8
911.0	Lookout Rocks *(1400')* vista	1268.1
910.3	Wind Gap, PA33 📖*p.144 (980')* .... R,L,w	1268.8
---	*right 1m*–to **Wind Gap, PA 18091** .... L,M,G,Lm	---
908.2	Private road *(1550')* .... R	1270.9
903.3	Wolf Rocks *(1620')* vista	1275.8
903.0	Old road *(1510')* power line adjacent .... R	1276.1
901.7	Fox Gap, PA191 *(1320')* .... R	1277.4
901.6	Unnamed trail *(1330')* crosses A.T., bulletin board	1277.5
901.4	Side trail *(1350')* right 0.8m to historic church site, telephone lines nearby..	1277.7

Pennsylvania-New Jersey

Miles from Katahdin	Features / Services		Miles from Springer
901.1	**Kirkridge Shelter** *(1500') sleeps 8 (1948)*	S,w	1278.0
---	*on A.T., spigot on blue-blazed trail, ←S13.8m|N31.2m→*		---
901.0	Grassy area *(1500')* vista to right	R	1278.1
900.4	Lunch Rocks *(1460')* right 50ft, vista		1278.7
899.5	Power lines *(1310')*		1279.6
899.2	Totts Gap *(1290')* towers nearby		1279.9
898.3	Pipeline right-of-way *(1365')*		1280.8
897.2	Mt. Minsi *(1461')*		1281.9
896.2	Lookout Rock *(820')* to the right, vista		1282.9
896.0	Eureka Creek *(470')* crosses A.T.	w	1283.1
895.4	Council Rock *(500')*		1283.7
895.1	Lake Lenape *(500')* pond to left, parking area		1284.0
894.9	Lake Road *(480')*	R	1284.2
894.7	**DELAWARE WATER GAP, PA 18327** 📖*p.145 (390')*	H,L,M,G,O,Lm,f	1284.4
894.5	Delaware River, Interstate 80 Bridge *(350')*	R	1284.6
---	*A.T. crosses river on bridge; Pennsylvania-New Jersey border*		---
893.5	Delaware Water Gap NRA Information Center *(360')*		1285.6
893.1	Interstate 80 *(360')* A.T. passes under, exit ramps		1286.0
892.9	Water pump *(360')* seasonal	w?	1286.2
892.8	Dunfield Creek *(380')* footbridge	w	1286.3
891.5	Trail to Holly Springs *(980')* right 0.2m to seasonal spring	w?	1287.6
---	*Beulaland Trail left 1.3m to Delaware River*		---
889.9	Backpacker Campsite *(1320')* no water	R,C	1289.2
---	**Notice!** No camping in Worthington State Forest except here.		---
888.6	Sunfish Pond 📖*p.146 (1382')* glacial pond on A.T. to right	w	1290.5
---	**Notice!** no swimming allowed.		---
888.3	Sunfish Pond outlet *(1380')*	w	1290.8
888.0	Turquoise Trail *(1500')* to the right		1291.1
887.9	Garvey Spring Trail *(1500')* left 600ft to seasonal spring	w?	1291.2
887.0	Stream *(1400')* crosses A.T.	w	1292.1
886.8	Herbert Hiller plaque *(1450')* left 35ft on rock		1292.3
886.3	Power line *(1500')*		1292.8
886.2	Viewpoint *(1480')* on A.T. at rock pile, vista		1292.9
885.8	Old woods road (Kaiser Road) *(1390')* right 0.3m to spring	R,w	1293.3
884.2	Camp Mohican Road 📖*p.146 (1120')* Yard Creek adjacent	R,w	1294.9
---	*left 0.25m–to Mohican Outdoor Center*	C,L,f,w	---
883.4	Viewpoint *(1480')* to the right		1295.7
883.2	Rattlesnake Swamp Trail *(1500')* left 0.5m to Catfish Pond		1295.9
881.8	Catfish Fire Tower *(1565')* vistas		1297.3

New Jersey

Miles from Katahdin	Features / Services		Miles from Springer
881.2	Rattlesnake Spring *(1500')* left 50ft on dirt road	R,w	1297.9
880.8	Millbrook-Blairstown Road *(1260')*	R	1298.3
880.4	Beaver pond outlet *(1250')* footbridge	w	1298.7
880.1	Powerline *(1460')* vista		1299.0
879.1	Trail to Camp No-Be-Bo-Sho *(1450')* to the right		1300.0
878.5	Old woods road *(1450')*	R	1300.6
876.9	Blue Mtn Lakes Road *p.146 (1300')* water pump to left	R,w	1302.2
---	**Notice!** *No camping from 0.5m S of here to Buttermilk Falls*		---
875.3	Woods road *(1300')* gravel surfaced	R	1303.8
---	*left to Harding Lake Rock Shelter archeological site (c. 3000 BC)*		---
874.9	Hemlock Pond Trail *(1380')* to the left		1304.2
874.0	Trail to Buttermilk Falls *(1560')* left 1.5m to falls		1305.1
872.6	Stream *(1350')* crosses A.T.	w	1306.5
872.1	Rattlesnake Mtn *(1492')* vista		1307.0
871.8	Stream *(1400')* crosses A.T.	w	1307.3
871.3	Woods road *(1420')* dirt surfaced	R	1307.8
869.9	**Brink Road Shelter** *(1310')* sleeps 5 (1970)	S,w	1309.2
---	*left 0.2m, spring 300ft behind shelter,* ←S31.2m | N6.6m→		---
869.6	Trail register *(1350')* to the right, attached to tree	w	1309.5
868.2	Jacob's Ladder Trail *(1300')* to the left		1310.9
867.5	Viewpoint *(1380')* on A.T., vista		1311.6
866.8	Road *(1350')* power line nearby	R	1312.3
866.3	Culvers Gap, US206 *p.146 (935')*	R,L,M,w	1312.8
---	*right 3.4m*–to **Branchville, NJ 07826**	L,M,G,w	---
865.8	Sunrise Mtn Road *(990')*	R	1313.3
865.3	Viewpoint *(1350')* on A.T., vista		1313.8
864.5	Viewpoint *(1500')* left 100ft to vista		1314.6
864.4	Culver Fire Tower *(1500')* vistas		1314.7
864.3	Tower Trail *(1490')* to the left, register on A.T.		1314.8
863.4	Stony Brook *(1300')* crosses A.T.	w	1315.7
863.3	**Gren Anderson Shelter** *(1320')* sleeps 8 (1958)	S,w	1315.8
---	*left 0.3m, spring 300ft beyond shelter,* ←S6.6m | N5.8m→		---
861.9	Tinsley Trail *(1420')* to the left		1317.2
860.9	Sunrise Mtn *(1653')* pavilion, vistas, no water		1318.2
---	**Notice!** *no overnight camping or fires permitted at pavilion*		---
860.1	Crigger Road *(1400')* dirt surfaced	R	1319.0
859.5	Stone walls *(1380')* A.T. crosses walls		1319.6
858.2	Swenson Road *(1420')*	R	1320.9

New Jersey

Miles from Katahdin	Features / Services		Miles from Springer
857.5	**Mashipacong Shelter** *(1425') sleeps 8 (1936)*	S	1321.6
---	*on A.T., no water, ←S5.8m | N2.9m→*		---
857.3	Deckertown Turnpike *(1400') parking area*	R	1321.8
856.6	Iris Trail *(1430') crosses A.T.*		1322.5
856.5	Register *(1430') to the left on tree*		1322.6
856.2	Woods road *(1320') pipeline right-of-way adjacent*	R	1322.9
855.4	Iris Trail *(1460') follows woods road*		1323.7
854.6	**Rutherford Shelter** *(1345') sleeps 6 (1967)*	S,w	1324.5
---	*right 0.4m, spring on path to shelter, ←S2.9m | N4.3m→*		---
852.9	Blue Dot Trail *(1620') left to Sawmill Lake*		1326.2
852.0	NJ23, High Point State Park 🕮 *p.147 (1500')*	R,C,L,M,G	1327.1
851.0	Observation platform *(1680') vista (NYC visible)*		1328.1
850.8	Monument Trail *(1600') right to High Point Monument*		1328.3
850.3	**High Point Shelter** *(1280') sleeps 8 (1936)*	S,w	1328.8
---	*right 450ft, spring 250ft behind shelter, ←S4.3m | N12.4m→*		---
850.0	Stream *(1220') crosses A.T., intermittent*	w?	1329.1
849.0	County Road 519 *(1180') paved*	R	1330.1
848.4	Stream *(1000') crosses A.T.*	w	1330.7
848.3	Stream *(980') crosses A.T.*	w	1330.8
848.2	Courtwright Road *(950') dirt/gravel surfaced*	R	1330.9
847.8	Barbed-wire fences *(1000') A.T. crosses on stiles*		1331.3
847.6	Pond *(900') to the left*	w	1331.5
847.3	Stream *(850') bridge, puncheons*	w	1331.8
847.1	Ferguson Road 519 *(820') paved*	R	1332.0
---	*A.T. follows New Jersey-New York border north for several miles*		---
846.5	Stream *(790') swampy area*	w	1332.6
846.4	Gemmer Road *(780')*	R	1332.7
846.3	Stream *(770') footbridge*	w	1332.8
846.1	Stream *(760') footbridge*	w	1333.0
845.7	Stream *(610') footbridge*	w	1333.4
845.4	Goodrich Road *(620')*	R	1333.7
845.2	Pond and dam *(700') A.T. crosses at spillway*	w	1333.9
845.0	Trail to Murray property 🕮 *p.147 (660') marked by sign*	w	1334.1
844.9	Goldsmith Road *(650') stream adjacent*	R,w	1334.2
844.8	Vernie Swamp *(640') A.T. crosses on puncheons*		1334.3
844.4	Goldsmith Lane *(680') dirt surfaced*	R	1334.7
844.1	Unionville Road, County Road 651 *(640')*	R	1335.0
843.9	Quarry Road *(640')*	R	1335.2
843.2	Lott Road 🕮 *p.147 (600') pond on north side*	R,w	1335.9
---	*left 0.4m–to* **UNIONVILLE, NY 10988**	H?,C,M,G	---

2000'
1000'
0'
Mashipacong Shelter — Rutherford Shelter — High Point Shelter — Lott Rd. (Unionville)

New Jersey

842.2	NJ284 *(420')* stream adjacent .... R,w	1336.9
841.7	Oil City Road *(380')* aka *Lower Road* .... R	1337.4
841.1	Stream *(380')* .... w	1338.0
840.9	State Line Road *(380')* aka *Oil City Road* .... R	1338.2
840.7	Walkill River *(380')* *A.T. crosses on bridge* .... w	1338.4
840.4	Walkill Natl. Wildlife Preserve *(380')* *former sod farm*	1338.7
838.4	Walkill Road *(380')* aka *Liberty Corners Road* .... R,w?	1340.7
---	*water 150ft north of road, on blue-blazed side trail to the left*	---
837.9	**Pochuck Mtn Shelter** *(840')* *sleeps 6 (1989)* .... S	1341.2
---	*left 500ft, no water (see Walkill Road above),* ←*S12.4m*	*N11.6m*→	---
836.9	Viewpoint *(1180')* on *A.T.*	1342.2
836.4	Pochuck Mtn *(1200')* *15yds left to overlook*	1342.7
836.0	Woods road *(1000')* *dirt surfaced* .... R	1343.1
835.8	Stream *(990')* *A.T. crosses on stepping stones* .... w	1343.3
835.5	Stream *(800')* *footbridge* .... w	1343.6
835.2	County Road 565 📖*p.147* *(700')* .... R	1343.9
---	*left 1.1m–to* **GLENWOOD, NJ 07418** .... L,G?	---
834.5	Old woods road *(780')* *dirt surfaced* .... R	1344.6
834.1	Viewpoint *(700')* on *A.T.*	1345.0
833.7	County Road 517 *(410')* .... R	1345.4
---	*left 1.1m to Glenwood (see County Road 565 above)*	---
833.0	Pochuck Creek *(380')* *suspension bridge, raised walkway* .... w	1346.1
832.3	Canal Road 565 *(380')* .... R	1346.8
832.0	Wawayanda Creek *(380')* .... w	1347.1
831.5	Railroad tracks *(400')*	1347.6
831.4	NJ94 📖*p.147* *(450')* .... R,L	1347.7
---	*right 2.4m–to* **VERNON, NJ 07462** .... H,M,G,Lm	---
831.2	Quarry road *(500')* .... R	1347.9
830.1	Trail to Pinwheel's Vista *(1300')* *left 0.1m to overlook*	1349.0
830.0	Wawayanda Mtn *(1340')*	1349.1
---	*Wawayanda Ridge Trail right 0.8m to overlook*	---
829.6	Woods road *(1020')* .... R	1349.5
829.4	Streams *(1000')* *A.T. crosses several on footbridges* .... w	1349.7
828.7	Luthers Rock *(1235')* *vista*	1350.4
828.6	Stream *(1200')* *A.T. crosses on stepping stones* .... w	1350.5
828.3	Barrett Road *(1240')* *steps, stream* .... R,w	1350.8
827.5	Stream *(1170')* *crosses A.T.* .... w	1351.6
827.2	Iron Mtn Road *(1150')* .... R,w	1351.9
---	*A.T. crosses the Doublekill (a stream) on iron bridge*	---

New Jersey-New York

Miles from Katahdin	Features / Services	Miles from Springer
826.5	Wawayanda Road *(1200')* .... R	1352.6
826.3	**Wawayanda Shelter** *(1200') sleeps 6 (1990)* .... S,w	1352.8
---	*left 0.1m, water (see note below), ←S11.6m	N12.0m→*	---
826.2	Trail to Wawayanda State Park Hqs. *(1200') right 0.4m* .... w	1352.9
---	*rest rooms; if closed, water from hose at maintenance yard*	---
826.1	Stream *(1190') footbridge* .... w	1353.0
825.9	Warwick Turnpike 📖*p.148 (1140') left 2.6m to supermarket*................. R	1353.2
825.7	Old road *(1240')* .... R	1353.4
825.4	Stream *(1250') crosses A.T.* .... w	1353.7
824.6	Stream *(1200') intermittent* .... w?	1354.5
824.5	Long House Road *(1200') aka Brady Road* .... R	1354.6
823.8	Stream *(1250') footbridge* .... w	1355.3
823.4	Long House Creek *(1180') footbridge* .... w	1355.7
823.0	Stream *(1260') A.T. crosses on rocks, seasonal* .... w	1356.1
822.6	Ernest Walter Trail *(1370') to the right*	1356.5
822.5	Bearfort Mtn *(1380') vista*	1356.6
822.1	State Line Trail *(1395') New Jersey-New York border*	1357.0
821.9	Trail register *(1400') to the right on tree*	1357.2
---	**Notice!** *camping along the A.T. in New York is restricted in some*	---
---	*locations, be alert for posted regulations; fires are permitted only*	---
---	*at shelters and official campsites with fire rings*	---
821.6	Prospect Rock *(1433') vista*	1357.5
820.6	Furnace Brook *(1200') crosses A.T.* .... w	1358.5
819.0	Cascade Brook *(1180') crosses A.T.* .... w	1360.1
818.2	Greenwood Lake Vista Trail 📖*p.148 (1240') blue blazed to right*.............	1360.9
816.7	Power lines *(1100')*	1362.4
816.4	NY17A 📖*p.148 (1110')* .... R	1362.7
---	*right 2m*–to **Greenwood Lake, NY 10925** .... L,M,G	---
---	*left 1.6m*–to **Bellvale, NY 10912** .... G	---
---	*left 3.5m*–to **Warwick, NY 10990** .... L,G,Lm	---
815.1	Eastern Pinnacles *(1294') vistas*	1364.0
814.8	Stream *(1120') crosses A.T.* .... w	1364.3
814.6	Cat Rocks *(1050') vistas*	1364.5
814.4	Stream *(1070') crosses A.T.* .... w	1364.7
814.3	**Wildcat Shelter** *(1180') sleeps 8 (1992)*... S,w	1364.8
---	*left 0.1m, spring near shelter, ←S12.0m	N14.3m→*	---
812.8	Lakes Road *(680') aka Monroe Road* .... R	1366.3
812.6	Stream *(630') crosses A.T.* .... w	1366.5
---	**Notice!** *use blue-blazed bypass if low areas are flooded*	---

New York

812.5	Fitzgerald Falls *(820')* .... w	1366.6
---	**Notice!** *no overnight camping or fires permitted at falls*	---
812.4	Streams *(845') A.T. crosses several* .... w	1366.7
811.3	Allis Trail *(1250') right to NY17A*	1367.8
810.5	Mombasha High Point *(1280') vistas (NYC visible south)*	1368.6
809.3	West Mombasha Road *(990')* .... R	1369.8
809.2	Stream *(990') crosses A.T.* .... w	1369.9
808.9	Stream *(1020') crosses A.T.* .... w	1370.2
808.4	Buchanan Mtn *(1142') vistas*	1370.7
808.1	Streams *(1000') A.T. crosses several* .... w	1371.0
807.6	East Mombasha Road *(800')* .... R	1371.5
806.9	Little Dam Lake *(750') bridge* .... w	1372.2
806.2	Orange Turnpike *(800') right 0.5m to piped spring (on left)* .... R,w	1372.9
805.5	Arden Mtn *(1180')*	1373.6
805.2	Trail register *(1150') to the right on tree*	1373.9
804.4	NY17/Arden Valley Road 🕮 *p.148 (550')* .... R	1374.7
---	*left 0.7m*–to **Arden, NY 10910** .... post office closed	---
---	*right 2.1m*–to **Southfields, NY 10975** .... L,M	---
804.2	New York State Thruway overpass *(560') railroad tracks* .... R	1374.9
---	*southern boundary of Harriman State Park* 🕮 *p.148*	---
803.3	Green Pond Mtn *(1200')*	1375.8
802.8	Island Pond Road *(980')* .... R	1376.3
802.7	Island Pond outlet *(970') footbridge* .... w	1376.4
802.4	Crooked Road *(1100')* .... R	1376.7
802.1	Lemon Squeezer *(1140')*	1377.0
801.9	Island Pond Mtn *(1303')*	1377.2
801.5	Long Path *(1240') crosses A.T.*	1377.6
801.4	Stream *(1250') intermittent* .... w	1377.7
800.7	Surebridge Brook/Surebridge Mine Road *(1200')* .... R,w	1378.4
800.0	**Fingerboard Shelter** *(1300') sleeps 8 (1928), no privy* .... S,w	1379.1
---	*right 300ft, water 0.5m on blue-blazed trail,* ←*S14.3m* | *N5.3m*→	---
799.4	Fingerboard Mtn *(1328')*	1379.7
798.9	Arden Valley Road *(1196')* .... R	1380.2
---	*right 0.3m*–to Lake Tiorati Circle (rest rooms, swimming area) .... w	---
796.8	Stream *(1000') footbridge* .... w	1382.3
796.7	Seven Lakes Drive *(830')* .... R	1382.4
795.5	Ramapo-Dunderberg Trail *(1180') right to Lake Tiorati Circle*	1383.6
794.7	**William Brien Memorial Shelter** *(1070') sleeps 8 (1933), no privy* ...... S,w?	1384.4
---	*on A.T., spring 150ft in front (unreliable),* ←*S5.3m* | *N3.1m*→	---
793.3	Black Mtn *(1160') vista (NYC visible)*	1385.8

New York

792.9	1779 Trail *(800') crosses A.T.*	1386.2
792.7	Old woods road *(720')* .... R	1386.4
792.6	Palisades Interstate Parkway *(680') divided highway* .... R	1386.5
---	*left 0.4m*–to visitor center (rest rooms) .... w?	---
---	*southern boundary of Bear Mountain State Park* 📖 *p.149*	---
792.4	Beechy Bottom Brook *(680') footbridge* .... w	1386.7
---	*spring to the right facing (upstream) on north side of Beechy Bottom*	---
---	*Brook; northbounders, get water here for West Mtn Shelter*	---
792.3	Stream *(670') intermittent* .... w	1386.8
792.0	Beechy Bottom Road *(700') used as bike path* .... R	1387.1
791.6	**West Mtn Shelter** *(1240') sleeps 8 (1928), no privy* .... S	1387.5
---	*right 0.6m, no water, ←S3.1m	N31.0m→*	---
790.9	Viewpoint *(1100') on A.T., vistas*	1388.2
790.3	Fawn Trail *(750') to the left*	1388.8
790.1	1777 Trail *(700') on woods road* .... R	1389.0
790.0	Seven Lakes Drive *(650')* .... R	1389.1
789.5	Perkins Drive *(950') to Bear Mtn summit* .... R	1389.6
788.4	Bear Mtn *(1305')* Perkins Tower, vistas, seasonal water fountain .... w?	1390.7
---	*Southbounders, get water for West Mtn Shelter if fountain working*	---
788.3	Joseph Bartha plaque *(1300')*	1390.8
788.1	Scenic Drive *(1250')* A.T. crosses r d several times .... R	1391.0
787.1	Suffern-Bear Mtn Trail *(750')*	1392.0
786.9	Stream *(300') crosses A.T.* .... w	1392.2
786.8	Park maintenance road *(260')* .... R	1392.3
786.7	Ski jump *(250') A.T. passes under*	1392.4
786.6	**Bear Mountain, NY 10911** 📖 *p.149 (155') Hessian Lake* ....L?,w	1392.5
786.2	Pedestrian tunnel under US9W *(145')*	1392.9
---	*if tunnel closed, continue on shore of Hessian Lake, turn right, cross*	---
---	*US9W, then follow sidewalk to tollgate at end of Bear Mtn Bridge;*	---
---	*directions reversed for southbounders if museum gates closed*	---
785.9	Trailside Museums & Wildlife Center *(135')*	1393.2
---	*lowest point on entire A.T. (124') is in front of black bear exhibit*	---
785.8	Hudson River, Bear Mtn Bridge 📖 *p.149 (180')* .... R	1393.3
---	*left 0.8m*–to **FORT MONTGOMERY, NY 10922** .... L,M,G?	---
---	*northern boundary of Harriman and Bear Mtn State Parks*	---
785.1	NY9D *(180')* .... R	1394.0
784.6	Woods road *(700')* .... R	1394.5
---	*Camp Smith Trail right 0.6m to Anthony's Nose, vistas*	---
783.6	Hemlock Springs Campsite *(550') to the right* .... C,w	1395.5
783.4	South Mtn Pass *(460') aka Manitou Road* .... R	1395.7

New York

Miles from Katahdin	Features / Services	Miles from Springer
782.4	Osborn Loop Trail *(820')* to the left, rejoins A.T. north .... R	1396.7
781.1	Viewpoint *(900')* left 100ft to vista	1398.0
780.0	US9/NY403 📖 *p.150 (400')* stile on south side .... R	1399.1
---	right 4.5m–to **Peekskill, NY 10566** .... L,M,G,Lm	---
779.8	Old Highland Turnpike *(470')* paved .... R	1399.3
779.5	Graymoor entrance road 📖 *p.150 (520')* paved .... R	1399.6
---	right 0.2m–to Graymoor Friary *(pavilion, showers)* .... C,w	---
779.4	Old West Point Road *(515')* .... R	1399.7
778.7	Trail to shrine *(835')* to the right, vista	1400.4
777.5	Denning Hill *(900')*	1401.6
776.7	Old Albany Post Road, Chapman Road *(620')* .... R	1402.4
775.7	Canopus Hill *(820')* vista	1403.4
775.0	Canopus Hill Road *(420')* .... R	1404.1
774.0	South Highland Road *(650')* aka Phillips Brook Road .... R	1405.1
772.8	Stream *(700')* crosses A.T. .... w	1406.3
772.5	Catfish Loop Trail *(950')* crosses A.T., rejoins north	1406.6
771.3	Dennytown Road *(830')* water pump at building *(seasonal)* .... R,C,w?	1407.8
---	Dennytown Group Camp *(no sign)* left 0.5m, then left 0.1m on dirt road	---
770.6	Stream *(790')* Catfish Loop Trail, rejoins A.T. south .... w	1408.5
769.2	Sunk Mine Road *(800')* .... R	1409.9
769.1	Stream *(740')* footbridge .... w	1410.0
768.0	Three Lakes Trail *(800')* crosses A.T.	1411.1
767.6	NY301 📖 *p.150 (900')* Canopus Lake .... R	1411.5
---	right 0.8m–to Clarence Fahnestock State Park .... C,w	---
767.3	Trail register *(1000')* to the right on tree	1411.8
767.0	Fahnestock Trail *(1080')* to the left	1412.1
766.7	Stream *(1100')* crosses A.T. .... w	1412.4
765.6	Stream *(1020')* crosses A.T. .... w	1413.5
765.3	Viewpoint *(1200')* on A.T., vista	1413.8
764.8	Stream *(980')* crosses A.T. .... w	1414.3
763.4	Shenandoah Mtn *(1282')* vista	1415.7
763.0	Long Hill Road *(1060')* .... R	1416.1
762.4	Power lines *(1000')*	1416.7
761.9	Shenandoah Tenting Area *(905')* left 0.1m to campsite .... C,w	1417.2
761.5	Stream *(580')* crosses A.T. .... w	1417.6
760.8	Stream *(360')* bridge .... w	1418.3
760.6	**RPH Shelter** *(350')* sleeps 6 *(1982)* .... S,w	1418.5
---	on A.T., water *(need to purify)* at shelter, ←S31.0m	N9.0m→	---
760.5	Hortontown Road *(365')* .... R	1418.6

New York

Miles from Katahdin	Features / Services	Miles from Springer
760.4	Stream *(400')* footbridge .... w	1418.7
760.3	Taconic State Parkway *(500') A.T. under parkway on road* .... R	1418.8
759.3	Viewpoint *(910') on A.T., vista*	1419.8
759.0	Stream *(910') crosses A.T.* .... w	1420.1
757.7	Viewpoint *(1050') rock steps, vista*	1421.4
757.1	Hosner Mtn Road *(500') stream, bridge* .... R,w	1422.0
756.0	Stormville Mtn *(1050')*	1423.1
755.5	NY52 📖 *p.150 (800') right 0.4m to store* .... R,M,G	1423.6
755.0	Stream *(980') crosses A.T.* .... w	1424.1
754.9	Viewpoint *(1000') on A.T. in cleared field, vista*	1424.2
754.5	Stormville Mtn Road *(970')* .... R	1424.6
754.3	Mountain Top Road *(970')* .... R	1424.8
---	*A.T. crosses over Interstate 84 on road (no exits)*	---
754.1	Grape Hollow Road *(970') A.T. crosses guardrail* .... R	1425.0
752.2	Stream *(1200') crosses A.T.* .... w	1426.9
751.9	Mt. Egbert *(1329') vistas*	1427.2
751.6	**Morgan Stewart Shelter** *(1285') sleeps 6 (1984)* .... S,w	1427.5
---	*right 25yds, water from well 380ft downhill, ←S9.0m	N7.8m→*	---
751.3	Viewpoint *(1300') on A.T., vista*	1427.8
750.5	Depot Hill Road *(1280') dirt surfaced* .... R	1428.6
749.9	Stream *(1260') crosses A.T.* .... w	1429.2
748.7	Railroad tracks *(750') Whaley Lake Stream adjacent* .... w	1430.4
748.6	Old Route 55 *(750')* .... R	1430.5
748.3	NY55 📖 *p.150 (720')* .... R	1430.8
---	*left 3.1m*–to **Poughquag, NY 12570** .... L,M,G	---
747.1	Nuclear Lake outlet *(760') lake to right* .... w	1432.0
744.8	Penny Road *(1070')* .... R	1434.3
744.3	West Mtn *(1200')*	1434.8
743.8	**Telephone Pioneers Shelter** *(910') sleeps 6 (1988)* .... S,w?	1435.3
---	*right 0.1m, stream nearby (intermittent), ←S7.8m	N8.7m→*	---
743.1	County Road 20/West Dover Road 📖 *p.151 (600') Dover Oak* .... R	1436.0
---	*right 3m*–to **PAWLING, NY 12564** .... C,M,G,O,Lm	---
742.2	Corbin Hill *(770')*	1436.9
741.1	Swamp River *(460') bridge* .... w	1438.0
740.8	Appalachian Trail Station 📖 *p.151 (480') railroad tracks*	1438.3
740.7	NY22 📖 *p.151 (480') right 0.5m to store* .... R,M,G	1438.4
740.5	Hurds Corner Road *(480') old water tower to right* .... R	1438.6
740.3	Stream *(620') bridge* .... w	1438.8
739.9	Stream *(700') register nearby* .... w	1439.2

New York-Connecticut

739.0	Red Trail *(900') to the left, rejoins A.T.*	1440.1
738.8	Stream *(900') crosses A.T.* .... w	1440.3
738.5	Yellow Trail *(940') stream adjacent* .... w	1440.6
---	*right on Yellow Trail to entrance of Pawling Nature Preserve*	---
738.1	Green Trail *(870') to the left*	1441.0
737.2	Yellow Trail *(880') to the right to Pawling Nature Preserve*	1441.9
735.9	Streams *(750') A.T. crosses several* .... w	1443.2
735.5	Leather Hill Road *(750')* .... R	1443.6
735.1	**Wiley (Webatuck) Shelter** *(740') sleeps 6 (1940)* .... S,w	1444.0
---	*on A.T., pump (purify) 0.1m north on A.T., ←S8.7m│N4.0m→*	---
735.0	Pump *(700') water source for Wiley Shelter* .... w	1444.1
734.9	Duell Hollow Road *(600')* .... R	1444.2
734.8	Duell Hollow Brook *(400')* .... w	1444.3
---	**Notice!** *camping along the A.T. in New York is restricted in some*	---
---	*locations, be alert for posted regulations; fires are permitted only*	---
---	*at shelters and official campsites with fire rings*	---
733.9	Hoyt Road 📖*p.152 (400') New York-Connecticut border* .... R	1445.2
---	**Notice!** *camping in Connecticut is permitted only at designated*	---
---	*sites, and no fires are permitted anywhere. Ridgerunners patrol*	---
---	*during summer months and most spring and fall weekends*	---
733.2	CT55 📖*p.152 (490')* left 3.3m–to **Wingdale, NY 12594**................ L,M,G	1445.9
732.1	Ten Mile Hill *(1000')*	1447.0
732.0	Herrick Trail *(1000') to the right*	1447.1
731.6	Spring *(600') seasonal* .... w?	1447.5
731.4	Old woods road *(550')* .... R	1447.7
731.1	**Ten Mile River Lean-to** *(290') sleeps 6 (1996) tent sites* .... S,w	1448.0
---	*right 200ft, pump 0.1m north on A.T., ←S4.0m│N8.4m→*	---
731.0	Campsite/water pump *(290') right 100ft at end of bridge* .... C,w	1448.1
730.9	Ten Mile River *(280') Ned Anderson Bridge* .... w	1448.2
730.7	Power lines *(295')*	1448.4
729.5	Schaghticoke Road/Bulls Bridge Road 📖*p.152 (350')* .... R	1449.6
---	*right 0.4m (on Bulls Bridge Road)–to US7* .... G,w	---
---	*A.T. loops back into New York for approximately 2.3 miles*	---
727.8	Schaghticoke Mtn *(1330')*	1451.3
726.2	Indian Rocks *(1320') vista*	1452.9
---	*A.T. passes through Schaghticoke Indian Reservation*	---
725.9	Dry Gulch *(1000') ravine*	1453.2
725.6	Schaghticoke Mtn Campsite *(990') to the left* .... C,w	1453.5
723.7	Thayer Brook *(950') crosses A.T.* .... w	1455.4

Connecticut

Miles from Katahdin	Features / Services	Miles from Springer
722.7	**Mt. Algo Lean-to** *(655') sleeps 6 (1986)* .... S,w	1456.4
---	*left 200ft, water from stream, ←S8.4m	N7.3m→*	---
722.4	CT341 📖 *p.152 (350') Kent School campus* .... R	1456.7
---	*right 0.5m–to* **KENT, CT 06757** .... H?,L,M,G,O,Lm,f	---
722.3	Macedonia Brook *(350') footbridge* .... w	1456.8
721.8	Numeral Rock Trail *(750') right to CT341*	1457.3
721.6	Viewpoint *(800') to the right, vista*	1457.5
719.6	Skiff Mtn Road *(780')* .... R	1459.5
718.9	Caleb's Peak *(1160') vistas*	1460.2
718.2	St. Johns Ledges *(895') vistas, rock steps*	1460.9
717.7	River Road *(425')* .... R	1461.4
717.1	Stream *(425') crosses A.T.* .... w	1462.0
716.1	Red pine plantation *(430') "pink" trees to the right*	1463.0
715.4	**Stewart Hollow Brook Lean-to** *(400') sleeps 6 (1980s)* .... S,w	1463.7
---	*left 100ft, stream 200ft south on A.T., ←S7.3m	N10.0m→*	---
715.0	Stony Brook Campsite *(435') to the left at Stony Brook* .... C,w	1464.1
713.0	River Road *(435') spring 25ft to the right on road* .... R,w	1466.1
712.8	Dawn Hill Road *(700')* .... R	1466.3
712.2	Silver Hill Campsite *(1000') to the right, water pump, vista* .... C,w	1466.9
711.4	Silver Hill *(1110') vista*	1467.7
711.3	CT4 📖 *p.153 (670')* .... R	1467.8
---	*right 0.9m–to* **CORNWALL BRIDGE, CT 06754** .... L,M,G,O,f	---
711.2	Guinea Brook *(690') crosses A.T. Note high water bypass route* .... w	1467.9
---	*Bypass: 0.5m right on CT4, then left 0.5 on Old Sharon Rd.*	---
711.1	Old Sharon Road *(700') right to Cornwall Bridge, CT* .... R	1468.0
711.0	Bread Loaf Mtn *(800')*	1468.1
709.9	Hatch Brook *(880') crosses A.T.* .... w	1469.2
709.2	Pine Knob Loop Trail 📖 *p.153 (1170') rejoins A.T. north*	1469.9
---	*right 1m–to Housatonic Meadows State Park* .... C,w	---
708.8	Caesar Brook Campsite *(800') Caesar Road* .... C,w	1470.3
707.4	Old woods road *(1050')* .... R	1471.7
706.6	Carse Brook *(800') crosses A.T.* .... w	1472.5
706.5	West Cornwall Road 📖 *p.153 (800')* .... R	1472.6
---	*right 2.2m–to* **West Cornwall, CT 06796** .... M	---
---	*left 4.6m–to* **Sharon, CT 06069** .... L,M,G,Lm	---
705.4	**Pine Swamp Brook Lean-to** *(1075') sleeps 6 (1989)* .... S,w	1473.7
---	*right 100ft, stream beyond shelter, ←S10.0m	N12.3m→*	---
704.5	Sharon Mtn Road *(1070')* .... R	1474.6
704.2	Mt. Easter *(1350')*	1474.9
703.1	Stream *(1190') crosses A.T., seasonal* .... w?	1476.0

Connecticut

Miles from Katahdin	Features / Services		Miles from Springer
703.0	Sharon Mtn Campsite *(1210')*	C	1476.1
700.2	Trail to Belter's Campsite *(770') 0.2m right*	C,w	1478.9
699.8	US7/CT112 *(550') stile*	R	1479.3
699.2	Housatonic River/US7 📖 *p.153 (500') A.T. crosses on bridge*	R,L?,M	1479.9
699.1	Mohawk Trail *(550') right 0.2m to US7*		1480.0
697.3	Hydroelectric plant *(550') to the left*	w	1481.8
---	*shower available at vine-covered building next to transformers*		---
697.2	Iron Bridge over Housatonic River 📖 *p.153 (550')*	w	1481.9
---	*right 0.5m–to* **Falls Village, CT 06031**	C?,M,w	---
696.6	Housatonic River Road *(750')*	R	1482.5
---	*right on blue-blazed trail to Great Falls (swimming area)*		---
696.1	Spring *(860') right 25ft, seasonal*	w?	1483.0
693.8	Prospect Mtn *(1475')*		1485.3
693.1	**Limestone Springs Lean-to** *(980') sleeps 6 (1986)*	S,w	1486.0
---	*left 0.5m, stream behind shelter, ←S12.3m	N7.5m→*		---
693.0	Rand's View *(1375') to the right, vista*		1486.1
692.5	Giant's Thumb *(1265') geologic formation*		1486.6
692.2	Viewpoint *(1190') "Billy's View"*		1486.9
689.8	US44 *(700')*	R	1489.3
689.7	Lower Cobble Road 📖 *p.154 (680') A.T. turns right off US44*	R	1489.4
---	*left 0.5m (on US44)–to* **SALISBURY, CT 06068**	L,M,G,f	---
---	*left 2.5m (on US44)–to* **Lakeville, CT 06031**	M	---
689.0	CT41 *(680') Undermountain Road*	R	1490.1
---	*left 0.8m to Salisbury, left 2.8m to Lakeville (see above)*		---
688.8	Plateau Campsite *(700') to the left, spring unreliable*	C,w?	1490.3
687.2	Stream *(1150') crosses A.T.*	w	1491.9
686.5	Lions Head Trail *(1550') to the left*		1492.6
686.3	Lion's Head *(1738')*		1492.8
685.6	**Riga Lean-to** *(1610') sleeps 6 (1960s), tent sites*	S,w	1493.5
---	*right 0.1m, spring on path to shelter, ←S7.5m	N1.2m→*		---
685.0	Ball Brook Campsite *(1705')*	C,w	1494.1
684.4	**Brassie Brook Lean-to** *(1705') sleeps 6 (1980s)*	S,w	1494.7
---	*right 200ft, stream behind shelter, ←S1.2m	N8.8m→*		---
683.9	Undermountain Trail *(1820') right 1.9m to CT41*		1495.2
683.7	Bear Mtn Road *(1900')*	R	1495.4
683.0	Bear Mtn *(2316') rock observation tower*		1496.1
---	**Notice!** camping in Connecticut is permitted only at designated		---
---	sites, and no fires are permitted anywhere. Ridgerunners patrol		---
---	during summer months and most spring and fall weekends		---

Massachusetts

Miles from Katahdin	Features / Services		Miles from Springer
682.4	Connecticut-Massachusetts border *(1850')unmarked*		1496.7
682.3	Paradise Lane Trail *(1600') to the right*		1496.8
682.2	Sawmill Brook *(1540') aka Sages Ravine Brook*	w	1496.9
681.6	Sages Ravine Brook Campsite *(1380') caretaker (no fee)*	C,w	1497.5
680.4	Spring *(1420') on A.T. to the left*	w	1498.7
680.3	Laurel Ridge Campsite *(1650') to the left*	C,w	1498.8
678.5	Race Mtn *(2430') vistas*		1500.6
677.4	Race Brook Falls Trail *(1980') 0.4m right to tent platforms*	C,w	1501.7
676.7	Mt. Everett *(2602') vista*		1502.4
676.4	Summit road *(2450')*	R	1502.7
676.0	Trail to Guilder Pond *(2042') to the left, picnic area*	w	1503.1
---	**Notice!** no camping or swimming permitted at pond		---
675.6	**Hemlocks Lean-to** *(1905') sleeps 10 (1999) Glen Brook crosses A.T.*	S,w	1503.5
---	*right 0.1m, water from stream, ←S8.8m | N500ft→*		---
675.5	**Glen Brook Lean-to** *(1900') sleeps 6 (1960s) tent platforms*	S,w	1503.6
---	*right 0.2m, water from strea, ←S500ft | N14.3m→*		---
674.9	Elbow Trail *(1780') right 1.5m to MA41*		1504.2
674.4	Mt. Bushnell *(1835')*		1504.7
673.2	The Jug End *(1750') vistas*		1505.9
672.1	Jug End Road *(850') right 0.2m to spring, on right*	R	1507.0
671.2	MA41 📖 *p.154 (620')*	R	1507.9
---	*left 1.2m*–to **SOUTH EGREMONT, MA 01258** .... L,M,G		---
669.6	Hubbard Brook *(620') bridge*	w	1509.5
669.4	South Egremont Road *(700') Shay's Rebellion Monument*	R	1509.7
668.2	West Sheffield Road *(620') aka West Road*	R	1510.9
667.8	Railroad tracks *(620')*		1511.3
667.6	US7 📖 *p.154 (620')*	R	1511.5
---	*left 1.8m*–to business district .... M,G,Lm		---
---	*left 3.1m*–to **Great Barrington, MA 01230** .... L,M,G,Lm		---
---	*right 2.8m*–to **Sheffield, MA 01257** .... M,G		---
666.7	Housatonic River *(610') A.T. crosses on Kellogg Road bridge*	R,w	1512.4
666.3	Boardman Street *(750')*	R	1512.8
665.7	June Mtn *(1210') vistas*		1513.4
664.7	Homes Road *(1100') aka Brush Hill Road*	R	1514.4
663.9	Spring *(1605') intermittent*	w?	1515.2
663.3	East Mtn *(1800')*		1515.8
661.2	**Tom Leonard Lean-to** *(1540') sleeps 10 (1970)*	S,w	1517.9
---	*right 150ft, spring downhill in Ice Gulch, ←S14.3m | N5.3m→*		---

Massachusetts

Miles from Katahdin	Features / Services		Miles from Springer
660.1	Lake Buel Road *(1100')*	R	1519.0
659.7	Stream *(1000') A.T. crosses on old dam*	w	1519.4
659.2	MA23 📖*p.155 (1000') left 1m to Lake Buel Road*	R,H,Lm	1519.9
658.7	Stream *(1350') intermittent*	w?	1520.4
658.2	Bog bridges *(1520')*		1520.9
658.0	Blue Hill Road *(1500') aka Stony Brook Road*	R	1521.1
657.2	Benedict Pond 📖*p.155 (1610') left to swimming area*	C,w	1521.9
656.8	Stream *(1780') swamp outlet, footbridge*	w	1522.3
656.2	Power line *(1680')*		1522.9
656.0	Spring *(1690') on A.T. to the right*	w	1523.1
655.9	**Mt. Wilcox South Lean-to** *(1720') sleeps 12 (1930, 2007)*	S,w	1523.2
---	*right 250ft, spring on path to shelter, ←S5.3m | N1.8m→*		---
654.7	Stream *(1800') beaver dam*	w	1524.4
654.1	**Mt. Wilcox North Lean-to** *(2100') sleeps 10 (1930s)*	S,w	1525.0
---	*right 0.3m, stream behind shelter, ←S1.8m | N14.0m→*		---
653.6	Trail for motorcycles *(1850') crosses A.T.*		1525.5
653.5	Beartown Mtn Road *(1805')*	R	1525.6
653.0	Stream *(1700') beaver dam*	w	1526.1
650.3	Fernside Road *(1200')*	R	1528.8
650.0	Shaker Campsite *(995')*	C	1529.1
649.9	Stream *(990') crosses A.T.*	w	1529.2
648.2	Jerusalem Road *(1100') spring to left, on left*	R,w	1530.9
647.9	Streams *(910') footbridges, intermittent*	w?	1531.2
647.2	Hop Brook *(900') bridge*	w	1531.9
647.1	Main Road 📖*p.155 (930')*	R	1532.0
---	*left 0.9m–to* **TYRINGHAM, MA 01264**	C?,L,f	---
645.2	Webster Road *(1800')*	R	1533.9
643.7	Spring *(1790') 0.1m left*	w	1535.4
642.8	Goose Pond Road *(1650')*	R	1536.3
642.6	Cooper Brook *(1620') footbridge*	w	1536.5
640.9	Stream *(1500') Upper Goose Pond to left*	w	1538.2
640.4	Old chimney and plaque *(1520') site of rod & gun club*		1538.7
640.1	**Upper Goose Pond Cabin** 📖*p.155 (1515') caretaker, fee*	S,w	1539.0
---	*left 0.5m, water at cabin, ←S14.0m | N8.8m→*		---
639.5	Viewpoint *(1720') on A.T.*		1539.6
---	***Notice!*** *no overnight camping or fires permitted at overlook*		---
638.9	Interstate 90/Mass. Turnpike *(1400') A.T. crosses on bridge*	R	1540.2
638.8	Stream *(1400') footbridge*	w	1540.3
638.5	US20, Jacob's Ladder Highway 📖*p.155 (1400')*	R,L	1540.6
---	*left 5m–to* **Lee, MA 01238**	L,M,G,Lm	---

2000' — Mt. Wilcox N. Lean-to · I-90

1000' — Mt. Wilcox S. Lean-to · Tyringham · Upper Goose Pond Cabin

Massachusetts

Miles from Katahdin	Features / Services		Miles from Springer
638.3	Power line *(1520')*		1540.8
637.7	Tyne Road *(1500')* aka Becket Road	R	1541.4
637.2	Becket Mtn *(2180')*		1541.9
636.2	Walling Mtn *(2220')*		1542.9
635.4	Finerty Pond *(1900')* outlet	w	1543.7
634.6	Old logging road *(1950')*	R	1544.5
634.1	Streams *(1820')* several cross A.T.	w	1545.0
633.1	County Road *(1850')*	R	1546.0
632.9	Bald Top *(2040')*		1546.2
632.4	Motorcycle-ATV trail *(2000')*		1546.7
631.3	**October Mtn Lean-to** *(1950') sleeps 12 (1980s)*	S,w?	1547.8
---	*left 200ft, intermittent stream at shelter, ←S8.8m | N8.8m→*		---
630.6	West Branch Road *(1950')*	R	1548.5
630.2	Woods road *(2000')*	R	1548.9
629.1	Pittsfield Road 📖*p.155 (2000')* aka Washington Mtn Road	R,C?,w	1550.0
---	*right 5m–to* **Becket, MA 01223** *no hiker services*		---
627.1	Stream *(1900')* crosses A.T.	w	1552.0
625.9	Blotz Road *(1800')*	R	1553.2
625.2	Warner Mtn *(2050')*		1553.9
622.6	Power lines *(1870')*		1556.5
622.5	**Kay Wood Lean-to** *(1860') sleeps 10 (1980s)*	S,w	1556.6
---	*right 800ft, stream downhill in front, ←S8.8m | N16.7m→*		---
622.2	Grange Hall Road *(1650')*	R	1556.9
622.0	Stream *(1550')* crosses A.T.	w	1557.1
621.3	Day Mtn *(1750')*		1557.8
620.1	Railroad tracks *(1250')*		1559.0
620.0	Depot Street *(1250')* water spigot at 83 Depot Street	R,w	1559.1
619.5	**DALTON, MA 01226** 📖*p.156 (1200')* MA8/9	R,L,M,G,Lm	1559.6
618.5	Gulf Road *(1220')*	R	1560.6
615.2	Power line *(1960')*		1563.9
614.8	Crystal Mtn Campsite *(2100')* right 0.2m to campsite	C,w	1564.3
614.4	Stream *(2050')* crosses A.T., outlet from Gore Pond	w	1564.7
613.9	Old logging road *(2200')*	R	1565.2
611.9	Trail to The Cobbles *(1800')* to the left, vista		1567.2
611.1	Furnace Hill Road *(980')*	R	1568.0
610.9	Church Street *(960')*	R	1568.2
610.8	Hoosic River *(960')* A.T. crosses on bridge	R	1568.3
610.7	Cheshire post office *(960')* to the left	R	1568.4
610.2	**CHESHIRE, MA 01225** 📖*p.157 (1000')* MA8	R,H,L,M,G,O,f	1568.9
609.4	Outlook Avenue *(1300')*	R	1569.7

Massachusetts

Miles from Katahdin	Features / Services	Miles from Springer
606.7	Old Adams Road *(2300')* multi-use trail crosses A.T.	1572.4
605.8	**Mark Noepel Lean-to** *(2800') sleeps 10 (1985)* .... S,w	1573.3
---	*right 700ft, water from Bassett Brook, ←S16.7m	N6.6m→*	---
605.2	Jones Nose Trail *(3140') to the left*	1573.9
604.4	Streams *(3100') several cross A.T., intermittent* .... w?	1574.7
603.5	Rockwell Road *(3120') parking area* .... R	1575.6
603.2	Rockwell Road *(3200')* .... R	1575.9
---	*Cheshire Harbor Trail to the right, Hopper Trail to the left*	---
603.0	Rockwell Road/Notch Road/Summit Road *(3250') pond* .... R	1576.1
602.5	Mt. Greylock 📖*p.157 (3491') War Memorial Tower*	1576.6
---	*on summit*–Bascom Lodge (closed until 2009)	---
---	***Notice!*** *no camping or fires (including stoves) permitted on summit*	---
602.0	Thunderbolt Trail *(3100') to the right*	1577.1
601.9	Bellows Pipe Trail *(3090') to the right*	1577.2
---	*steep descent 1m to Bellows Pipe Lean-to (not an A.T. shelter)*	---
601.2	Mt. Fitch *(3110')*	1577.9
600.4	Bernard Farm Trail *(2900') 0.3m left to spring at Notch Road* .... w	1578.7
600.2	Mt. Williams *(2950') register*	1578.9
599.3	Notch Road *(2300')* .... R	1579.8
599.2	**Wilbur Clearing Lean-to** *(2300') sleeps 8 (1970) Money Brook Trail* ...... S,w	1579.9
---	*left 0.3m, spring beyond shelter, ←S6.6m	N9.9m→*	---
599.0	Mt. Prospect Trail *(2450') to the left*	1580.1
597.1	Pattison Road *(900')* .... R	1582.0
596.7	Phelps Avenue *(670')* .... R	1582.4
596.2	MA2, State Road 📖*p.158 (650')* .... R,L?,G,Lm	1582.9
---	*left 2.6m–to* **WILLIAMSTOWN, MA 01267** .... C?,L,M,O,Lm,f	---
---	*right 2.5m–to* **North Adams, MA 01247** .... L,M,G,Lm	---
596.1	Hoosic River *(650') railroad tracks, footbridge*	1583.0
596.0	Massachusetts Avenue *(660')* .... R	1583.1
595.9	Sherman Brook *(900') A.T. borders stream north* .... w	1583.2
595.0	Power line *(1050')*	1584.1
594.6	Trail to Sherman Brook Campsite *(1300') left 0.1m, platforms* .... C,w	1584.5
---	*Pete's Spring to the right on blue-blazed trail*	---
594.4	Trail to Sherman Brook Campsite *(1380') left 0.1m, platforms* .... C,w	1584.7
593.4	Pine Cobble Trail *(2100') left 1.9m to Williamstown, MA*	1585.7
593.1	'98 Trail *(2200') to the left*	1586.0
592.9	Eph's Lookout *(2250') vista*	1586.2
592.6	Old woods road *(2260')* .... R	1586.5

Vermont

Miles from Katahdin	Features / Services	Miles from Springer
592.1	Massachusetts-Vermont border 📖 *p.159 (2330')*	1587.0
---	*southern terminus of the Long Trail; northbounders, read about*	---
---	*Green Mtn Club caretaker program and fee locations in notes*	---
591.7	Stream *(2100') crosses A.T.* .... w	1587.4
589.5	Woods road *(2130') Broad Brook Trail left* .... R	1589.6
589.3	**Seth Warner Shelter** *(2180') sleeps 8 (1965) tent sites* .... S,C,w	1589.8
---	*left 0.2m, stream beyond shelter,* ←*S9.9m	N7.2m*→	---
589.0	County Road *(2250') power line adjacent* .... R	1590.1
588.0	Ed's Spring *(2850') boxed, 100ft right* .... w	1591.1
587.6	Unnamed Peak *(3070') view to S*	1591.5
587.2	Power line *(2900')*	1591.9
586.3	Roaring Branch *(2490') crosses A.T.* .... w	1592.8
585.1	Consultation Peak *(2840')*	1594.0
584.1	Woods Road *(2300')* .... R	1595.0
582.8	Woods Road *(2200')* .... R	1596.3
582.6	Stamford Stream *(2040') A.T. borders stream* .... w	1596.5
582.1	**Congdon Shelter** *(2060') sleeps 8 (1967) tent sites* .... S,w	1597.0
---	*on A.T., stream near shelter,* ←*S7.2m	N5.9m*→	---
581.5	Woods road *(2150')* .... R	1597.6
581.0	Stream *(2250') crosses A.T.* .... w	1598.1
579.6	Harmon Hill *(2325') vista*	1599.5
577.8	VT9 📖 *p.159 (1360')* .... R	1601.3
---	*left 5.1m–to* **BENNINGTON, VT 05201** .... L,M,G,O,Lm,f	---
---	*right 3m–to private campground* .... C,G	---
577.1	Split Rock *(1900') A.T. passes through cleft*	1602.0
576.9	Woods road *(2050')* .... R	1602.2
576.7	Woods road *(2100')* .... R	1602.4
576.2	**Melville Nauheim Shelter** *(2330') sleeps 8 (1977)* .... S,w	1602.9
---	*right 100yds, stream north on A.T.,* ←*S5.9m	N8.5m*→	---
576.1	Stream *(2500') crosses A.T.* .... w	1603.0
575.6	Maple Hill *(2620') power line*	1603.5
575.1	Stream *(2500') crosses A.T.* .... w	1604.0
575.0	Stream *(2490') crosses A.T.* .... w	1604.1
574.6	Hell Hollow Brook *(2480')* .... w	1604.5
---	**Notice!** *no camping or fires permitted along stream; last reliable*	---
---	*water source north until spring at Goddard Shelter*	---
573.4	Porcupine Lookout *(2815') vista*	1605.7
572.4	Little Pond Mtn *(3100')*	1606.7

Vermont

572.0	Little Pond Lookout *(3060')* vista	1607.1
570.2	Glastenbury Lookout *(2870')* vista	1608.9
569.9	Old woods road *(2800')* .... R	1609.2
567.7	**Goddard Shelter** *(3540') sleeps 10 (2005) West Ridge Trail left* .... S,w	1611.4
---	*on A.T., spring at shelter, ←S8.5m|N4.3m→*	---
---	***Notice!** last reliable water source south until Hell Hollow Brook*	---
567.4	Glastenbury Mtn *(3748')* observation tower	1611.7
---	***Notice!** no camping or fires permitted on summit*	---
566.1	Big Rock *(3150')*	1613.0
563.4	**Kid Gore Shelter** *(2795') sleeps 8 (1971)* .... S,w	1615.7
---	*right 0.1m, spring at shelter, ←S4.3m|N4.6m→*	---
---	*stream on A.T. at site of former Caughnawaga Shelter* .... w	---
563.0	Stream *(2690')* crosses A.T. .... w	1616.1
559.7	South Alder Brook *(2600')* crosses A.T. .... w	1619.4
558.8	**Story Spring Shelter** *(2810') sleeps 8 (1963)* .... S,w	1620.3
---	*on A.T., spring at shelter, ←S4.6m|N10.4m→*	---
557.3	USFS Road 71 *(2500')* .... R	1621.8
556.2	Black Brook *(2350')* footbridge, woods road .... R,w	1622.9
555.6	Stream *(2300')* crosses A.T. .... w	1623.5
555.2	Stratton-Arlington Road *(2340')* aka Kelley Stand Road .... R	1623.9
555.1	East Branch of Deerfield River *(2335')* .... R,w	1624.0
553.7	Woods road *(2620')* gravel surfaced .... R	1625.4
552.0	Spring *(3500')* on A.T. to the left .... w	1627.1
551.4	Stratton Mtn 📖 *p.160 (3936')* fire tower, caretaker cabin	1627.7
---	***Notice!** no camping or fires permitted on summit*	---
549.4	Woods road *(2550')* .... R	1629.7
548.9	Stream *(2490')* crosses A.T. .... w	1630.2
548.4	Stratton Pond 📖 *p.160 (2550')* GMC caretaker .... w	1630.7
---	**Stratton Pond Shelter** *(2550') sleeps 16 (1999) fee* .... S,w	---
---	*left 0.2m on Stratton Pond Trail, spring below, S10.4m|N4.9m→*	---
---	*(0.1m right on Lye Brook Trail, following south shore of Stratton*	---
---	*Pond, water usually available from spring)*	---
548.2	North Shore Trail *(2555')* left 0.5m to N. Shore Tenting Area, fee .... C,w	1630.9
546.3	Winhall River *(2300')* bridge, woods road .... R,w	1632.8
543.5	**William B. Douglas Shelter** *(2210') sleeps 10 (1956)* .... S,w	1635.6
---	*left 0.5m on Branch Pond Trail, stream, ←S4.9m|N3.0m→*	---
543.4	Stream/woods road *(2200')* .... R,w	1635.7
543.3	Old Rootville Road *(2230')* gravel surfaced .... R	1635.8

Vermont

542.6	Prospect Rock *(2080') 150ft left, vista*	1636.5
542.0	Stream *(2380') crosses A.T.* .... w	1637.1
541.6	Stream *(2300') crosses A.T.* .... w	1637.5
540.5	**Spruce Peak Shelter** *(2180') sleeps 14 (1983)* .... S,w	1638.6
---	*left 400ft, spring at shelter,* ←*S3.0m* | *N4.8m*→	---
540.1	Trail to Spruce Peak summit *(2060') 400ft left, vista*	1639.0
539.6	Stream *(1750') crosses A.T., power line* .... w	1639.5
537.9	Stream *(1780') crosses A.T., power line nearby* .... w	1641.2
537.7	VT 11/30 📖 *p.161 (1800') parking area* .... R	1641.4
---	*left 5.5m–to* **MANCHESTER CENTER, VT 05255** .... L,M,G,O,Lm,f	---
537.6	Stream *(1870') footbridge* .... w	1641.5
535.8	Stream *(2500') crosses A.T.* .... w	1643.3
535.7	**Bromley Shelter** *(2560') sleeps 12 (2003) tent platforms* .... S,w	1643.4
---	*on A.T., stream 0.1m south on A.T.,* ←*S4.8m* | *N8.1m*→	---
534.7	Bromley Mtn 📖 *p.162 (3260') warming hut* .... C?	1644.4
532.2	Mad Tom Notch, USFS Road 21 *(2446') hand pump* .... R,w	1646.9
530.6	Styles Peak *(3395') vista*	1648.5
528.9	Peru Peak *(3429') vista to the right*	1650.2
527.6	**Peru Peak Shelter** *(2605') sleeps 10 (renovated 2000), fee* .... S,w	1651.5
---	*on A.T., stream at shelter,* ←*S8.1m* | *N4.7m*→	---
527.4	Stream *(2600') crosses A.T.* .... w	1651.7
527.3	Stream *(2610') crosses A.T.* .... w	1651.8
527.2	Old woods road *(2650')* .... R	1651.9
527.1	Griffith Lake Tenting Area *(2500') GMC caretaker, fee* .... C,w	1652.0
526.9	Old Job Trail *(2500') to the right*	1652.2
---	*right 4.3m to Old Job Shelter (see below), rejoins A.T. north*	---
526.8	Lake Trail *(2500') to the left*	1652.3
526.3	Woods road *(2650')* .... R	1652.8
525.0	Baker Peak Trail *(2780') to the left*	1654.1
524.9	Baker Peak *(2850') vista*	1654.2
523.1	Woods road *(2400')* .... R	1656.0
522.9	**Lost Pond Shelter** *(2230') (rebuilt 2009)* .... w	1656.2
---	*left 0.1m, stream by shelter,* ←*S4.7m* | *N1.5m*→	---
521.4	**Old Job Shelter** *(1665') sleeps 8 (1935)* .... S,w	1657.7
---	*right 1m on old roadbed, stream at shelter,* ←*S1.5m* | *N0.2m*→	---
521.2	**Big Branch Shelter** *(1460') sleeps 8 (1963)* .... S,w	1657.9
---	*on A.T., stream at shelter,* ←*S0.2m* | *N3.0m*→	---
521.0	Woods road *(1500')* .... R	1658.1

Vermont

Miles from Katahdin	Features / Services		Miles from Springer
520.1	Big Black Branch *(1500')* bridge	w	1659.0
519.9	Danby-Landgrove Road, USFS Road 10 📖*p.162 (1500')*	R	1659.2
---	*left 3.5m*–to **Danby, VT 05739**	L,M,G	---
519.8	Old logging road *(1690')*	R	1659.3
518.2	**Lula Tye Shelter** *(1920') sleeps 8 (1962), fee*	S,w	1660.9
---	*right 150ft, spring 0.4m north on A.T., ←S3.0m | N0.7m→*		---
518.0	Little Rock Pond Loop Trail *(1900')* to the left, rejoins A.T. north		1661.1
517.9	Little Rock Pond Tenting Area *(1900')* GMC caretaker, fee	C	1661.2
517.8	Spring *(1900')* on A.T. to right	w	1661.3
517.6	Homer Stone Brook Trail *(1900')*		1661.5
517.5	**Little Rock Pond Shelter** *(1920') sleeps 8 (1962), fee*	S,w	1661.6
---	*right 100ft, spring 0.3m south on A.T., ←S0.7m | N4.4m→*		---
516.6	Homer Stone Brook *(1925')* crosses A.T.	w	1662.5
516.4	Old woods road *(2000')*	R	1662.7
514.8	White Rocks Mtn *(2680')* left 100yds to spring	w	1664.3
514.6	White Rocks Cliffs *(2400')* vista		1664.5
513.1	**Greenwall Shelter** *(2025') sleeps 8 (1962)*	S,w	1666.0
---	*right 0.3m, water on blue-blazed trail, ←S4.4m | N5.1m→*		---
512.5	Bully Brook *(1760')* crosses A.T.	w	1666.6
---	*Keewaydin Trail left 0.4m to White Rocks Picnic Area*		---
511.7	Sugar Hill Road *(1660')*	R	1667.4
511.6	VT140, Wallingford Gulf Road 📖*p.162 (1560') Roaring Brook*	R,w	1667.5
---	*left 2.8m*–to **Wallingford, VT 05773**	L,M,G	---
509.5	Bear Mtn *(2240')*		1669.6
508.4	Power line *(1650')*		1670.7
508.0	**Minerva Hinchey Shelter** *(1530') sleeps 10 (renovated 2006)*	S,w	1671.1
---	*right 230ft, stream south of shelter, ←S5.1m | N3.7m→*		---
507.4	Spring Lake Clearing *(1625')*		1671.7
505.4	Mill River, Clarendon Gorge *(850')* suspension bridge	w	1673.7
---	**Notice!** *no overnight camping permitted either side of gorge*		
505.3	VT103 📖*p.162 (860')* railroad tracks	R,M,G	1673.8
---	*left 4.2m*–to **North Clarendon, VT 05759**	L	---
505.2	Power line *(900')*		1673.9
504.9	Clarendon Lookout *(1000')* vista		1674.2
504.3	**Clarendon Shelter** *(1390') sleeps 10 (1952)*	S,w	1674.8
---	*on A.T., stream beyond shelter, ←S3.7m | N5.8m→*		---
503.8	Beacon Hill *(1760')* aviation beacon		1675.3
503.4	Lottery Road *(1720')*	R	1675.7

Vermont

Miles from Katahdin	Features / Services		Miles from Springer
503.0	Hermit Spring *(1700')* on A.T., seasonal	w?	1676.1
501.7	Keiffer Road *(1505')*	R	1677.4
501.5	Cold River *(1440')* A.T. borders	w	1677.6
501.4	Lower Cold River Road *(1450')* bridge	R,w	1677.7
500.6	Gould Brook *(1480')* crosses A.T.	w	1678.5
499.9	Upper Cold River Road *(1670')*	R,w	1679.2
499.3	Woods road *(1800')* bridge	R,w	1679.8
498.6	Robinson Brook/woods road *(1860')* bridge	R,w	1680.5
498.5	**Governor Clement Shelter** *(1850')* sleeps 12 *(1929)*	S,w	1680.6
---	*on A.T., stream near shelter, ←S5.8m	N4.3m→*	---
---	***Notice!*** *nearby road now gated, but historically a problem area*	---
498.4	Stream *(2500')* crosses A.T.	w	1680.7
497.5	Stream *(3000')* crosses A.T.	w	1681.6
496.0	Shrewsbury Peak Trail *(3500')* to the right		1683.1
494.3	Killington Peak Trail 📖 *p.162 (3870')* right 0.2m to summit	M?,w	1684.8
494.2	**Cooper Lodge** *(3850')* sleeps 16 *(1939)* slated for demolition	S,w?	1684.9
---	*on A.T., intermittent spring near shelter, ←S4.3m	N2.5m→*	---
---	***Notice!*** *no camping permitted from here north to Maine Junction*	---
491.7	**Pico Camp** *(3510')* sleeps 12 *(1959)* Sherburne Pass Trail	S,w	1687.4
---	*right 0.5m, spring at shelter, ←S2.5m	N1.9m→*	---
489.8	**Churchill Scott Shelter** *(2560')* sleeps 8 *(2002)* tent platform, no fires	S,w	1689.3
---	*left 0.1m, spring 0.1m below shelter, ←S1.9m	N2.9m→*	---
489.7	Mendon Lookout *(2400')* vista		1689.4
489.3	Streams *(2300')* two streams cross A.T.	w	1689.8
487.9	US4 (near Sherburne Pass) 📖 *p.163 (1880')*	R	1691.2
---	*right 0.9m–to private inn*	L,M,Lm,w	---
---	*left 8.6m–to* **RUTLAND, VT 05701**	H,L,M,G,O,Lm,f	---
---	*right 2.2m to Killington (see VT100 below)*	L,M,G	---
486.9	**Tucker-Johnson Shelter** *(2300')* sleeps 8 *(1969)* Maine Junction	S,w	1692.2
---	*left (on Long Trail) 0.4m, spring at shelter, ←S2.9m	N9.0m→*	---
---	*A.T. contiguous with the Long Trail south from here to the MA/VT border*	---
---	***Notice!*** *no camping permitted from here to Cooper Lodge*	---
486.8	Deer Leap Trail *(2320')* right to overlook, rejoins A.T.		1692.3
486.0	Sherburne Pass Trail *(2440')* right 0.5m to Sherburne Pass		1693.1
485.7	Ben's Balcony *(2100')* right 50ft to vista		1693.4
484.7	Gifford Woods State Park 📖 *p.164 (1700')* showers, fee	C,w	1694.4
484.6	VT100 📖 *p.164 (1690')*	R	1694.5
---	*right 0.7m–to* **KILLINGTON, VT 05751**	L,M,G	---

Vermont

Miles from Katahdin	Features / Services		Miles from Springer
483.9	Kent Pond 🕮 *p.164 (1680') swimming area, lodge*	L,M,w	1695.2
483.5	Thundering Brook Road *(1685')*	R	1695.6
482.3	Ottauquechee River *(1220') A.T. crosses on bridge*	w	1696.8
482.2	River Road *(1214')*	R	1696.9
481.9	Stream *(2000') crosses A.T.*	w	1697.2
481.2	Power line *(2300')*		1697.9
480.7	Woods road *(2350')*	R	1698.4
479.7	Old logging road *(2500')*	R	1699.4
478.9	Quimby Mtn *(2620')*		1700.2
478.7	Streams/old logging roads *(2200') several cross A.T.*	R,w	1700.4
477.9	**Stony Brook Shelter** *(1760') sleeps 8 (1997)*	S,w	1701.2
---	*right 0.1m, stream at shelter, ←S9.0m|N9.9m→*		---
477.3	Stony Brook Road *(1500') Stony Brook*	R	1701.8
477.2	Mink Brook *(1700') crosses A.T.*	w	1701.9
476.4	Pond *(1820')*	w	1702.7
475.1	Continental Divide *(2320') sag on ridge*		1704.0
474.0	Stream *(2000') crosses A.T.*	w	1705.1
473.6	Old logging roads *(2100') several cross A.T.*	R	1705.5
473.2	Chateauquay Road *(2000') Locust Creek*	R,w	1705.9
472.8	Stream *(2250') crosses A.T.*	w	1706.3
472.5	Lakota Lake Lookout *(2450')*		1706.6
472.3	Woods road *(2400')*	R	1706.8
470.4	Trail to The Lookout 🕮 *p.164 (2415') observation deck*		1708.7
469.6	Lookout Farm Road *(2225')*	R	1709.5
469.5	King Cabin Road *(2200')*	R	1709.6
469.0	Don's Rock *(2400')*		1710.1
468.5	Sawyer Hill *(2500')*		1710.6
468.0	**Wintturi Shelter** *(1900') sleeps 8 (1994)*	S,w	1711.1
---	*left 0.2m, spring at shelter, ←S9.9m|N11.6m→*		---
467.4	Old woods road *(1700')*	R	1711.7
466.8	Old woods road *(1300')*	R	1712.3
465.1	Electric fence *(1000')*		1714.0
464.2	VT12, Barnard Gulf Road 🕮 *p.164 (882')*	R	1714.9
---	*right 4.4m–to* **Woodstock, VT 05091**	G,L,M,Lm	---
---	***Notice!*** *no camping or fires ¼ mile either side of road*		---
462.7	Woodstock Stage Road 🕮 *p.165 (770') aka Barnard Brook Rd*	R	1716.4
---	*right 1m–to* **SOUTH POMFRET, VT 05067**	M?,G	---
461.9	Town Highway 38 *(980') dirt surfaced*	R	1717.2

Vermont

Miles from Katahdin	Features / Services	Miles from Springer
461.2	Bartlett Brook Road *(1050') stream* .... R	1717.9
460.7	Stream *(1030') crosses A.T.* .... w	1718.4
460.5	Pomfret-South Pomfret Road *(990')* .... R	1718.6
460.1	Old woods road *(1390')* .... R	1719.0
459.6	Spring *(1500') right 50ft* .... w	1719.5
458.7	Cloudland Road *(1390')* .... R	1720.4
458.5	Trail to ***Cloudland Shelter*** 📖*p.165 (1430') left 0.5m* ....C,w	1720.6
458.2	Powerline *(1480')*	1720.9
456.7	Thistle Hill *(1700')*	1722.4
456.6	Woods road *(1600') snowmobile trail* .... R	1722.5
456.4	**Thistle Hill Shelter** *(1640') sleeps 8 (1995)* .... S,w	1722.7
---	*right 0.1m, stream near shelter, ←S11.6m|N8.8m→*	---
456.0	Stream *(1500') crosses A.T.* .... w	1723.1
455.6	Arms Hill *(1650')*	1723.5
454.9	Joe Ranger Road *(1360')* .... R	1724.2
454.6	Bunker Hill *(1415')*	1724.5
454.1	Woods road *(1280')* .... R	1725.0
453.9	Woods road *(1000')* .... R	1725.2
452.5	Quechee-West Hartford Road *(500')* .... R	1726.6
451.7	White River *(400') A.T. crosses on bridge* .... w	1727.4
451.6	**WEST HARTFORD, VT 05084** 📖*p.165 (400') VT14* .... R,C?	1727.5
451.0	Tigertown Road *(600') railroad tracks* .... R	1728.1
450.9	Interstate 89 *(620') A.T. uses underpass, no exits* .... R	1728.2
450.2	Podunk Brook *(800') Podunk Road* .... R,w	1728.9
450.0	Woods road *(810')* .... R	1729.1
449.3	Logging road *(1000') East Fork of Podunk Brook* .... R,w	1729.8
448.7	Snowmobile trail *(1300')*	1730.4
448.3	Griggs Mtn *(1580')*	1730.8
448.1	Stream *(1500') crosses A.T.* .... w	1731.0
448.0	Old woods road *(1430')* .... R	1731.1
447.6	**Happy Hill Shelter** *(1400') sleeps 8 (1998)* .... S,w	1731.5
---	*right 0.1m, seasonal spring near shelter, ←S8.8m|N7.3m→*	---
447.5	William Tucker Trail *(1425')*	1731.6
446.0	Newton Lane *(1100')* .... R	1733.1
444.7	Power line *(1150')*	1734.4
444.1	Elm Street *(900')* .... R	1735.0
443.8	Hopson Road *(750')* .... R	1735.3
443.5	Bloody Brook *(550') crosses A.T.* .... w	1735.6

Vermont-New Hampshire

Miles from Katahdin	Features / Services		Miles from Springer
443.3	**NORWICH, VT 05055** 📖 *p.165 (515') Hwy. 5*	R,L,M,G?	1735.8
443.1	Interstate 91 *(430') A.T. passes under on Hwy. 10-A*	R	1736.0
442.3	Connecticut River *(400') A.T. crosses on bridge*	R	1736.8
2179.1	*Vermont-New Hampshire border*		
441.8	**HANOVER, NH 03755** 📖 *p.166 (425')*	H,L,M,G,Lm,O,f	1737.3
440.9	Spring *(500') seasonal*	w?	1738.2
440.3	**Velvet Rocks Shelter** *(1040') sleeps 6 (renovated 2006)*	S,w	1738.8
---	*left 0.2m, spring 0.2m beyond shelter, ←S7.3m	N9.5m→*		---
439.8	Ledyard Spring Trail *(1220') left 0.2m to spring*	w	1739.3
439.2	Trescott Road Trail *(880')*		1739.9
438.1	Pond *(800') beaver dam, bridge*	w	1741.0
437.3	Trescott Road 📖 *p.167 (920')*	R	1741.8
---	*right 0.8m–to **Etna, NH 03750***	H,L,M,G,Lm,f	---
435.9	Etna-Hanover Center Road 📖 *p.167 (880')*	R	1743.2
---	*right 0.8m–to **Etna, NH 03750***	H,L,M,G,Lm,f	---
433.9	Cory Road *(1280')*	R	1745.2
433.4	Three-Mile Road *(1390')*	R	1745.7
433.2	Mink Brook *(1320') crosses A.T.*	w	1745.9
431.6	South Peak of Moose Mtn *(2250')*		1747.5
430.8	**Moose Mtn Shelter** *(1850') sleeps 8 (2004)*	S,w	1748.3
---	*right 300ft on loop, spring/stream at A.T., ←S9.5m	N5.7m→*		---
429.6	North Peak of Moose Mtn *(2300')*		1749.5
428.9	South Fork of Hewes Brook *(970')*	w	1750.2
427.6	Goose Pond Road *(920')*	R	1751.5
427.2	Old logging road *(1250')*	R	1751.9
425.6	Holts Ledge *(2100') peregrine falcon rookery*		1753.5
425.1	**Trapper John Shelter** *(1345') sleeps 6 (1990s) tent sites*	S,w	1754.0
---	*left 0.2m, stream at shelter, ←S5.7m	N6.7m→*		---
424.2	Lyme-Dorchester Road 📖 *p.167 (880') road forks*	R,w	1754.9
---	*left 1.2m–to **Lyme Center, NH 03769***	ATC regional office	---
---	*left 3.2m–to **Lyme, NH 03768***	L,M,G	---
422.3	Grant Brook *(1150') crosses A.T.*	w	1756.8
422.2	Lyme-Dorchester Road *(1160') Smarts Mtn Ranger Trail*	R	1756.9
420.4	Stream *(2200') crosses A.T.*	w	1758.7
418.9	Smarts Mtn Ranger Trail *(2700') joins A.T., ends at summit*		1760.2
418.5	Smarts Mtn Tent site *(3200') right 500ft*	C,w	1760.6
418.4	**Firewarden's Cabin** *(3240') sleeps 8, fire tower, vistas*	S,w	1760.7
---	*on A.T., Mike Murphy Spring near shelter, ←S6.7m	N5.3m→*		---
418.3	Clark Pond Loop Trail *(3200') to the left, rejoins A.T. south*		1760.8

New Hampshire

Miles from Katahdin	Features / Services		Miles from Springer
414.5	South Jacobs Brook *(1450') bridge*	w	1764.6
414.1	Eastman Ledges *(2010') vista*		1765.0
413.9	North Jacobs Brook *(1800') bridge*	w	1765.2
413.1	**Hexacuba Shelter** *(2180') sleeps 8 (1989)*	S,w	1766.0
---	*right 0.3m, stream on path to shelter, ←S5.3m|N7.3m→*		---
411.7	Mt. Cube *(2911') vistas*		1767.4
411.2	Trail to North Cube *(2300') to the right, vistas*		1767.9
410.0	Brackett Brook *(1650') crosses A.T.*	w	1769.1
408.7	Logging road *(1580') gravel surfaced*	R	1770.4
408.2	NH25A 📖 *p.167 (900')*	R	1770.9
---	*right 4.2m–*to **Wentworth, NH 03282**	G	---
406.4	Cape Moonshine Road *(1500') Atwell Hill Road*	R	1772.7
405.8	**Ore Hill Shelter** *(1800') sleeps 8 (2000)*	S,w	1773.3
---	*right 0.1m, stream downhill from shelter, ←S7.3m|N8.4m→*		---
405.4	Spring *(1650') to the right on blue-blazed trail*	w	1773.7
404.8	Ore Hill *(1870')*		1774.3
403.4	NH25C *(1500')*	R	1775.7
---	*right 4m to Warren (see NH25 below)*		---
403.2	Stream *(1500') crosses A.T.*	w	1775.9
400.9	Mt. Mist *(2200') vista to the right 0.2n north of summit*		1778.2
400.4	Trail to Webster Slide Mtn *(1550') to the left*		1778.7
400.3	Hairy Root Spring *(1530') on A.T., seasonal*	w	1778.8
400.1	Wachipauka Pond *(1500') A.T. skirts pond*	w	1779.0
399.4	Wyatt Hill *(1700')*		1779.7
398.5	NH25 📖 *p.167 (1140')*	R	1780.6
---	*right 0.5m–*to **GLENCLIFF, NH 03238**	H,f	---
---	*right 5m–*to **Warren, NH 03279**	M,G	---
398.4	Oliverian Brook *(1140') ford*	w	1780.7
---	**Alternate!** *Northbounders, if water level is dangerous for fording*		---
---	*Oliverian Brook, go right on NH25 past Glencliff post office,*		---
---	*turn left on Sanitarium Road, go 1m to where A.T. crosses,*		---
---	*then right. Southbounders, backtrack and reverse directions*		---
397.4	**Jeffers Brook Shelter** *(1350') sleeps 10 (1970s)*	S,w	1781.7
---	*left 500ft, stream in front of shelter, ←S8.4m|N6.8m→*		---
397.2	USFS Road 19 *(1450')*	R	1781.9
397.1	Sanitarium Road *(1550') paved, stile*	R	1782.0
396.8	Stream *(1800') crosses A.T.*	w	1782.3
396.7	Hurricane Trail *(1900') right 5.1m to DOC Ravine Lodge*		1782.4

New Hampshire

396.6	Stream *(2000')* crosses A.T. .... w	1782.5
395.6	Stream *(3100')* crosses A.T.	1783.5
393.8	Trail to South Peak, Mt. Moosilauke *(4523')* Carriage Road	1785.3
393.5	Viewpoint *(4580')* right 50ft to vista	1785.6
---	*A.T. above treeline for first time northbound; last time southbound*	---
392.8	Mt. Moosilauke *(4802')* panoramic vista	1786.3
---	*Gorge Brook Trail right 3.6m to DOC Ravine Lodge*	---
391.5	Spring *(4400')* on A.T. to the left at Jobildunc Ravine .... w	1787.6
390.9	Ridge Trail *(4200')* right 5.1m to DOC Ravine Lodge	1788.2
390.6	**Beaver Brook Shelter** *(3650')* sleeps 10 *(1980s)* .... S,w	1788.5
---	*left 200ft, stream beyond shelter, ←S6.8m	N9.1m→*	---
389.2	Stream *(1830')* footbridge .... w	1789.9
389.1	Stream *(1825')* bridge .... w	1790.0
389.0	Kinsman Notch, NH112 p.168 *(1812')* .... R	1790.1
---	*right 0.5m–to Lost River Reservation .... snack bar*	---
---	*right 5m to North Woodstock (see Franconia Notch below)*	---
---	*See regulations for A.T. hikers using the White Mountains* 📖 *p.168;*	---
---	*also, Appalachian Mountain Club* 📖 *p.168 management section*	---
---	*begins for northbounders, read about AMC fee locations in notes*	---
388.3	Dilly Trail *(2630')* right 0.8m to Lost River Reservation	1790.8
385.7	Gordon Pond Trail *(2850')* right 0.3m to pond .... w	1793.4
385.4	Stream *(3230')* crosses A.T. .... w	1793.7
385.3	South Peak of Mt. Wolf *(3360')*	1793.8
384.4	East Peak of Mt. Wolf *(3478')* right 100ft to summit	1794.7
382.5	Reel Brook Trail *(2390')* to the left	1796.6
381.5	**Eliza Brook Shelter** *(2500')* sleeps 8 *(1993)*, Eliza Brook adjacent .... S,w	1797.6
---	*left 200ft, stream near shelter, ←S9.1m	N4.0m→*	---
---	*(camping at designated areas only, walk only on in-site trails)*	---
380.7	Stream *(2800')* Eliza Brook .... w	1798.4
380.2	Stream *(3450')* Harrington Pond to the left .... w	1798.9
379.0	South Kinsman *(4358')* ascent/descent involves rock scramble	1800.1
378.1	North Kinsman *(4293')* vistas	1801.0
377.7	Mt. Kinsman Trail *(3800')* to the left	1801.4
377.5	**Kinsman Pond Campsite** *(3750')* sleeps 15 *(2007)*, fee .... S,C,w	1801.6
---	*right 500ft, water from pond, ←S4.0m	N15.1m→*	---
376.4	Stream *(2700')* crosses A.T. .... w	1802.7

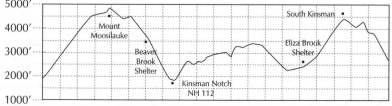

New Hampshire

Miles from Katahdin	Features / Services		Miles from Springer
375.6	AMC-Lonesome Lake Hut 📖 p.169 (2760') fee	L,M,w	1803.5
---	*Around-Lonesome-Lake Trail left 0.3m, then right 1.2m on Lonesome*		---
---	*Lake Trail to Lafayette Place CG (see Franconia Notch Bike Path below)*		---
374.8	Kinsman Pond Trail *(2370') to the right, rejoins A.T. south*		1804.3
374.3	Cascade Brook *(2180') Basin-Cascade Trail left*	w	1804.8
372.9	Whitehouse Brook *(1500') crosses A.T.*	w	1806.2
372.7	Franconia Notch, Interstate 93/US3 📖 p.169 (1450')	R,w	1806.4
---	*A.T. goes under Interstate 93/US3, borders Pemigawasset River*		---
---	*right 5.8m*–to **NORTH WOODSTOCK, NH 03262**	L,M,G,Lm	---
---	*right 4.5m*–to **Lincoln, NH 03251**	M,G,O,f	---
372.6	Franconia Notch Bike Path 📖 p.170 (1450') Pemigawassett River	R,w	1806.5
---	*left 2.5m*–to Lafayette Place Campground (fee)	C,w	---
---	*right 1m*–to The Flume Visitor Center	M	---
372.4	Stream *(1500') crosses A.T.*	w	1806.7
372.1	Flume Side Trail *(2390') right 3.8m to Mt. Flume*		1807.0
370.8	Stream *(3210') crosses A.T.*	w	1808.3
370.1	Liberty Spring Tent site 📖 p.170 (3800') AMC caretaker, fee	C,w	1809.0
369.8	Franconia Ridge Trail *(4250') right 0.3m to Liberty Mtn summit*		1809.3
---	**Notice!** *A.T. mostly above treeline on Franconia Range* 📖 p.155		---
369.0	Little Haystack Mtn *(4760') vistas*		1810.1
---	*Falling Waters Trail left 2.8m to Lafayette Place Campground*		---
367.3	Mt. Lincoln *(5089') vistas*		1811.8
366.3	Mt. Lafayette 📖 p.170 (5249') vistas		1812.8
---	*Greenleaf Trail left 1m to AMC-Greenleaf Hut (fee)*	L,M,w	---
365.9	North Peak of Mt. Lafayette *(5080') vistas*		1813.2
365.6	Skookumchuck Trail *(4700') to the left*		1813.5
363.5	Garfield Pond *(3800') to the left*		1815.6
362.8	Mt. Garfield *(4488') vista*		1816.3
362.6	Garfield Trail *(4150') to the left*		1816.5
362.4	**Garfield Ridge Campsite** *(3500') sleeps 12 (1970), fee*	S,C,w	1816.7
---	*left 500ft, spring at A.T. junction, ←S15.1m | N5.5m→*		---
361.9	Franconia Brook Trail *(3450') to the right*		1817.2
---	*right 2.2m to 13 Falls Tent Site (AMC caretaker, fee)*		---
360.4	Gale River Trail *(3400') to the left*		1818.7
359.7	AMC-Galehead Hut 📖 p.170 (3820') fee	L,M,w	1819.4
358.9	South Twin Mtn *(4902') North Twin Spur left*		1820.2
356.9	**Guyot Campsite** *(4560') sleeps 12 (1977), fee, tent platforms*	S,C,w	1822.2
---	*right 0.7m (on Bondcliff Trail), spring, ←S5.5m | N9.0m→*		---

New Hampshire

Miles from Katahdin	Features / Services	Miles from Springer

Miles from Katahdin	Features / Services	Miles from Springer
356.7	Mt. Guyot *(4560')* vista	1822.4
355.6	Trail to Zealand Mtn *(4000')* left 0.1m to summit	1823.5
354.4	Trail to Zeacliff Pond *(3800')* right 0.1m to pond .... w	1824.7
354.1	Zeacliff Trail *(3650')* to the right, rejoins A.T. north	1825.0
353.9	Stream *(3590')* crosses A.T. .... w	1825.2
352.8	Whitewall Brook *(2605')* Lend-a-Hand Trail left .... w	1826.3
352.7	AMC-Zealand Falls Hut 📖 *p.170 (2450')* fee, *Zealand Falls* .... L,M,w	1826.4
352.3	Whitewall Mtn *(2500')* A.T. follows old railroad bed	1826.8
351.0	Zeacliff Trail *(2470')* to the right, rejoins A.T. south	1828.1
350.4	Thoreau Falls Trail *(2430')* to the right	1828.7
349.9	Shoal Pond Trail *(2620')* right 0.8m to pond	1829.2
349.6	Stream *(2750')* crosses A.T. .... w	1829.5
347.9	**Ethan Pond Campsite** *(2950')* sleeps 10 (1970s), fee, tent platforms .. S,C,w	1831.2
---	*left 500ft, water from pond, ←S9.0m | N42.0m→*	---
346.9	Willey Range Trail *(2690')* left 0.1m to Kedron Brook .... w	1832.2
346.6	Kedron Flume Trail *(2300')* to the left	1832.5
345.5	Arethusa-Ripley Falls Trail *(1620')* right 0.4m to Ripley Falls .... w	1833.6
345.4	Willey House Station Road *(1300')* railroad tracks .... R	1833.7
345.0	Crawford Notch, US302 📖 *p.170 (1277')* Presidential Range .... R	1834.1
---	*left 1m*–to Willey House .... snack bar	---
---	*left 3.7m*–to Highland Lodge at Crawford Notch .... L,M	---
---	*right 1.5m*–to Dry River Campground C	---
---	*right 3m*–to private campground .... H,C,L,G,f	---
344.9	Saco River *(1270')* bridge .... w	1834.2
343.1	Webster Cliffs *(3330')* vistas	1836.0
341.7	Mt. Webster *(3910')* Webster Fork of Webster-Jackson Trail left	1837.4
340.3	Mt. Jackson *(4052')* Jackson Fork of Webster-Jackson Trail left	1838.8
338.6	AMC-Mizpah Spring Hut/Nauman Tent Site 📖 *p.171 (3800')* fee .... C,L,M,w	1840.5
---	*Mt. Clinton Trail right, Mizpah Cutoff to Crawford Path left*	---
338.3	South Peak of Mt. Clinton *(4180')*	1840.8
337.8	Mt. Clinton *(4310')* aka Mt. Pierce	1841.3
---	**Notice!** *A.T. mostly above treeline for next 12.7 miles north*	---
337.6	Mt. Eisenhower Loop *(4450')* to the left, rejoins A.T.	1841.5
335.7	Edmonds Path *(4500')* to the left	1843.4
335.6	Spring *(4700')* on A.T. .... w	1843.5
335.3	Mt. Franklin *(5004')*	1843.8
334.9	Monroe Loop *(5120')* to the left, rejoins A.T.	1844.2

84   *The Thru-hiker's Handbook 2010*

New Hampshire

Miles from Katahdin	Features / Services	Miles from Springer
334.3	Dry River Trail *(5080') to the right*	1844.8
333.8	AMC-Lakes of the Clouds Hut 📖*p.171 (5000') fee* .... H,L,M,w	1845.3
---	*"The Dungeon" bunk room for long-distance hikers only (fee)*	---
332.9	Davis Path *(5700') to the right*	1846.2
332.8	Westside Trail *(5700') to the left*	1846.3
332.6	Gulfside Trail *(5800') to the left*	1846.5
332.4	Mt. Washington 📖*p.171 (6288') Summit House* .... R,M,w	1846.7
---	*on summit–***Mt. Washington, NH 03589** .... post office	---
---	*Mt. Washington Auto Road descends 8m to NH16; right 1.7m on*	---
---	*Tuckerman Ravine Trail* 📖 *p.171 to Hermit Lake Shelters and*	---
---	*Tent Sites (caretaker, fee); 4.1m to Pinkham Notch Camp*	---
332.1	Cog Railroad tracks *(6150')*	1847.0
331.7	Westside Trail *(5500') to the left*	1847.4
331.4	Mt. Clay Loop *(5050') to the right, rejoins A.T. north*	1847.7
331.3	Jewell Trail *(5030') to the left*	1847.8
331.0	Greenough Spring *(5000') to the left, unreliable* .... w?	1848.1
330.4	Sphinx Trail *(5200') to the right*	1848.7
329.9	Cornice Trail *(5350') to the left*	1849.2
329.8	Monticello Lawn *(5400') Jefferson Loop to the left*	1849.3
329.4	Six Husbands Trail *(5260') left to Mt. Jefferson summit*	1849.7
329.0	Edmands Col *(5000') right 30yds to Gulfside Spring* .... C,w	1850.1
---	*Randolph Path left 0.2m to Spaulding Spring; 1.1m to The Perch*	---
---	*Shelter (RMC caretaker, fee); see Randolph Mountain Club* 📖 *p.156*	---
328.3	Israel Ridge Path *(5180') left 0.9m to Perch Shelter (see above)* .... C,w	1850.8
328.0	Spring *(5150') on A.T., seasonal* .... w	1851.1
327.8	Trail to Mt. Adams *(5450') right 0.4m to summit, vistas*	1851.3
327.7	Thunderstorm Junction *(5510') 10ft rock cairn* .... C,L,w	1851.4
---	*Lowe's Path left 1.2m to Gray Knob Cabin (RMC caretaker, fee),*	---
---	*right 0.3m to Mt. Adams; Spur Trail left 1.1m to Crag Camp Cabin*	---
---	*(RMC caretaker, fee); see Randolph Mountain Club* 📖 *p.171*	---
327.0	Air Line *(5000') right 0.8m to Mt. Adams summit*	1852.1
326.9	Snyder Brook *(4850') crosses A.T.* .... w	1852.2
326.8	AMC-Madison Spring Hut 📖*p.172 (4820') fee* .... C,L,M,w	1852.3
---	*Valley Way Trail left 0.6m to USFS tent platforms (spring, no fee)*	---
326.3	Mt. Madison *(5363') Watson Path left*	1852.8
326.1	Howker Ridge Trail *(5100') to the left*	1853.0
325.8	Osgood Junction *(4850') Parapet Trail right, Webster Trail left*	1853.3
---	**Notice!** *A.T. mostly above treeline for next 12.7 miles south*	---
---	*A.T. sparsely blazed from 4000' level to Auto Road* 📖 *p.172*	---

Elevation profile from 4000' to 7000' showing Lake of the Clouds Hut, Mount Washington, and Madison Hut.

New Hampshire

Miles from Katahdin	Features / Services		Miles from Springer
323.8	USFS Osgood Tent Site *(2550') tent platforms, spring (no fee)*	C,w	1855.3
---	*Osgood Trail right 2.6m to NH16 (near Camp Dodge)*		---
323.2	Parapet Brook *(2450') crosses A.T.*	w	1855.9
323.0	West Branch of Peabody River *(2300') suspension bridge*	w	1856.1
---	*Great Gulf Trail follows Peabody River upstream*		---
---	*Numerous streams cross A.T. in this area*		---
321.0	Viewpoint *(2820')* left 0.1m to Lowe's Bald Spot, vista		1858.1
---	**Notice!** *A.T. sparsely blazed south to 4000' level* 📖 *p.172*		---
320.8	Mt. Washington Auto Road *(2750') left to NH16*	R	1858.3
320.7	Nelson Crag Trail *(2700') to the right*		1858.4
320.6	Stream *(2600') crosses A.T.*	w	1858.5
320.5	Raymond Path *(2580') to the right*		1858.6
319.6	Stream *(2150') crosses A.T.*	w	1859.5
319.1	Pinkham Notch Camp 📖 *p.172 (2050') lodge (fee)*	L,M,G?,f	1860.0
---	*right 2.4m on Tuckerman Ravine Trail* 📖 *p.172 to Hermit Lake Shelters*		---
---	*and Tent Sites (caretaker, fee); 3.6m to Mt. Washington summit*		---
319.0	Pinkham Notch, NH16 📖 *p.172 (2035')*	R	1860.1
---	*right 15m–to* **Intervale, NH 03845**	O	---
---	*right 17m–to* **North Conway, NH 03860**	L,M,G,Lm,O	---
---	*left 4m–to Camp Dodge (AMC trail crew headquarters)*		---
---	**Notice!** *no camping permitted ¼ mile either side of NH16*		---
318.1	Wildcat Ridge Trail *(2080') right 0.1m to NH16*		1861.0
316.3	Wildcat Peak E *(4041')*		1862.8
---	*A.T. passes near Wildcat Mountain Chair Lift* 📖 *p.172*	M	---
316.0	Wildcat Peak D *(4063') observation platform*		1863.1
315.7	Wildcat Col *(3780')*		1863.4
315.0	Wildcat Peak C *(4270')*		1864.1
314.5	Wildcat Peak B *(4270')*		1864.6
314.0	Wildcat Peak A *(4380')*		1865.1
313.2	Carter Notch *(3390') Nineteen-Mile Brook Trail left*		1865.9
313.1	Nineteen-Mile Brook Trail *(3290') to the right*		1866.0
---	*right 0.2m–to AMC-Carter Notch Hut* 📖 *p.172 (fee)*	L,w	---
312.7	Viewpoint *(4000')*		1866.4
312.4	Spring *(4200') on A.T.*	w	1866.7
311.9	Carter Dome *(4832') Rainbow Trail right*		1867.2
311.5	Black Angel Trail *(4560') to the right*		1867.6
311.1	Mt. Hight *(4675') vistas*		1868.0
310.5	Zeta Pass *(3990') spring on A.T., Carter Dome Trail left*	w	1868.6

New Hampshire

Miles from Katahdin	Features / Services	Miles from Springer
309.7	South Carter Mtn (4458')	1869.4
308.4	Middle Carter Mtn (4600')	1870.7
307.8	North Carter Trail (4505') to the left	1871.3
307.6	North Carter Mtn (4530')	1871.5
305.9	**Imp Campsite** (3250') sleeps 16 (1980s), fee, tent platforms .... S,C,w	1873.2
---	left 500ft, stream near shelter, ←S42.0m | N6.1m→	---
305.2	Stony Brook Trail (3150') to the left, Moriah Brook Trail right	1873.9
303.8	Carter-Moriah Trail (3950') left 0.2m to Mt. Moriah summit	1875.3
---	Carter-Moriah Trail descends left 4.7m to US2 near Gorham	---
302.9	Middle Moriah Mtn (3620')	1876.2
302.4	Kenduskeag Trail (3380') to the right	1876.7
301.3	Rattle River (1700') footbridge	1877.8
300.2	East Branch of Rattle River (1500') footbridge .... w	1878.9
299.8	**Rattle River Shelter** (1260') sleeps 8 (1980s) .... S,w	1879.3
---	on A.T., stream near shelter, ←S6.1m | N13.7m→	---
297.9	US2 📖 p.173 (760') Rattle River .... R	1881.2
---	left 3.6m–to **GORHAM, NH 03581** .... H,L,M,G,O,Lm,f	---
297.8	North Road (760') US2 intersection .... R	1881.3
297.7	Railroad tracks (755')	1881.4
297.6	Androscoggin River (750') A.T. crosses on Leadmine Bridge .... R	1881.5
297.4	Hogan Road (780') .... R	1881.7
296.4	Stream (1480') logging road adjacent .... R,w	1882.7
294.3	Mt. Hayes (2555') vista	1884.8
294.0	Mahoosuc Trail (2500') left 0.2m to Mt. Hayes summit	1885.1
---	Mahoosuc Trail descends left 3.3m to US2 near Gorham	---
293.0	Spring (1960') on A.T. .... w	1886.1
292.1	Cascade Mtn (2631')	1887.0
291.0	Trident Col Tent Site (2000') left 500ft (tent pads, spring) .... C,w	1888.1
290.0	Page Pond (2220') A.T. crosses beaver dam .... w	1889.1
289.4	Wocket Ledge (2300') vista	1889.7
288.7	Left Branch of Peabody Brook (2750') crosses A.T. .... w	1890.4
288.3	Dream Lake (2650') A.T. crosses at inlet. .... w	1890.8
---	Peabody Brook Trail right 300ft to Dryad Falls	---
286.8	Moss Pond (2590') .... w	1892.3
286.1	**Gentian Pond Shelter** (2166') sleeps 14 (1974) tent platforms .... S,w	1893.0
---	right 0.2m, water on blue-blazed trail, ←S13.7m | N5.2m→	---
---	Austin Brook Trail right 3.3m to North Road	---

New Hampshire-Maine

284.7	Stream *(2500') crosses A.T.* .... w		1894.4
283.3	Mt. Success *(3565')*		1895.8
282.7	Success Trail *(3215') to the left*		1896.4
281.4	New Hampshire-Maine border *(2972')*		1897.7
---	**Important!** *Stay on log-plank walkways to protect alpine areas*		---
280.9	**Carlo Col Shelter** *(2945') sleeps 8 (1980s), tent platforms* .... S,C,w		1898.2
---	*left 0.3m, spring near shelter,* ←*S5.2m* | *N4.4m*→		---
280.5	Mt. Carlo *(3565') vista*		1898.6
280.1	West Peak of Goose Eye Mtn *(3854') left 0.1m to summit vista*		1899.0
---	*Goose Eye Trail left 3.2m to Success Pond Road*		---
278.8	Wright Trail, South Fork *(3700') to the right*		1900.3
278.7	East Peak of Goose Eye Mtn *(3790')*		1900.4
278.6	Wright Trail, North Fork *(3550') to the right*		1900.5
277.5	North Peak of Goose Eye Mtn *(3675')*		1901.6
276.5	**Full Goose Shelter** *(3030') sleeps 8 (1978), tent platforms* .... S,C,w		1902.6
---	*right 250ft, stream near shelter,* ←*S4.4m* | *N5.1m*→		---
276.0	South Peak of Fulling Mtn *(3395') vista*		1903.1
275.0	Mahoosuc Notch 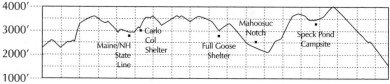 *p.174 (2480') southern end*		1904.1
---	*Mahoosuc Notch Trail left 2.5m to Success Pond Road*		---
273.9	Mahoosuc Notch *(2150') northern end, Bull Branch* .... C,w		1905.2
273.4	Stream *(2600') crosses A.T.* .... w		1905.7
272.3	Mahoosuc Arm *(3770') vistas*		1906.8
---	*Joe May Cut-off Trail left 0.3m to Speck Pond Trail*		---
271.7	Speck Pond Brook *(3400') outlet from pond* .... w		1907.4
271.4	**Speck Pond Shelter** *(3440') sleeps 8 (1978), fee, tent platforms* .... S,C,w		1907.7
---	*right 250ft, stream near shelter,* ←*S5.1m* | *N6.9m*→		---
---	*Speck Pond Trail left 3.6m to Success Pond Road*		---
270.8	Spring *(3600') right 100ft, seasonal* .... w		1908.3
270.3	Loop to Old Speck Mtn *(3985') rejoins A.T. north as Link Trail*		1908.8
---	*right 0.3m to Old Speck summit, observation deck, vistas*		---
268.5	Eyebrow Trail *(2550') loop rejoins A.T. south*		1910.6
---	*Eyebrow Trail left 0.1m to 825' cliff called "The Eyebrows"*		---
268.4	Stream *(2500') to the right* .... w		1910.7
267.9	Stream *(1580') crosses A.T.* .... w		1911.2
267.5	Eyebrow Trail *(1525') to the left, loop rejoins A.T. north*		1911.6
---	*Appalachian Mountain Club* *p.168 management section begins*		---
---	*for southbounders; read notes about fee locations in NH notes;*		---
---	*see regulations for using the White Mountains* *p.168*		---

Maine

Miles from Katahdin	Features / Services	Miles from Springer

Miles from Katahdin	Features / Services	Miles from Springer
266.8	Grafton Notch, ME26 🕮 *p.174 (1495') parking area* .... R	1912.3
---	*right 17m*–to **Bethel, ME 04217** .... H,L,M,G,O,Lm,f	---
266.7	Table Rock Trail *(1550') loop rejoins A.T. north*	1912.4
264.5	**Baldpate Lean-to** *(2660') sleeps 8 (1995)* .... S,w	1914.6
---	*right 200yds, stream on blue-blazed trail, ←S6.9m│N3.5m→*	---
263.7	West Peak of Baldpate Mtn *(3662') vista*	1915.4
262.8	East Peak of Baldpate Mtn *(3810') vistas*	1916.3
262.3	Little Baldpate Mtn *(3450') vista*	1916.8
261.0	**Frye Notch Lean-to** *(2280') sleeps 6 (1983)* .... S,w	1918.1
---	*on A.T., stream in front of shelter, ←S3.5m│N10.5m→*	---
260.5	Surplus Mtn *(2870') A.T. skirts summit*	1918.6
257.3	West Branch of Ellis River *(1350') crosses A.T.* .... w	1921.8
---	*Cascade Trail right 200ft to Dunn Notch Falls, rejoins A.T. north*	---
---	*just south of East B Hill Road (see below); left 0.2m to upper falls*	---
256.6	Stream *(1480') Cascade Trail to the right, rejoins A.T. south* .... w	1922.5
256.5	East B Hill Road 🕮 *p.174 (1485') aka Upton Road* .... R	1922.6
---	*right 8m*–to **ANDOVER, ME 04216** .... H,L,M,G,Lm,f	---
254.7	Surplus Pond *(2050') Burroughs Brook* .... w	1924.4
254.6	Spring *(2050') left 200ft on old road, piped* .... C,w	1924.5
---	**Notice!** *no campfires permitted in Surplus Pond area*	---
251.8	North Peak of Wyman Mtn *(2920') vista*	1927.3
250.9	Stream *(2620') crosses A.T.* .... w	1928.2
250.5	**Hall Mtn Lean-to** *(2650') sleeps 6 (1978), tent platforms* .... S,w	1928.6
---	*on A.T., spring south on A.T., ←S10.5m│N12.8m→*	---
249.2	Stream *(1120') crosses A.T.* .... w	1929.9
249.1	Sawyer Notch *(1095') Sawyer Brook (ford), old logging road* .... R,w	1930.0
248.2	Moody Mtn *(2440') right 100ft to overlook*	1930.9
247.1	Stream *(1990') crosses A.T.* .... w	1932.0
246.4	South Arm Road 🕮 *p.175 (1410') Black Brook (ford)* .... R,C,w	1932.7
---	*on A.T.–campsites along stream (spring 0.3m to right on road)*	---
---	*left 8m*–to campground .... C,G?,Lm	---
---	*right 9m to Andover (see East B Hill Road above)*	---
245.8	Viewpoint *(2300') on A.T.*	1933.3
243.6	Old Blue *(3600') vistas*	1935.5
240.4	Bemis Stream Trail *(3320') to the right*	1938.7
239.4	West Peak of Bemis Mtn *(3580') vista*	1939.7
239.3	East Peak of Bemis Mtn *(3532')*	1939.8
238.1	Third Peak, Bemis Range *(3115')*	1941.0

Maine

Miles from Katahdin	Features / Services		Miles from Springer
237.7	**Bemis Mtn Lean-to** *(2800') sleeps 8 (1988)*	S,w?	1941.4
---	*right 100ft, seasonal spring at shelter, ←S12.8m|N8.3m→*		---
236.2	Second Peak, Bemis Range *(2915') vistas*		1942.9
235.3	First Peak, Bemis Range *(2604') cairn*		1943.8
234.2	Spring *(1515') on A.T. to the right*	w	1944.9
234.0	Woods road *(1500') gravel surfaced*	R	1945.1
233.9	Bemis Stream *(1495') ford*	w	1945.2
---	*A.T. fords two channels of stream, watch blazes carefully*		---
233.1	ME17 *(2200')*	R	1946.0
232.3	Spruce Mtn *(2530')*		1946.8
231.5	Moxie Pond *(2420') A.T. skirts to the left*	w	1947.6
230.4	Viewpoint at Bates Ledge *(2700') on A.T.*		1948.7
229.7	Long Pond *(2330') sand beach, swimming area*	w	1949.4
229.4	**Sabbath Day Pond Lean-to** *(2390') sleeps 8 (1993), tent platforms*	S,w	1949.7
---	*on A.T., water from pond, ←S8.3m|N11.2m→*		---
228.9	Old woods road *(2400')*	R	1950.2
227.7	Power lines *(2820')*		1951.4
224.8	Little Swift River Pond Campsite *(2460') spring 100ft right*	C,w	1954.3
223.6	Chandler Mill Stream *(2100') crosses A.T.*	w	1955.5
222.1	South Pond *(2174') to the right*	w	1957.0
220.0	ME4 📖 *p.175 (1600')*	R	1959.1
---	*left 9m–*to **RANGELEY, ME 04970**	H,L,M,G,O,Lm,f	---
219.9	Sandy River *(1600') footbridge*	w	1959.2
219.3	Woods road *(1850') gravel surfaced*	R	1959.8
218.8	Old woods road *(1900')*	R	1960.3
218.5	Stream *(2070') crosses A.T.*	w	1960.6
218.2	**Piazza Rock Lean-to** *(2065') sleeps 8 (1993), tent platforms*	S,C,w	1960.9
---	*right 200ft, stream near shelter, ←S11.2m|N8.9m→*		---
---	*Piazza Rock Trail right 200yds to Piazza Rock formation*		---
217.3	Ethel Pond *(2200') to the right*	w	1961.8
216.9	Saddleback Stream *(2300') crosses A.T.*	w	1962.2
216.8	Mud Pond *(2325') to the left*	w	1962.3
216.3	Eddy Pond *(2680') inlet stream crosses A.T.*	w	1962.8
---	**Notice!** *no overnight camping or fires permitted at pond*		---
216.1	Logging road *(2700') gravel surfaced*	R,w	1963.0
---	*right on road to spring (on left side of road in low area)*		---
214.3	Saddleback Mtn *(4120') vistas, view of Katahdin*		1964.8
212.7	The Horn *(4040') vistas*		1966.4

Maine

Miles from Katahdin	Features / Services		Miles from Springer
210.7	Saddleback Junior *(3655')* vistas		1968.4
210.3	Stream *(3190')* crosses A.T. .... w		1968.8
209.3	**Poplar Ridge Lean-to** *(2960')* sleeps 6 *(1991)* no tent sites .... S,w		1969.8
---	*on A.T., stream in front of shelter, ←S8.9m	N8.0m→*		---
208.8	Poplar Ridge *(3120')* vista		1970.3
206.6	Orbeton Stream *(1550')* ford .... w		1972.5
206.5	Old woods road *(1600')* .... R		1972.6
205.8	Sluice Brook *(2100')* crosses A.T. .... w		1973.3
205.0	Logging road *(2300')* .... R		1974.1
204.6	Perham Stream *(2290')* logging road adjacent .... R,w		1974.5
203.5	Lone Mtn *(3260')* vista		1975.6
202.4	Mt. Abraham Trail *(3370')* right 1.7m to summit		1976.7
---	*side trail offers spectacular vistas mostly above treeline*		---
201.3	**Spaulding Mtn Lean-to** *(3140')* sleeps 8 *(1989)* .... S,w		1977.8
---	*left 150ft, stream near shelter, ←S8.0m	N18.6m→*		---
200.5	Trail to Spaulding Mtn *(4000')* right 175ft to summit, no views		1978.6
199.8	Bronze plaque *(3600')* on rock to the left		1979.3
198.4	Sugarloaf Mtn Trail 🕮 *p.176 (3650')* .... C?,w		1980.7
---	*Sugarloaf Mtn Trail right 0.2m to spring; 0,5m to a summit house*		---
197.8	Stream *(3600')* crosses A.T. .... w		1981.3
197.0	Viewpoint *(3450')* to the right		1982.1
196.2	South Branch of Carabassett River *(2100')* ford .... w		1982.9
196.1	Caribou Valley Road *(2220')* .... R		1983.0
195.1	Crocker Cirque Campsite *(2710')* right 0.2m, platforms, stream .... C,w		1984.0
194.6	Stream *(3600')* intermittent .... w?		1984.5
194.0	South Crocker Mtn *(4040')*		1985.1
193.0	North Crocker Mtn *(4228')*		1986.1
192.0	Stream *(3450')* crosses A.T. .... w		1987.1
189.9	Stream *(2500')* crosses A.T. .... w		1989.2
187.8	ME27 🕮 *p.176 (1400')* power lines .... R		1991.3
---	*left 5m–to* **STRATTON, ME 04982** .... H,L,M,G,Lm,f		---
187.0	Stratton Brook Pond Road *(1395')* .... R		1992.1
186.9	Old logging road *(1390')* gravel surfaced .... R		1992.2
186.8	Stratton Brook *(1390')* footbridge .... w		1992.3
186.7	Old woods road *(1420')* .... R		1992.4
185.9	Cranberry Stream Campsite *(1350')* right 200ft, stream .... C,w		1993.2
---	**Notice!** *no open fires permitted, backpacking stoves only*		---
184.6	Bigelow Range Trail *(2440')* left 4.6m to Stratton		1994.5

Elevation profile: 4000', 3000', 2000', 1000' — Sugarloaf Side Trail, Crocker Mt., Poplar Ridge Lean-to, Spaulding Mt. Lean-to, Caribou Valley Road, Me. 27 Stratton

Maine

Miles from Katahdin	Features / Services	Miles from Springer
183.5	Viewpoint *(2500')* to the right	1995.6
183.0	Viewpoint *(3000')* to the right	1996.1
182.9	Horns Pond Trail *(3200')* to the right	1996.2
182.7	**Horns Pond Lean-tos** *(3160') sleep 16 (1997), tent platforms* ....S,C,w	1996.4
---	*on A.T., spring near shelter, ←S18.6m	N10.2m→*	---
---	**Notice!** *no open campfires permitted, backpacking stoves only*	---
182.4	Spring *(3400')* on A.T. .... w	1996.7
182.3	Trail to North Horn *(3792')* left 0.2m to summit	1996.8
182.2	South Horn *(3805')* vista	1996.9
180.1	West Peak of Bigelow Mtn *(4145')* vistas	1999.0
179.8	Avery Memorial Campsite *(3815') platforms, caretaker (no fee)* .... C,w	1999.3
---	*spring 0.2m north on A.T.; Fire Warden's Trail right to spring,*	---
---	*also 1m to Moose Falls Campsite, stream (very steep descent);*	---
---	**Notice!** *no open fires permitted, backpacking stoves only*	---
179.6	Spring *(3900')* on A.T., boxed .... w	1999.5
179.4	Avery Peak *(4090')* vista	1999.7
178.6	Old Man's Head *(3300')* right 0.1m, vista	2000.5
177.5	Safford Brook Trail *(2250')* to the left	2001.6
177.4	Safford Notch Campsite *(2230')* right 0.3m, platforms, stream .... C,w	2001.7
174.2	Little Bigelow Mtn *(3010')* vistas	2004.9
172.5	**Little Bigelow Lean-to** *(1760') sleeps 8 (1986) "The Tubs"* .... S,w	2006.6
---	*left 0.1m, spring on path to shelter, ←S10.2m	N7.3m→*	---
171.1	East Flagstaff Road *(1200')* .... R	2008.0
171.0	Bog Brook Road *(1200')* .... R	2008.1
170.9	Bog Brook *(1190')* footbridges .... w	2008.2
170.5	Flagstaff Lake *(1190')* A.T. skirts shoreline .... w	2008.6
168.7	Long Falls Dam Road *(1225')* .... R	2010.4
168.6	Jerome Brook *(1220')* footbridge .... w	2010.5
168.3	Logging road *(1300')* gravel surfaced .... R	2010.8
167.0	Roundtop Mtn *(1760')*	2012.1
166.2	Stream *(1360')* crosses A.T. .... w	2012.9
165.9	West Carry Pond *(1320')* to the left .... w	2013.2
165.2	**West Carry Pond Lean-to** *(1340') sleeps 8 (1989) swimming* .... S,w	2013.9
---	*right 100ft, springhouse near shelter, ←S7.3m	N10.0m→*	---
164.5	Arnold Point *(1340')* to the left, sand beach, swimming area .... w	2014.6
163.0	Arnold Swamp *(1250')* log-plank walkways .... w	2016.1
162.8	Woods road *(1250')* .... R	2016.3
162.7	Woods road junction *(1250')* .... R	2016.4

Maine

Miles from Katahdin	Features / Services		Miles from Springer
162.6	Sandy Stream *(1250')* *A.T. crosses on woods road*	R,w	2016.5
161.8	Logging road *(1250') gravel surfaced*	R	2017.3
161.1	East Carry Pond *(1130') to the right*	w	2018.0
159.4	Logging road *(1300') gravel surfaced*	R	2019.7
158.7	North Branch of Carrying Place Stream *(1150') crosses A.T.*	w	2020.4
158.2	Spring *(1200') on A.T. to the right*	w	2020.9
155.2	**Pierce Pond Lean-to** *(1160') sleeps 6 (1970) swimming*	S,w	2023.9
---	*on A.T., water on blue-blazed trail at dam, ←S10.0m|N9.7m→*		---
155.1	Pierce Pond *(1140') outlet, A.T. crosses on dam*	w	2024.0
---	*right 0.1m on blue-blazed trail to stream, 0.3m to Harrison Camps*		---
154.8	Trail to Harrison Camps 📖*p.176 (1100') 0.1m right*	L,M,w	2024.3
154.5	Woods road *(1000')*	R	2024.6
154.0	Trail to Pierce Pond Stream *(920') right 0.1m to waterfall*	w	2025.1
153.8	Trail to Pierce Pond Stream *(900') right 0.1m to pool*	w	2025.3
153.4	Otter Pond Stream *(850') ford*	w	2025.7
151.6	Kennebec River, south bank 📖*p.176 (490') ferry service*	w	2027.5
---	**Notice!** *no camping or fires permitted along banks of river*		---
151.5	Kennebec River, north bank *(490') ferry service, see above*	w	2027.6
151.2	US201 📖*p.177 (520') parking area*	R,H,C,L,M,G?,f	2027.9
---	*opposite where A.T. (going north) reaches US201, follow paved Main*		---
---	*Street*–to **CARATUNK, ME 04925**	post office only	---
148.5	Holly Brook *(920') crosses A.T.*	w	2030.6
147.8	Stream *(1040') crosses A.T.*	w	2031.3
147.1	Logging road *(1200')*	R	2032.0
146.6	Holly Brook *(1350') crosses A.T.*	w	2032.5
146.1	Logging road *(1390') gravel surfaced*	R	2033.0
145.9	Old logging road *(1370') parking area*	R	2033.2
145.5	**Pleasant Pond Lean-to** *(1320') sleeps 6 (renovated 1991) swimming*	S,w	2033.6
---	*right 0.1m, stream near shelter, ←S9.7m|N9.0m→*		---
145.3	Trail to Pleasant Pond *(1340') right 0.2m to beach, swimming area*	w	2033.8
144.2	Pleasant Pond Mtn *(2470') vistas*		2034.9
139.8	Stream *(1050') crosses A.T.*	w	2039.3
139.5	Power lines *(1000')*		2039.6
139.4	Woods road *(1000')*	R	2039.7
139.3	Baker Stream *(970') Moxie Pond (Joe's Hole), ford*	w	2039.8
138.9	Power lines *(1000')*		2040.2
138.2	Joe's Hole Brook *(1200') crosses A.T.*	w	2040.9
136.8	Bald Mtn Brook Campsite *(1260') Bald Mtn Brook*	C,w	2042.3

Maine

Miles from Katahdin	Features / Services	Miles from Springer
136.5	**Bald Mtn Brook Lean-to** *(1300') sleeps 8 (1994)* .... S,w	2042.6
---	*right 500ft, water from stream, ←S9.0m	N4.1m→*	---
136.1	Moxie Bald bypass *(2200')* to the left, rejoins A.T. north	2043.0
134.5	Moxie Bald Mtn *(2629')* vistas (view of Katahdin)	2044.6
134.2	Moxie Bald bypass *(2400')* to the left, rejoins A.T. south .... w	2044.9
---	*spring to the left on bypass trail at base of rocks*	---
133.5	Trail to North Peak, Moxie Bald Mtn *(2350')* left 0.7m to summit	2045.6
132.4	**Moxie Bald Lean-to** *(1220') sleeps 6 (1958) swimming* .... S,w	2046.7
---	*right 150ft, water from pond in front, ←S4.1m	N8.9m→*	---
130.9	Woods road *(1250')* .... R	2048.2
130.3	Bald Mtn Stream *(1250')* crosses A.T. .... w	2048.8
127.0	Marble Brook *(950')* old road adjacent .... R,w	2052.1
126.6	West Branch of Piscataquis River *(940')* ford .... w	2052.5
---	*A.T. borders West Branch of Piscataquis River for several miles north*	---
123.5	**Horseshoe Canyon Lean-to** *(870') sleeps 8 (1991)* .... S,w	2055.6
---	*left 0.1m, water from stream, ←S8.9m	N12.0m→*	---
123.3	Trail to Horseshoe Canyon Lean-to *(780')* left 0.1m (see above)	2055.8
121.2	East Branch of Piscataquis River *(650')* ford .... w	2057.9
120.8	Shirley-Blanchard Road *(900')* paved .... R	2058.3
119.3	Logging road *(900')* .... R	2059.8
117.8	Trail to Lake Hebron *(900')* to the right	2061.3
---	*right 0.3m on blue-blazed trail (old roadbed) to parking area on*	---
---	*Pleasant Road, then left 1.7m to Monson (see ME15 below)*	---
116.7	Buck Hill *(1390')*	2062.4
115.9	Trail to Doughty Pond *(950')* left 0.1m to pond .... w	2063.2
114.5	ME15 📖 *p.177 (1215')* parking area .... R	2064.6
---	*right 3.5m–to* **MONSON, ME 04464** .... H,C,L,M,G,Lm,f	---
---	*Northbounders, you are entering the 100-Mile Wilderness* 📖 *p.178,*	---
---	*read information about resupplying in the notes section*	---
114.4	Spectacle Pond *(1230')* Goodell Brook, ford .... w	2064.7
113.6	Old Stage Road *(1250')* .... R	2065.5
113.3	Bell Pond *(1250')* to the left .... w	2065.8
113.2	Power line *(1300')*	2065.9
112.6	Trail to Lily Pond *(1150')* right 0.1m to pond	2066.5
111.5	**Leeman Brook Lean-to** *(1060') sleeps 6 (1987)* .... S,w	2067.6
---	*left 100ft, water from stream, ←S12.0m	N7.4m→*	---
110.7	Stream *(1140')* North Pond outlet .... w	2068.4
110.3	North Pond Road *(1100')* .... R	2068.8

Maine

109.3	Mud Pond *(1090')* *to the right*	w	2069.8
108.2	James Brook *(920')* *crosses A.T.*	w	2070.9
108.0	Woods road *(1000')* *gravel surfaced*	R	2071.1
107.9	Little Wilson Falls *(840')* *left 100ft to 60' falls*	w	2071.2
107.7	Little Wilson Stream *(750')* *ford*	w	2071.4
107.4	Beaver Dam *(850')* *200yds in length, A.T. crosses dam*	w	2071.7
107.3	Woods road *(870')* *gravel surfaced*	R	2071.8
105.4	Big Wilson Road *(570')*	R	2073.7
105.3	Thompson Brook *(550')* *crosses A.T.*	w	2073.8
104.8	Big Wilson Stream *(600')* *ford*	w	2074.3
---	***Alternate!*** *if water level dangerous, hike downstream 1.5m, cross*		---
---	*stream on highway bridge, follow bank upstream to rejoin A.T.*		---
104.5	Canadian Pacific Railroad tracks *(900')* ***Caution!*** *fast trains*		2074.6
104.1	**Wilson Valley Lean-to** *(1045')* *sleeps 6 (1993)*	S,w	2075.0
---	*right 175ft, spring near shelter, ←S7.4m	N4.7m→*		---
103.5	Old logging road *(1165')*	R	2075.6
102.9	Viewpoint *(1260')* *vista*		2076.2
102.6	Rocky slope *(1200')* *A.T. crosses 175-yard-long scree field*		2076.5
100.9	Wilbur Brook *(650')* *crosses A.T.*	w	2078.2
100.8	Vaughn Stream *(650')* *waterfall to right*	w	2078.3
100.3	Bodfish Farm-Long Pond Road *(630')*	R	2078.8
100.2	Long Pond Stream *(620')* *ford*	w	2078.9
99.5	Trail to Slugundy Gorge *(900')* *left 0.1m to falls*	w	2079.6
99.4	**Long Pond Stream Lean-to** *(940')* *sleeps 8 (1991)*	S,w	2079.7
---	*left 200ft, water from stream, ←S4.7m	N4.0m→*		---
98.3	Barren Slide *(1990')* *right 225ft to overlook*		2080.8
98.1	Barren Ledges *(1980')* *to the right, vista*		2081.0
96.3	Barren Mtn *(2660')* *fire tower, vistas*		2082.8
95.4	**Cloud Pond Lean-to** *(2420')* *sleeps 6 (1992)*	S,w	2083.7
---	*right 0.3m, water from pond, ←S4.0m	N6.9m→*		---
93.9	Stream *(2400')* *crosses A.T.*	w	2085.2
93.3	Fourth Mtn *(2380')*		2085.8
92.5	Stream *(1745')* *crosses A.T., intermittent*	w?	2086.6
92.0	Viewpoint *(1900')* *ledges*		2087.1
90.8	Third Mtn *(1920')* *Monument Cliff, vista*		2088.3
90.2	Stream *(1770')* *crosses A.T., old road adjacent*	w	2088.9
---	*right 0.2m on side trail to West Chairback Pond*		---
88.9	Columbus Mtn *(2325')* *ledge, vista*		2090.2

Maine

88.5	**Chairback Gap Lean-to** *(1930') sleeps 6 (1954)* .... S,w	2090.6
---	*on A.T., spring below shelter in front, ←S6.9m	N9.9m→*	---
88.0	Chairback Mtn *(2180') vistas*	2091.1
87.6	Viewpoint *(1970') ledges*	2091.5
85.8	Trail to East Chairback Pond *(1630') left 0.2m to pond* .... w	2093.3
85.3	Spring/stream *(1250') on A.T. to the right* .... w	2093.8
84.6	Woods road *(750')* .... R	2094.5
84.1	West Branch of Pleasant River *(630') ford* .... w	2095.0
83.9	Trail to Hay Brook *(670') to the right* .... w	2095.2
83.8	The Hermitage *(695') right 200ft*	2095.3
---	**Notice!** *no camping or fires permitted in Hermitage area*	---
82.8	Gulf Hagas Trail 📖*p.178 (915') to the left, rejoins A.T. north* .... w	2096.3
---	**Notice!** *no camping or fires permitted in Gulf Hagas*	---
82.1	Gulf Hagas Cut-off Trail *(1100') see Gulf Hagas Trail above*	2097.0
78.6	**Carl A. Newhall Lean-to** *(1860') sleeps 6 (1986)* .... S,w	2100.5
---	*left 200ft, stream south of shelter, ←S9.9m	N7.2m→*	---
77.7	Gulf Hagas Mtn *(2680')*	2101.4
76.8	Sidney Tappan Campsite *(2425') spring 150yds right* .... C,w	2102.3
76.1	West Peak *(3178') vista*	2103.0
74.5	Hay Mtn *(3245')*	2104.6
73.9	White Brook Trail *(3100') right 0.5m to spring* .... w	2105.2
72.8	White Cap Mtn *(3650') vistas (view of Katahdin)*	2106.3
71.8	Viewpoint *(3200') to the left*	2107.3
71.4	**Logan Brook Lean-to** *(2480') sleeps 6 (1983)* .... S,w	2107.7
---	*on A.T., stream at shelter, ←S7.2m	N3.6m→*	---
69.8	Woods road *(1625')* .... R	2109.3
69.3	B Inlet Brook *(1375')* .... w	2109.8
67.8	**East Branch Lean-to** *(1225') sleeps 8 (1996)* .... S,w	2111.3
---	*left 0.1m, water from stream, ←S3.6m	N8.1m→*	---
67.5	East Branch of Pleasant River *(1210') ford* .... w	2111.6
65.9	Mountain View Pond *(1640')* .... w	2113.2
65.6	Spring *(1630') to the right* .... w	2113.5
64.3	Little Boardman Mtn *(1980') left 100yds to summit*	2114.8
62.9	Kokadjo-B Pond Road *(1390') gravel surfaced* .... R	2116.2
62.0	Crawford Pond *(1270') sand beach* .... w	2117.1
---	**Notice!** *no camping or fires permitted at Crawford Pond*	---
61.3	Stream *(1270') outlet of Crawford Pond* .... w	2117.8

Maine

Miles from Katahdin	Features / Services		Miles from Springer
59.7	**Cooper Brook Falls Lean-to** *(880') sleeps 6 (1956) swimming*	S,w	2119.4
---	*right 100ft, stream 0.2m north on A.T.,* ←S8.1m｜N11.4m→		---
59.5	Stream *(910') crosses A.T.*	w	2119.6
56.0	Jo-Mary Road *(655') Cooper Brook*	R,w	2123.1
54.7	Trail to Cooper Pond *(600') right 0.2m to pond*	w	2124.4
54.5	Spring *(590') to the right, seasonal*	w?	2124.6
53.4	Logging road *(590') Cooper Brook*	R,w	2125.7
53.1	Mud Pond *(585') outlets streams cross A.T.*	w	2126.0
52.4	Old logging road *(500')*	R	2126.7
51.8	Antlers Campsite *(500') right 300ft, vistas*	C,w	2127.3
50.6	Stream *(520') inlet for Lower Jo-Mary Lake*	w	2128.5
50.3	Trail to Potaywadjo Ridge *(525') left 1m to vista*		2128.8
50.1	Lower Jo-Mary Lake *(520') right 100ft to sand beach*	w	2129.0
48.3	**Potaywadjo Spring Lean-to** *(710') sleeps 8 (1995)*	S,w	2130.8
---	*right 200ft, spring on path to shelter,* ←S11.4m｜N10.1m→		---
47.8	Twitchell Brook *(530') logging road*	w	2131.3
47.7	Trail to Pemadumcook Lake *(530') right 100ft (view of Katahdin)*	w	2131.4
46.9	Deer Brook *(525') crosses A.T.*	w	2132.2
46.0	Logging road *(520') gravel surfaced*	R	2133.1
45.9	Mahar Tote Road 📖*p.178 (520') grassy surfaced*	R	2133.2
---	*right 0.9m (follow blue blazes)–to private camp*	L,M,G,f	---
45.8	Branch of Nahmakanta Stream *(520') crosses A.T.*	w	2133.3
44.4	Tumbledown Dick Stream *(525') crosses A.T.*	w	2134.7
44.0	Nahmakanta Stream Campsite *(575') to the left*	C,w	2135.1
42.2	Trail to Nahmakanta Stream *(580') to the right*	w	2136.9
41.4	Spring *(700') on A.T. to the right*	w	2137.7
41.1	Woods road *(700') gravel surfaced*	R	2138.0
40.8	Nahmakanta Lake, south end *(650') right 100ft to beach*	C,R,w	2138.3
39.9	Prentiss Brook *(670') crosses A.T.*	w	2139.2
38.6	Nahmakanta Lake, north end *(650') right 50ft to sand beach*	w	2140.5
38.3	Wadleigh Stream *(680') crosses A.T.*	w	2140.8
38.2	**Wadleigh Stream Lean-to** *(685') sleeps 6 (1981)*	S,w	2140.9
---	*left 25ft, stream in front of shelter,* ←S10.1m｜N8.1m→		---
36.3	Nesuntabunt Mtn *(1520') right 200ft to vista (view of Katahdin)*		2142.8
35.8	Viewpoint *(1260') excellent view of Katahdin*		2143.3
35.1	Woods road *(1040') gravel surfaced*	R	2144.0
34.2	Crescent Pond *(1035') south end, trail is near pond for 0.4m*	w	2144.9
33.5	Pollywog Gorge *(682') left 30yds to overlook*		2145.6

Maine

Miles from Katahdin	Features / Services		Miles from Springer
32.5	Pollywog Stream *(682')* *logging road, bridge*	w	2146.6
30.5	Stream *(1020')* *crosses A.T.*	w	2148.6
30.1	**Rainbow Stream Lean-to** *(1020')* *sleeps 6 (1971)*	S,w	2149.0
---	*on A.T., stream in front of shelter,* ←S8.1m	N11.5m→	---
28.1	Rainbow Lake, south end *(1100')* *left to dam (view of Katahdin)*	w	2151.0
26.3	Rainbow Spring Campsite *(1120')* *right 150ft to campsites*	C,w	2152.8
---	*Rainbow Spring across A.T. near shore of Rainbow Lake*		---
24.8	Trail to camp *(1115')* *to the left (private, do not trespass)*		2154.3
24.6	Trail to Rainbow Mtn *(1120')* *right 1.1m to summit, vista*		2154.5
22.9	Rainbow Lake, north end *(1100')*	w	2156.2
22.8	Trail to Little/Big Beaver Ponds *(1130')* *to the right*	w	2156.3
21.1	Rainbow Ledges *(1517')* *view of Katahdin*		2158.0
18.6	**Hurd Brook Lean-to** *(710')* *sleeps 6 (1959)*	S,w	2160.5
---	*on A.T., stream in front of shelter,* ←S11.5m	N13.4m→	---
17.9	Spring *(750')* *on A.T.*	w	2161.2
15.3	Golden Road *(600')* *aka Greenville-Millinocket Road*	R	2163.8
---	*Southbounders, you are entering the 100-Mile Wilderness* 📖 *p.163,*		---
---	*read information about resupplying in the notes section*		---
15.1	Abol Bridge 📖*p.179 (588')* *West Branch of Penobscot River*	R	2164.0
---	**Caution!** *wide-load trucks on bridge, use pedestrian walkway only*		---
---	*on A.T.–campground/camp store*	C,G,snacks	---
---	*across road from store–Abol Pines Camping Area (fee)*	C,w	---
14.8	Trail leaves gravel road *(600')*		2164.3
14.4	Abol Stream *(605')* *footbridge*	w	2164.7
---	*Baxter State Park* 📖 *p.179 boundary, read regulations for thru-hikers*		---
---	**Notice!** *camping at designated sites only, no pets permitted in park*		---
14.3	Information Board 📖*p.179 (605')* *with reservation sheet*		2164.8
---	*Northbounders, sign up for a thru-hiker-only space at "The Birches"*		---
---	*Abol Pond Trail right 4.4m to "The Birches" Campsite*		---
14.0	Katahdin Stream *(600')* *crosses A.T.*	w	2165.1
13.5	Stream *(600')* *crosses A.T.*	w	2165.6
13.2	Foss and Knowlton Brook *(600')* *crosses A.T.*	w	2165.9
12.7	Oxbow Lake *(585')*	w	2166.4
11.0	Pine Point *(600')* *Nesowadnehunk Falls left*	w	2168.1
10.7	Nesowadnehunk Stream *(650')* *ford, high water trail south of crossing*	w	2168.4
9.7	Nesowadnehunk Stream *(770')* *ford, high water trail*	w	2169.4
8.8	Trail to Big Niagara Falls *(850')* *150ft left*	w	2170.3
8.5	Trail to Little Niagara Falls *(920')* *200ft left*	w	2170.6

Maine

Miles from Katahdin	Features / Services		Miles from Springer
7.7	Daicey Pond Nature Trail *(1100')*		2171.4
7.6	Daicey Pond Campground 📖*p.180 (1100')* .... w		2171.5
---	*right 0.1m to ranger station, weather bulletin board*		---
7.1	Grassy Pond Trail *(1105') south end*		2172.0
6.4	Grassy Pond Trail *(1105') north end* .... w		2172.7
6.1	Tracy Pond *(1100') A.T. crosses outlet* .... w		2173.0
5.3	Perimeter Road *(1090') A.T. follows road* .... R		2173.8
5.2	Katahdin Stream Campground 📖*p.180 (1070')* .... w		2173.9
---	**Notice!** *check in at the ranger station to confirm overnight stay at "The*		---
---	*Birches" campsite; mandatory sign in/sign out for summiting Katahdin;*		---
---	*go right across footbridge to ranger station, weather information*		---
---	**"The Birches" Campsite** 📖*p.180 (1070') thru-hikers only* .... S,C		---
---	*right 0.3m (on Tote Road), water from stream, S13.4m|none→*		---
4.2	The Owl Trail *(1570') left 2.2m to The Owl summit*		2174.9
4.1	Katahdin Stream *(1510') A.T. crosses on footbridge* .... w		2175.0
---	**Notice!** *last dependable water source on A.T. for summiting*		---
4.0	Katahdin Stream Falls *(1530') to the left* .... w?		2175.1
3.1	Stream *(2450') intermittent* .... w?		2176.0
2.4	Hunt Spur *(3400') treeline*		2176.7
1.6	The Gateway *(4600') Tableland begins*		2177.5
1.0	Thoreau Spring *(4627') intermittent* .... w?		2178.1
0.0	Baxter Peak, Katahdin 📖*p.180 (5268') sign, cairn, plaque* .... terminus		2179.1

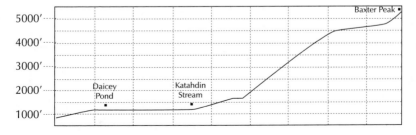

Thru-hiker Notes

Notes in this section provide additional information about features listed in Section 1, which contains the mileage tables. The symbol 📖 *p.142* in the mileage tables indicates that additional information about a feature is available in these "Thru-hiker Notes," on the page indicated by the number that follows the little open-book symbol (in this example, on page 142). Notes in this section are arranged in geographical order from Georgia to Maine, just like the mileage tables, and are cross referenced back to the mileage tables. The symbol 📖 *p.11* in this section indicates that the feature can be found in the "Mileage Tables" on the page indicated by the number that follows the little open-book symbol (in this example, on page 11).

Most of the information in this section is descriptive information about services in towns—the expanded details about services represented by the coded abbreviations shown to the right in the mileage tables. The format for describing services will vary from town to town since each town is somewhat different. In general, though, basic town services are listed in this order: hiker hostels or equivalents, campgrounds or camping places, commercial lodging facilities, places to eat, grocery stores, outfitters, laundry facilities, stove fuel sources, and then all other services.

Businesses and services that have been serving hikers the longest are usually listed first in each category. The businesses and services listed in this guide lean towards those considered "hiker friendly" by past A.T. hikers. A few services are not listed because the providers do not want to be overwhelmed with hikers, preferring their services to be advertised by word of mouth. Don't worry, you'll hear about them.

A few people who provide shuttles have been listed, mostly at their request. There are people who provide shuttles in almost every town, often on an informal basis. You can usually find shuttlers by contacting local service providers. The Appalachian Trail Conservancy also has a list of shuttle providers on their web site.

Prices for overnight lodging generally ***do not include tax***, which can be 10% or more in some locations. Prices are as up-to-date as possible, but are subject to change. Generally, the cheaper lodgings in each town will always be listed, although what qualifies as "cheap" depends a lot on the area. Expensive facilities are only listed if the establishment in question welcomes hikers. You can feel comfortable about splurging in such a place, although it's a good idea to make an effort to fit in.

Places that do not allow smoking and/or alcohol consumption on premises are so noted, as are places that do not accept credit cards. In most cases, it has been noted whether an establishment accepts pets. It may be worth double-checking if you have a dog, as policies regarding pets sometimes change.

Post-office information for the most frequently used towns is provided in this section with the town's description (also see the quick-reference "Post Office Information" section in the back of this book which lists information for the post offices most frequently used by thru-hikers from Georgia to Maine).

Getting to the southern terminus—If you have your own transportation, see directions to the trailhead on the Georgia AT Club's site, <*www.georgia-atclub.org/directions/html*>. It may be a good idea to ask about road conditions locally if you wish to start at USFS 42. If you need to arrange transportation, Josh and Leigh Saint at the Hiker Hostel (7693 Highway 19N, P. O. Box 802, Dahlonega, GA 30533; 770-312-7342) <*www.hikerhostel. com*> offer a "thru-hiker's special" including pickup in Gainesville or at the MARTA station near Atlanta, a bunk, breakfast, fuel, and drop-off at either Amicalola Falls or USFS 42 for $72, will hold maildrop packages. Alternatively, consult <*www.georgia-atclub. org*> for possible shuttles. *Nearby outfitters*—North Georgia Mountain Outfitters (1215 Industrial Blvd., East Ellijay, GA 30539; 706-698-HIKE <*www.hikenorthgeorgia.com*>); The Outside World (471 Quill Dr., Dawsonville, GA 30534; 866-375-2628); Mountain Crossings at Neels Gap (706-745-6095; see listing under Neels Gap, below).

Amicalola Falls State Park 🕮 *p. 4* ... (418 Amicalola Lodge Rd., Dawsonville, GA 30534; 706-265-4703; <*www.gastateparks.org*>); derives its name from a Cherokee word meaning "tumbling waters." Its beautiful falls plunge 729 feet in seven cascades. *Visitor Center*—open 7 days, 8:30am-5pm; vending machines, rest rooms, an outside public telephone, some hiking supplies. Sign the register at the visitor center, where you can check for thru-hikers who have signed in ahead of you. The park will hold packages sent by mail or UPS to the address shown above (packages are held at the visitor center). Specify on the package that it is being sent to a thru-hiker. Camping is prohibited except at the park campsites, which are $25 per night with shower for tenters. Coin-operated laundry for campground guests. All vehicles entering the park must pay a $3 parking fee unless only dropping someone off. Dogs are permitted on leash only. Cottages are booked far in advance, but rooms are usually available in the lodge early in the year when thru-hikers start their hikes. *Amicalola Lodge*—rates start at $100 weekdays, $110 weekends (lower before March 1); 1-800-573-9656 or 706-265-8888 for reservations; with the Maple Restaurant in the lodge (open for B/L/D 7 days); ATM. *Max Epperson Shelter*—available to thru-hikers free of charge, located 500 feet beyond the visitor center on the Appalachian Approach Trail. Water is available from the visitor center rest rooms, which are left open at night, or from a water fountain near the rest rooms. A shower is located in the nearby day use area. *Len Foote Hike Inn*—located about five miles from the park by way of the lime green-blazed Hike Inn Trail which begins near the lodge, and about 4.3 miles by trail from the summit of Springer Mtn. For reservations, call 800-581-8032 or inquire at the park visitor center. Rates $97S/140D, includes dinner and breakfast; work for stay may be possible. *Southbounders*—Congratulations for finishing your hike (see note on page 165). Don't forget to sign the register in the visitor center and ask for a list of people offering shuttles to Atlanta or Gainesville where you can make travel connections for heading home.

The Approach Trail—an 8.8 mile blue-blazed trail leading to the summit of Springer Mountain, called the Appalachian Approach Trail inside the park, recently relocated to pass directly by the falls. The Approach Trail starts at the stone arch behind the visitor center, passes the "Golden Anniversary Maple," and immediately turns sharp left following the Bottom of the Falls Trail. It then passes the Max Epperson shelter (on the right), the falls, and the lodge entrance road before leaving the park and heading toward the southern terminus. You can cut off the steep first mile of the Approach Trail by taking the paved Top of Falls Road to the falls. At the falls parking area, take the road to the lodge, which intersects the approach trail at a yellow crosswalk before you reach the lodge. Be sure to fill your water bottles at the visitor center or lodge before leaving the park, since the Approach Trail has few dependable water sources. Once underway, do not get caught up in the initial enthusiasm of your trip and wear yourself out before you reach Frosty Mountain, as have all too many eager thru-hikers in past years. Take it easy at first and enjoy the walk to Springer, which can be quite delightful on a sunny spring day.

Springer Mtn 📖 *p. 5* ... southernmost of the Blue Ridge Mountains and terminus of the Appalachian Trail since 1958. The Appalachian Trail begins at the bronze Georgia AT Club plaque mounted on a summit rock, with sunset vista to the west. White blazes begin at the plaque and extend for more than two thousand miles to Katahdin. Nearby is the more recent USFS plaque on a boulder housing the official Georgia AT Club sign-in register, which will find its way to the club's archives at summer's end. In the early days, thru-hikers picked up a pebble from Springer to be carried the distance and placed on the cairn atop Katahdin. Overnight camping is prohibited on the summit.

Stover Creek 📖 *p. 5* ... a rare stand of virgin hemlocks borders the creek. The trees were too remote to be harvested, unlike most forests along the A.T., which have been cut at least two or three times. To envision what the Great American Forest was like when European settlers arrived, double the height and triple the girth of every tree you see, then imagine a dense forest of such trees stretching unbroken from Alabama to Nova Scotia. If you feel a tinge of sadness at the loss of such grandeur, consider that future generations will feel the same about what remains today if we let it slip away.

Woody Gap, GA60 📖 *p. 5* ... *On A.T.*–roadside picnic area; spring on north side of the road beyond parking area, 500 feet off A.T. on side trail to the left. ➔ *right 6m*–to Hiker Hostel (see "getting to the southern terminus," above) first driveway past junction of GA60 and US19; hostel offers bunks $16, private rooms $38 (2 people), includes linens, towel, internet access, breakfast; laundry $3; Coleman, canister fuel, and denatured alcohol by the ounce; will hold maildrop packages; shuttles to area trailheads by arrangement. Between 2/22 and 4/25, the Hiker Hostel offers pickup at Woody Gap at 5PM every day. ↺ *left 1.9m*–to **SUCHES, GA 30572**: *Post office hours:* Mon-Fri 7:30am-11:30am and 1pm-4:30pm; Sat 7:30am-11:30am, 706-747-2611. Small store (closed Sunday). ▪ Two Wheels Only Motorcycle Resort (706) 747-5151. Camping and shower $7, open Apr/Nov, breakfast, L/D weekends ▪ medical clinic: open 8:30-4 M-Th, walk-ins before noon if possible.

Neels Gap, US19 📖 *p. 6* ... *On A.T.*–Mountain Crossings at Neels Gap, located in the historic Walasi-Yi Center (9710 Gainesville Hwy., Blairsville, GA 30512; 706-745-6095; <www.mountaincrossings.com>): the only building the A.T. goes through, so you can't miss it; hostel, backpacking store and small grocery section, open 7 days year-round; owned by Winton Porter. Hostel available on first-come first served basis, holds up to 16 people, bunk with shower and towel $15 per night; call ahead for cabin reservations; no dogs in hostel but kennels available. The backpacking store is well-stocked with hiking gear, clothing, trail guides, stove fuels, first-aid supplies, repair items, *etc.* If you need some equipment advice, set up an appointment with the staff when you arrive. The grocery section is intentionally stocked for thru-hikers, with standard backpacking staples, freeze-dried foods, some health foods, fruit, ice cream, sodas, and hot coffee. You should be able to resupply here. Mountain Crossings will hold packages for hikers, a $1 handling fee is charged at time of pickup; shower $3.50, coin-operated laundromat; UPS and postal service pickup and delivery weekdays; outside public telephone. Check with staff about shuttle services to towns and other locations in northern Georgia. *Also on US19*: ➲ *right* *0.2m*–Blood Mountain Cabins (9894 Gainesville Highway, Blairsville, GA 30512; 706-745-9454 or 800-284-6866) *<www.bloodmountain.com>* cabins $60 hiker rate (must arrive on foot), for entire cabin which accomodates up to 4 people, showers, kitchens, satellite TV, no pets. Call ahead. ☾ *left 2m*–to Vogel State Park (706-745-2628): cabins $85 with one bed, $95 with two, walk-in campsites $12 per night including shower, camp store with limited hiker supplies, coin-operated laundromat, public telephone, and $3 per person showers for thru-hikers. ☾ *left 3.5m*–to Goose Creek Cabins (7061 US19/129, Blairsville, GA 30514; 706-745-5111; *<www.goosecreekcabins.com>*): cabins with kitchen and fireplace for $25 per person ($35 up for private cabin), tent sites with shower $10, shower and towel without stay $2; laundry services for $5 per load; game room and public telephone; free shuttle to and from A.T. at Neels Gap for all guests, shuttle to nearby restaurant $3 per person, other points for fee; will hold packages (please send UPS); owned by Keith and Retter Bailey. ☾ *left 14m*–to **Blairsville, GA 30512**: motels, restaurants, two supermarkets (both good for long-term resupply), laundromats, bank, ATM, regional medical clinic. ➲ *right 17m*–to **Dahlonega, GA 30533**: a large town with all services.

Testnatee Gap, GA348 📖 *p. 6* ... historians believe John Muir, the famous naturalist and conservationist, crossed the mountains here on his famous thousand-mile walk from the Ohio River to the Gulf of Mexico in 1867-68.

Unicoi Gap, GA75 📖 *p. 7* ... ☾ *left 11m*–to **HIAWASSEE, GA 30546**, a hiker friendly town with all services. *Post office hours:* Mon-Fri 8:30am-5pm, Sat 8:30am-noon; 706-896-3632. *Lodging*—Hiawassee Inn (193 S Main St., Hiawassee, GA 30546; 706-896-4121, 706-896-1725): $39.95 single, $5 per additional person, laundry $3.00 per load, pets $10 extra, will hold mail packages, free shuttle to and from Unicoi and Dicks Creek trail heads, long distance shuttling can be arranged for a fee, showers $3.00, free continental breakfast, 1 bicycle available for use • Holiday Inn Express (300 Big Sky Dr., Hiawassee, GA 30546; 706-896-8884): seasonal hiker discount may be available, no pets, pool, spa, will hold maildrop packages, coin-operated laundry for guests only (free detergent); free bicycles available for use around town • Mull's Motel (213 N. Main St., Hiawassee, GA 30546; 706-896-4195): $50 up, no pets, will hold maildrop packages for guests only, manager "Miss Cordie" (who is a repository of local lore) can arrange shuttles back to A.T. and to northern Georgia locations. *Places to eat*—Georgia Mountain Restaurant: hearty country-style meals, hearty breakfast, daily specials • Daniel's Steakhouse: inexpensive meals, AYCE buffet, open 7 days • McDonalds • Subway • China Grill • Monte Alban (Mexican) • Mango's (Cuban) • Smoke Rings BBQ • Zaxby's *Other Services*—Dill's Food City: good for long-term resupply; open 7 days

• Ingles Supermarket: good for long-term resupply, open 7 days • laundromats: two in town, one open 7 days year-round • banks w/ATM • hospital, clinic • library. ➔ *right 10m*–to **Helen, GA 30545**: *Post office hours:* Mon-Fri 9-5, Sat 9-12, 706-878-2422. Alpine themed tourist village; rates for lodging increase substantially after Memorial Day weekend; lodging is expensive and very hard to find during fall "leaf season." *Services*—Helendorf River Inn (1-800-445-2271): Sun-Thur Dec-Mar $25, Apr-May 27 and Nov $35. May 28-Sep $45 (weekends, holidays, and during October Fest substantially higher; pets $10 extra; laundry on premises • Hofbrau Riverfront Hotel (1-800-830-3977): Nov 15-Memorial Day $69 up per room; pets $10 extra • Super 8 Motel (706-878-2191) and Best Western Motel (706-878-2111): $39 for special hiker's room at Super 8 ($45 at Best Western), otherwise rooms are $75 up at both; rates higher on weekends; no pets; internet terminal in lobby; deluxe breakfast; free shuttle when available • Econolodge (1-800-443-6488): weekdays Nov-May $60 per two-person room, add $10 for weekends; no pets allowed • numerous restaurants within walking distance, most open year-round • Betty's Country Store: good for long-term resupply, fresh produce in season, bulk food items, baked goods; open 7 days, year-round • laundromat, next door to Super 8: open 7 days, year-round.

Dicks Creek Gap, US76 📖 *p. 8* ... *On A.T.*–picnic tables, parking area, trash can, small stream. ◖ *left 11m*–to **HIAWASSEE, GA** (see above). ◖ *left 3.5m*–to The Blueberry Patch (5038 Hwy. 76 East, Hiawassee, GA 30546, 706-896-4893): a Christian ministry operated by former thru-hiker Gary Poteat and wife Lennie; open Feb 15-Apr 30; check-in time is after 10am and before 6pm. Hostel offers bunk or tent site (up to ten people can be accommodated), shower, laundry service, country-style breakfast (rated number one on trail in Backpacker Magazine, June 2006), and shuttle back to Dicks Creek Gap only at 9:30am; hostel depends on donations for its continued operation. Coleman fuel and denatured alcohol by the ounce. No alcoholic beverages, tobacco products, or drugs are permitted on the premises; no pets can be accommodated; will hold maildrop packages.

Rock Gap, USFS Road 67 📖 *p. 9* ... where A.T. reaches but does not cross paved road. ➔ *right 0.5m*–(on blue-blazed trail) to the Wasalik Poplar (now dead), once the second largest yellow poplar tree in the world. ◖ *left 1.4m*–to USFS Standing Indian Campground: campsites $16, showers, public telephone, closed until May 1 due to construction, volunteer caretakers on duty.

A Distinct and Separate Trail

The Appalachian Trail became an official trail with passage of the National Trails System Act in 1968. Its termini were established as Springer Mountain in Georgia and Katahdin in Maine, and its official route is recorded in the *Federal Register*. This makes the A.T. a distinct and separate trail, having legal status that cannot be changed by any individual or group but only by an act of Congress. Furthermore, the A.T. is not part of an "eastern continental trail," which doesn't even exist officially, though it is possible to walk continuously from Florida to Canada using state highways and five distinct and separate hiking trails.

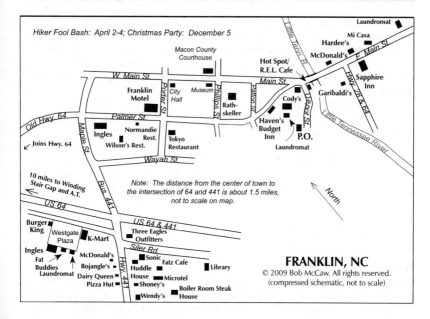

Hiker Fool Bash: April 2-4; Christmas Party: December 5

Laundromat

Mi Casa

Hardee's

Macon County Courthouse

McDonald's

E. Main St.

Hot Spot/ R.E.L. Cafe

Sapphire Inn

W. Main St.

Main St.

Garibaldi's

Hwy. 441 Bus. Rd

Franklin Motel

City Hall

Museum

Porter St.

Phillips St.

Cody's

Little Tennessee River

Patton St.

Rath-skeller

Palmer St.

Haven's Budget Inn

Maple St.

Ingles

Normandie Rest.

Tokyo Restaurant

P.O.

Old Hwy. 64

Joins Hwy. 64

Wilson's Rest.

Laundromat

Wayah St.

10 miles to Winding Stair Gap and A.T.

Note: The distance from the center of town to the intersection of 64 and 441 is about 1.5 miles, not to scale on map.

North

US 64

Bus. 441

US 64 & 441

Burger King

Westgate Plaza

K-Mart

Three Eagles Outfitters

FRANKLIN, NC

Ingles

McDonald's

Siler Rd.

Fat Buddies

Bojangle's

Sonic

Hwy. 441

Fatz Cafe

Library

© 2009 Bob McCaw. All rights reserved.

(compressed schematic, not to scale)

Laundromat

Dairy Queen

Huddle House

Microtel

Pizza Hut

Shoney's

Boiler Room Steak House

Wendy's

Winding Stair Gap, US64 📖 *p. 9* ... where explorer Hernando De Soto is believed to have passed through on his way to the Mississippi River in 1540. *On A.T.–piped spring to the right in parking area.* ➲ *right 10m–*to **FRANKLIN, NC 28734**: *Post office hours:* Mon-Fri 8:30am-5pm, Sat 9am-noon, 828-524-3219; area was originally called "Nikwasi" by the Cherokees, who believed this location is where their ancestors originated at the beginning of time.   Franklin has business districts downtown and near the US64/441 intersection. *In downtown area*—Haven's Budget Inn (433 E. Palmer St., Franklin, NC 28734; 828-524-4403; <www.havensbudgetinn.com>) and Sapphire Inn (761 E. Main St., Franklin, NC 28734; 828-524-4406): $39.95   single, each additional person $5, laundry facility on site with free soap, internet access, $10 for small dog, $15 for large dog ▪ Franklin Motel (17 W. Palmer St., Franklin, NC 28734; 1-800-433-5507): hiker rate, $42 single, $5 per additional person), small dogs $10 extra, large dogs $15; will hold maildrop packages, Coleman and denatured alcohol by the ounce. Budget Inn, Sapphire Inn, and Franklin Motel are owned by Ron Haven, great friend to hikers, offers shuttle back to A.T. and 4 PM shuttle around town; will hold maildrop packages for guests only. ▪ Ingles Supermarket: good for long-term resupply; open 7 days ▪ bank w/ ATM ▪ hospital ▪ *Places to eat*—near the river, R.E.L. Cafe, Cody's Original Roadhouse, Rathskeller Coffee House, Mi Casa and Garibaldi's Mexican have been recommended. At other end of downtown, Wilson's Restaurant   has been recommended for good value, Normandie Cafe serves breakfast and lunch.   *Shuttles*—Ron Haven (828-524-4403) is usually at Winding Stair Gap at 9am and 11am (and often at other times, call ahead) each day in March and April to offer hikers a free shuttle into Franklin. He leaves downtown Franklin for the gap about 8:30am and 10:30am each morning for free ride back to the gap. *Near US64/441 intersection*—in Westgate Plaza *(0.5 miles west)*: Ingles Supermarket: good for long-term resupply, open 7 days ▪ Fat Buddy's Ribs

& BBQ ▪ Burger King ▪ K-Mart ▪ laundromat (open 24 hours, 7 days) ▪ pharmacy. On US 441: Three Eagles Outfitters (78 Siler Rd., Franklin, NC 28734; 828-524-9061): full-service backpacking store, Coleman and denatured alcohol by the ounce; will hold maildrop packages; open 7 days. ▪ Microtel Inn (81 Allman Dr., Franklin, NC 28734; 1-888-403-1700): $42S $54D (after Apr 30, rates increase to $53S $63D), pets $20 extra, will hold maildrop packages ▪ A number of restaurants and fast food outlets lie within 0.5 miles of US 64 on US 441 south (see map). ▪ Library, 819 Siler Rd., is 0.8 miles from outfitter. *Special event*—April 1st Hiker Fool Bash: Apr 2-4, music and food; call 828-524-4406 or 4403; Christmas Party Dec 5.

US19 📖 *p. 10* ... *On A.T.*–Nantahala Outdoor Center (13077 Hwy. 19W, Bryson City, NC 28713; 828-488-2175; <www.noc.com>): on the Nantahala River where A.T. crosses on a footbridge, a white water rafting center friendly to hikers. Center offers bunk rooms in "base camp," motel rooms, outfitter store, restaurants, public telephone, laundry (cold water wash only); shower in base camp $2, coin-op in rest rooms. Store will hold maildrop packages (clearly label with real name, the phrase "Hold for A.T. Hiker," and a hold-until date). Note: there is no nearby post office. *Services*—bunk with hot shower, no linens, $17 per person; motel rooms with private bath, $54 and up (prices increase after May 1, again June 1); pets are $5 extra in base camp, not allowed in motel ▪ River's End Restaurant: pizza, burgers, home-style meals ▪ Slow Joe's Cafe: open Apr-Oct ▪ Relia's Garden and Paddlers Pub, fine dining, opens about mid-May ▪ Outfitter Store: backpacking clothing and gear; Coleman and denatured alcohol by the ounce; food section with freeze dried, typical hiker foods, snacks; hiking pole repair, laundry detergent; maildrop packages are held in basement, ask at the check-out counter ▪ Rafting: trips for about $30, also, raft rentals to individuals ▪ Shuttles: check the information board or office for anyone available to do area shuttles, or ask at store. *Also on US19*: ➔ *right 1m*–to Nantahala Food Mart and Wesser Cottages (1-800-468-7238; <www.carolinaoutfitters.com>): food mart has basic hiker supplies. Lodging: private cabins with linens, bath, basic kitchen for $50D, $10 per additional person, pets OK in one unit; check in at Nantahala Food Mart; call for free shuttle to and from NOC. ➔ *right 12m*–to **Bryson City, NC 28713**: Sleep Inn (828-488-0326): $65 up weekdays, no pets ▪ Jimmy Macs: breakfast, daily luncheon specials ▪ Everett St. Diner: vegetarian meals ▪ Burger King ▪ Pizza Hut ▪ Bryson City IGA: good for long-term resupply ▪ Ingles Supermarket: good for long-term resupply ▪ laundromat: open 24 hours, 7 days ▪ banks w/ATMs.

Stecoah Gap, NC143 📖 *p. 11* ... *On A.T.*–picnic table, water from piped spring. Directions to spring: From picnic table, go left (west) 450 feet on highway to a gated private road. Take a faint grassy road just **above** the private road for about 500 feet to the piped spring on the left. ➔ *right 0.8m, then 0.4m up driveway*–to Appalachian Inn (300 Knoll Top, Robbinsville, NC 28771; 828-479-8450, <www.appalachianinn.com>): B&B in a log home in a beautiful setting, $125 and up includes breakfast. Town shuttles and laundry available; maildrop packages held for guests. 15% discount with this book. ◖ *left 10m*–to **Robbinsville, NC 28771**: mountain town featured in he 1994 movie "Nell," has motel, restaurants, including Mexican, Chinese, BBQ, McDonald's, Subway, etc., Ingles Market (good for long-term resupply), bank with ATM and laundromat.

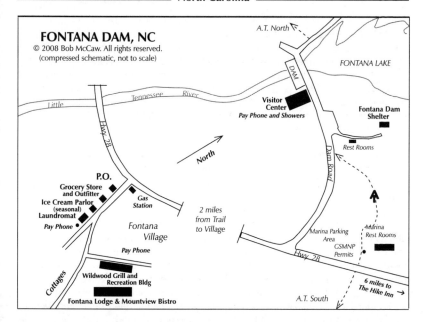

FONTANA DAM, NC
© 2008 Bob McCaw. All rights reserved.
(compressed schematic, not to scale)

A.T. North

FONTANA LAKE

DAM

Tennessee River

Little

Visitor
Center
Pay Phone and Showers

Fontana Dam
Shelter

Hwy 28

North

Rest Rooms

Dam Road

P.O.
Grocery Store
and Outfitter
Ice Cream Parlor
(seasonal)
Laundromat
Pay Phone

*Gas
Station*

*2 miles
from Trail
to Village*

*Fontana
Village*

Pay Phone

Marina Parking
Area

*Marina
Rest Rooms*

GSMNP
Permits

Hwy 28

Cottages

Wildwood Grill and
Recreation Bldg

Fontana Lodge & Mountview Bistro

A.T. South

*6 miles to
The Hike Inn →*

NC28 📖 *p. 11 ... On A.T.*–information board with GSMNP self-registration permit slips (located on north side of highway near rest room building in the marina parking lot); telephone at information board is a house phone that connects to Fontana Village Resorts only (dial "0" for shuttle information); regular public phone is located at the dam's visitor center. ➲ *right 6m*–to The Hike Inn (3204 Fontana Rd., Fontana Dam, NC 28733; 828-479-3677; *<www.thehikeinn.com>*): a hikers only lodging facility (five rooms, can accommodate up to ten hikers) Thru-hiker/Long distance hiker package is $60S $75D, reservations required and check-in by 4p.m., includes private room with bath, pick up and drop off at dam, one load of laundry and trip to Robbinsville (5-7p.m.) for dinner and re-supply. Call for pick up at dam visitor center. Section/Day hiker rate $40 for room only. Limit of one or two hikers per room with 9a.m. check-out for all hikers. Mail held for guests only ($30 service charge for non-guests that includes delivery to dam area only, other locations extra). Also available are Coleman and alcohol fuels, shuttles covering Amicalola to Erwin,TN, including all airports, bus stations and car rentals. All shuttles by arrangement. Open Feb15-Jul 9 and Sep1-Nov30, other dates by reservation only. No credit cards, No pets. Owned by friendly Jeff and Nancy Hoch, enjoying their seventeenth year of service to the A.T. hiking community; enjoy a personal tour of their prehistoric artifact museum during your stay. ☾ *left 2m*–to **FONTANA DAM, NC 28733**: *Post office hours:* Mon-Fri 8:30-3; 828-498-2315; a private resort community with visitor services, similar to NOC, not an actual town. *Services*—Fontana Village Resort (1-800-849-2258; *<www.fontanavillage.com>*): primarily geared toward summer activities, some facilities may not be open if harsh winter weather extends into early spring. The village offers cottages with full kitchen and bath; motel rooms at the Fontana Lodge are available for $60S/D. Rates available from Feb 1 to Apr 19, subject to availability outside of these dates. Pets are allowed in cottages with $100 pet fee nonrefundable, but not in motel. Meals are available at the lodge's Mountview Bistro. The shopping area has a small grocery store, post office, outfitter, ice cream parlor (summer only) and laundromat (open 7 days, change and detergent available at grocery store or Lodge). A recreation building with game room and grill is available to all guests; grill is open Apr-Oct. *Outfitter/stove fuel*—Hazel Creek Outfitters features a full-service backpacking store with gear and clothing, Coleman and denatured alcohol by the ounce, first-aid supplies, hiker food, etc., with a 10% discount given to thru-hikers. *Shuttle*—A shuttle service between the dam and village is available for $3. Dial "0" on Fontana A.T. crossing "house phone" at the information board near the marina rest rooms, or call the main number from the public telephone atop the dam; shuttle operates from early spring through late fall.

Fontana Dam 📖 *p. 11* ... 480 feet high, cornerstone in the network of dams built by the Tennessee Valley Authority during the Great Depression in the last century and the highest dam east of the Mississippi. *On A.T.*–Fontana Dam Visitor Center: open daily mid-April-Oct 31 atop the dam, offering sodas, candy, souvenirs, and film; no hiker resupply foods offered. A public pay phone and GSMNP self-registration permit slips are located on the south end of the dam's rest room building. Showers for use by thru-hikers are provided at no charge, water usually hot or at least lukewarm for first few hikers.

Thru-hiker Permits—Thru-hikers must have a backcountry permit to use the A.T. in the Great Smoky Mtns. Natl. Park. You are considered a thru-hiker for park purposes if you begin your hike at least 50 miles outside the park, hike through the park on the A.T., and end your hike 50 miles beyond the opposite boundary. Northbounders can pick up a park permit at the self-registration board located on the spillway side of the Fontana Dam visitor center. Southbounders can pick up a permit at the USFS office in Hot Springs during weekdays only. The permit slip should be retained in your possession while in the park; up to $5000 fine if caught without a permit. A thru-hiker permit allows you seven consecutive nights and eight days to transit the park without designating a specific location for each night.

Great Smoky Mountains National Park (GSMNP) 📖 *p. 11* ... The A.T. enters the park at Fontana Dam, climbs to the ridge line, then follows it for seventy miles, exiting the park at Davenport Gap. Twelve shelters are located on the A.T. for overnight use by park visitors (see below). There are an estimated 1600 black bears inside the park, one of the highest bear population densities in the country, and there are more varieties of trees and shrubs within the park than can be found in all of Europe, a truly magnificent forest environment that is protected from logging and other commercial uses forever.

Regulations—The following regulations apply to you as a visitor traversing the park using a thru-hiker permit:
• You are required to stay overnight on the A.T. route. Any overnight side trip to a backcountry area off the Trail (e.g., LeConte Shelter) voids your permit; overnight departure to resupply in Gatlinburg or Cherokee does not void your permit.
• You are required to use only the shelter system for overnight camping. Four sleeping spaces in each shelter are reserved exclusively for thru-hikers on a first-come, first-served basis from Apr 1-Jun 1.

• You are not permitted to stay more than one night in the same shelter, even if space is available, unless sick or injured.

• You are required to tent within sight of a shelter if there is no sleeping space available inside. Park regulations and common sense require that you use bear-proof food-storage cables for any food and odorous materials where cables are provided, or hang your food bag inside at fenced shelters with no cables.

• You are required to use designated areas for sanitation at shelters, a privy if available or, if no privy is provided, a location at least 500 feet from the shelter area.

• You are required to carry out all of your garbage. Do not ever leave garbage, food items, or gear in shelters for someone else to carry out.

Pets in the Smokies—No pets are allowed in Great Smoky Mtns. Natl. Park (up to $5000 fine). You can have your pet picked up at one end of the park, boarded, and delivered to the other end by using a kennel service: Loving Care Kennels (3779 Tinker Hollow Rd., Pigeon Forge, TN 37863; 865-453-2028), owned by Lida O'Neill, licensed. One dog $250, two $400 (for however long it takes you to pass through park); will hold and deliver maildrop packages at no charge and help with shopping for supplies ▪ Rippling Water Kennel (828-488-2091; <www.ripplingwaterkennel.net>): located 10 miles from Wesser, owned by David and Peggy Roderick, licensed; call them for current rates; reservations strongly recommended ▪ Standing Bear Farm (see entry under Green Corner Road, below) 423-487-0014 offers dog kennels, $15 per night plus $120 pickup fee. ▪ The Hike Inn (in the North Carolina section under "NC28") do not board themselves but can help you make arrangements for boarding your dogs.

Information or Emergency—call the Backcountry Information Office at 865-436-1297 (9am-noon); or in case of an emergency, call 865-436-1230; also see the park's website for additional information about the park <www.nps.gov/grsm/>.

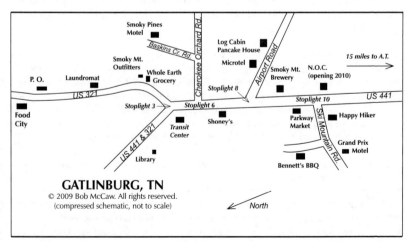

GATLINBURG, TN
© 2009 Bob McCaw. All rights reserved.
(compressed schematic, not to scale)

Newfound Gap, US441 📖 *p. 13 ... On A.T.*–rest rooms, parking area, and Rockefeller Memorial where FDR dedicated Great Smoky Mtns Natl. Park in 1934. ☾ *left 14m*–to

Park Headquarters; one mile farther to **GATLINBURG, TN 37738**: *Post office hours:*
Mon-Fri 9am-5pm, Sat 9am-11am; 865-436-3229. The contrast between the Park and
the tourist center of Gatlinburg is startling. The town's center is a strip with numbered
stoplights as reference points. Stoplight #10 is at the park entrance. One mile away
at stoplight #3, US 321 branches right, goes up a hill, and leads to the post office and
supermarket in about 2 more miles. The Gatlinburg Trolley serves the entire area, and
saves a lot of steps to the post office or supermarket. A few services recommended
by recent thru-hikers are highlighted below, but note that there are hundreds of tourist
services to meet just about any need and budget. *Lodging*—Grand Prix Motel (865-436-
4561): $42, internet, mail drops accepted, laundry on premises, go left at stoplight #10
on Ski Mountain Road to motel, shuttles to Clingman's Dome $40 (up to 4 people) ▪
Microtel Gatlinburg (865-436-0107): near stoplight #8, $45S/$50D and up hiker rate,
(prices may be higher if their is a special event in town); small pets $10 extra ▪ Smoky
Pines Motel (865-436-5327) recommended as inexpensive and friendly. *Places to eat*—
lots of fast food and chains line the main strip. A few places recommended by hikers:
Smoky Mountain Brewery: steaks, ribs, Italian specialties ▪ Log Cabin Pancake House:
breakfast ▪ Bennett's BBQ ▪ Shoney's: breakfast buffet. *Other services*—Food City:
good for long-term resupply, open 7 days; near post office ▪ Parkway Market: good for
short-term resupply ▪ Whole Earth Grocery (near stoplight #3): natural foods, closed
Sun ▪ The Wash Tub (on US 321 about a mile from stoplight #3): 24-hour laundromat ▪
ATMs ▪ library has relocated to a side street beyond stoplight #3. *Outfitter/stove fuel*—
The Happy Hiker (near stoplight #10 at 905 River Rd., Suite 5, Gatlinburg, TN 37738;
865-436-6000; <www.happyhiker.com>): full-service backpacking store, Coleman by
the ounce, denatured alcohol, other fuels, repair services, will hold maildrop packages;
open 7 days, get your picture added to the "Wall of Thru-hikers"; see "White Blaze
Day" below ▪ Smoky Mountain Outfitters (469 Brookside Village Way, Gatlinburg, TN
37738, near stoplight #3; 865-430-2267): full-service backpacking store, Coleman
by the ounce, denatured alcohol, other fuels, will hold maildrop packages; shuttles by
arrangement; 10% discount for thru-hikers; open 7 days; located in log cabin in Winery
Square. ▪ The Nantahala Outdoor Center is opening The Great Outpost, an outfitter,
April 3-4, 2010. *White Blaze Day*—a benefit Trail party with food, backpacking reps,
and music, all to raise money for the A.T.; takes place at The Happy Hiker outfitter
store, date to be announced. ➲ *right 21m*–to **Cherokee, NC 28719**: headquarters of
the eastern Cherokee Nation. Most hikers who go to town at Newfound Gap go to
Gatlinburg; however, a number of fairly inexpensive motels and restaurants are located
in Cherokee on the road to GSMNP, including Comfort Suites (828-497-3500) $59S/D
(rates increase after Apr 1), laundry on premises, no pets.

Davenport Gap, TN32/NC284 📖 *p. 14* ... ➲ *right 1.5m*–to Big Creek Ranger Station:
telephone (for 911 and park reservations only), water, campground, rest rooms; ranger
hours vary. Southbounders: it is probably possible to get a park permit here, but it will
save you a lot of steps to get one at Bluff Mt. Outfitters in Hot Springs!

Green Corner Road 📖 *p. 15* ... also called Waterville School Road on some older maps,
gravel surfaced ◒ *left 200yds*–to Standing Bear Farm (4255 Green Corner Rd., Hartford,
TN 37753; 423-487-0014; <http://standingbearfarm.tripod.com>): a restored 1920s
backwoods homestead with a hiker bunkhouse, cabin, or tent sites, each available on

first-come first served basis, $15 per tent, $15 for bunkhouse, $20 for cabin, includes hot shower, laundry facilities (washtub and dryer), and telephone; kitchen with refrigerator, microwave, coffee maker; camp store, good for short-term resupply; also ready-to-cook pizza and sandwiches; Coleman and denatured alcohol by the ounce; shuttles available; pets welcome. Will hold maildrop packages; packages unclaimed after 60 days will be opened and put in hiker box. Hostel open year-round. Internet available, $1 per 15 minutes. Dog kennel $15 per night, pickup at Fontana Dam $120.

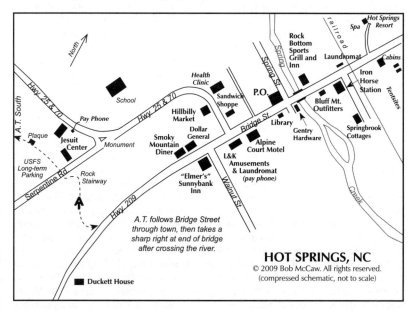

HOT SPRINGS, NC

HOT SPRINGS, NC 28743 📖 *p. 16* ... *Post office hours:* Mon-Fri 8:30am-11:30am and 1pm-4pm, Sat 8:30am-10:30am; 828-622-3242; a true Trail town, small, friendly, everything you need within walking distance. *Hostel*—"Elmer's" Sunnybank Inn (26 Walnut St., P. O. Box 233, Hot Springs, NC 28743; 828-622-7206): legendary among A.T. hikers, hosted by Elmer Hall since 1978 in white Victorian house with "Balladry" historical marker in front. Rates: bed with linens, bath and towel $20 for thru-hikers only; meals are gourmet vegetarian, organic, and no one ever goes away hungry, breakfast $6, family-style dinner $10; check in at door on back porch, work exchange possible; well-equipped music room, extensive progressive and environmental library; will hold maildrop packages. *Other lodging*—Duckett House Inn (P. O. Box 441, Hot Springs, NC 28743; 828-622-7621; <www.ducketthouseinn.com>): a large Victorian house with long driveway and red roof. Rates: $45 per person includes linens, bath or shower, and breakfast; bunkhouse with foam mattresses including shower $15; work exchange possible, dogs on leash only (call ahead to discuss), will hold maildrop packages for guests who have placed reservation with deposit. • Alpine Court Motel (828-622-3231): $45S $66D and up, no pets, no credit cards • Rock Bottom Sports Grill and Inn (145 Bridge St., Hot Springs, NC 28743; 828-622-0001) Rooms $50 for hikers with 10% discount on food ▪ Iron Horse Station (24 S. Andrews Ave., Hot Springs, NC 28743; 866-402-9377) hiker special $50 in March and April ▪ Springbrook Cottages (828-622-7385) special hiker rate $60S/D, $70 for three, $80 for four, pets OK with $25 fee. ▪ Hot Springs Resort Cabins Campground & Spa (828-622-7676; <*www.nchotsprings.com*>): private cabins on the river $45-$70 (up to four people, some units have half bath); tent sites $5 per thru-hiker (on foot) per night; shower without stay $5; pets on leash only; camp store has hot food, pizza, subs, sandwiches, limited grocery items. ▪ There are several other B&Bs in town. ***Places to eat***—Smoky Mountain Diner: breakfast, burgers, pizza, daily luncheon specials; owned by former long-distance hiker Genia Snelson (her Trail name is "Biscuits") ▪ Rock Bottom Sports Grill: entrees $10-19, sandwiches $4-11, open 11-10 seven days, bar menu 10-closing ▪ Iron Horse Station: entrees $8-22 with blue plate special under $10 ▪ Sandwich Shoppe, popular with locals. ***Groceries***—Bluff Mountain Outfitters: food section geared for thru-hikers (good for long-term resupply); natural and organic fresh fruit in season, energy bars, ice cream, *etc*) ▪ Hillbilly Market: good for short-term resupply, no credit cards, closed Sun ▪ Dollar General: some hiker supplies. ***Outfitter/stove fuel***—Bluff Mountain Outfitters (152 Bridge St., P. O. Box 114, Hot Springs, NC 28743; 828-622-7162; <*www.bluffmountain.com*>): full-service backpacking store with gear and clothing, Coleman and denatured alcohol by the ounce, public-access internet terminal, telephone cards, books, postcards, UPS and FedEx office, will hold maildrop packages, shuttles to anywhere between Springer and Damascus. ***Other services***—two laundromats: one at L&K Amusements (get detergent and change at the checkout counter) and the Wash Tub near railroad tracks ▪ bank ▪ ATM inside at Bluff Mountain Outfitters or outside at bank ▪ Hot Springs Clinic. ***The Hot Springs***—Hot Springs Spa: mineral waters at 102°F, hourly rates: (daytime) $12 one person $25 two to three people; (evening) $30 1-3 people, four people $40; open year-round, 10am-10pm (later on weekends). ***Southbounders***—pick up GSMNP permit at Bluff Mountain Outfitters.

Log Cabin Road 📖 *p. 16* ... ☾ *left 0.6m*–to Hemlock Hollow Farm (645 Chandler Circle, Greeneville, TN 37743; 423-787-0917; <*www.hemlockhollow.net*>): heated bunkhouse $20 w/ hot shower, kitchenette, cabins $48 (two people) with refrigerator, microwave, coffeepot and linens, shower w/ towel; tent sites under roof $12 w/ shower; shower without stay $3; pets $2, will hold maildrop packages, internet $3 per 15 minutes, meals possible by arrangement; outfitter with good selection of food aimed at hikers (long term resupply possible), fresh fruit, groceries, all fuels, shuttles and slackpacking by arrangement, free ride back to trailhead, free coffeefor guests, water refilled. Visa/ MC accepted.

Sams Gap, I-26 📖 *p. 17* ... ☽ *right 2.9m*–Little Creek Cafe: open daily. Side road leading east to cafe and west to Erwin is reportedly a very tough hitch.

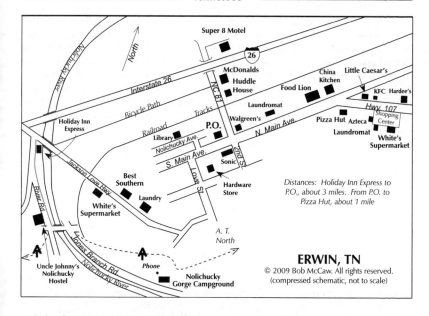

Distances: Holiday Inn Express to P.O., about 3 miles. From P.O. to Pizza Hut, about 1 mile

ERWIN, TN

Nolichucky River, Chestoa Bridge 📖 *p. 18* ... where Davy Crockett and Andrew Jackson are known to have attended frontier gatherings held along the river. ⊂ *at A.T.*–Uncle Johnny's Nolichucky Hostel (151 River Rd., Erwin, TN 37650; 423-735-0548; <*www. unclejohnnys.net*>): bunkhouse $15, cabins or private rooms $20-$45S, $40-65D, tenting $8; shower with towel, toiletries included in stay, shower without stay $4; laundry $4, internet, telephone and fax service, some hot foods. Nolichucky Outfitters, on premises, carries packs, tents, tarps, stoves, filters, socks, accessory and repair items, Coleman and denatured alcohol by the ounce, selection of hiker foods. Will hold maildrop packages, free shuttles to and from town for guests and to area trailheads for a fee, free bicycles for trips to town, work exchange possible; open year round. ⊂ *left 3.8m*–to **ERWIN, TN 37650**: *Post office hours:* Mon-Fri 8:30am-4:45pm, Sat 10am-noon; 423-743-9422; a friendly town but rather spread out; be prepared for some walking if you don't get a ride. *Lodging*—Holiday Inn Express (2002 Temple Hill Rd., Erwin, TN 37650; 423-743-4100): $70S/D hiker rate includes breakfast, no pets, laundry on premises, will hold maildrop packages, internet ▪ Best Southern Motel (1315 Jackson Love Hwy., Erwin, TN 37650; 423-743-6438): $46S/$56D, no pets; will hold maildrop packages ▪ Super 8 Motel (1101 N. Buffalo St., Erwin, TN 37650; 423-743-0200): $49S/$59D, internet, will hold maildrop packages, no pets. *Places to eat*—Sonic Drive-In ▪ China Kitchen ▪ McDonald's ▪ Hardee's ▪ KFC ▪ Pizza Hut ▪ Little Caesar's. In the past, there have been fast food outlets near the Holiday Inn Express, but they are closed as of press time. *Groceries*—White's Supermarket (two locations): both good for long-term resupply, open 7 days; ATM available at Main St. location ▪ Food Lion Supermarket: good for long-term resupply, open 7 days ▪ Walgreen's has some food items *Other services*— laundromats: open 24 hours, 7 days ▪ Baker's Shoe Repair: one-day service, gear repairs, insoles, closed Sun and Mon ▪ banks ▪ library ▪ hospital. *Nearby town*—Johnson City,

TN: Mahoney's Outfitters (423-282-8889): a full-service outfitter.

Jones Branch 📖 *p. 18* ... where A.T. crosses a small footbridge over Jones Branch and ascends to the left. ➔ *right 300ft (on side trail, just before the footbridge, leading across Jones Branch Road)*–to Nolichucky Gorge Campground & Cabins (#1 Jones Branch Rd., Erwin, TN 37650; 423-743-8876; *<www.nolichucky.com>*): hostel with bunk bed for $12; tent sites $10; cabin-tents on platforms $12; primitive cabins $75 (up to six people); shower and towel without stay $2; will hold maildrop packages for guests only; shuttles available to area trailheads, longer distances by arrangement.

Greasy Creek Gap 📖 *p. 19* ... marked by sign (higher than eye level) at large clearing with campsites and old jeep road that looks like a ditch crossing Trail. A blue-blazed trail to left that leads 300 yards to a spring. ➔ *right 0.6m (on jeep road going down)*–to Greasy Creek Friendly (1827 Greasy Creek Rd., Bakersville, NC 28705; 828-688-9948): bed in house $15, bunkhouse $10, tent site $7.50, all include shower; shower without stay $3; laundry; meals available for overnight guests (can cater to vegetarians, too); trail store with basic supplies, hiker food items (Lipton's, snacks, ice cream, *etc.*); Coleman and denatured alcohol by the ounce; will hold maildrop packages; shuttles to local trailheads, long-distance shuttles by arrangement; safe parking for section hikers; pets outside on leash only. Directions: Look for "Greasy Creek Gap" sign on tree. Go downhill (on North Carolina side) following unused jeep road, take first left, and then the next right, go past old barn and around metal gate to first house on right.

Roan High Bluff 📖 *p. 19* ... On A.T.–parking area and water fountain (summer only); at far end of parking area, the Cloudland Rhododendron Gardens, with trail through natural area of Catawba rhododendron, offers spectacular displays in season.

Carvers Gap, TN143/NC261 📖 *p. 19* ... On A.T.–spring and privy to the left, beyond parking area. North of gap you will be crossing the oldest rocks to be seen on the entire Trail, estimated to be 2.5 billion years old. ◖ *left 8.7m*–to Roan Mountain State Park: tent sites available April 15 to October 15, $11 for hikers on foot, hot showers for guests, laundromat. Cabins available year round, about $90 and up depending on date.

US19E 📖 *p. 20* ... ◖ *left 0.3m*–to Mountain Harbour Bed & Breakfast (9151 Highway 19E, Roan Mountain, TN 37687; 1-866-772-9494; *<www.mountainharbour.net>*): hiker cabin/hostel over barn for $18 per person, semi-private king-size bed $35, includes linens, shower with towel, full kitchen, wood-burning stove, video library; tent sites with shower for $8; B&B rooms $80 up; shower without stay $3 w/towel; laundry $5 per load for guests; Coleman and denatured alcohol by the ounce, will hold maildrop packages (free for guests, $5 for non-guests); breakfast available for $9 during peak hiker season; town shuttle $5, other shuttles by arrangement, secure overnight parking for $5 per day ($2 per day if using shuttle); open year-round. ◖ *left 3.4m*–to **ROAN MOUNTAIN, TN 37687**: *Post office hours*: Mon-Fri 8am-noon and 1pm-4pm, Sat 7:30am-9:30am; 423-772-3014. *Services*—Cloudland Market and Roan Mt. Supermarket (good for long-term resupply) ▪ Snack Shack ▪ Bob's Dairyland ▪ Highlander BBQ ▪ Subway ▪ pharmacy ▪ medical clinic ▪ bank w/ATM. ➔ *right 0.5m*–to King of the Road Restaurant & Steakhouse: open Apr-Nov, Thur-Sat for dinner, Sun for lunch. ➔ *right 1.2m*–to J's Market: good for long-term resupply, Coleman by the ounce, public pay phone out front, closed Sun ➔ *right 2.5m*–to **ELK PARK, NC 28622**: *Post office hours*: Mon-Fri 7:30am-noon and 1:30pm-4:15pm, Sat 7:30am-11am; 828-733-5711. *Services*—grocery store: good for short-term resupply ▪ hardware store: Coleman by the ounce ▪ Times Square Diner.

Laurel Fork 📖 *p. 21* ... ☾ *left 0.3m (0.5 miles south of Laurel Fork crossing, look for tree bench with vista, 200 feet farther, take side trail at green/white AT sign downhill under power line. Alternatively, just north of signed Laurel Fork hand-railed bridge, take mostly level blue blazed trail along creek 0.4m. Do not walk driveway (private property and mean dogs))*—to Vango & Abby's Memorial Hostel: rustic, no indoor toilet, two outhouses. Pets okay. Always open electric heated bunkroom w/stove & sink, internet, trail library, sleeps 6. When caretaker present: shower $3, wash $3, dryer $3, misc. hiker-food resupply & beverages. Suggested donation $5/night w/o heat, $10 using heat. Quiet hours 10pm - 8am. Shuttles and secure parking available. Contact info: scott_vandam@hotmail.com, 256-783-5060, PO Box 185, Roan Mtn, TN 37687. No maildrops.

Dennis Cove Road 📖 *p. 21* ... ☾ *left 0.2m*–to Kincora Hiker's Hostel (1278 Dennis Cove Rd., Hampton, TN 37658; 423-725-4409): hostel in log cabin offers bunk beds and tree house; tenting on the lawn is available; kitchen facilities provided; laundry available; $4 per night is requested as a donation; hostel may be used as a maildrop; shuttles to nearby locations by arrangement; Coleman by the ounce, denatured alcohol, owned by Bob Peoples. *Notice!*—If you would like to do some Trail maintenance with A.T. club members, check with Bob when you arrive. For a day of work, you can earn a handsome patch to display on your pack, plus you get the satisfaction of having put something back into the system. ➔ *right 0.5m*–to Laurel Fork Lodge Campground and Hostel (1511 Dennis Cove Rd., Hampton, TN 37658; 423-725-5988): offers tent sites for $6 or hiker bunkhouse for $10 (include AM coffee, shower, towel, kitchen privileges, mail drops); private cabins $30 (max. 3 people); dial-up internet access; laundry $3.00; short-term resupply and cold sodas, ice cream, etc. before Trail Days; Coleman and denatured alcohol by the ounce; will hold maildrop packages ($5 if no stay); pets welcome; shuttles can be arranged; open March to October.

Laurel Fork blue-blaze 📖 *p. 22* ... *left 1.0m*–to Brown's Supermarket and other Hampton locations (see US 321, below).

US321 📖 *p. 22* ... *On A.T.*–Shook Branch Picnic Area: a USFS recreation and boating area on Watauga Lake, with beach, picnic tables, water fountains, and rest rooms just off US321. Water is turned off if there is a danger of freezing temperatures. ☾ *left 1.8m*–to Brown's Supermarket & Hardware (613 Hwy. 321, Hampton, TN 37658; 423-725-2411 or 2262): good for long-term resupply, Coleman and denatured alcohol by the ounce, will hold maildrop packages, open Mon-Sat (owner Sutton Brown will open on Sunday for thru-hikers only); public telephone outside store ▪ Braemar Castle Hostel & Guest House: bunk room, kitchen facilities, and reading room. Bunk with shower $15 per person, shower without stay $2, private rooms $20 up, pets outside; located about a block from Brown's Grocery across the road, you can check in at the grocery; shuttle back to Trail by owner Sutton Brown, a friend of hikers. ▪ Hillbilly Bob's BBQ and Catfish Shack ▪ internet cafe ☾ *left 2.6m*–to **HAMPTON, TN 37658**: *Post office hours:* Mon-Fri 7:30am-11:30am, 12:30pm-4pm, Sat 8am-10am; 423-725-2177; Copper Kettle

Restaurant ▪ Quarterback's BBQ ▪ Ice House Saloon and Grill ▪ McDonald's ▪ Subway ▪ Pizza Plus ▪ bank w/ATM ▪ ATM (inside at Texaco) ▪ medical clinic. **Nearby lodging**— Creekside Chalet and Iron Mt. Inn B&B (423-768-2446), call for pickup from trail at Shook Branch, $10. Creekside Chalet features hot tub, washer/dryer, full kitchen, $50 per person per night (sleeps 5). Iron Mt. Inn rooms $110-175 (ask about hiker rates), with full breakfast and bottomless cookie jar.

Low Gap, US421 📖 *p. 23 ... On A.T.*–piped spring and picnic table at roadside, parking area. ➲ *right 3m*–to **Shady Valley, TN 37688**: essentially an intersection with two small stores (both good for short-term resupply), one with a country restaurant, stores open 7 days year around. **Lodging**—Switchback Creek Motorcycle Campground (570 Wallace Rd., Shady Valley, TN 37688; 407-484-3388): cabins $40, tenting $12, bath house with free washer/dryer (donations appreciated). Call for ride; campground is about 2.5 miles from AT and 1.5 miles from town.

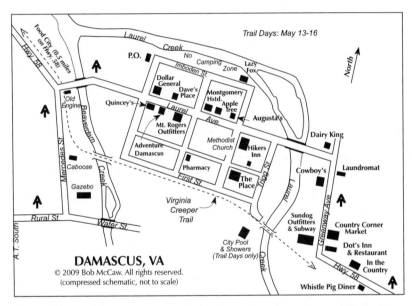

DAMASCUS, VA
© 2009 Bob McCaw. All rights reserved.
(compressed schematic, not to scale)

DAMASCUS, VA 24236 📖 *p. 23 ... Post office hours:* Mon-Fri 8:30am-1pm and 2pm-4:30pm, Sat 9am-11am; 276-475-3411; "the friendliest town on the Appalachian Trail," hosts "Trail Days" (see below). **The Place**—a Methodist hostel located in an old house behind the church, usually open Apr-Nov; rooms with bunks, common room, bathrooms with hot showers, back porch for cooking (no cooking inside building), and tenting in yard. The hostel is for overnight use by hikers and cyclists only (no family or friends); no dogs on premises. A $3 donation per night is requested, with two-night limit unless sick or injured. Absolutely no alcohol is permitted on the property; please keep noise to a minimum, especially after dark; hikers are responsible for housekeeping, please do your part. **Other lodging**—Dave's Place: hiker hostel, $10 per person; hot shower; shower without stay $2; parking $2 per day; check in at Mt. Rogers Outfitters;

absolutely no alcohol on premises ▪ Hikers' Inn (276-475-3788): bunk room $25 per person, with mattress, linens, hot shower, private room $35S/$45D, shared bath, pets OK; rooms in private home $65S/D or $55 per night for two nights, no credit cards accepted ▪ Lazy Fox Inn (276-475-5838): large rooms $65S/D with shared bath, $75S/D with private bath, full breakfast, pets outside ▪ Apple Tree B&B (145 E. Laurel Ave, P. O. Box 878, Damascus, VA 24236; 877-362-7753 or 276-475-5261; <*www.appletreebnb. com*>): $85S/D and up, private bath, pet friendly with verification of vaccination, full breakfast, no smoking, computer access, will hold maildrop packages for guests, owner does laundry $4 per load, phone access. ▪ Augusta's Appalachian Inn (125 Laurel Ave., P. O. Box 160, Damascus, VA 24236; 276-475-3565<*www.augustasappalachianinn. com*>): $90 up, will hold maildrop packages for guests only, free laundry, long distance, internet ▪ Montgomery Homestead Inn (103 Laurel Ave., Damascus, VA 24236; 276-475-3053 <*www.montgomeryhomestead.com*>): $65S/D and up, no pets, no smoking, no alcohol, will hold maildrop packages for guests only *Places to eat*—Quincey's: pizza, Italian, and American ▪ Cowboy's: fast food, cafeteria-style, luncheon specials, eat-in or take-out, burgers, subs, breakfast, luncheon specials on weekdays; open 7 days ▪ Dairy King: breakfast, home-style meals all day or until everything is gone, burgers, ice, cream, custard, pies ▪ Dot's Inn & Cafe: country cooking, homemade biscuits and gravy, burgers and fries anytime, daily luncheon specials, closed Sun ▪ In the Country: breakfast, soups and sandwiches ▪ Subway. *Groceries*—Food City Supermarket: good for long-term resupply, open 7 days; located 0.7 mile west on Hwy. 58 ▪ Country Corner Market: good for long-term resupply, deli; open 7 days ▪ The Dollar Store: good for long-term resupply, with a good variety of inexpensive trail foods and sample-sized items); open 7 days. *Outfitters*—Mt. Rogers Outfitters (110 Laurel Avenue, Damascus, VA 24236; 276-475-5416; <*www.mtrogersoutfitters.com*>): full-service backpacking store with wide range of gear and clothing; stove and pack repairs; Coleman and denatured alcohol by the ounce, other fuels; shuttles to area trailheads, will hold maildrop packages; open 7 days; operated by Jeff Patrick and his dad Dave ("Damascus Dave" of '90), who have been serving the A.T. and thru-hiking communities for more than seventeen years ▪ Sundog Outfitters (331 Douglas Dr., Damascus, VA 24236; 276-475-6252; <*www.sundogoutfitter.com*>): backpacking gear and clothing, hiker food, repairs, Coleman and denatured alcohol by the ounce, will hold maildrop packages; shuttles to area trailheads by arrangement, open 7 days. ▪ Adventure Damascus (P.O. Box 1113, 128 W. Laurel Ave., Damascus, VA 24236;888-595-2453 or 276-475-6262 <www. adventuredamascus.com>): catering to thru-hikers with backpacking gear, a hiker food section, denatured alcohol and Coleman fuel by the ounce, other fuels, bike rentals, will hold UPS and maildrop packages, shuttles to area trailheads by arrangement, $2 showers ($4 with towel), open 7 days year round *Other services*—laundromat: open 24 hours ▪ bank w/ATM; also ATM at Cowboy's ▪ pharmacy ▪ library is moving to a new facility near where AT comes into Damascus ▪ "Tow", a local trail angel, lets hikers use the phone on his porch at 204 Douglas Drive (near Cowboy's, look for the trail paraphenalia). *Trail Days*—an enormously popular annual hiker festival, scheduled for May 13-16 this year. During Trail Days, arriving hikers should check in at the campground provided for hikers on South Shady Avenue (behind the old rock school). Alumni hikers are requested to leave The Place for use by first-time thru-hikers who are hiking into Damascus. *Point of interest*—Virginia Creeper Trail: multi-use for horse, bike, and foot travel on the old "Creeper" railroad bed; several places in town rent mountain bikes. *Nearby town*—Abingdon, VA (14 miles west, motels and services are all near intersection of US58 and I-81): Holiday Lodge (276-628-2114): $36 up, laundry, pets allowed ▪ Quality Inn ▪ Comfort Inn ▪ Holiday Inn Express ▪ Cracker Barrel Restaurant ▪ McDonald's ▪ Pizza Hut ▪ Wolf Hill Plaza: drug store, discount department store; large supermarket next door.

VA600, Elk Garden 📖 *p. 24* ... ⊂ *left 3.5m*–to the Konnarock (Virginia) commmunity with a convenience store and restaurant, 1.7 miles further to Konnarock Medical Center. ⊃ *right 3.4m*–to **Whitetop, VA 24292**: small convenience store.

Grayson Highlands State Park 📖 *p. 24* ... *On A.T.*–likened to the grasslands of Montana, speckled with magnificent rock outcroppings and blessed with plenty of sky. Herds of feral ponies roam the park. Many are fairly tame, but as with all wild animals, it is best not to feed them. Camping along the Trail is prohibited inside the park. A dirt road to the right at Massie Gap leads off the ridge to a parking area. Water can be obtained by following this road to a fence, turning right at the fence, then going several hundred feet to a small spring; unmarked. A camp store at the park campground is more than two miles from the A.T., rarely open for those who make the trek.

Dickey Gap, VA650/VA16 📖 *p. 25* ... where A.T. crosses VA650, the entrance road to the USFS Hurricane Campground; with VA16, a primary highway, visible 150ft to the right. ⊃ *right 2.6m* (on VA16)–to **TROUTDALE, VA 24378**: *Post office hours:* Mon-Fri 8:15am-noon and 1pm-4:30pm, Sat 8:15am-11:30am; 276-677-3221. *Services*— Troutdale Baptist Hostel (276-677-4278): bunkhouse and campsites, rest rooms; hot shower and towel, pets okay outside; no alcohol on premises; check in time is from 8am until 6pm; open Mar 15-Nov 15. Donations are welcomed. Church services begin at 10am on Sun, 7pm on Wed, and you are welcome in hiker attire ▪ Jerry's Kitchen and Goods (10973 Troutdale Highway, Troutdale, VA 24378; 276-677-3010) varied menu with pizza, buffets on the weekends, mail drops accepted, Coleman and denatured alcohol by ounce, selection of hiker foods in small store, internet, shuttles available, open 7 days. Owners Jerry and Susana Bartley very friendly to hikers. ▪ Fox Hill Inn And Cabins (276-677-3313; <www.foxhillinn.net>); 2.3 miles south of Jerry's Kitchen & Goods. 4 miles south of Dickey's Gap. Hiker rates (thru-hikers only, 4/1-7/15, subject to change) $75S/D, $20 per additional person. Children under 18 free in parent's room. Price includes breakfast, you may use the kitchen to prepare lunches or evening meals. Dinner arrangements can be made with the innkeepers. No pets. Shuttle rides to and from trailheads or Jerry's Kitchen & Goods when available. ▪ bank w/ATM.

VA16 📖 *p. 26* ... *On A.T.*–Mt. Rogers National Recreation Area HQ: visitor center, maps for sale; open 7 days, Mem Day-Labor Day; weekdays only remainder of year. Rest rooms and drink machine are located in inside hallway; water available from spigot across the driveway opposite the front entrance. A public pay phone is available on the front porch. ⊂ *left 5.9m*-**Marion, VA 24354**: large town with all services. Post office, library and Francis Marion Hotel are in center of town near intersection of VA16 and US11. Supermarkets, several moderately priced motels, fast food are about one mile north of center ▪ Royal Inn (435 S. Main St., Marion VA 24354; 276-783-8511): $35S/$39D, pets OK, 0.5m south of center ▪ Virginia House Inn (1419 N. Main St., Marion, VA 24354; 276-783-5112): $30S $40D, pets $7 extra, will hold maildrop packages, north of town near supermarkets ▪ Food Lion, Ingles Supermarkets, Wal-Mart: all good for long-term resupply, open 7 days ▪ laundromat 0.5m north of center ▪ ATMs (one inside at Wal-Mart). ➲ *right 3.2m*–to **Sugar Grove, VA 24375**: Sugar Grove Diner (276-677-3351) and small grocery store. Large rooms available at diner, $59, shuttles available. Call ahead for availability. ▪ The Konnarock base camp is about a mile down Route 601; contact ATC's Blacksburg office (540-961-5551) in advance if you wish to include a week of Trail work in your A.T. thru-hiking experience.

US11/VA683 📖 *p. 26* ... *On A.T.*-Relax Inn (7253 Lee Hwy., Exit 54, Rural Retreat, VA 24368; 276-783-5811): $40S/$45D, more for 3 or more persons, coin laundry (get detergent in office), pets $10 extra, will hold maildrop packages for guests ($5 fee), shuttles to area locations by arrangement ▪ The Barn Restaurant: country-style Southern breakfast, daily luncheon specials; open 7 days; internet ▪ Village Truckstop (Shell station): good for short-term resupply, may offer Coleman by the ounce; open 7 days ▪ short order restaurant in Exxon station ▪ public pay phone. *Hostel*—Happy Hiker Hollow (276-783-3754): operated by thru-hikers Rambunny and Aqua. Space is limited and reservations are essential; please call ahead. Shuttles, slackpacking, laundry, internet, long distance phone, showers and eats. Long term parking for sectioners. Northbounders call from Troutdale for reservations. Southbounders call before Chestnut Shelter. ◖ *left 3.5m*–to **ATKINS, VA 24311**: *Post office hours:* Mon-Fri 9-1 and 2:30pm-4pm, Sat 9:30am-11am; 276-783-5551; Atkins Grocery good for long-term resupply, closed Sun ▪ laundromat ▪ bank w/ATM.

VA615 📖 *p. 28* ... Deer Trail Campground (599 Gullion Fork Rd., Wytheville, VA 24382; 276-228-3636): call for pickup (fee charged), tent sites $18, cabins $45D/$55 for 4, camp store stocked with hiker supplies, showers, heated pool, maildrops accepted.

US21/52 📖 *p. 28* ... ➲ *right 2.5m*–to **BLAND, VA 24315**: *Post office hours:* Mon-Fri 8am-11:30am and noon-4pm, Sat 9am-11am; 276-688-3751. *Services in town*–Bruce's Market: good for long-term resupply; hot lunch daily; open 7 days ▪ Bland Square Restaurant (in Citgo station): home-style meals, open weekdays only ▪ bank w/ATM ▪ library; *Near I-77 interchange (up hill 0.7m from town)*–Big Walker Motel (276-688-3331): $58S/D, pets allowed ▪ Dollar General ▪ ATM at Kangaroo Station ▪ Subway ▪ Dairy Queen ▪ no laundry facilities at motel or in town. ◖ *left 1.8m*–to **Bastian, VA 24314**: health clinic. Pizza Plus (276-688-3332; delivers to Bland), Front Porch Grille and convenience store near I-77 interchange beyond town.

VA608 📖 *p. 28* ... ➲ *right 0.8m*–to small grocery store, closed Sun.

VA606 📖 *p. 28* ... ◖ *left 0.4m*–to Trent's Grocery: good for short-term resupply, snack foods, drinks, restaurant/deli section (pizza, sandwiches, *etc.*), Coleman by the ounce, denatured alcohol, water from faucet on side of store, picnic table, and outside public telephone; campsites with hot shower and laundry $6 per person; open 7 days.

Sugar Run Gap, Sugar Run Road 📖 *p. 29* ... ➲ *right 0.5m (turn right on dirt road, bear left at the fork, and go 0.5 mile down the road to Woods Hole on right)*–to Woods Hole Hostel (3696 Sugar Run Rd. Pearisburg, VA 24134; 540-921-3444; *<www.woodsholehostel.com>*). An old homestead discovered by Roy and Tillie Wood while Roy was doing a study on elk in 1940. The two opened the hostel in 1986. Roy passed away in

1987. Tillie continued hosting thru hikers for 21 years. She passed away in 2007. Her granddaughter, Neville and husband, Michael are continuing her legacy now offering massage, healing arts, & retreats. Woods Hole is an 1880's chestnut-log cabin and hiker's bunkhouse on 100 acres. The bunkhouse has mattresses in the loft, electricity, and solar shower, $10 PP suggested donation. Two indoor rooms: $35S/$45D long distance hiker rate, $55S/$65D Reg Rate. Family style dinner, $12 and authentic southern breakfast, $6.50 in the main cabin. Yoga at 5pm. Shuttles, WiFi internet, telephone, laundry, sodas, candy bars, pizza, smoothies, granola, juice, home baked cookies, coffee/tea, coleman fuel, fuel canisters, and denatured alcohol available. Pet friendly. Will hold packages:

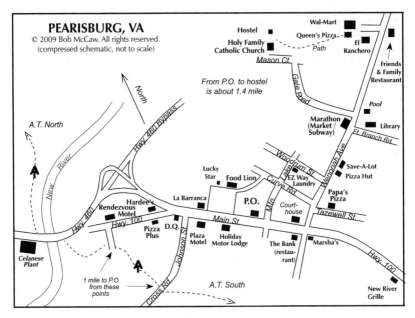

PEARISBURG, VA 24134 📖 *p. 29 ... Post office hours:* Mon-Fri 9am-4:30pm, Sat 10am-noon; will answer knock until 5:30pm weekdays if anyone working; 540-921-1100; a large, hiker friendly town proud of its long association with the Trail. The A.T. crosses Cross Road (a back road) and then a side street off Hwy. 100 very near the Rendezvous Motel. From both crossings, it is about 1 mile to the center of town and then about another 1.5 miles to the church hostel and Wal-mart. **Hostel**—Holy Family Hostel (516 Mason Court Dr., Pearisburg, VA 24134): $10 per person per night, open Apr to Oct, operated by the Church of the Holy Family; sleeping loft, stove and refrigerator, shower, deck, expansive lawn that can be used for tenting; no alcoholic beverages or pets are permitted on the property; normal stay is two overnights (if you need to stay longer, check with priest); cannot accept mail drops; no friends, relatives, or other visitors permitted for overnight stay. **Other lodging**—Rendezvous Motel (795 N. Main St., Pearisburg, VA 24134; 540-921-2636): $40S/$50D, laundry on premises, will hold maildrop packages, free long-distance calling for guests only; Coleman and denatured alcohol by the ounce. Shuttles into town and elsewhere as time permits ▪ Plaza Motel

(415 N. Main St., Pearisburg, VA 24134; 540-921-2591): $45S/$55D including tax, special room for up to 6 hikers ($55 for two, $5 each additional person up to a total of six), will hold maildrop packages for guests, will do laundry for guests, Coleman and denatured alcohol by the ounce, no pets ▪ Holiday Motor Lodge (401 N. Main St., Pearisburg, VA 24134; 540-921-1551): $34S/$42.50D and up, internet, will hold maildrop packages, pets OK. *Places to eat*—*In town:* Lucky Star Chinese Restaurant, AYCE ▪ The Bank, fine dining ▪ Hardee's ▪ Dairy Queen ▪ La Barranca (Mexican) ▪ Pizza Plus ▪ Pizza Hut ▪ New River Grille, steaks, seafood, open 11-8 Tue-Sat, lunch on Sun. *Near Wal-Mart*–Friends & Family Restaurant ▪ Wendy's ▪ Subway ▪ Queen's Pizza (recommended) ▪ El Ranchero. *Groceries*—Food Lion Supermarket: good for long-term resupply; open 24 hours ▪ Wal-Mart Superstore/Food Store: supermarket: good for long-term resupply, deli (if staying at the hostel use the shortcut trail that leads direct to the shopping area) ▪ Save-A-Lot Food Mart: bulk discount foods, open 7 days ▪ 7-Day Market: in the Marathon station, good for short-term resupply, snacks; open daily. Note that Wade's Supermarket has closed. *Other services*—Don Raines, 540-921-7433, shuttles Damascus to Troutville ▪ EZ Way Laundromat: open 7 days ▪ hospital ▪ municipal pool: snack bar, on Wenonah Avenue, open Mem Day-Labor Day ▪ library (on Ft. Branch Rd. off Wenonah Ave.): internet access terminals. *Nearby town*—Blacksburg, VA, a large college town, is about 25 miles east on US460, offers many services including outfitters, Backcountry Ski & Sports (540-552-6400; across from hospital), Dick's Sporting Goods (540-265-0861; near the mall).

VA42, Sinking Creek Valley 📖 *p. 31* ... ➔ *right 8m*–to **Newport, VA 24128**: small grocery store on road between Blacksburg and Pearisburg. No other services.

Keffer Oak 📖 *p. 31* ... large white oak 18-plus feet around in Sinking Creek Valley, with stile attached; estimated to be more than 300 years old.

VA624 📖 *p. 32* ... ◖ *left 0.3m*–to VA311, then left 500 feet to Catawba Grocery: good for short-term resupply, breakfast, pizza, hot dogs, sandwiches, rest rooms, outside pay phone; open 7 days.

VA311 📖 *p. 32* ... ◖ *left 1m*–to **CATAWBA, VA 24070**: *Post office hours:* Mon-Fri 7:30am-noon and 1pm-5pm, Sat 8am-10:30am; 540-384-6011. *Services*—The Homeplace Restaurant: family-style AYCE dinners (fried chicken, country ham, roast beef, vegetables, biscuits, cobblers) about $13-15; open Thur-Fri 4-8, Sat 3-8, Sun 11-6, closed July 4th; hikers welcomed as adding to the ambiance. Excellent southern style food; many hikers time their hikes to make sure they eat here. ▪ Catawba Valley General Store: good for short-term resupply, pizza, sandwiches, deli, Coleman and denatured alcohol by the ounce, closed Sun; camping is allowed in nearby field and pole barn, ask at store.

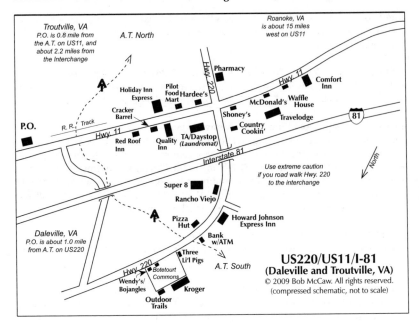

Troutville, VA
P.O. is 0.8 mile from
the A.T. on US11, and
about 2.2 miles from
the Interchange

A.T. North

Roanoke, VA
is about 15 miles
west on US11

Pharmacy

Comfort Inn

Holiday Inn Express

Pilot Food Mart

Hardee's

McDonald's

Waffle House

Cracker Barrel

Shoney's

Travelodge

P.O.

R. R. Track

Hwy 11

Red Roof Inn

Quality Inn

TA/Daystop (Laundromat)

Country Cookin'

Interstate 81

Use extreme caution
if you road walk Hwy. 220
to the interchange

Super 8

Rancho Viejo

Pizza Hut

Howard Johnson Express Inn

Daleville, VA
P.O. is about 1.0 mile
from A.T. on US220

Bank w/ATM

Three Li'l Pigs

A.T. South

Hwy 220

Botetourt Commons

Wendy's/ Bojangles

Kroger

Outdoor Trails

US220/US11/I-81
(Daleville and Troutville, VA)
© 2009 Bob McCaw. All rights reserved.
(compressed schematic, not to scale)

US220 📖 *p. 33* ... The A.T. first crosses US220, goes under I-81 on a back road, then crosses US11 near Troutville. Access to services (except post office) is easier via US220. *On A.T.*–Howard Johnson Express Inn (437 Roanoke Rd., Daleville, VA 24083; 540-992-1234): $55 (up to 2 people, includes full hot breakfast), laundry, pets $10 extra, business center with internet, will hold maildrop packages for guests only ▪ Super 8 (446 Roanoke Rd., Daleville, VA 24083; 540-992-3000): $59S/D; continental breakfast; coin-operated laundry on premises, will hold maildrop packages for guests, internet; no pets ▪ Pizza Hut ▪ Rancho Viejo Mexican Restaurant: offers daily luncheon buffet, open 7 days ▪ bank w/ATM. ☜ *left 0.3m*–to Botetourt Commons: Kroger Supermarket: good for long-term resupply, open 7 days ▪ Outdoor Trails (28 Kingston Dr., Daleville, VA 24083; 540-992-5850): a full-service outfitter with backpacking gear and clothing, Coleman and denatured alcohol by the ounce, other fuels; will hold maildrop packages; internet access; shuttles to area trailheads by arrangement; open year-round, closed Sunday ▪ Three Li'l Pigs BBQ ▪ Wendy's ▪ Bojangle's. ☞ *right 0.3m*–to I-81 interchange area: Travelodge (540-992-6700): hiker rate $45S/D, pets $6 extra ▪ Daystop Motel has closed ▪ Holiday Inn Express (540-966-4444): $110S/D, breakfast, no pets ▪ Red Roof Inn (540-992-5055) $58S/D, pets OK ▪ Comfort Inn (540-992-5600) $40S, pets $25, internet in lobby ▪ public shower at TA Travel Center for $9 and at Pilot Truckstop for $8, both with towel furnished ▪ Shoney's: AYCE breakfast buffet ▪ Country Cookin' Restaurant: home-style meals with AYCE salad-vegetable-bread-desert buffet; open 7 days ▪ McDonald's ▪ Taco Bell ▪ Hardee's ▪ Waffle House ▪ Cracker Barrel ▪ Subway in Pilot Food Mart ▪ 24-hour full-service laundromat inside at TA Travel Center ▪ pharmacy ▪ bank w/ATM ☜ *left 1m*–to **DALEVILLE, VA 24083**: *Post office hours:* Mon-Fri 8am-5pm, Sat 8am-noon; 540-992-4422; note that some businesses listed above will hold maildrop packages for overnight guests, but it is a good idea to call ahead to verify. *Nearby town (about 14m south)*—Roanoke, VA: large city with bus and airline service.

US11 📖 *p. 33* ... ☚ *left 0.7m*–to **TROUTVILLE, VA 24175**: *Post office hours:* Mon-Fri 9-12, 1-5, Sat 9-11; 540-992-1472: Thriftway Supermarket: good for long-term resupply, closed Sun ▪ bank w/ATM. ☛ *right 1.5m*–to I-81 interchange area (see US220, above).

Bearwallow Gap, VA43/Blue Ridge Parkway 📖 *p. 34* ... ☛ *right 5m*-north on Blue Ridge Parkway to Peaks of Otter Recreation Area (800-542-5927): Peaks of Otter Lodge ($115 up) with restaurant, no pets. Park service campground, sites $16, with camp store (limited supplies); open May-Oct. ☚ *left 5m*–to **Buchanan, VA**. *In town*—restaurants ▪ grocery store: good for short-term resupply ▪ laundromat ▪ bank w/ ATM. *At I-81 interchange (2.7 miles north of Buchanan)*—Wattstull Motel (540-254-1551): $58 and up, pets $10 each. Past hikers have reported that hitching can be difficult.

VA614 📖 *p. 34* ... ☛ *right 0.3m*–to VA618, then left 0.1 mile to Middle Creek Picnic Area with pavilion and well. Camp store 1.0 mile up VA 618 (follow signs). ☚ *left 4.5m*–to Wattstull Motel (see entry above).

US501/VA130 📖 *p. 36* ... ☛ *right 4.9m (stay on VA130 at fork)*–to Wildwood Campground (6252 Elon Rd., Monroe, VA 24574; 434-299-5228): tent sites $20 per site and up, cabins $55 and up per night (up to 4 people; two-night minimum on weekends), laundromat for guests only, camp store with microwave meals, ice cream, Coleman and denatured alcohol by the ounce, will hold maildrop packages; shuttle back to Trail. ☚ *left 5.9m*–to **Glasgow, VA 24555**: *Post office hours:* Mon-Fri 8am-11:30am, 12:30pm-4:30pm, Sat 8:30am-10:30am; 540-258-2852. *Services*—Grocery Express: good for long-term resupply, Coleman and denatured alcohol by the ounce, open 7 days ▪ laundromat: open year-around, 7 days ▪ Dollar General Store: some hiker-type food items ▪ bank w/ATM. ▪ Inquire locally about possible camping. ☛ *right 5.1m (on US501)*–to **Big Island, VA 24526**: *Post office hours:* Mon-Fri 8:30am-12:30pm and 1:30pm-4:30pm, Sat 8am-10am; 434-299-5072. *Services*—H&H Food Market: good for short-term resupply, short order food, open daily, outside telephone ▪ Sharon's Pizza and More ▪ bank w/ATM ▪ medical center.

US60 📖 *p. 37* ... ☚ *left 9m*–to **Buena Vista, VA 24416**. Buena (byoo-nah) Vista is rather spread out. From center of town at intersection of US60 and US501, Budget Inn is 0.25m west on US60, Buena Vista motel 0.5m east on US60, Food Lion 1.5m west on 60, park and most restauarnts are about 1.5m east on US501. *Post office hours:* Mon-Fri 8:30am-4:30pm; 540-261-8959. *Services*—Budget Inn (540-261-2156) <www.budgetinnbv.com>: $45S/$55D, laundry, pets $10 extra; may be able to arrange shuttles to and from trail (fee) ▪ Buena Vista Motel (540-261-2138): $45S/D and up, no pets ▪ Glen Maury Park Campground (540-261-7321) shower, pool, campsite $22 per tent ▪ Captain Tim's Galley (near Buena Vista Motel) ▪ Burger King ▪ Todd's BBQ ▪ Nick's Italian Restaurant ▪ Domino's Pizza ▪ Hardee's ▪ Subway (in Budget Inn) ▪ Food Lion Supermarket: good for long-term resupply, open year-around, 7 days ▪ bank w/ATM ▪ laundromats: open 7 days.

Fish Hatchery Road 📖 *p. 38* ... unpaved, looks like jeep road. **☾** *left 1.6m* (passing the fish hatchery on the way to intersection with VA56, then left 0.9 mile)–to **MONTEBELLO, VA 24464**: *Post office hours:* Mon-Fri 8-12, 12:30-4:30, Sat 9am-noon; 540-377-9218. *Services*—Montebello Camping & Fishing Resort (540-377-2650): $10 tent site, cabins $45 up; cafe planned; laundromat; shower without stay $3.50; store good for short-term resupply, stove fuel; ▪ Dutch Haus B&B (655 Fork Mountain Ln., Montebello, VA 24464; 540-377-2119; <*www.dutchhaus.com*>): open year-round, southbounders call after Oct 31; $30 per person (special rate for thru-hikers on foot), includes breakfast and laundry service; dinner extra by arrangement; free lunch 11am-1pm May 1-Jun 30; no smoking; will hold maildrop packages; internet access; shuttles to area trailheads by arrangement.

VA56, Tye River 📖 *p. 38* ... On A.T.–campsites and swimming holes available across the suspension bridge. **☾** *left 4.1m*–to Crabtree Falls Campground (540-377-2066): tent sites $24, cabins for $50, camp store, laundry, hot showers, campground open year-around.

Rusty's Hard Time Hollow 📖 *p. 38* ... a pre-civil war homestead which is Rusty's home and back to basic mountain farm including many farm animals. Unlike any other place to stay. "Where you can be yourself" as Rusty puts it. Enjoyed by thousands since Rusty started welcoming Thru-Hikers and cyclists in 1982. The bunkhouse and barn will sleep several dozen hikers. There is a full hiker kitchen/porch, cold spring with drinks and a rain water shower. Also you can purchase a unique "Hollow" t-shirt, a collectible in thru-hiker circles. Past hikers will tell you that Rusty is a very generous individual, the kind of person who will give you the shirt off his back. Kick back and relax, keeping in mind that this is Rusty's farm and it takes a lot of work on his part to keep it ready for hikers. So pitch in and help out if you see something that needs attention. Donations needed and appreciated since Rusty has no other means to keep the hollow open for visitors. Rides to Sherando Lake on hot days to cool off. No dogs allowed because of free ranging farm animals. Rides back to the trail when you are ready to go (during the day). No alcohol or illegal drugs allowed. Directions: From Maupin Field Shelter, go back to the A.T. turn left and follow the dirt access fire road 1.2 miles to the Blue Ridge

Trail Magic

Thru-hikers all enjoy the kindness and generosity of people who provide a cold drink on a hot day or "real" food after days of hiker fare. When providing such "trail magic", it is very important to be careful to protect the trail and follow Leave No Trace principles. The Appalachian Trail Conservancy has common sense guidelines for providing trail magic; here is a partial list:

● Locate events in developed areas on durable surfaces.
● Be present if you provide food or drink.
● Restore the site after you are finished.
● Forego alcoholic beverages.
● Be hospitable to all.

For more details, please visit *www.appalachiantrail.org/trailmagic*.

Parkway, turn left (South) on the parkway and go 1.2 miles to Rusty pipe gate on the left. Gate has his name and A.T. stickers on one end. Signs on the driveway are for your information and entertainment(!).

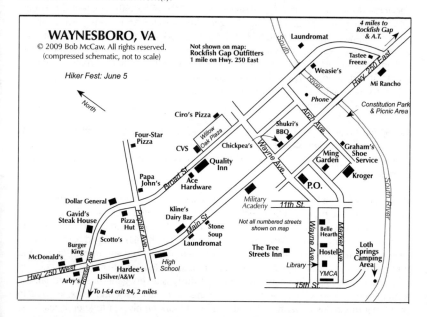

WAYNESBORO, VA
© 2009 Bob McCaw. All rights reserved.
(compressed schematic, not to scale)

Hiker Fest: June 5

North

Not shown on map:
Rockfish Gap Outfitters
1 mile on Hwy. 250 East

4 miles to
Rockfish Gap
& A.T.

Laundromat

Tastee Freeze

Weasie's

Mi Rancho

Phone

Constitution Park
& Picnic Area

Ciro's Pizza

Four-Star Pizza

CVS

Chickpea's

Shukri's BBQ

Willow Oak Plaza

Graham's Shoe Service

Ming Garden

Quality Inn

Papa John's

Ace Hardware

Kroger

P.O.

Dollar General

Military Academy

11th St.

Gavid's Steak House

Kline's Dairy Bar

Pizza Hut

Scotto's

Stone Soup Laundromat

Not all numbered streets shown on map

Belle Hearth

Burger King

McDonald's

The Tree Streets Inn

Hostel

Loth Springs Camping Area

Hardee's

LJSilver/A&W

Arby's

High School

Library

YMCA

15th St.

To I-64 exit 94, 2 miles

Hwy 250 West

South River

Arch Ave.

Wayne Ave.

Broad St.

Poplar Ave.

Main St.

Market St.

Rockfish Gap, Interstate 64/US250 📖 *p. 39* ... Trail crosses I-64 and US 250 on the Blue Ridge Parkway. A list of telephone numbers for a free shuttle into town is posted on the door of the tourist information center south of the gap. This is a project of the local "Trail Angel Network" organized to assist A.T. thru-hikers. ☾ *left 0.2 miles from info center*–to The Inn at Afton (1-800-860-8559): $65S/D, will hold UPS packages addressed c/o Inn at Afton, Jct. I-64 & US250, Waynesboro, VA 22980 (clearly mark "hold for hiker"); restuarant is being remodeled, may open by summer 2010. ☾ *left 0.7m on US 250*–to Colony Motel (540-942-4156): hiker rate $60, all rooms have refrigerator, pool, no pets. ☾ *left 4.5m on US 250*–to **WAYNESBORO, VA 22980**: *Post office hours:* Mon-Fri 9am-5pm; 540-942-7320; one of the largest Trail towns you will visit during your hike, prides itself on "hospitality in the valley," has all major services needed by thru-hikers. *Hostel*—Grace Lutheran Church (on S. Wayne Avenue about three blocks beyond the post office) offers a supervised hostel for long-distance hikers in the basement of the church building, open mid-May to about June 21, closed Sunday nights; check-in 5pm-8pm; checkout 9am but church will store packs for those staying another night; two-night limit unless sick or injured; max. 15 hikers at a time. Hostel offers lounge with big screen VCR/DVD, air conditioning, internet access, hot showers, use of kitchen, snacks, and continental breakfast. Members of the congregation host a Thursday night supper for hikers in residence followed by an optional Vesper service. No pets, drugs, alcohol, smoking, or foul language are allowed, of course. You should show your appreciation for this hostel by leaving a donation. *Camping*—Loth Springs

Camping Area: free private tent sites on the South River behind the YMCA, check in at the Y's front desk, showers, rest rooms available inside at main building (in summer open weekdays until 10pm, weekends until 7pm); portatoilets usually available when building closed. **Lodging**—Quality Inn (540-942-1171): $49S/$59D, higher on weekends, pets $10 extra, continental breakfast ▪ The Tree Streets Inn (421 Walnut Ave., Waynesboro, VA 22980; 540-949-4484): a B&B with comfortable rooms in family atmosphere $75S/D includes breakfast, will hold maildrop packages for guests only; call for pickup at Rockfish Gap, ride back to Trail. No pets. ▪ Belle Hearth B&B (320 S. Wayne Ave, Waynesboro, VA 22980; 540-943-1910) <www.bellehearth.com>: $75S and up includes breakfast, laundry options, no pets, no smoking, pool, will hold mail drop packages for guests only; ride back to Trail. **Places to eat** (near downtown)—Weasie's Kitchen: home-cooked meals, AYCE pancakes, open 7 days ▪ Colby's on Main Street ▪ Ciro's Pizza ▪ Ming Garden: buffet, recommended ▪ Papa John's ▪ Chickpeas Greek Restaurant ▪ Rick's BBQ ▪ Shukri's BBQ ▪ Stone Soup Books serves soup, has internet, is a very popular hiker hangout ▪ Mi Rancho, large portions, inexpensive. **Places to eat** (1 mile west of downtown)—Gavid's Steak House with AYCE salad-fruit-food bar ▪ Scotto's Italian Restaurant ▪ fast food outlets ▪ Four-Star Pizza. **Groceries**—Kroger Supermarket: good for long-term resupply, deli, hot meals to take out, open 7 days, 24 hours. **Laundromats**—B Z Laundromat: two locations, one near fire station, one near fast food district, open daily. **Outfitter/stove fuel**—Rockfish Gap Outfitters (540-943-1461): full-service outfitter with backpacking gear and clothing, Coleman and denatured alcohol by the ounce, other fuels; also information about local and long-distance shuttle services; store opens 10am Mon-Sat, noon on Sun ▪ Ace Hardware: Coleman and denatured alcohol by the ounce. **Other services**—Graham's Shoe Service: overnight boot and pack repair, insoles, closed Sun ▪ banks w/ATMs ▪ pharmacies ▪ hospital ▪ library with free internet access for thru-hikers ▪ movie theater ▪ Waynesboro YMCA: showers $2 with towel, free camping in field at Loth Springs behind the main building (see above), possible free use of pool and other membership courtesies will be extended by the Y for thru-hikers. **Special event**—"Hiker Fest," to be held on June 5 this year at Grace Lutheran Church hostel on S. Wayne Avenue, activities will include an AYCE spaghetti dinner (minimal charge), free Trail video, and shuttle to the local movie theater after dinner, also prizes and free movie tickets will be awarded at the event; for more information contact the Waynesboro Trail Angels at 540-942-6644. **Shuttles back to gap**—a list of people you can call for a free shuttle back to the A.T. is posted at the library, YMCA front desk, and at many lodging facilities in Waynesboro. ◐ left 5.8m on I-64—fast food outlets, chain motels, restaurants and Wal-Mart are located near I-64 Exit 94. This area lacks Waynesboro's personality, but can meet hiker needs. It is also about 2 miles south of the intersection of Main and Rosser in Waynesboro (see map).

Shenandoah Natl. Park (SNP) ▢ p. 39 ... containing 290 square miles of reclaimed backcountry connected by more than 500 miles of hiking trails. The A.T. runs the length of the park, with a smooth, wide treadway and moderate grades most of the distance. Along the way, animals conditioned by years of protection are plentiful and seem tame. Skyline Drive is crossed frequently, usually at scenic overlooks, and, to the delight of many hikers, restaurants, camp stores, and shelters are never far away.

Thru-hiker Permits—Thru-hikers must obtain a backcountry camping permit before entering the park, with permits for northbounders available at a self-registration information board on the A.T. north of Rockfish Gap or at the Rockfish Gap entrance station on Skyline Drive, which is accessible from the A.T. on a blue-blazed side trail to the left at the information board. Southbounders can pick up a permit at an information board located on the A.T. just after crossing the park's northern boundary.

Regulations—Shelters for overnight use are called "huts," with hut use restricted to those who have backcountry permits on a first-served basis. Bunk space is available to the rated capacity of each hut. Except in case of emergency, stay is limited to one night. If a hut is full, you must camp, but your campsite cannot be located ...

• Within 10 yards of a stream or other natural water source.

• Within 50 yards of building ruins including foundations, chimneys, and walls.

• Within 50 yards of another camping party or "no camping" post or sign.

• Within 100 yards from a hut, cabin, or day-use shelter (some huts have designated overflow camping areas you may use).

• Within ¼ mile of a paved road, park boundary, or park facility (e.g., campground, picnic area, visitor center, lodge, wayside or restaurant).

If designated facilities are provided for sanitation, use them. If no facilities are provided, solid human waste must be buried in a cat hole at least three inches deep. Defecation within 20 yards of streams, trails, or roads is prohibited. Backcountry campfires are permitted at huts only. Pets must be leashed at all times inside park boundaries, and are not permitted inside any buildings in the park or on some side trails. When you pick up your permit, check the information board for any change in these regulations.

Concession Services—Concessions are run by ARAMARK (800-778-2851; <*www.visitshenandoah.com*>), more information and promotions can be found at the website. Campsites can be reserved by phone at 877-444-6777 or online at <*www.recreation.gov*>, except Lewis Mountain, which is not on the reservation system.

Park Information or Emergency—call the park office at 540-999-3500; also see the park's website for additional information about the park <*www.nps.gov/shen/*>. The emergency number is 800-732-0911.

Shuttles—Mountain & Valley Shuttle Service, Rodney Ketterman ("Rodman") and Jim Austin ("Skyline"), based near Luray, 1-877-789-3210, <www.mvshuttle.com>, offers shuttles anywhere between Duncannon, Pa and Daleville Va. Also serves nearby airports, Amtrak, Greyhound. Operates fully insured, late-model vehicles, offers trail logistics, town assistance (one-day notice appreciated). Holds Commercial Use Authorization to shuttle hikers in SNP, Virginia DMV for-hire operating authority. Free limited rustic camping for shuttle clients night before or upon conclusion of hike, on-site parking at base camp (A.T.-style shelter, picnic table, BBQ grill, fire pit, hot shower, flush toilet; not a hostel). Also offers lodge-to-lodge hiking vacation package in SNP. Accepts Visa, MasterCard, Discover (at time of phone reservation only).

Loft Mtn Campground 📖 *p. 40* ... *On A.T.*—campground actually bordered by the Trail for more than a mile. You can follow a side trail (continue straight ahead at first concrete mile marker you encounter) through the amphitheater to the camp store, or stay on the A.T. for 0.7 mile to another marker indicating the camp store 250 feet to the left. The store has a limited hiker-food selection, coin-operated laundromat, pay showers, and picnic tables; open mid-May through late Oct, camp store open 9am-5:30pm, showers and laundry until 8pm. Campsites $15. From the store, the paved entrance road leads about 0.8 mile to the right to Loft Mountain Wayside: short-order menu, milk shakes; open Sat-Sun only April through early May, full time 9am-5:30pm beginning early May through late Oct.

Swift Run Gap, US 33/Skyline Drive - mile 65.5 📖 *p. 41* ... ☾ *left 2.6m* to Country View Motel (540-298-0025) $40 up, pets OK, possible shuttles to trail and town, maildrop packages accepted for guests, send to 19974 Spotswood Trail, Elkton, VA 22827. ▪ Misty Mountain Motel (540-298-9771) $43-53, up to 4 people, no pets, no smoking ▪ convenience store ▪ Swift Run Campground, public swimming pool ☾*left 6.4m to* **Elkton, VA 22827**: *Post office hours:* Mon-Fri 8:30am-4:30pm, Sat 9am-11am; 540-298-7772. Elkton Motel (540-298-1463) $39S/$46D, no pets ▪ Dollar General ▪ Pizza Hut ▪ McDonald's ▪ several diners in town ▪ Food Lion 2 miles beyond town on US 33.

Lewis Mountain Campground 📖 *p. 41* ... *On A.T.*–campground similar to Loft Mountain, but smaller. The camp store can be reached via a side trail to the left through the campground; store has a limited food selection, coin-operated laundromat and pay showers inside, drink machine and public telephone on porch; open 4/9-11/7, 9am-5pm, until 8pm summer months. Campsites $15. A group tent-cabin (four bunks and an antique wood stove) may be available for about $20, ask at store. Cabins are available, $89 and up, pets $10 extra, 10% weekday hiker discount subject to availability. Primitive tent cabin with bunks, $30.

Lewis Spring 📖 *p. 41* ... *On A.T.*– spring house to the left off A.T., 0.6 mile farther down is Lewis Falls. ➔ *right 0.2m*–to Big Meadows Wayside: store, restaurant, and park visitor center. The store (reasonably good hiker-food selection but expensive) is open late Apr-Nov, 9am-5:30pm, until 8pm during summer months. The restaurant with dining room and grill is also open 9am-5:30pm, until 8pm during summer months. An outside public pay phone and ATM are available nearby. The adjacent Harry F. Byrd Visitor Interpretive Center features exhibits and movies about the history and wildlife of the park.

Big Meadows 📖 *p. 41* ... *On A.T.*–a large complex, A.T. borders the camping-picnic-amphitheater area. Big Meadows Lodge: rooms and cabins (Sun-Thur $84 up, weekends $94 up, pets $25 extra) open late Apr-early Nov; dining room offers home-style cooking, breakfast 7:30-10, lunch 12-2, dinner 5:30-9; taproom with entertainment and lighter menu; telephone in lobby. Campsites $20 ($17 in early spring and late fall), with pay showers and laundromat. A level mile away (via the paved entrance road to Skyline Drive) is the Big Meadows Wayside described above.

Skyland Road, north 📖 *p. 42* ... marked by sign pointing to "Dining Room" on the road just before reaching the Stony Man Nature Trail parking area. ☾ *left 0.3m*–to Skyland Lodge and Restaurant. Rooms $74 up, $84 up on weekends; ATM. The restaurant is open April 1 through late Nov (breakfast 7:30-10:30, lunch 12-2, dinner 5:30-9); breakfast comes highly recommended by several past thru-hikers); taproom also serves food.

Thornton Gap, US 211/Skyline Drive - mile 31.5 📖 *p. 42* ... ➲ *right 0.1m*–The former Panorama wayside is being torn down as of this writing, to be replaced by rest rooms and a telephone by 2009. **Shuttles**—Mountain & Valley Shuttle Service (877-789-3210). See listing under information for Shenandoah Nat'l Park, above. ◐ *left 9m*–to **Luray, VA 22835**: *Post office hours:* Mon-Fri 8:30am-4:30pm; 540-743-2100. Center of town, recommended to hikers, has all services in compact area. **Places to stay**—Best Western Inn (410 W. Main St., Luray, VA 22835; 540-743-6511): $70-160, maildrop accepted, pets $20 extra ▪ Budget Inn (320 W. Main St., Luray, VA 22835; 540-743-5176): $49 up, pets $5 extra, maildrops accepted ▪ Cardinal Inn (888-648-4633): $59 up, no pets. **Other Services**—Farmer's Foods (in East Luray Shopping Center): good for long-term resupply ▪ laundromat ▪ several restaurants. **Outfitters**—Appalachian Outdoors Adventures (540-743-7400): outdoor-recreation store, Coleman and denatured alcohol by the ounce; open year-around, closed Tues, opens at noon Sun.

Elkwallow Gap, Skyline Drive - mile 23.9 📖 *p. 43* ... ➲ *right 0.1m*–to Elkwallow Wayside Store & Grill: limited groceries, burgers, Mountain Blackberry shake, picnic tables, rest rooms, and outside public telephone; open early Apr-Oct, 9am-5:30pm, until 6:30pm during summer and Oct weekends; grill closes at 5:30pm.

Tuscarora Trail 📖 *p. 43* ... leads left 0.8 mile to Mathews Arm Campground: tent sites $15, no shower or laundry. The Big Blue-Tuscarora Trail extends northward from this junction for 220 miles until it eventually rejoins the A.T. near Duncannon, Pennsylvania.

Compton Gap Trail 📖 *p. 43* ... *right 0.5m: at concrete post labelled "Chester Gap, Va. 610", A.T. goes left, Compton Gap Trail is straight ahead)*–to Front Royal Terrapin Station Hostel (304 Chester Gap Rd., Chester Gap, VA 22623; 540-539-0509 or 540-631-0777 <gratefulgg@hotmail.com>): first house on left on paved road, enter in back through marked gate. Bunk with mattress and sheets, $19S/$34D, additional nights $16S/$30D, discounted rates for groups, including shower with soap and shampoo, free internet, free town shuttle. Fuel, snacks, and ice cream on-site. Mail drop packages held for guests.

Night-hiker's Guide

Schedule of Major Meteor Showers in 2010

Jan 3-4: Quandtrantids, 40 per hour, moderately bright, bluish (max. activity Jan 3, NE)
Apr 21-22: April Lyrids, 10-20 per hour, moderately bright (max. activity Apr 22, E)
May 5-6: Eta Aquarids, 20 per hour, moderately bright (max. activity May 6, E)
Jul 28-29: Delta Aquarids, 20 per hour, moderately bright (max. activity Jul 28, SE)
Aug 12-13: Perseids, 60 per hour, fairly bright, streaking (max. activity Aug 12, NE)
Oct 21-22: Orionids, 10-15 per hour, moderately bright, swift (max. activity Oct 21, E)
Nov 17-18: Leonids, 10 per hour, moderately bright, streaking (max. activity Nov 17, E)
Dec 13-14: Geminids, 75 per hour, fairly bright yellowish, swift (max. activity Dec 14, SE)

Find a viewing site away from lights and unobstructed; lie down and look straight up to the heavens; best viewing time is from midnight to dawn.

Full Moons in 2010

Jan 30, Feb 28, Mar 30, Apr 28, May 27, Jun 26, Jul 26, Aug 24, Sep 23, Oct 23, Nov 22, Dec 21

Shuttle and slackpacking available. Owned by Mike Evans (AT '95, PCT '98). Please be quiet when entering to avoid disturbing neighbors. Open May 2 to July 10.

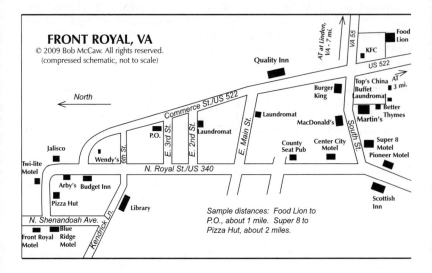

FRONT ROYAL, VA
© 2009 Bob McCaw. All rights reserved.
(compressed schematic, not to scale)

North

Sample distances: Food Lion to P.O., about 1 mile. Super 8 to Pizza Hut, about 2 miles.

US522 📖 *p. 44* ... **☾** *left 4m*–to **FRONT ROYAL, VA 22630**: *Post office hours:* Mon-Fri 8:30am-5pm, Sat 8:30am-1pm; 540-635-8482; weekends in spring and summer are often crowded, best to hit town on weekdays. *Lodging*—Super 8 Motel (540-636-4888): $53S $58D for hikers (add $6 weekends), pets $10 extra ▪ Scottish Inns (540-636-6168): $45 and up, pets $10 extra ▪ Pioneer Motel (540-635-4784): $49S/$55D, $10 extra for pets ▪ Quality Inn (540-635-3161): $65S/D, pets are $15 extra; pre-arrange a shuttle back to Trail at US522 when you first check in, internet, continental breakfast ▪ Center City Motel (540-635-4050): $40S/$45D (higher weekends), no pets. ▪ Several motels lie about 2 miles north, including Blue Ridge Motel (540-636-7200): $35S/$45D (add $10 weekends), no pets. *Places to eat*—many restaurants within walking distance of motels, some mentioned by hikers are: County Seat Pub & Eatery: breakfast and lunch Mon-Fri ▪ South Street Grill: country-style meals ▪ Dean's Steak House. *Also,* Pizza Hut, McDonald's, KFC, Burger King, Little Caesar's, Wendy's, Arby's, Jalisco Mexican, Tastee Freeze, Top's China Buffet. *Groceries*—Food Lion Supermarket: good for long-term resupply, deli; open 7 days ▪ Martin's Food Store: good for long-term resupply, open 7 days ▪ Better Thymes Natural Foods: open 7 days. *Other services*—several laundromats: open 7 days, year-round ▪ banks w/ATMs ▪ hardware store sells Coleman fuel by the ounce ▪ hospital ▪ K-mart (in Royal Plaza).

National Zoo, southern boundary 📖 *p. 44* ... *On A.T.*–The National Zoo's Conservation and Research Center at Front Royal is home for many rare and endangered animals from all over the world. Formerly a U.S. Army military reservation, the buildings and lands cover thousands of acres. Exotic birds comprise a major part of the collection, and herd animals adapt particularly well to the rolling landscape. The species recovery program here is world renowned. A nearby facility, part of a former U.S. Army Cavalry Remount Station, is used to train dogs and agents for DEA duties.

Manassas Gap, VA55/VA725 📖 *p. 44* ... ⊂ *left 1.2m*–to **LINDEN, VA 22642**: *Post office hours:* Mon-Fri 8am-noon and 1pm-5pm, Sat 8am-noon; 540-636-9936; will hold packages for 15 days maximum, so call to let the postmaster know if you are running behind schedule. *Services*—Monterey Store: good for short-term resupply; open 7 days
▪ outside pay phone.

Wooden park bench 📖 *p. 44* ... located right on the A.T., used to mark the trail that leads to the park. ⊃ *right 1.7m*–(on blue-blazed trail) to Sky Meadows State Park: visitor center with soda machine, tent sites $13 (campground 2.5 miles from A.T.), telephone, no laundry or showers; open year-round. The park naturalist leads nature hikes on the Trail during summer months.

Ashby Gap, US50 📖 *p. 44* ... rock wall just before highway marks boundary surveyed by 19-year-old George Washington. ⊃ *right 1.2m*–Ashby Inn (540-592-3900), dinner 6-9 M-S, Sunday brunch, entrees about $25-34. Rooms $155 up.

Bears Den Rocks 📖 *p. 45* ... On A.T.–viewpoint offers vista of Shenandoah River Valley. ⊃ *right 0.2m*–to Bears Den Hostel (18393 Blue Ridge Mountain Rd., Bluemont, VA 20135, 540-554-8708; <www.bearsdencenter.org>): a 26-bed hostel owned by ATC and operated by the PATC. Hostel offers bunk, sheet sleepsack, shower and towel, and cooking privileges in well-equipped kitchen, $15 for hikers on foot; camping on lawn for $10 per person includes inside privileges. Showers $3 for non-guests. Laundry and detergent available for $3 per load. Hostel store stocks trail foods (several days resupply possible), ready-to-cook pizza and breakfast foods; Coleman and denatured alcohol available for donation. Telephone with free domestic long distance and internet access are available; will hold maildrop packages sent c/o Bears Den Hostel as above. Water is available from an outside spigot through a window to the right of the hiker entrance at the back of the building. The Center is open year-round (gate for drive in access open 8am-10pm). A private room is $55 per couple, $18 for each extra person. Ask about the thru-hiker special, which includes a bunk bed, laundry privileges, a Tombstone pizza, B&J ice cream, and soda, all for $27.50 plus tax. Note: hikers can enter the hiker room during the day, but the hostel, store and kitchen are not available until 5 PM,.

Snickers Gap, VA7/VA679 📖 *p. 45* ... A.T. follows VA7 for short distance, then turns right onto VA679 for about 50 yards before entering the woods. ⊂ *left 0.3m (downhill on VA679)*–to Horseshoe Curve Restaurant: third-generation family pub with sandwiches, burgers, and fries; open Tues-Sat noon-late, Sun until 7pm, closed Mon and major holidays; will fill water bottles. ⊂ *left 1m*–to restaurant and small grocery store.

Trail to Blackburn A.T. Center 📖 *p. 45* ... ⊃ *right 0.2m (on side trail that descends steeply on switchbacks)*–to Blackburn A.T. Center, a Potomac A.T. Club facility, staffed by caretakers year-around. Open to hikers free of charge, donations are appreciated. The main center building has a large, screened porch, sofas, picnic table, and public telephone (540-338-9028). Water is available year-round from an outside spigot next to the steps. A small cabin near the main building serves as a hiker hostel with bunk beds and a wood stove;

also overflow tent sites are available nearby; shower is a solar type located on the lawn. The monuments of Washington, D.C. are visible from the lawn on clear days.

Keys Gap, WV9 📖 *p. 46* ... ☾ *left 0.3m*–to mini-mart and bar/pizza place.➔ *right 0.3m across state line*–to convenience store.

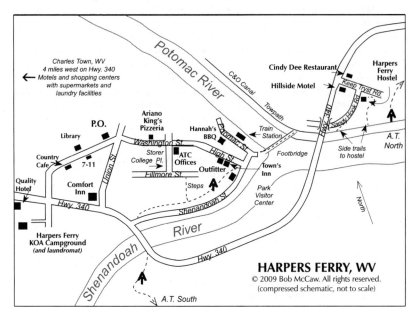

HARPERS FERRY, WV
© 2009 Bob McCaw. All rights reserved.
(compressed schematic, not to scale)

HARPERS FERRY, WV 25425 📖 *p. 46* ... *Post-office hours:* Mon-Fri 8am-4pm, Sat 9am-noon; 304-535-2479; headquarters of the Appalachian Trail Conservancy and the psychological halfway point for most thru-hikers. The town itself, founded in 1747, is dominated by the Harpers Ferry National Historical Park. There is a friendly outfitter and a number of places to stay and eat in or near town, but the nearest grocery store is several miles away. **ATC Headquarters**—ATC offices are open year-round, 9am-5pm. A staff member or volunteer will greet you and take your picture for the photo album. You can sign the hikers' register and check the letter box for mail and messages. An up-to-date listing of services and bus schedules in the Harpers Ferry area can be found on the hiker's table. In the visitor area, guidebooks, maps, and other Trail items are on sale; internet access and hiker telephone, Coleman fuel and denatured alcohol for a donation. **Hostels**—Town's Inn (175 and 179 High St., Harpers Ferry, WV 25425, 877-489-2447): a hostel in a beautiful 1840s-era house in the historic district next to the outfitter. Bunk room, $30, $35-40 for semi-private room, $120 for 4-bed private room with private bath, laundry $5/load. ▪ Harpers Ferry Hostel: across the Potomac River (see listing below). **Other lodging**—Comfort Inn (304-535-6391): $85S/D Mon-Thur (weekends higher), no pets ▪ Quality Hotel (304-535-6302): $88-121. Two pet friendly rooms, $50 extra ▪ Harpers Ferry KOA Campground (304-535-6895): full-service campground, cabins $58 up, tent sites $34 up; shower, camp store, pool, laundromat (8am-10pm), game room, other amenities. **Places to eat**—Ariano's King's Pizzeria: pizza, subs, pasta dinners; open 7 days ▪ Country Cafe ▪ There are several rather pricey restaurants in the historic district, Hannah's BBQ on Potomac Street reportedly has generous portions. **Groceries**—outfitter's store stocks food items; nearest supermarkets are in shopping centers on Highway 340 (see below). **Outfitter/stove fuel**—Outfitter at Harpers Ferry (189 High St., P. O. Box 1231, Harpers Ferry, WV 25425; 304-535-2087; <*www.theoutfitteratharpersferry.com*>): full-service backpacking store with gear and clothing, complete line of footwear and foot care products, small repairs, hiker-food section in the Outfitter's Store on Potomac Street (Lipton, Ramens, tuna, chicken, basic staples, Pop-Tarts, Snickers, Cliff Bars, *etc.*), Coleman and denatured alcohol by the ounce, other fuels, bike rentals, first-aid and personal-care/hygiene products, will hold and send maildrop packages; can arrange shuttles to area Trailheads; open 7 days. **Other services**—convenience stores ▪ bank w/ATM ▪ nearest laundromats at KOA and in shopping center on Hwy. 340 (see below). **Transportation**—Pan Tran (304-263-0876; <*www.pantran.com*>) provides local bus service from the ATC offices to Charles Town via Hwy. 340, buses run Mon-Fri, fare $1.50; schedule and route map are posted on hiker information board at ATC ▪ Amtrak (800-USA-RAIL; <*www.amtrak.com*>), trains to Washington, D.C., about $11 one way. **Harpers Ferry National Historical Park**—Exhibits and guided tours will acquaint you with the history of the Harpers Ferry area, most famous for John Brown's raid during the Civil War. Adjacent to the park are shops and a few restaurants mostly geared to automobile tourists. The route of the A.T. passes Jefferson Rock in the middle of town. Thomas Jefferson stood on this rock in 1793 and later wrote enticingly to a friend in France, "This view is worth a voyage across the Atlantic!" **Nearby town**—Charles Town, WV (with shopping malls 4 miles west on US340): Food Lion in Somerset Village Shopping Center: good for long-term resupply ▪ Super Wal-Mart and laundromat in Charles Town Plaza ▪ Martin's Food Store, good for long-term resupply, open 7 days ▪ several motels near Martin's ▪ bank w/ATM ▪ hospital.

Blue-blazed trail 📖 *p. 46* ... ☾ *left 0.5m*–to Harpers Ferry Hostel (19123 Sandy Hook Rd., Knoxville, MD 21758; 301-834-7652; <*www.harpersferryhostel.org*>): offers air-conditioned bunk rooms, kitchen, and hot showers; open Apr 15-Nov 15 (check in 5pm-10pm, check out 10am, open all day May 29-Sept 7). Bunk room $16-20, tenting on lawn is $10 per person, access to inside facilities and shower additional $3; laundry with detergent $4 per load including soap. Pets okay outside, no alcohol permitted on premises; will hold maildrop packages (must have photo-ID for pickup and stay); guest phone with free domestic calls; internet. Directions: Follow the A.T. (towpath) 0.2 miles beyond US340 bridge, then take a blue-blazed side trail to the left (crossing railroad track) 0.3 mile to the hostel; watch carefully for speeding trains. Another unofficial blue-blazed side trail to the left off the canal towpath leads to the back of the hostel property. *Beyond hostel* (go right, then left on Keep Tryst Road): Hillside Motel (301-834-8144): $45S $55D, no pets ($5 higher on weekends) ▪ Cindy Dee Restaurant: home-style food, open 24 hours ▪ convenience store: open 7 days.

Gathland State Park 📖 *p. 46* ... *On A.T.*–rest room building with drink machine on far side of building away from the Trail; water, usually available year-round, and picnic pavilion on north side of road that bisects the park make this a good place to cook dinner if you are heading for Crampton Gap Shelter, where water source can be unreliable in dry years, or you may want to carry water from here; park notable for its unique and distinctive stone monument to war correspondents.

Dahlgren Back Pack Campground 📖 *p. 47* ... *On A.T.*–the only place on the A.T. with state-provided 24-hour rest rooms, showers, picnic tables, and a camping area; all free. Watch your gear here, since nearby US40A provides easy public access.

Turners Gap, US40A 📖 *p. 47* ... ☾ *at A.T.*–Old South Mountain Inn: fine dining, prime rib, seafood, vegetarian entrees, good wine list; open 5-9 Tues-Fri, Sat 12-8, Sun 10:30-8, closed Mon; several U.S. presidents have visited here during the inn's 200-year history. Hikers are welcome (you can shower at nearby Dahlgren Campground first). ☾ *left 2m*–to **Boonsboro, MD 21713**: *Post office hours:* Mon-Fri 9-1, 2-5, Sat 9am-12am; 301-432-6861. restaurants ▪ Weis Grocery (far side of town): good for long-term resupply ▪ laundromat ▪ bank w/ATM.

Interstate 70 📖 *p. 47* ... *On A.T.*–footbridge over I-70 where drivers in cars and trucks often honk their horns and wave at thru-hikers. At the northern end of the footbridge, the A.T. turns sharply left and passes under the US40 bridge. If you go up the bank to US40: ☾ *left 0.4m*–to Greenbrier State Park with $25 tent sites, camp store, showers and swimming; opens Memorial Day. Across the road from the park is the Dogpatch Tavern, a favorite spot for local bikers, offering country cooking and hospitality to thru-hikers; open 7 days.

Wolfsville Road 📖 *p. 47* ... ☾ *left 0.3m*–to The Free State Hiker Hostel (11626 Wolfsville Rd., Smithsburg, MD 21783; 301-824-2407; <*www.freestatehiker.com*>): with climate-controlled bunk room $32, includes linens, shower, telephone, internet access; no pets or alcohol; open Mar 15-Nov 15, two-night maximum; operated by thru-hiker Ken Berry; will hold mail drop packages, $2 fee for non-guests. ☾ *left 2.4m*–to **Smithsburg, MD 21783**: *Post office hours:* Mon-Fri 8:30am-1pm and 2pm-4:30pm, Sat 8:30am-12pm; 301-824-2828. Dixie Eatery: home-cooked meals, luncheon specials; closed Sun ▪ Smithsburg Market: good for long-term resupply; open 7 days ▪ laundromat, open 7 days. ☾ *left 2.1 miles (turn left at bottom of hill on MD 64)*–Smithsburg Plaza with Food Lion Supermarket (good for long-term resupply), convenience store, medical center, bank w/ATM, pharmacy, hardware store.

Pen-Mar Park 📖 *p. 48* ... *On A.T.*–featuring sunset and picnic pavilions and rest rooms. The sunset pavilion overlooks Maryland and Pennsylvania farmland to the west. Nearby, an A.T. sign and American flag make a good place to have your picture made for the folks back home. A public pay phone is located in the ranger office, which along with the rest rooms, is locked when the ranger leaves at about 8pm. No camping is permitted in the park (up to $500 fine). Weekends and holidays often feature special events and music. Unofficial campsites are reportedly located on the A.T. just north of the park, off to the right, but you'll need to carry water from the park. ➲ *right 2.1m from park or 1.5m from Buena Vista Road*–to **Cascade, MD 21719**: *Post office hours:* Mon-Fri 8am-1pm and 2pm-5pm, Sat 8am-12pm; 301-241-3403. ▪ Vince's New York Pizza ▪ Sanders Market (good for long-term resupply, closed Sun). Directions: go to liquor store near end of Buena Vista road, then east past pizza place to P.O., then left to store.

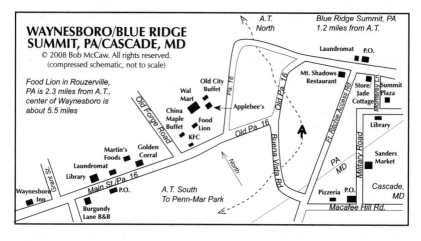

WAYNESBORO/BLUE RIDGE SUMMIT, PA/CASCADE, MD
© 2008 Bob McCaw. All rights reserved.
(compressed schematic, not to scale)

Food Lion in Rouzerville, PA is 2.3 miles from A.T., center of Waynesboro is about 5.5 miles

Old PA16 📖 *p. 48* ... Best route on foot to Blue Ridge Summit and Waynesboro, PA. ➲ *right 1.2m*–to **Blue Ridge Summit, PA 17214**: *Post office hours:* Mon-Fri 8-4, Sat 9am-11:30am; 717-794-2335. Mountain Shadows Restaurant ▪ Jade Cottage (Korean and Thai) ▪ Laundromat ▪ Blue Ridge Mini-Mart: open 24 hours ▪ Summit Plaza Restaurant: home-cooked meals, open 7 days ▪ library ⊂ *left 2.3m*–to a sprawling shopping area, off PA 16, with Food Lion: good for long-term resupply ▪ Wal-Mart ▪ KFC ▪ China Maple Buffet ▪ Old City Buffet ▪ Applebee's ▪ more restaurants nearby ⊂ *left 3.3m*–Golden Corral (AYCE) ▪ Martin's Supermarket. ⊂ *left 5m*–to **Waynesboro, PA 17268**: *Post office hours:* Mon-Fri 8:30-5pm, Sat 9am-12pm; 717-762-1513. Waynesboro Inn (239 W. Main St., Waynesboro, PA 17268; 717-762-9113): 2009 rates: $72S/$82D, pets $20 extra; call ahead as the property may be out of business or changing management ▪ Burgundy Lane B&B (717-762-8112): $85 per room (up to two people), internet, laundry, will pick up and shuttle back to Trail, no charge. Shuttles around town and to area trailheads by arrangement ▪ restaurants and fast food outlets scattered along PA 16 between Food Lion and center of town ▪ laundromat: open 7 days ▪ bank w/ATM ▪ pharmacy ▪ hardware store ▪ hospital.

PA16 📖 *p. 48* ... alternate route to Blue Ridge Summit and Waynesboro, PA. PA 16 is a busy road with narrow shoulders, tough for motorists to pick up hitchhikers.

PA233 📖 *p. 49* ... ➲ *right 1.2m*–to **South Mountain, PA 17261**: *Post office hours:* Mon-Fri 8:30am-1pm and 2pm-4:45pm, Sat 8:30am-11:30am; 717-749-5833; Bar and grill in South Mountain Hotel. No lodging. Store has closed.

US30 📖 *p. 49* ... ⊂ *left 0.5m*–to Taormina's Italian Restaurant (717-352-8503), closed Mon; ⊂ *left 0.9m*–to Henicle's Market: good for long-term resupply, deli; open daily. ⊂ *left 3.5m*–to **Fayetteville, PA 17222**: Scottish Inn-Rite Spot Motel (5651 Lincoln Way East, Fayetteville, PA 17222; 717-352-2144): $55S/$62D, pets $10 extra; will hold maildrop packages; shuttles to and from A.T. for guests, slackpacking and other shuttles by arrangement, office center with internet, restaurant on premises ▪ Flamingo

Restaurant: home-style meals, open 7 days ▪ coin-operated laundromat ▪ doctor ▪ bank w/ATM. Historic Gettysburg is 14 miles east on US30.

Caledonia State Park 📖 *p. 49 ... On A.T.*–picnic area, rest rooms, telephone, and campsites for $21-$27 per site (non-resident) with shower, up to 5 people per site, pets allowed in some sites; shower without stay $3. Also, pool with safe place to store pack and concession stand with fast food and snacks; open 7 days during summer months; $4 pool fee. The historic Thaddeus Stevens blacksmith shop is located near the park's entrance on US30.

Pine Grove Furnace State Park 📖 *p. 50 ...* campground with tent sites $10-$14 per site, up to 5 people per site; free Fuller Lake swimming area during summer months (open daily, concession stand nearby), and furnace used to smelt iron during the Revolutionary and Civil Wars. Public telephones are available at park office and lake concession building. Thru-hiking dogs may pass through on leash, and are permitted to stay overnight at campsites ($2 per pet extra); no alcohol permitted. The park is open from 8am to dusk year-round (concession facilities open Mem Day-Labor Day). *Hostel*—Ironmaster's Mansion Hostel (1212 Pine Grove Rd., Gardners, PA 17324; 717-486-7575): on A.T. to your left in large brick building dating back to 1820; ask to see the "secret" room used on the Underground Railroad. Bunk with shower and kitchen privileges $27 for thru-hikers ($24 for Hostels International members), includes linens, towel, internet, satellite TV; shower for non-guests $4; laundry $4 (free detergent); piano for guests; no pets allowed; will hold maildrop packages (don't send "signature requested"); the hostel building is closed 9:30am-5pm, check in 5pm-9pm; limited food may be available; Coleman and denatured alcohol by the ounce. *Campstore*—Pine Grove Furnace Store: adjacent to hostel, home of the "Half-Gallon Club." Anyone who has hiked here from Georgia or Maine may join this thru-hiker tradition. All you have to do is buy a half-gallon of ice cream as soon as you arrive and eat it as fast as you can. You are permitted to wash it down with hot coffee or soda if you have the stomach for it! Store good for very short-term resupply; open daily Mem Day-Labor Day and weekends in May and Sept-Oct.

Midpoint marker 📖 *p. 50 ... On A.T.*–located just north of Pine Grove Furnace State Park, erected by a 1985 thru-hiker. This isn't the actual halfway point. Due to trail relocations, the halfway point changes each year. This year, it's about four miles south of here.

Trail to Pine Grove Road 📖 *p. 50 ...* ☾ *left 0.7m*–to Mountain Creek Campground (717-486-7681): cabins $45 up; individual tent sites $25 and up; showers, laundromat, camp store, snack shack, public telephone; open Apr-Nov.

Pine Grove Road 📖 *p. 50 ...* ☾ *left 0.3m*–to Cherokee Family Campground (717-486-8000): campground has tent sites, pool, hot showers, $25 per site (up to two people); outside pay phone; camp store has Coleman fuel (only pint cans); open 7 days; deli.

PA34 📖 *p. 50 ...* ☽ *right 0.2m*–to Green Mountain General Store: good for short-term resupply, deli section, some fresh fruits and produce in season, Coleman fuel (usually pint cans stocked); open 7 days.

PA94 📖 *p.50* ... ➲ *left 2.0m*–to the Holly Inn Restaurant and Motel (717-486-3823) hiker rate $55, internet, rides often available to and from trail, continental breakfast; restaurant open 7 days for lunch and dinner ➲ *left 2.5m*–to **Mt. Holly Springs, PA 17065:** several family-style restaurants ▪ sandwich/sub shop ▪ Dollar General ▪ laundromat ▪ bank w/ATM.

Backpacker's Campsite 📖 *p. 51* ... ➲ *right 0.1m*–(look for sign) to the Backpacker's Campsite, a free (but railroad noisy) primitive camping area on the south edge of Boiling Springs provided by the Cumberland Valley A.T. Club; portatoilets provided Memorial Day-Labor Day. Water can be obtained at the ATC Regional Office (0.4 miles north on the A.T. in Boiling Springs), from a spigot on building by the oil tank. **Notice!**—no camping is allowed along the A.T. in the Cumberland Valley between Alec Kennedy Shelter and Darlington Shelter, with this one exception on the outskirts of Boiling Springs.

BOILING SPRINGS, PA 17007 📖 *p. 51* ... *Post office hours:* Mon-Fri 8am-4:30pm, Sat 8am-noon; 717-258-6668; an 18th-century iron-industry settlement that became a 19th-century tourist village and recreational area. Today, it is a quiet little residential community listed in the National Register of Historic Places. The springs are some of the largest in Pennsylvania, with a flow of 22-million gallons bubbling up per day (the local high school teams are known as "The Bubblers"; the water is actually 53°F, just appears to be boiling). The A.T. was routed through town in 1990, and its residents have finally adapted to the flow of hiker traffic that passes through each summer. *Lodging*—Gelinas Manor B&B (717-258-6584): $79D up (only one room at this price, call to reserve); internet; laundry $6, shuttles by arrangement (or call 717-249-3718); no pets, packs must be kept in protected area outside ▪ Garmanhaus B&B (717-258-3980): $50S/$75D up, weekends $25 higher, tenting allowed in back yard for $1 donation with no access to rest room or other inside amenities (public portatoilet usually located at lake in summer) ▪ Other lodging options are sometimes made available by local residents; check the message board at the ATC office. *Places to eat*—J.C.'s Countrytime Cafe ▪ Boiling Springs Tavern: dinner reservations usually required; open Tues-Sat ▪ Anile's Pizza. *Other services*—Karn's Grocery Store: good for long-term resupply; open 7 days ▪ ATMs at bank and convenience store ▪ Boiling Springs Pool: admission about $9 ($2 discount if you show this book), open Mem Day-Labor Day; $1 for shower only for hikers ▪ ATC Regional Office (717-258-5771) with swing on porch and grassy yard borders A.T. City ordinances forbid camping. Water is available from spigot behind building.

US11, Harrisburg Pike 📖 *p. 51* ... crossed on $1 million pedestrian footbridge spanning the highway. ➲ *left 0.2m*–to Super 8 Motel (717-249-7000): $45S/$50D weekdays, laundry, pets $10 extra ▪ America's Best Inn (717-245-2242): $55S/D weekdays, pets $25 extra, laundry ▪ The motels listed are the closest ones to the trail, but many tourist facilities are located along US11 west of the A.T. ➲ *left 0.7m*–to truck stop: restaurant, laundromat, showers, phones, small store; open 24 hours. Note: Lodging without reservations unavailable or more expensive on summer weekends, when special events draw thousands of visitors.

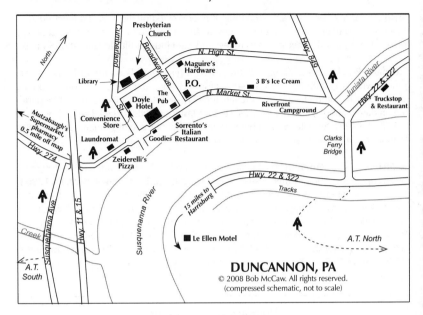

North

Presbyterian
Church

Cumberland

Broadway Ave

N. High St.

Hwy 849

Juniata River

Library

Maguire's
Hardware

P.O.

3 B's Ice Cream

Hwy 22 & 322

Truckstop
& Restaurant

Doyle
Hotel

The
Pub

N. Market St.

Riverfront
Campground

St.

Mutzabaugh's
Supermarket,
pharmacy,
0.5 mile off map

Convenience
Store

Laundromat

Sorrento's
Italian
Goodies Restaurant

Clarks
Ferry
Bridge

Hwy 274

Zeiderelli's
Pizza

Susquehanna River

Hwy. 22 & 322

Tracks

Hwy 11 & 15

15 miles to
Harrisburg

Creek

Susquehanna Ave

Le Ellen Motel

A.T. North

A.T.
South

DUNCANNON, PA

DUNCANNON, PA 17020 📖 *p. 52 ... Post office hours:* Mon-Fri 8am-4:30pm, Sat 9am-noon; 717-834-3332; friendly town once called "the jewel of the Susquehanna." ***Doyle Hotel***—(7 N. Market St., Duncannon, PA 17020; 717-834-6789): an ancient hotel built by Anheuser Busch, staying here and swapping tales in the bar is a thru-hiker tradition. Rooms $25S, $7.50 per additional person, pets allowed, includes internet. Check in 11am-11pm (or Sun noon-8pm); will hold maildrop packages. The restaurant and bar features cajun and home-style meals with a Southern flair; open 11am-9pm, Sunday 12-6; coin-operated laundry for hikers; 4pm shuttles to supermarket. ***Other lodging***— Riverfront Campground (717-834-5252): tent sites $3.50 per person, hot showers, snacks, check in before dark; campsites next to railroad tracks (noisy at times).There are no motels near town, closest are the Red Carpet Inn (717-834-3320) and Stardust Motel (717-834-3191), several miles north on US 11, and the Le Ellen Motel (717-921-8715), about 3 miles from town across the river on US 22 (a scary looking road walk.) ***Places to eat***—Sorrento's Italian Restaurant: pizza, subs, stromboli ▪ Goodies, breakfast ▪ Zeiderelli's Pizza ▪ The Pub ▪ All-America Truck Plaza Restuarant (on highway north of town) family-style, open 24 hours ▪ 3B's Ice Cream Shop. ***Groceries***—Mutzabaugh's Market: full-service supermarket, good for long-term resupply, open 7 days (store runs hiker shuttle from Doyle mid-afternoon during peak thru-hiker season, ask at bar about schedule) ▪ laundromat: open 7 days ▪ convenience store, open 24 hours. ***Other services***—Duncannon Presbyterian Church (3 High St.) offers internet access, snacks and cold drinks to hikers ▪ Coleman by the ounce at hardware store ▪ bank w/ATM ▪ ***Nearby town***—Harrisburg, PA (15 miles southeast): large city, many services. Wildware Backcountry (717-564-8008) gear and clothing, repair services; open 7 days.

Susquehanna River 📖 *p. 52* ... the longest river crossed by the Trail at a length of 444 miles. Connecticut River is second longest at 411 miles; Potomac, third longest at 383 miles; James, fourth longest at 340 miles; and the Hudson, fifth longest at 315 miles.

Lickdale, PA 📖 *p. 53* ... ☞ *right 2.4m to I-81 interchange*–Days Inn (3 Everest Lane, Jonestown, PA 17038; 717-865-4064) call for rates (discount if you mention this book), small dogs OK, internet, laundry ▪ Quality Inn (717-865-6600) about $80-110 (depending on date), laundry, internet, pets $10 extra ▪ fast food outlets ▪ Lickdale Campground (717-865-6411): tent sites $25, cabin $52 (up to 4 people, two night minimum, no pets), laundry facilities, camp store, showers and bath house ▪ No post office.

PA501 📖 *p. 53* ... Amy and Fritz Holland (570-345-1119) offer shuttles up to 200 miles by arrangement. Their former hostel has closed. ☜ *left 3.3m*–to **Pine Grove, PA 17963**: Services are spread over a large area; this is not an easy place to resupply. *Center of town*—Do's Pizza ▪ Original Italian Pizza (570-345-5432, delivers to 501 Shelter) ▪ small markets ▪ laundromat. *North of town (a mile or more)*—Berger's Market and BG's Value Market (good for long-term resupply; open 7 days) ▪ Sholl's Family Restaurant, AYCE, closed Monday. *Near I-81 (2.5 miles south of town on PA443)*—Econolodge (570-345-4099) $55S/$60D, pets $10 extra in smoking rooms only ▪ Colony Lodge (570-345-8095) ▪ Hampton Inn (570-345-4505) ▪ McDonald's ▪ Arby's.

Holidays and Occasions

The following is a list of holidays and special occasions that will be observed in 2010. Dates indicated by an asterisk (*) have been designated as official federal holidays, which means that all post offices will be closed on those dates.

January 1* .... New Year's Day	July 4* .... Independence Day
January 18* .... MLK, Jr. Birthday	September 6* .... Labor Day
February 14 .... Valentine Day	September 9 .... Rosh Hashanah
February 15* .... Presidents Day	September 18 .... Yom Kippur
March 14 .... Daylight Savings Time (begins)	September 22 .... Autumnal Equinox
March 17 .... St. Patrick's Day	October 11* .... Columbus Day
March 20 .... Vernal Equinox	October 31 .... Halloween
March 31 .... Passover	November 7 .... Daylight Savings Time (ends)
April 4 .... Easter Sunday	November 11* .... Veterans Day
April 22 .... Earth Day	November 25* .... Thanksgiving Day
May 9 .... Mother's Day	December 2 .... Hanukkah
May 31* .... Memorial Day	December 21 .... Winter Solstice
June 20 .... Father's Day	December 25 .... Christmas Day
June 21 .... Summer Solstice	

Shartlesville-Cross Mtn Road 📖 *p. 54* ... the road to Shartlesville is grassy and overgrown where it interesects the A.T. The road is nondescript, but can be identified by a six foot high sign marking "A.T. north and south" for the beneift of people on the side road. Follow this grassy road 100yds right, and it becomes a well-maintained gravel road that leads to a gate in about a mile. ➲ *right 3.6m*–to **Shartlesville, PA 19554:** Scottish Inn (610-488-1578): about $49S/$59D depending on day, pets $10 extra ▪ Dutch Motel (610-488-1479) rates $40S/$47D weekdays, $15 higher weekends ▪ Haag's Hotel (610-488-6692) $40S/$50D, Pennsylvania Dutch-style meals ▪ several convenience stores ▪ bank w/ATM. Shartlesville can also be reached via Marshall's Path. Nearby roads are lightly travelled and hitching may be difficult.

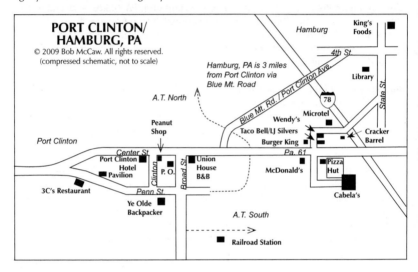

PORT CLINTON, PA 19549 📖 *p. 54* ... *Post office hours:* Mon-Fri 7:30am-12:30pm and 2pm-5pm, Sat 8am-11am; 610-562-3787; on the Schuylkill River. Twelve-year-old Daniel Boone, born south of here, once got lost and camped overnight on the riverbank near where the Trail crosses a bridge into town. The A.T. was routed through the town in 1928; town now bills itself as the "buzzard capital of the Northeast" and welcomes A.T. hikers. ***Town pavilion***—a covered wooden structure available for use by long distance hikers only, one night stay maximum. No alcohol is allowed; please help support his policy. Water is available from a nearby hand pump (or often bottled water is provided by local "Trail angels" if pump not working), and a privy is usually located across the road near the river. As you enter town, turn left on Penn Street and follow the blue-blazes to the large pavilion, on the right one block beyond Ravine Street. Do not use the adjacent private swimming pool. ***Lodging***—Port Clinton Hotel (610-562-3354): rooms $49S/$62D ($10 towel and key deposit refundable); shared bath; outside fenced area for pets; dining room open for lunch and dinner (owners request you shower before dining), closed Mon; coin-operated laundry on premises (check in at bar) ▪ Union House B&B; status is uncertain at press time. ***Outfitter***—Ye Olde Backpacker (45 Penn St., Port Clinton PA 19549, 610-562-2322): full service outfitter with Coleman and denatured alcohol by the ounce. Local transportation and shuttles available, will hold maildrop packages (please send UPS or FedEx). Open 9-8 Mon-Sat, 10-5 Sun. **Other services**—3C's Restaurant: open 5am-3pm Mon-Fri, weekends 6am-2pm ▪ The Peanut Shop: trail mixes, ATM inside; open 7 days ▪ Capitol Trailways no longer stops in Port Clinton. ➲ *right 1.8m on PA 61*–to *I-78 interchange*: Cabela's (610-929-7000) huge outfitter mainly oriented towards hunting and fishing, will come over to pick up hikers at pavilion if someone is free to drive the van, may give shuttles back to Port Clinton, open 7 days ▪ fast food outlets and chain restaurants ▪ convenience stores ▪ Microtel (610-562-4234): $85S/$100D, pets $10 extra.

Blue Mountain Road 📖 *p. 54* ... ➲ *right 3m* to **Hamburg, PA 19526**: ▪ several restaurants ▪ Kings Food Market: good for long-term resupply ▪ laundromat ▪ library ▪ bank w/ ATM ▪ health clinic. Alternate route: Hamburg is 1.5 miles from Cabela's via Industrial Drive and State Street. **Outfitter**—Tom Schaeffer's Recreation & Sports Center (610-562-3071), camping supply store on Hwy. 61, closed Sun.

Blue Rocks Trail 📖 *p. 55* ... ➲ *right 1.4m*–to Blue Rocks Campground (610-756-6366) <*www.bluerockscampground.com*>: cabins $50 up, campsites $30 per tent, showers, coin-operated laundry, pets on leash with updated shots, camp store with hiking items, catch-and-release fishing pond; open Apr-Nov 1. Blue Rocks formation is on the camp property.

Hawk Mtn Road 📖 *p. 55* ... ➲ *right 0.2m*–to Eckville Shelter. ☾ *left 1.4m*–to Hawk Mountain Sanctuary: internationally recognized mecca for hawk watchers and a center for raptor research, visitor area has exhibits and viewing windows; open 7 days, $5-$7 admission fee charged for use of nature trails. The fall hawk migrations are an awesome sight. Between mid-August and mid-December, observers will record 20,000 hawks, eagles, and falcons passing over Hawk Mountain, more than 150 a day!

PA309, Blue Mtn Summit 📖 *p. 55* ... *On A.T.*-Blue Mountain B&B (570-386-2003): lodging $90 up, possible discount on weekdays subject to availability; restaurant open Thur-Sun for lunch and dinner; thru-hikers allowed to tent behind restaurant with permission only, water spigot on southwest corner of building. Shuttles possible by prior arrangement.

Lehigh Gap, PA 873 📖 *p. 56* ... before crossing bridge. ➲ *right 2.4m*–to **Slatington, PA 18080**: *Post office hours:* Mon-Fri 8:30am-5pm, Sat 8:30am-noon; 610-767-2182. **Services**—Fine Lodging (700 Main St., Slatington, PA 18080; 610-760-0700): $39 up for regular room; air-conditioned room $4 extra; Coleman and denatured alcohol; shuttle to and from the Trail (please call a day or two ahead as there is no full-time front desk); shuttle to outfitter and other services by arrangement; will hold maildrop packages (be sure to put c/o Fine Lodging on box); shower without stay $3; no alcohol ▪ Slatington Diner ▪ Mama's Pizza ▪ Corner Store (good for short-term resupply, deli) ▪ Horner's Laundry (open 7 days) ▪ pharmacy ▪ bank w/ATM. Services in Walnutport (see below) are less than a mile from Slatington across bridge.

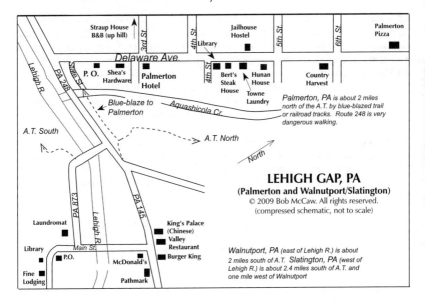

LEHIGH GAP, PA
(Palmerton and Walnutport/Slatington)
© 2009 Bob McCaw. All rights reserved.
(compressed schematic, not to scale)

Lehig Gap, PA 248/PA145 📖 *p. 56* ... ***Notice!*** PA 248 is a very busy highway with narrow shoulders. Palmerton may be reached on foot by the well marked blue blaze 0.1 miles north of PA 248 (not recommended after 4PM, when the road is gated and there is no access to State St.) or by jumping the guardrail on PA 248 and following the railroad tracks by the river into town. ☾ *left 2m*–to **PALMERTON, PA 18071**: *Post office hours:* Mon-Fri 8:30am-5pm, Sat 8:30am-noon; 610-826-2286. ***"Jailhouse hostel"***—city allows hikers to stay in basement room of borough hall (the old police station at 443 Delaware Ave.), no charge; one-night limit unless under a doctor's care; hikers on foot only, no bicycle or automobile assisted hikers. Check in before 4:30pm at the clerk's window (after 4:30pm, check in at nearby police station or flag down officer on patrol), photo ID required. Hot showers are available. Cooking must be done outside the building. No pets are allowed inside, and dogs cannot run free under the town leash law. The hostel has a 10pm curfew, strictly enforced. No alcohol or drunken behavior permitted on premises. ***Lodging***—The Straup House B&B (610-826-5430; <*www.thestrauphousebb. com*>): $50 up, no pets; call ahead for availability and directions.▪ Palmerton Hotel (610-826-5454): rooms are generally rented monthly, but may be available for about $65 if one is vacant. No pets, restaurant in hotel. ***Places to eat***—Bert's Steak House: home-style meals, cheese steaks, soups; open 7 days ▪ Palmerton Pizza: pizza, subs; open 7 days ▪ Simply Something: luncheon, wraps, *etc.* ▪ Hunan House: Chinese eat-in or takeout, open 7 days. ***Groceries***—Country Harvest Supermarket: good for long-term resupply; open 7 days. ***Other services***—Towne Laundry: open 7 days, closed holidays ▪ banks w/ATMs ▪ pharmacy ▪ Palmerton Hardware: Coleman by the gallon ▪ hospital ▪ library. ☽ *right 2.0m*–to **Walnutport, PA 18088** (historic Lehigh Canal area)**:** King's Palace, AYCE at lunch ▪ Valley Restaurant, pizza ▪ Burger King ▪ Pathmark Foods, good for long-term resupply ▪ bank w/ATM.

Little Gap 📖 *p. 56* ... ⟳ *left 1.5m*–to village of Little Gap: Roth House B&B (4285 Little Gap Road, Palmerton, PA 18071, 610-824-5341, <*www.bbonline.com/pa/roth*>): call for rates, will hold maildrop packages, ride to and from trail if someone available, no pets ▪ Covered Bridge Inn, dinner 7 days, lunch on weekends ➲ *right 1.5m*–to **Danielsville, PA 18038**: Filbert B&B (610-428-3300; <*www.filbertbnb.com*>): $75 up, includes hearty breakfast and ride to and from trail at Little Gap (rides to other trailhead for fee), with stop at store and post office; laundry service available; local Italian restaurant delivers ▪ drive-in restaurant ▪ small grocery store, good for short-term resupply.

Smith Gap Road 📖 *p. 56* ... ⟳ *left 1.0m*–to Blue Mountain Dome: where you can usually get water from an outside spigot at rear of the house, free cold shower outside, pets welcome; overnight stay with permission; if home, owner John "Mechanical Man" Stempa will give ride back to the Trail. John is very active with the local hiking clubs and blazed the trail to Stempa spring.

Wind Gap, PA33 📖 *p. 56* ... ⟳ *left 0.1m*–to the Gateway Motel (610-863-4959): $55S/$65D, pets $7 extra, friendly owner will often give rides to nearby restaurants and laundry; sodas available inside, hikers invited to fill water bottles. ➲ *right 1.6m*–to **Wind Gap, PA 18091**: *Post office hours:* Mon-Fri 8:30am-5pm, Sat 8:30am-12pm; 610-863-6206. Post office on right 0.8 mile from A.T., business district with services listed below is about a mile beyond the post office. *Lodging*—Travel Inn (610-863-4146): rates vary, best to call ahead, pets generally $10 extra; located near business district. *Places to eat*—Wind Gap Diner ▪ Three Brothers Pizza ▪ The Beer Stein ▪ Hong Kong Restaurant (for takeout orders, call locally 863-9309) ▪ Four Seasons Pizzeria ▪ One-Stop Italian Deli & Bakery ▪ J&R's Smokehouse Restaurant: steaks, ribs, seafood ▪ Arby's ▪ McDonald's ▪ Burger King. *Groceries*—Giant Food Store, good for long-term resupply; open 7 days, year-round. *Other Services*—laundromats ▪ bank w/ATM.

NWS Wind Chill Chart
updated with 2001 re-calibration

National Weather Service	Temperature (°F)												
Wind (mph)	**35**	**30**	**25**	**20**	**15**	**10**	**5**	**0**	**-5**	**-10**	**-15**	**-20**	**-25**
5	31	25	19	13	7	1	-5	-11	-16	-22	-28	-34	-40
10	27	21	15	9	3	-4	-10	-16	-22	-28	-35	-41	-47
15	25	19	13	6	0	-7	-13	-19	-26	-32	-39	-45	-51
20	24	17	11	4	-2	-9	-15	-22	-29	-35	-42	-48	-55
25	23	16	9	3	-4	-11	-17	-24	-31	-37	-44	-51	-58
30	22	15	8	1	-5	-12	-19	-26	-33	-39	-46	-53	-60
35	21	14	7	0	-7	-14	-21	-27	-34	-41	-48	-55	-62
40	20	13	6	-1	-8	-15	-22	-29	-36	-43	-50	-57	-64

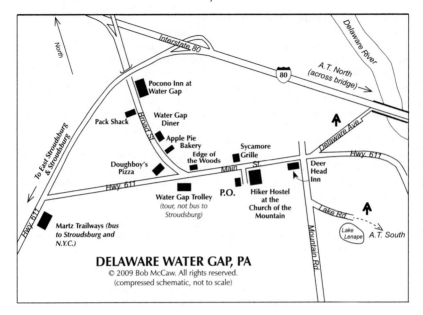

DELAWARE WATER GAP, PA

© 2009 Bob McCaw. All rights reserved.
(compressed schematic, not to scale)

DELAWARE WATER GAP, PA 18327 📖 *p. 57* ... *Post office hours:* Mon-Fri 8:30am-noon and 1pm-4:45pm, Sat 8:30am-11:30am; 570-476-0304. Delaware Water Gap is a small village with an outfitter, restaurants, and places to stay. Groceries and other services are available in downtown Stroudsburg, a large town several miles away. The Pack Shack runs a shuttle service once a day to Stroudsburg and bus service is available (see below). Locals recommend using Pocono Cab (570-424-2800). ***Hostel***—provided by the Presbyterian Church of the Mountain (Pastor Karen Nickels, 570-476-0345) and operated year-round for long-distance hikers only (not for group use, and long-distance hikers with vehicle support should use area motels or campgrounds). The hostel has a basement room with bunks, hot shower and towels, and a sitting room. If crowded, hikers may use the Matthew Kolb Shelter behind annex or pitch tents on the church lawn. A $5 donation is requested for the second night; two night limit; stay beyond two nights only with permission of pastor. Sunday worship service is at 10am, and you are welcome in hiker attire. Free Sunday afternoon concerts (often jazz) are held in June-August. Friendly "Pastor Karen" is available to help with any problems you may be having (with one exception, she won't pick up mail, so don't call ahead to ask, and do not send mail to the church). The church piano is available for musical hikers missing the ivories; when office open, internet access is available for $1 per half hour. Note that no alcohol or alcoholic behavior is permitted on premises; if you think you might need help, an Alcoholics Anonymous chapter meets in the church's activity building at 8pm on Wed and Sun evenings. ***Lodging***—Pocono Inn at Water Gap (570-476-0000): $69 weekends, $10 extra for pets, $10 extra on weekends. ***Places to eat***—Water Gap Diner: varied menu (American, Italian, Greek, seafood, burgers, homemade bread, pies), daily specials; open 7 days, open 24 hours (summer) ▪ Doughboy's Pizza ▪ Sycamore Grille, upscale ▪ Apple Pie Bakery, popular with hikers, offers baked goods, fruit, ice cream, and light meals. **Outfitter/stove fuel**—Edge of the Woods Outfitters (570-421-6681): full-service backpacking store, Coleman and denatured alcohol by the ounce, organic trail foods ▪ The Pack Shack (570-424-8533): primary business is canoe trips, but offers some hiker items. Shuttles available once a day to Stroudsburg and to other points by arrangement. **Points of interest**—The Deer Head Inn: elegant rooms, fine dining and recognized as a regional jazz center ▪ The Water Gap Trolley: a one-hour ride that touches the scenic and historic points and others sites of interest. **Nearby town**—Stroudsburg, PA: large, but easy to navigate because most services are available in the center, including: Pocono Inne Town (570-421-2200); $98 most weekdays, in town center, no pets ▪ Budget Host Inn (570-424-1771); moderately priced for the area, call for rates, guest laundry, easy walk to center, no pets ▪ many restaurants ▪ small shopping mall at 3rd and McConnell Streets with a Shop-Rite Supermarket (good for long-term resupply, deli; open 7 days, in-store ATM). ▪ Dunkelberger's Sports Outfitters (570-421-7950) with a backpacking section ▪ Main St. Laundromat between 5th and 6th. Stroud Mall, outside center, is accessible by bus. **Local bus service**—The "Pocono Pony" bus runs weekdays every two hours from the Martz Bus Terminal, goes to many points in Stroudsburg. Fare $1.25. For schedule and route information, see <www.gomcta.com> or the bulletin board at the church hostel.

Sunfish Pond 📖 *p. 57* ... the first glacial pond encountered going north on the A.T. In the late 1960s, local power companies were prevented from using it industrially by the "Save Sunfish Pond" campaign, an early environmentalist cause. Today, the pond is a popular spot with hikers and often crowded on sunny weekends. Swimming is not allowed. Camping in Worthington State Forest, roughly the southernmost 8 miles of the A.T. in New Jersey, is only allowed at the Backpacker Campsite south of Sunfish Pond.

Camp Mohican Road 📖 *p. 57* ... ◖ *left 0.3m*–(at dirt road with small A.T. sign and hiker register) to Mohican Outdoor Center (50 Camp Mohican Rd., Blairstown, NJ 07825; 908-362-5670), operated by AMC as a retreat center for groups. Thru-hikers can stay overnight in a cabin with bunk for $25 per person including shower and towel, tent sites free for thru-hikers only. Shower and towel $3 if tenting. Camp store has snack items and soda, Coleman and denatured alcohol by the ounce; will hold maildrop packages (must be sent UPS). Deli section open June 1 to September 1. Weekends are often filled to capacity with groups, so your best bet for bunk space is during the week, but camping on the lawn is always available. Check in at entrance lodge before 6pm or call ahead to make other arrangements, water is available at lodge from spigot near garage across road.

Blue Mtn Lakes Road 📖 *p. 58* ... *On A.T.*–water pump to the left on south side of road; no camping is allowed from 0.5 miles south of the road to a point just south of the side trail to Buttermilk Falls. In the past, the YMCA let hikers stay in a nearby lean-to on National Park Service property. The YMCA, however, no longer operates here and the Park Service advises that the facility is no longer maintained.

Culvers Gap, US206 📖 *p. 58* ... *Near A.T.*–Gyp's Tavern (pizza, short-order menu; overlooking Kittatinny Lake) welcomes hikers ▪ Kevin's Steakhouse, very hiker friendly. Burgers, steak and seafood $10-$25, open 4-10 Wed-Sun ▪ Joe to Go Cafe ◖ *left 1.9m*–to Forest Motel (973-948-5456) $50S/$60D, pets $20 extra ▪ Fratelli's Italian

Restaurant ➲ *right 2.5m*–to Cobman Ridge Motel (973-948-3459) $60S/$65D, no pets. *Also right on US206*—Blue Ribbon, bar and grill (0.6m) ▪ Jumboland Diner (1.2m) ▪ Dale's Market: good for long-term resupply (1.6m).

NJ23, High Point State Park 📖 *p. 59* ... *On A.T.*-High Point State Park (1480 State Route 23, Sussex, N.J. 07461; 973-875-4800): headquarters building with information desk, rest rooms, outside water fountain and pay phone; will hold maildrop packages; open 7 days, 9am-4pm, year around. About a mile from the Trail, the park offers swimming in Lake Marcia, hot showers, concession stand (open 10am-6pm summer months), a picnic area, and High Point monument. Campsites available at Sawmill Pond, $20/night. Rangers here are very friendly to thru-hikers. ➲ *right 1.3m*–to High Point Country Inn (1328 Rt. 23, Wantage, NJ 07461; 973-702-1860): $79S $89D; prices include four shuttles, *e.g.*, shuttle to and from Trail and to and from grocery store, restaurant, or any point within seven miles of inn; call for pickup from the park; laundry $7; will hold maildrop packages; deli and pizza shuttle available. ◖ *left 4m*–to I-84 interchange near Port Jervis, NY. Comfort Inn (845-856-6611) ▪ ShopRite Supermarket ▪ fast-food restaurants ▪ Short Line bus to New York City, schedules at <*www.coachusa.com*>.

Trail to Murray property 📖 *p. 59* ... ◖ *left 0.2m*—look for "water" sign on Goldsmith Road; water available from well, tenting, outside shower. The outbuilding which had served as a "shelter" is closed as of last report.

Lott Road 📖 *p. 59* ... small man-made pond on north side. ◖ *left 0.5m* passing a cemetery to **UNIONVILLE, NY 10988**: *Post office hours:* Mon-Fri 8am-11:30am and 1pm-5pm, Sat 9am-noon; 845-726-3535. *Services*—Back Track Inn: burgers, pizza, salads; open noon-2am, 7 days; and "hostel" (which is really a converted storage room, very narrow bunks are actually shelves) for $3 per person, no rest room facilities when inn closed, very basic; no credit cards ▪ Horler's General Store: good for long-term resupply, deli, baked goods; open 7 days ▪ water fountain and portatoilet in village park during summer months; hikers invited to camp overnight in park (get permission at the friendly town office or call 845-726-3681 to register) ▪ Dick Ludwick, a great friend of hikers, offers laundry, shower, and warm hospitality at "The Out House" to all hikers who end their day at Unionville. Call 845-726-3894 for directions. ▪ outside pay phone near post office.

County Road 565 📖 *p. 60* ... ◖ *left 1.1m*–to **GLENWOOD, NJ 07418**: *Post office hours:* Mon-Fri 7:30am-5pm, Sat 10am-12pm; 973-764-2616; Apple Valley Inn (973-764-3735) call for rates; includes breakfast; shuttles to and from nearby A.T. trailheads for guests only; will hold maildrop packages for guests only (call for permission to send) ▪ Pochuck Farmer's Market: produce in season, deli, outside pay phone; open 7 days.

NJ94 📖 *p. 60* ... ◖ *left 0.1m*–to Heaven Hill Farm with ice cream, baked goods, fresh fruits and produce in season, honey, jams, sodas, and good well water; open daily; drop gear at hiker area with picnic table in back. ➲ *right 1.4m*–to Appalachian Motel (973-764-6070): $69S $89D, pets $20 extra, $10 higher weekends. Call for pickup from trailheads at NJ94 or County 565 ➲ *right 2.4m*–to **VERNON, NJ 07462**: *Post office hours:* Mon-Fri 8:30am-5pm, Sat 9:30am-12:30pm; 973-764-9056. *Hostel*—St. Thomas Episcopal Church (973-764-7506): hikers sleep on floor, hot shower, laundry on premises, refrigerator, microwave (and kitchen facilities with permission), internet, no pets; $10 donation; 12 hikers maximum; operates Apr-Sept but thru-hikers not usually turned away other months. **Note**—If the hostel is full, hikers may camp overnight behind the firehouse in the center of town, with water and rest rooms available during the summer months. **Services**—several restaurants, pizzerias ▪ A&P 24-Hour Supermarket: good for long-term resupply; open 7 days ▪ laundromat 1.2 miles outside town on County 644 ▪ bank w/ATM ▪ natural food store.

Warwick Turnpike 📖 *p. 61* ... ☛ *left 2.6m*–ShopRite Supermarket in Warwick, NY, good for long-term resupply. It is easier to get to the supermarket by this road than by NY17A.

Greenwood Lake Vista Trail 📖 *p. 61* ... ☛ *right 1.1m*–shortest route to **Greenwood Lake, NY 10925**: *Post office hours:* Mon-Fri 8-5, Sat 9-12; 845-477-7328. **Lodging**—Anton's on the Lake (7 Waterstone Rd., Greenwood Lake, NY 10925; 845-477-0010): near village; hiker rate $75S/D, higher on Sat; laundry available; will hold maildrop packages; call for pickup from trail at 17A, slackpacking available; no pets or smoking ▪ Breezy Point Inn (620 Jersey Ave., Greenwood Lake, NY 10925; 845-477-8100) 0.5 miles south of village on lake, $85D, restaurant, live music Fri/Sat. **Other services**—Market Basket Deli: good for short-term resupply ▪ hardware store ▪ several restaurants ▪ library

NY17A 📖 *p. 61* ... ☛ *left 0.1m*–to Bellvale Farms: homemade ice cream, picnic tables, water from hose. ☛ *right 2.0m*–to **Greenwood Lake, NY 10925** (*see listing above)* ☛ *left 1.6m*–to **Bellvale, NY 10912**: grocery store (good for short-term resupply). ☛ *left 3.5m*–to **Warwick, NY 10990**: a very nice town, but incoveniently spread out. *Post office hours:* Mon-Fri 8:30-5, Sat 9-4; 845-986-0271. **Lodging**—Warwick Motel (845-986-6656, on 17A about halfway from A.T. to town): newly remodeled after fire, $79 up, pool, continental breakfast. ▪ Frank's Pizza ▪ ShopRite Supermarket (left 2 miles at intersection of NY 17A and NY 94, see Warwick Turnpike, above) ▪ laundromats ▪ library ▪ bank w/ATM.

NY17 📖 *p. 62* ... site of the nation's first nature trail specifically denoted as such, constructed in the early 1900s about a mile south of where the A.T. crosses road. *On A.T.-emergency phone.* ☛ *right 2.1m*–to **Southfields, NY 10975**: *Post office hours:* Mon-Fri 8am-noon and 1pm-5pm, Sat 8:30am-11:30am; 845-351-2628 ▪ Tuxedo Motel (845-351-4747): $45S/$50D, no pets ▪ Corner Deli/Pizzeria: pizza, sandwiches. ☛ *left 2.0m*–to Harriman train station, easiest nearby access to New York City, see <www.njtransit.com> for schedules. ☛ *left 3.4m*–to **Harriman, NY**: American Budget Inn (845-783-3211) $66S/$70D, pets OK ▪ Americas Best Value Inn (845-928-2266) $69S/D, higher weekends, no pets ▪ laundromat ▪ Two large mall-like areas with Wal-Mart (good for long-term resupply) ▪ Chili's ▪ Wendy's. Note: post office in Arden, NY has closed and there is nothing else there.

Harriman State Park 📖 *p. 62* ... New York's second-largest park, encompassing 46,000 beautiful wooded acres; entered when you pass over New York State Thruway. The flora and fauna in the park are different from any other section on the A.T., and the terrain has many small ascents and descents.

Bear Mountain State Park 📖 *p. 63* ... part of the Palisades Interstate Park system, a pioneering outdoor recreation project, a state effort that complemented federal efforts in the early part of the twentieth century. The land for Bear Mountain State Park was donated by the Harriman family. The first sections of footpath specifically built for the Appalachian Trail project were constructed in this park in 1922-23. Although much of the original route has been rerouted over the years, you are often literally walking on Trail history in this area. The park is mostly undeveloped, but there are vending machines on top of Bear Mountain and concession stands near Hessian Lake.

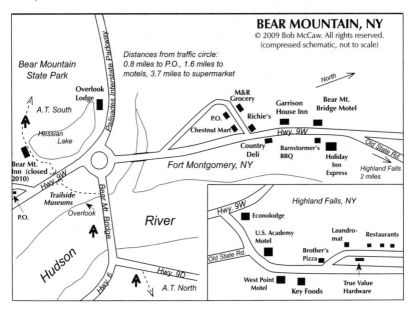

Bear Mountain, NY 10911 📖 *p. 63* ... The post office is open limited hours, the one in nearby Fort Montgomery is probably better for mail drops. Short Line bus to New York, see <*www.coachusa.com*> for schedules. ***Lodging in Bear Mt. State Park***—The Bear Mountain Inn is being renovated and will probably not reopen in 2010 ▪ Overlook Lodge (845-786-2731), in state park near traffic circle, $110S/$139D, continental breakfast. ***Trailside Museums & Wildlife Center***—the A.T. runs through this facility. Built in 1927, it features the nation's oldest continuously used nature trail, featuring local fauna and flora, and a small zoo. Admission is free for thru-hikers. At 124 feet above sea level, the path in front of the bear exhibit is the lowest point on the A.T. The Trailside Museum closes at 5PM, and no pets are allowed. If you arrive when the Museum is closed or are hiking with a dog, follow Hwy. 9W around the Trailside Museum between Hessian Lake and the Bear Mountain Bridge.

Hudson River, Bear Mountain Bridge 📖 *p. 63* ... The A.T. emerges from the Trailside Museum just west of the Bear Mountain Bridge. Facilities in Fort Montgomery and Highland Falls are reached by going a few hundred feet to a traffic circle, then north on

US 9W. ◖ *left 0.8m*–to **FORT MONTGOMERY, NY 10922**: *Post office hours:* Mon-Fri 8:30am-1pm, 2:30-5pm, Sat 8:30am-noon; 845-446-8459. *Near post office:* Country Deli ▪ convenience stores ▪ Richie's Little Place: dinner only. ◖ *left 1.2m on 9W*–Garrison House Inn (915 Route 9W, Fort Montgomery, NY 10922; 845-446-2322; *<www.thegar-risonhouse.com>*): B&B style accommodations, $50 hiker rate for whichever rooms are available, generally shared bath, continental breakfast, will hold maildrop packages. ◖ *left 1.8m on 9W*–Bear Mountain Bridge Motel (845-446-2472): $65S/$69D (rates may increase a bit on weekends), no pets; hiker friendly, local rides possible if time permits ▪ Holiday Inn Express (845-446-4277): $110S/D (special hiker rate, must carry this book), no pets, laundry on premises, will hold maildrop packages (please send UPS or FedEx) for guests ▪ Barnstormer's BBQ ▪ The Bagel Cafe: open 7 days ◖ *left 3.7 miles*– to **Highland Falls, NY 10928**: Key Food Marketplace (good for long-term resupply) ▪ Econolodge (845-446-9400) ▪ West Point Motel (845-446-4180) ▪ US Academy Motel (845-446-2021) ▪ laundromat ▪ restaurants ▪ bank w/ATM ▪ pharmacy ▪ library north of town. West Point and the U.S. Military Academy (with visitor center: hourly tours 10am-3:30pm, $6 per person) is two miles farther.

US9/NY403 📖 *p. 64* ... On *A.T.*–Appalachian Market, convenience store. ➲ *right 0.7m*–to The Stadium Sports Bar with burgers, wings, lots of sports memorabilia. ➲ *right 4.5m*–to **Peekskill, NY 10566**. Facilities in Peekskill exist, but are far from the trail and spread out over a large area. This is not an easy area for hikers to navigate and is not the best option to get to New York City. Super Stop & Shop supermarket is 1.4 miles east of center of town.

Graymoor entrance road 📖 *p. 64* ... ➲ *right 0.2m*–to Graymoor Spiritual Life Center (845-424-3671): home of the Franciscan Friars of the Atonement and birthplace of the Christian Unity movement in America. Thru-hikers have been welcomed here for decades. Hikers may use the campsite/shelter at the ball field, with water, cold shower, and covered picnic pavilion free of charge. Pizza delivery menu is posted. Directions: After crossing US9, go 0.5 mile on A.T. to the second paved road (entrance road), turn right, then bear left at fork.

NY301 📖 *p. 64* ... ➲ *right 0.8m*–to Clarence Fahnestock State Park: check in at park office, then go 0.2 mile to campground; tent sites $15 (fee **may** be waived for one night for thru-hikers), hot showers, and rest rooms; or at park entrance, turn left 0.3 mile to free Canopus Lake swimming area with beach, concession stand (open late June-Labor Day), rest rooms, hot showers (some find them cold), and picnic tables. No pets are allowed on the beach or in the picnic area.

NY52 📖 *p. 65* ... ➲ *right 0.4m* (then 0.1 mile on side road)–to Mountain Top Market with limited groceries, daily luncheon specials, sandwiches, subs, ice cream, public telephone, outside water spigot and a hiker register; open 7 days. Danny's Pizzeria II next to market.

NY55 📖 *p. 65* ... ◖ *left 1.6m*–pizzeria, convenience store. ◖ *left 2.6m*–to **Poughquag, NY 12570**: *Post office hours:* Mon-Fri 8:305, Sat 8:30-12; 845-724-4763. Pine Grove Motel (845-724-5151): $65S/$70D, no pets ◖ *left 3.6m*–Stop & Shop Supermarket (good for long-term resupply). ▪ There are several restaurants between the motel and supermarket; Beekman Square Restaurant has been recommended.

County Road 20/West Dover Road 📖 *p. 65* … On A.T.—large oak tree at roadside is known as the Dover Oak, may be the largest tree on the A.T. Both this tree and the Keffer Oak in Virginia are majestic trees worthy of the claim, and reminders of what the forest was like about 350 years ago. ➜ *right 3.1m*–to **PAWLING, NY 12564** (see NY22, below).

Appalachian Trail Station 📖 *p. 65* … On A.T.–just before NY22, weekends only, trains go to and from Grand Central Station. Schedules available by calling 1-800-METRO-INFO (nearest public pay phone at Tony's Deli, below) or at <www.mta.info>. Weekday service is available to and from Pawling, below.

Table of Magnetic Declinations

The magnetic north pole is located in northern Canada but is not in the same location as the geographic North Pole. This means that your compass, when it points to "north," is not necessarily pointing to true north (*i.e.*, the north shown on your map). The angular difference between magnetic north and geographic north is called magnetic declination. A line of 0° declination in the U.S. runs just east of the Mississippi River. When east of this 0° line, the declination is a negative number. To correct a magnetic compass reading to true geographic north, subtract the declination value for your location from the magnetic north reading at your location (and remember that subtracting a negative number is the same as adding the declination value to the magnetic north reading). This gives the true north heading. Listed below are some declination values for sample locations along the A.T. from Georgia to Maine. As you can see, the magnetic declination is minimal in Georgia, but becomes substantial in Maine. Adjust your compass readings accordingly!

Springer Mtn .... -4.19	Waynesboro .... -9.15	Manchester Ctr ..... -14.92
Fontana Dam .... -4.68	Harpers Ferry .... -10.38	Hanover .... -15.59
Hot Springs .... -5.60	Duncannon .... -11.25	Mt. Washington .... -16.43
Erwin .... -5.92	Del Water Gap .... -12.77	Gorham .... -16.50
Damascus .... -6.53	Bear Mountain ...... -13.64	Rangeley .... -17.03
Pearisburg .... -7.53	Kent .... -14.11	Monson .... -17.29
Troutville .... -8.22	Cheshire .... -14.62	Mt. Katahdin .... -17.78

NY22 📖 *p.65* … ➜ *right 0.5m*–to Tony's Deli with some groceries, sandwiches and subs, ice cream, sodas, hot coffee, and picnic tables out front, will fill water bottles for hikers; open 7 days. A public telephone and soda machine are available outside. ➜ *right 2.4m*–to village of **PAWLING, NY 12564**: *Post office hours:* Mon-Fri 8:30am-5pm, Sat 8:30-12:30; 845-855-2669. Note: due to budgetary cutbacks, there is no swimming at Murrow Park and hikers have reported that overnight stays are no longer allowed. **Services in the village**–Mama's Pizza ▪ Great Wall Chinese Takeout ▪ small farmer's market with fresh fruit and veggies open during summer months ▪ laundromat: open 7 days ▪ pharmacy ▪ banks w/ATM ▪ Pawling Cycle & Sports (845-855-9866): water filters, Coleman and denatured alcohol by the ounce; closed Mon. ▪ trains to New York, see *<www.mta.info>* for schedules. ***Supermarket***—Hannaford's supermarket about 2 miles south of Pawling on NY22. ☏ *left 2.2m*–to Duchess Motor Lodge (845-832-6400): $65S/D, laundry service available for guests only $5, no pets.

Hoyt Road or CT55 📖 *p. 66* ... ☏ *left 3.3m*–to **Wingdale, NY 12594**. Just north of intersection of NY55 and US22: laundromat ▪ restaurants ▪ pizzeria ▪ Wingdale Supermarket: good for long-term resupply ▪ bank w/ATM. Dutchess Motor Lodge (see above) is 1.4 miles south of this point. CT55 is probably an easier hitch.

Schaghticoke Road/Bulls Bridge Road 📖 *p. 66* ... ➲ *right 0.2m*–across an early 1800s covered bridge at a site where George Washington crossed, to Bull Bridge Country Store: good for short-term resupply, fresh fruit and produce in season, outside telephone; open 7 days; friendly owner will fill water bottles ▪ restaurant.

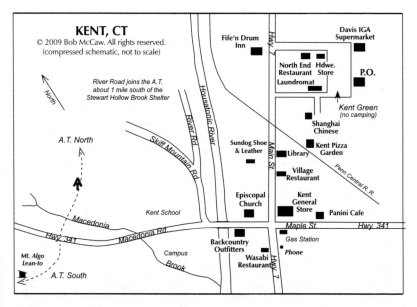

CT341 📖 *p. 67* ... ➲ *right 0.5m*–to **KENT, CT 06757**: *Post office hours:* Mon-Fri 8am-1pm and 2pm-5pm, Sat 8:30am-12:30pm; 860-927-3435; an upscale New England village with lots of activity on weekends. ***Lodging***—Fife'n Drum Inn (860-927-3509): special rates for hikers $95 up weekdays (up to two people; add $28 weekends), pets outside only, possible shuttle back to Trail; in the inn, restaurant with award-winning wine list; closed Tues (call ahead for Tues stay) ▪ Several expensive B&Bs lie north of town on US 7. ***Places to eat***—North End Restaurant: pizza, subs, dinner menu; open 7 days ▪ Kent Pizza Garden: pizza, grinders, charcoal-pit-cooked foods, vegetarian dishes; open 7 days ▪ Village Restaurant: casual, varied inexpensive menu ▪ Shanghai Chinese Restaurant: eat-in or take-out; open 7 days ▪ Panini Cafe: breakfast, soups, salads, ice cream; open 7 days ▪ Wasabi Chinese/Japanese Restaurant. ***Groceries***—Davis IGA Supermarket:

good for long-term resupply, deli, bakery; open 7 days ▪ Kent General Store: good for short-term resupply, sandwiches to go. **Outfitters/stove fuel**—Backcountry Outfitters (5 Bridge St., Kent, CT 06757; 860-927-3377): full-service outfitter with gear and clothing, Coleman and denatured alcohol by the ounce, other fuels; will hold maildrop packages (UPS/FedEx only, do not mail packages); information about shuttles to area trailheads available at desk; open 7 days. ▪ Sundog Shoe and Leather (25 N. Main St. in Kent Town Center; 860-927-0009) full ranger of footwear, open 7 days, 10% hiker discount. **Other services**—laundromat ▪ bank w/ATM **Note**—The rector of St. Andrews Episcopal Church, located at the intersection with US7 as you enter town on CT341, has let thru-hikers tent on the lawn in July and August if the facilities are not being used for church functions; get permission from pastor before camping.

CT4 📖 p. 67 ... ➲ right 0.9m–to **CORNWALL BRIDGE, CT 06754**: Post-office hours: Mon-Fri 8am-1pm and 2pm-5pm, Sat 9am-12:30pm; 860-672-6710. **Services**— Hitching Post Motel (860-672-6219): $65S/$75D (weekends $95S/D and up), laundry $5 per load, pets $5 extra ▪ Baird's General Store: good for short-term resupply, deli, sandwiches and grinders to go, take-out breakfast, outside public telephone; open 7 days ▪ Housatonic River Outfitters (860-672-1010): basic gear and clothing items, Coleman and denatured alcohol by the ounce, other fuels ▪ Cornwall Package Store: owned by Richard and Patty Bramley, hospitable people who invite you to stop and sign their hikers' register, the latter a tradition many thru-hikers find refreshing; closed Sun; outside water spigot available when store is closed. **Note**—Ask about the history of the bridge at the grocery or package store.

Pine Knob Loop Trail 📖 p. 67 ... ➲ right 1m–to Housatonic Meadows State Park: campsites $26, showers, swimming, public pay phone; open mid-April-Dec.

West Cornwall Road 📖 p. 67 ... ➲ right 2.2m–to **West Cornwall, CT 06796**: Wandering Moose Restaurant: family-style meals, sandwiches, closed Mon. ☾ left 4.6m–to **Sharon, CT 06069**: Sharon Motor Lodge (860-364-0036): $75S/D (must ask for hiker rate), no pets ▪ Trotta's Supermarket: good for long-term resupply, open 7 days ▪ laundromat: open 7 days ▪ Twin Oaks Cafe ▪ bank w/ATM.

Housatonic River/US7 📖 p. 68 ... The A.T. goes left on Warren Turnpike at school offices just after you cross the Housatonic River, or you can go: ➲ right 0.2m–(continue on US7, crossing over railroad tracks) to the Mountainside Cafe (860-824-7886), which is closed as of this writing, but may reopen by summer. The Mohawk Trail across from cafe leads 0.2 mile back to A.T.

Iron Bridge over Housatonic River 📖 p. 68 ... a classic from the Berlin Iron Bridge Company; at northern end of the bridge, 300 feet to left, is picnic area, privy, but no water. ➲ right 0.5m (go right, then left under railroad bridge, then right)–to **FALLS VILLAGE, CT 06031**: Post office hours: Mon-Fri 8:30am-1pm and 2pm-5pm, Sat 8:30am-noon; 860-824-7781: Toymakers Cafe: moderately-priced meals, outdoor picnic tables, free camping with permission; closed Mon-Wed but owners live on property and like hikers, so knock on upstairs back door (ask for Annie or Greg, or call 860-824-8169), they may open up for sandwiches and cold drinks; outside spigot for water anytime. Also in the village, bank w/ATM and outside telephone.

Lower Cobble Road 📖 *p. 68* ... ☾ *left 0.5m (from intersection of US 44 and Lower Cobble Road)*–to **SALISBURY, CT 06068**: *Post office hours:* Mon-Fri 8am-1pm and 2pm-5pm, Sat 9am-noon; 860-435-5072; the quintessential New England town with white-steepled church and shopping common, neat and compact and easy to get to everything by walking. *Services*—White Hart Inn (860-435-0030): $175 and up (hiker discount no longer available), no pets; tavern and restaurant ▪ Maria McCabe (4 Grove Street, 860-435-0593), opens her home to thru-hikers year-round, $35 per person includes shower, pets must be kept outside on porch; no credit cards (cash only), no work for stay; maildrop packages held for guests only, trips to laundromat and around town ▪ LaBonne's Market: good for long-term resupply, deli with sandwiches and grinders, full-service bakery, hot meals; open 7 days ▪ The Roast: specialty coffees, baked goods, homemade specialties ▪ bank w/ATM ▪ pharmacy ▪ The Auto Shop (near center of town) has Coleman fuel and stove alcohol. ☾ *left 2.5m*–(by continuing 2 miles beyond Salisbury on US44) to **Lakeville, CT 06031**: several restaurants ▪ bank with ATM ▪ laundromat. *Note*—if you continue 500 feet on Lower Cobble Road (where A.T. northbound leaves road) to St. Mary's Cemetery, water is available from spigot in front of large stone cross during warm-weather months.

MA41 📖 *p. 69* ... ☾ *left 1.2m*–to **SOUTH EGREMONT, MA 01258**: *Post office hours:* Mon-Fri 8:15-4pm, Sat 9-11:30; 413-528-1571. *Services*—The Egremont Inn (413-528-2111): $75S/D hiker rate (must arrive on foot, shuttles available to trailheads) weekdays, rates higher on weekends, breakfast included; inn's restaurant open Wed-Sun; pets allowed, $25 extra, subject to restrictions ▪ Country Market; good for short-term resupply ▪ Mom's Country Cafe.

US7 📖 *p. 69* ... Services are spread out along US7, with groceries on south side of Great Barrington, 2m north, and motels, restaurants and resupply in a compact area 4.5m north. ☾ *left 0.3m*–Route 7 Grille, dinner ☾ *left 1.8m*–to Big Y supermarket (good for long-term resupply) ▪ Guidos natural and organic foods ▪ Bizalion's Fine Foods ▪ laundromat, open 7 days. ☾ *left 3.1m*–to **GREAT BARRINGTON, MA 01230**: *Post office hours:* Mon-Fri 8:30-4:30, Sat 8:30am-12:30pm; 413-528-3670. Days Inn (372 Main St., Great Barrington, MA 01230; 413-528-3150) hiker rate $69 Sun-Thu subject to availability, weekends $139 and up; no pets ▪ restaurants ▪ Eagle Shoe & Boot Repair: closed Sun ▪ banks. *North of town (about 4.5m from A.T.)*– Monument Mountain Motel (413-528-3272): special rates from $50S $65D on Sun-Thur (weekend and holiday rates considerably higher); pets $20 extra; possible pickup from Trail if someone can break away ▪ Travelodge (413-528-2340): $55S/$60D (much higher weekends), coin laundry on site, continental breakfast, two rooms allow pets, $15 extra ▪ Lantern House Motel (413-528-2350): $55-150 ▪ Holiday Inn Express (877-863-4780) offers 25% discount to hikers, Comfort Inn (413-644-3200) has done the same in the past, but will be under new management in 2010 ▪ several restaurants ▪ Price Chopper Supermarket: good for long-term resupply, open 7 days ▪ laundromat ▪ banks w/ATM. ⊃ *right 3.2m*–to **Sheffield, MA 01257**: The Bridge Restaurant ▪ Gretta's Market and Deli: short-term resupply only ▪ bank (no ATM).

Transportation in the Berkshires—Berkshire Regional Transit Authority (800-292-2782) <*www.berkshirerta.com*> operates commuter bus service serving the Trail towns of Great

Barrington, Dalton, Cheshire, North Adams, Adams, and Williamstown, the peripheral towns of Pittsfield and Lee, and the Berkshire Mall, a large regional shopping center. Buses run Mon-Fri and Sat until 6pm (no Sunday service); fares $1.25 to $5. Drivers cannot make change, flag down bus anywhere you see one.

MA23 📖 *p. 70* ... ◖ *left 1.0m*–to East Mountain Retreat Center (8 Lake Buel Rd., Great Barrington, MA 01230; 413-528-6617): hostel for thru-hikers $10 per night includes shower, laundry $3, will hold UPS/FedEx packages (no mail); open Apr 15-Oct 15 (call for availability other dates); gates close at 10pm and everyone needs to be in camp and quiet by this hour. Directions: Turn left on MA23, go one mile to Lake Buel Road on left, look for obvious sign about 10 feet up road, follow driveway 0.5m to center; shopping area north of Great Barrington is located three miles from center.

Benedict Pond 📖 *p. 70* ... *On A.T.*–a beautiful glacial pond with swimming just off the Trail, or take the blue-blazed Pond Loop Trail 0.5 mile to a swimming area with beach, picnic tables, and a public telephone; tent sites are reservation only in summer.

Main Road 📖 *p. 70* ... first paved road northbounders come to after crossing the wooden bridge over Hop Brook. ◖ *left 0.9m*–to **TYRINGHAM, MA 01264**: *Post office hours:* Mon-Fri 9am-12:30 and 4pm-5:30pm, Sat 8:30am-12:30pm; 413-243-1225; a summer retreat for Mark Twain, among others. *Services*—Cobble View B&B (1-800-467-4136): call ahead for special hiker rates, no pets; sodas, ice cream available; Coleman by the ounce. Thru-hikers no longer have permission to stay in the town's fire pavilion.

Upper Goose Pond Cabin 📖 *p. 70* ... ◖ *left 0.5m*–to the cabin, an enclosed facility with bunk beds, gas stove and cooking utensils, outside privy, nearby swimming area, canoe, and a fireplace for cold nights. Volunteer caretakers (some former thru-hikers) are in residence from Memorial Day to mid-Sept, but only on weekends in autumn. Dontaions appreciated. If no caretaker is on duty, the cabin is locked, but camping is permitted.

US20, Jacob's Ladder Highway 📖 *p. 70* ... ◖ *left 5m*–to **Lee, MA 01238**. The center of Lee, where services are located, is 0.8 miles north of junction of US 20, MA 102 and Mass. Pike. Note: lodging is much higher or unavailable on summer weekends or during special events. *Towards center:* Sunset Motel (413-243-0302): $65 up, no pets • Super 8 (413-243-0143): $85S/$95D, no pets. *North of town:* Rodeway Inn (413-243-0813) $79S/D, no pets. *In center of town:* Price Chopper Supermarket: good for long-term resupply • several restaurants and fast food outlets near motels and in center of town • laundromat • health clinic • Greyhound bus service.

Pittsfield Road 📖 *p. 71* ... also called Washington Mountain Road. ◗ *right 0.1m*–to the home of "Cookie Lady" Marilyn Wiley (47 Washington Mountain Road, Washington, MA 01223; 413-623-5859), who lives on the left, behind the yellow building near the road. Marilyn and her husband Roy have a blueberry farm (ripe berries from July to autumn). An outside water spigot next to the front steps is available for hikers during the summer months. Overnight camping possible (ask first); will hold maildrop packages, but call ahead to make arrangements. Shuttles available from Connecticut to Manchester, Vt.

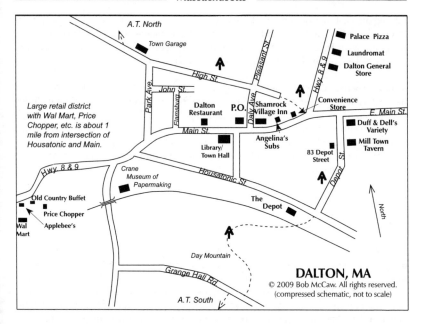

DALTON, MA
© 2009 Bob McCaw. All rights reserved.
(compressed schematic, not to scale)

DALTON, MA 01227 📖 *p. 71* ... *Post office hours:* Mon-Fri 8:30am-4:30pm, Sat 9am-noon; 413-684-0364. *Lodging*—Shamrock Village Inn (413-684-0860): $56S/$62D Sun-Thur (weekend rates about $10 higher), $80 pet deposit refundable ▪ Tom Levardi (83 Depot Street) has a sign in his front yard offering water and sometimes invites hikers to stay overnight; if no one home, water is available from a spigot, and the covered front porch is possibly available on a rainy night (be sure to tidy up any mess you make if you take Tom up on this courtesy). *Places to eat*—Dalton Restaurant: reasonably-priced meals; open Mon-Sat, Sun breakfast only ▪ Palace Pizza: open 7 days ▪ Mill Town Tavern: pizzas, grinders, Italian home-cooked ▪ Angelina's Subs: Italian subs ▪ Juice and Java Coffee Shop ▪ The Depot: restaurant in old train station; American-style food ▪ Duff & Del's Variety: good breakfast, reasonable prices; closed Sun. *Groceries*—Cumberland Farms: convenience store, limited hiker supplies, snacks; open daily ▪ Dalton General Store: eclectic, limited hiker supplies, deli, fruit, pastries; open 7 days. *Other services*—Dalton Laundromat: wash cloth and towel offered to anyone who wants to freshen up; on North Street (Hwy. 8/9 North), 0.3 mile from Trail ▪ bank w/ATM ▪ pharmacy ▪ library: internet access. *West of town*—Large shopping area with Price Chopper, Wal Mart, Applebee's and Old Country Buffet (AYCE) are located west on MA 9, about 1.6 miles from intersection of Park and High Streets or two miles from intersection of MA 8 and MA 9. Pittsfield, MA, 6 miles south on MA8A/9; bus service available.

CHESHIRE, MA 01225 📖 *p. 71* ... *Post-office hours:* Mon-Fri 7:30am-1pm and 2pm-4:30pm, Sat 8:30am-11:30am; 413-743-3184. *Hostels*—Mason Hill Hostel (195 West Mountain Road, 413-743-2492): 1/2 mile from post office, west of intersection of Church

St. and MA 8. Open for 2009 from April 1 through October 31. Two bunk beds in private room in barn each $25; private cabin with porch overlooking Kitchen Brook Gorge with double bed $50S/D; tent sites near Kitchen Brook $15S/D. Rates include shower. Individual services: shower $5; laundry $5; internet access $5. Private full bathroom in barn with tub/shower. Linens and towels included in all fees. Once daily resupply ride to town, and back to trail. Well behaved dogs okay. No drugs or alcohol. Cold drinks available for sale. No maildrop pacakges, please. ▪ St. Mary of the Assumption Catholic Church (413-743-2110): makes limited space available on floor year-round at no charge to hikers (maximum 10 hikers per night); stay limited to one night only, check in between 3:30pm and 8pm, must be out of the building by 9am. When you arrive, use the Father McAuliffe Hall entrance at rear of church, and, immediately upon arrival, sign the guest register and check the list of "house rules." Rest rooms available, but no bathing and no use of kitchen facilities. *Places to eat*—Cobble View Pub and Pizzeria, center of town on MA8 ▪ Bass Water Grille, 0.5 miles south on MA8, closed Mon. ▪ Diane's Twist (near post office) offers grinders, ice cream sundaes, snacks, sodas. *Groceries*—O'Connell's Convenience Store & Shell Station (on MA8 near where A.T. crosses): mini-convenience store, building hiker area with picnic table, water, other amenities; these folks are making a special effort to be hiker-friendly, so let them know what you need in the way of food and supplies. *Other services*—Coleman by the ounce at Reynold's General Store, closed Sun ▪ bank w/ATM. ➲ *right 0.8m–*(on Route 8) to Harbour House Inn B&B (413-743-8959) <*www.harbourhouseinn.com*>: $85 special hiker rate weekdays (weekends usually booked), no pets; laundry; internet access; local shuttles possible. ➲ *right 2.3m–*(on Route 8) to Berkshire Outfitters (413-743-5900; <*www.berkshireoutfitters.com*>): a white water and x-country skiing center with backpacking gear and clothing, Coleman and denatured alcohol by the ounce, other fuels; open 7 days. ➲ *right 4.3m on MA8–*to **Adams, MA**: Big Y Supermarket (good for long-term resupply), laundromat, restaurants. *Nearby towns*—BRTA bus runs to Adams, Pittsfield, and the Berkshire Mall (see information board across street from post office for schedule). Pittsfield is a large town with many services; Berkshire Mall has hundreds of retail stores including EMS (413-445-4967); catch bus on MA8. See information on BRTA on p. 141; no buses on Sunday.

Mt. Greylock 📖 *p. 72* ... *On A.T.–*highest point in Massachusetts, summit features the distinctive War Memorial and Bascom Lodge. Bascom Lodge (413-743-1591,<*www.bascomlodge.net*>): reopened in mid-2009, offers meals and lodging. Bunk beds are $35, private rooms $100 and up. The restaurant is open for B/L/D seven days, prices are moderate considering the altitude.

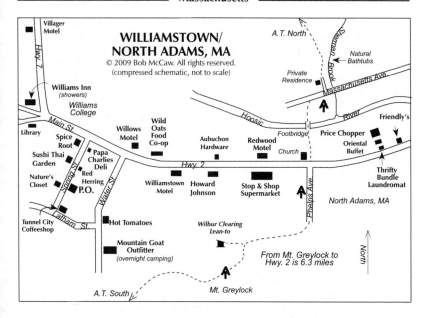

MA2 📖 *p. 72* ... services are spread out for several miles between the two downtown areas of Williamstown and North Adams. ◐ *left 0.3m*–to The Redwood Motel (413-664-4351): $70-150 (weekends higher), pets $30 extra ▪ Stop & Shop Supermarket:good for long-term resupply, pharmacy, bakery, bookstore, deli, banking on premises; open 7 days. ◑ *right 0.7m*–to Price Chopper Supermarket: good for long-term resupply, deli, pharmacy inside, open 7 days ▪ Oriental Buffet ▪ Thrifty Bundle Laundromat: open 7 days ▪ Friendly's: opens for breakfast, ice cream later ▪ pharmacy. ◐ *left 2.6m*–to **WILLIAMSTOWN, MA 01267**: *Post office hours:* Mon-Fri 8:30am-4:30pm, Sat 9am-noon; 413-458-3707; home of Williams College. **Lodging**–moderately priced options are: *Between A.T. and Williamstown*–Willows Motel (413-458-5768): $70S/$75D and up, no pets ▪ Williamstown Motel (413-458-5202): $59 up, weekends $69 up, call for shuttle from trail, two pet rooms, 10% discount in Spice Root restaurant ▪ Howard Johnson Express (413-458-8158): $69 up, internet, continental breakfast, no pets. *Two miles north of Williamstown on US7*–Villager Motel (413-458-4046): $45S/$55D, pets $10 extra. **Services**—*1.5m west of trail*–Colonial Plaza with Aubuchon Hardware, Chinese and Mexican restaurants. *Center of town*–Spice Root (Indian) ▪ Sushi Thai Garden ▪ Papa Charlie's Deli: cafeteria, sandwiches, frozen yogurt; open 7 days ▪ Tunnel City Coffee Shop ▪ Hot Tomatoes Restaurant: primarily pizza ▪ Subway ▪ The Mountain Goat (413-458-8445): full-service outfitter with backpacking gear and clothing, miscellaneous items, Coleman and denatured alcohol by the ounce; open 7 days; information about area transportation is available from staff at checkout counter ▪ Nature's Closet (61 Spring St., Williamstown, MA 01267) <www.naturescloset.net>: outdoor store oriented towards clothing and footwear, will hold maildrop packages; open 7 days. ▪ bank w/ATM ▪ pharmacy ▪ hardware store ▪ health clinic ▪ library ▪ bus service. **Shower only**—Williams Inn allows hikers to shower for $6, check at desk for

information. **Camping**—The Mountain Goat allows overnight camping in the store's back yard with permission, limited to two tents per night, no pets, no fires. **Clark Art Institute**—located 0.5 miles south of the library, famed for its many French-impressionist paintings (thirty by Renoir, for instance), and includes a fine collection of old-masters paintings as well as more modern paintings by Homer, Sargent, and Remington; galleries open Tues-Sun 10am-5pm. ➔ *right 2.5m*–to **North Adams, MA 01247:** *Post office hours:* Mon-Fri 8:30am-4:30pm, Sat 10am-12pm; 413-664-4554. In center: Holiday Inn (413-663-6500); $89 up, internet, laundry, no pets, hiker friendly ▪ shoe repair ▪ restaurants ▪ Big Y supermarket ▪ Massachusetts Museum of Contemporary Art: a project that encompasses a 27-building historic mill complex in North Adams converted into a multi-disciplinary regional center for visual, performing and media arts; $10 admission.

Massachusetts-Vermont border 📖 *p. 73* ... The Long Trail extends the length of Vermont from here to the Canadian border. The nation's first long-distance trail, it was mostly completed by 1921 when the A.T. was proposed. The two trails share the same treadway for more than a hundred miles before the A.T. turns east at Maine Junction just north of US4. The Long Trail is managed by the Green Mountain Club (802-244-7037; <*www.greenmountainclub.org*>). A caretaker program is used to manage heavy-use areas. The following sites will have a caretaker and charge a $5 fee for overnight use from early May through November: Stratton Pond Shelter and Campsite, Peru Peak Shelter, Griffith Lake Campsite, Lula Tye Shelter, and Little Rock Pond Shelter and Tenting Area. If you pay cash at Stratton Pond, Griffith Lake, or Little Rock Pond, you will get a receipt for one-night free stay at each of the other two sites (must be used within 7 days). Camping off-Trail is prohibited for ½ mile either side of the high-use facilities. GMC field personnel request that you camp only at designated sites.

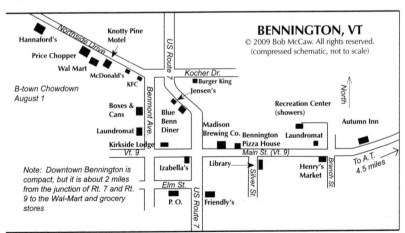

VT9 📖 *p. 73* ... ◐ *left 5.1m*–to **BENNINGTON, VT 05201:** *Post office hours:* Mon-Fri 8am-5pm, Sat 9am-2pm; 802-442-2421; increasingly friendly to thru-hikers in recent years. Free "yellow bicycles" are available from many local businesses to help

hikers get around, and the recreation center at 655 Gage Street offers free showers. *Lodging*—Knotty Pine Motel (130 Northside Dr., Bennington, VT 05201; 802-442-5487): $70S/D up, pets with permission, internet, will hold maildrop packages ▪ Kirkside Motor Lodge (802-447-7596): $69S-$129S/D, generally high on weekends and after Labor Day, no pets ▪ Autumn Inn Motel (802-447-7625): $55S/$65D (weekends add $10); laundry; pets OK; possible shuttle back to Trail if someone available *Places to eat (a partial list)*—South Street Cafe: pastries, sandwiches ▪ Izabella's Eatery: offers vegetarian ▪ Blue Benn Diner, recommended ▪ Madison Brewing Co., sandwiches to dinner ▪ Jensen's Restaurant: breakfast ▪ fast food outlets near intersection of Northside Drive and US7 ▪ Friendly's ▪ Bennington Pizza House. *Other services*—Price Chopper Supermarket and Hannaford's Superstore: both good for long-term resupply, are about 2 miles north of downtown ▪ Henry's Market: good for long-term resupply (on east side, closest grocery store to downtown) ▪ Boxes and Cans, 160 Benmont Ave., sells oddball groceries at huge discount ▪ Bennington Coin Laundry (near Henry's) ▪ Maytag Laundromat: open 7 days (closest to the post office) ▪ Marras Shoe Repair: closed Sun ▪ banks w/ATM ▪ hospital ▪ library ▪ Bennington Center for the Arts: Native American Arts ▪ Bennington Museum: Grandma Moses collection. ▪ Note that the outfitter has moved to Williamstown. *Special event*—B-Town Chowdown: free food and drink for thru-hikers, good music, August 1.

Stratton Mtn 📖 *p. 74* ... *On A.T.*–probable birthplace of the Appalachian Trail: Benton MacKaye said he first thought about an eastern continental trail while sitting in a tree on this summit. Summit has a fire tower and caretaker-naturalist cabin; no camping permitted. *Stratton Gondola*—0.7 mile from the A.T. on blue-blazed side trail; operates on 4th of July and Labor Day weekend during thru-hiking season. Restaurants and lodging are available at the base.

Stratton Pond: 📖 *p. 74* ... *On A.T.*–left off A.T. 0.2 mile on blue-blazed side trail to the Stratton Pond Shelter; swimming. About 0.3 mile north on A.T. is North Shore Tenting Area on the north side of the pond; caretaker on duty, $5 fee for overnight stay at shelter or tent site (see information about rates on p. 159).

2000 Miler Requirements

The designation "2,000 Miler" is earned by any person at the instant he or she has completed hiking the entire Appalachian Trail, whether they later choose to apply for recognition as such or not. The Appalachian Trail Conservancy recognizes anyone who reports completion of the entire Trail as a "2,000-miler." The term is a matter of tradition and convenience, based upon the original estimated length of the Trail. Conservancy policy is to operate on an honor system, assuming that those who apply for 2000-miler status have hiked all of the A.T. between Katahdin and Springer Mountain, either as a thru-hiker or in sections. In the event of an emergency, such as a flood, a forest fire, or an impending storm, blue-blazed trails or officially required road walks are viable substitutes for the white-blazed route. Issues of sequence, direction, speed, length of time or whether one carries a pack are not considered. ATC assumes that those who apply have made an honest effort to walk the entire Trail, even if they did not walk past every white blaze.

Vermont

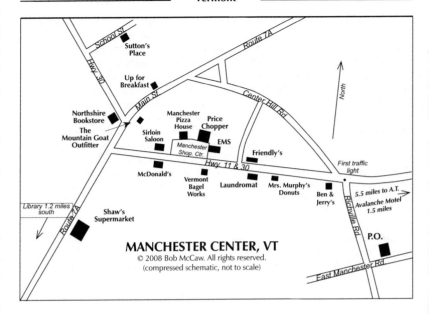

MANCHESTER CENTER, VT
© 2008 Bob McCaw. All rights reserved.
(compressed schematic, not to scale)

VT11/30 📖 *p. 75* ... On A.T.–parking area; usually an easy hitch to town from here if you keep your backpack visible. ◐ *left 5.5m*–to **MANCHESTER CENTER, VT 05255**: *Post office hours:* Mon-Fri 8:30am-4:30pm, Sat 9am-noon; 802-362-3070; a compact town with all hiker services (except for P.O. and library) within a few blocks of the center. The main post office is on the far edge of town, turn left at first traffic light on Highway 11/30 onto Richville Road). *Hostel*—Green Mountain House (330-388-6478): Reservations required, Jeff & Regina Taussig host hikers at their residence. Open 7/4-9/7, they offer hikers a bed, shower with towel, laundry, high speed internet and full hiker kitchen. Not a party place, no alcohol, no drugs. Shuttles from town & back to the trail in the morning. $15 per night suggested donation. *Lodging*—Note: there is a horse show in town from 7/7-8/15, motels are heavily booked and expensive. *In town:* Sutton's Place (50 School St., 802-362-1165): $55 private room, double occupancy $35 each, three in a room $28 each, all shared bath, no pets inside. *East on Hwy 11/30:* Avalanche Motor Lodge (2187 Depot Street, Manchester Center, VT 05255; 802-362-2622): $75S/D weekdays, pets okay, will hold maildrop packages; restaurant in motel; possible shuttle back to A.T.; rooms generally booked during horse show. There are several more motels east of town on Rt. 11/30 and north of town on Rt. 7A, mostly priced around $85-100 per night. *Potential lodging*—Ask the staff at EMS if any local residents are offering lodging, or if any local motels are offering unpublished summer specials for hikers. *Places to eat*—Manchester Pizza House: once *Skiing* magazine's "best pizza in town," pasta dinners, salads ▪ Sirloin Saloon: dinner only, prime rib, trout, salad bar with 30 items ▪ Friendly's ▪ Mrs. Murphy's Donuts & Coffee Shop: breakfast only (good place to pick up ride back to Trail from early-morning customers) ▪ Up for Breakfast: breakfast only, strawberry pancakes, wild-turkey hash, scones, coffees; painter Norman Rockwell's former hangout ▪ Vermont Bagel Works ▪ McDonald's ▪ Ben & Jerry's. *Groceries*—

The Thru-hiker's Handbook 2010

Price Chopper Supermarket: good for long-term resupply; deli, open 7 days ▪ Shaw's Supermarket: good for long-term resupply, deli section, bakery; open 7 days. *Outfitter/stove fuel*—The Mountain Goat: (4886 Main St., Manchester Center, VT 05255; 802-362-5159): full service outfitter with backpacking gear and clothing, Coleman and denatured alcohol by the ounce, repair service for stoves and filters, custom footbeds and orthotics, will hold maildrop packages; open 7 days year-round ▪ Eastern Mountain Sports (802-366-8082): full-service backpacking store, repair services, Coleman and denatured alcohol by the ounce, open 7 days year-round. *Other services*—laundromat, open year-round 7 days ▪ bank w/ATM ▪ Northshire Bookstore: huge selection, many thru-hikers think it the best on the Trail ▪ movie theater ▪ several factory outlets have featured outdoor clothing, boots, and hiking socks in recent years. ➲ *right 1.5m (follow Route 11)*–Bromley Sun Lodge (802-824-6941) $69 up, includes breakfast, laundry, restaurant/tavern, pool ▪ Johnny Seesaw's (800-424-2429) $50 Sun/Thu, $100 weekends, restaurant, will pick up and return to trail ▪ Bromley Market (good for short-term resupply) ▪ Bromley Base Lodge (see below)

Bromley Mtn 📖 *p. 75 ...* On A.T.–observation tower, and picnic table, but no water; nearby warming hut is usually left unlocked and may be used overnight by thru-hikers (if it remains clean). The Bromley summit lift is not in service during summer months, but you can follow it down to the Bromley Fun Park; open 7 days. Lower lift will take you to Bromley Base Lodge ($7.50 round trip, with lodge offering meals and snacks).

Danby-Landgrove Road, USFS Road 10 📖 *p. 76 ...* ◗ *left 3.5m*–to **Danby, VT 05739**: home of Nobel Prize-winning author Pearl Buck. Road lightly traveled, may be a tough hitch. *Services*—Nichols Store: good for short-term resupply ▪ Mt. Tabor Country Store: good for short-term resupply ▪ Alice's Someday Cafe (closed Mon/Tue) ▪ library. *North 2 miles from Danby on US 7:* The Otter Creek Campground (802-293-5041): tent sites $16 (up to two people), showers, camp store, laundry, Coleman by the pint; shuttles to area trailheads by arrangement.

VT140, Wallingford Gulf Road 📖 *p. 76 ...* ◗ *left 2.8m*–to **Wallingford, VT 05773**: Mom's Restaurant: home-style meals; open daily until 2pm ▪ Sal's Pizza ▪ Victorian Inn, fine dining, no lodging ▪ several convenience stores ▪ bank w/ATM.

VT103 📖 *p. 76 ...* ◗ *left 0.5m*–to the Whistle Stop Corner Restaurant. Open under new management, offers home style meals, ice cream, plan to be open 7 days in summer ◗ *left 1m*–to Clarendon General Store: good for short-term resupply, ice cream, sodas, snacks, and outside public telephone; open 7 days. ◗*left 7m*–to **RUTLAND, VT 05701** (see map and entry for US 4, below).

Killington Peak Trail: 📖 *p. 77 ...* ➲ *right 0.2m*–(straight up) to summit, where the state was christened "Verd-mont" (French for "green mountain") in 1763. The summit, mostly bare of vegetation, offers a panoramic vista of five states (Vermont, New Hampshire, New York, Massachusetts, Maine) and the southern provinces of Canada. Just below the summit is the Killington snack bar, with coffee, snacks, pastries, and fruit, all items priced to match the altitude; usually open 10am-4pm daily through Labor Day. You can take the chair lift down to the base lodge and resort area for about $14 per person round-trip, usually in operation Jul-Aug, 10am-4pm.

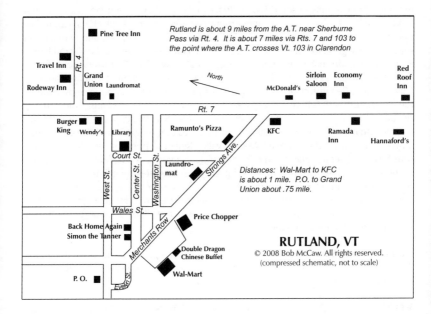

Pine Tree Inn

Rutland is about 9 miles from the A.T. near Sherburne Pass via Rt. 4. It is about 7 miles via Rts. 7 and 103 to the point where the A.T. crosses Vt. 103 in Clarendon

Travel Inn

Rt. 4

Grand Union Laundromat

Rodeway Inn

North

McDonald's

Sirloin Saloon

Economy Inn

Red Roof Inn

Rt. 7

Burger King

Wendy's

Library

Ramunto's Pizza

KFC

Ramada Inn

Hannaford's

Court St.

West St.

Center St.

Washington St.

Laundro-mat

Strongs Ave.

Distances: Wal-Mart to KFC is about 1 mile. P.O. to Grand Union about .75 mile.

Wales St.

Back Home Again
Simon the Tanner

Merchants Row

Price Chopper

RUTLAND, VT

© 2008 Bob McCaw. All rights reserved.
(compressed schematic, not to scale)

Double Dragon Chinese Buffet

P.O.

Evens St.

Wal-Mart

US4 📖 *p. 77* ... ➲ *right 0.8m*–to The Inn at Long Trail (Sherburne Pass, 709 Rt. 4, Killington, VT 05751; 802-775-7181): the first ski lodge in Vermont, built in 1939, operated by the McGrath family since 1977, open year-round except mid-Apr through mid-June. Rates (after 20% hiker discount, walk-ins only, reservations accepted but not with hiker discount, hiker rates good thru mid-Sept) $55S $68D includes hiker-sized breakfast; will hold UPS/FedEx packages only, do not send packages by mail. The inn has a bar, McGrath's Irish Pub (open 7 days, 11:30-midnight), featuring Guinness Stout served at the correct temperature and Long Trail Ale, both on tap; pub menu until 9pm. *Skiing* magazine said, "one of the liveliest, coziest pubs this side of Dublin"; coin-operated laundry on premises, water available for hikers from outside spigot. ◖ *left 0.8m*–to Edelweiss Lodge (802-775-5577): under new management, $59-$89, hot tub, pets OK in double room, breakfast and sandwiches available. ◖ *left 8.6m*–to **RUTLAND, VT 05701**: *Post office hours:* Mon-Fri 8am-5pm, Sat 8am-noon; 802-773-0222. Rutland is large town, but the downtown area is compact and most services hikers need are nearby. ***Hostel***—Back Home Again Hostel (23 Center St., Rutland, VT 05701; 802-775-9800; <www.twelvetribes.com>): operated by the Twelve Tribes community; $20 donation on weekends, work for stay possible on weekdays; separate dormitories for men and women, couples welcome but must sleep separately, includes sheets, shower and towel; coin-operated laundry and kitchenette; no pets (kennel available, $5); no alcohol or smoking permitted on premises; will hold maildrop packages; check in at cafe by same name (or call 773-0160 for check in on Sat when cafe is closed). ***Other lodging*** *(near town on US4)*—Rodeway Inn (802-773-9176): $54S/$59D, pets $10 extra, rates $15 higher weekends ▪ Pine Tree Lodge (802-773-2442); $49S/D ($69 weekends), pets allowed in some rooms ▪ Travel Inn (802-775-4348); $35S/$39D ($9 more weekends), pets in some rooms. *Places to eat*—many restaurants in town, fast food on US7 ▪ Double Dragon Chinese Buffet, near Wal-Mart ▪ Back Home Again Cafe (see hostel, above). *Other services*—Grand Union, Price Chopper, and Hannaford's supermarkets: good for long-term resupply ▪ The Laundry Basket: next to Grand Union ▪ another laundromat near Price Chopper ▪ banks w/ATM. *Outfitters/stove fuel*—Mountain Travelers Hike and Ski (802-775-0814): good selection of gear and clothing; Coleman and denatured alcohol by the ounce; open 7 days (Sun noon-5pm) ▪ Simon the Tanner (802-282-4016): backpacking gear, cold-weather clothing, Coleman and denatured alcohol by the ounce, other fuels; closed Sat; located next door to hostel. *Nearby town*—community of Killington is 2.2 miles to the right, shorter to access from VT100 (see below). *Bus service*—Marble Valley Regional Transit <www.thebus.com> runs buses between Rutland and Killington roughly every 2 hours, fare $2, stops at Inn at the Long Trail, see website for schedules. *Special event*—Long Trail Festival: at the State Fair Grounds in Rutland, Aug 6-8; music, food, special presentations about hiking and other outdoor activities; camping in secure area from Friday night to Monday morning, $5 for the weekend, rest rooms and water available. Opportunity to help with trail maintenance on Sunday.

Gifford Woods State Park: 📖 *p. 77* ... *On A.T.*–Trail passes through camping area. Tent sites $18 up, pay showers, water available at no charge; lean-to usually available by reservation only, open mid-May-October 15.

VT100 📖 *p. 77* ... ➲ *right 0.4m to US4*–to **KILLINGTON, VT 05751**: *Post office hours:* Mon-Fri 8:30am-4:30pm, Sat 8:30am-noon; 802-775-4247. *Outfitter*–Base Camp Outfitters (2363 Rt. 4, Killington, VT 05751; 802-775-0166) full-service outfitter, Coleman and denatured alcohol by the ounce, mail drop packages accepted. *Services*—Killington Motel (802-773-9535): $60S/D, call for trail pickup and possible special hiker rate, rates may be higher on weekends and during fall foliage season, continental breakfast, no pets ▪ Greenbrier Inn (802-775-1575) $70S/$85D, continental breakfast, no smoking, no pets ▪ Killington Deli and Marketplace: small neighborhood grocery store, good for short-term resupply, sandwiches, fresh bagels daily; open 7 days ▪ library on River Rd. ▪ ATM ▪ outside pay phone.

Kent Pond 📖 *p. 78* ... ➲ *right 200ft*–to Mountain Meadows Lodge (285 Thundering Brook Rd., Killington, VT 05751; 802-775-1010; <www.mountainmeadowslodge. com>): $59 per room (up to 2 people) for hikers includes breakfast, no pets in rooms, will hold maildrop packages for hikers, even if not staying overnight; summer weekends are usually full. Hikers may purchase a special hiker "lunch" for $9 available anytime, and a special hiker dinner is available for $10 up. Owners are hiker-friendly.

Trail to The Lookout 📖 *p. 78* ... ☾ *left 900ft*–to a cabin with an observation platform on the roof. The cabin is private property, may have notice allowing hikers to stay when unoccupied, but there is no water anywhere nearby; register box is provided on a tree on the A.T. for guests to sign. If you do camp here overnight, be a good guest and clean up any mess you make.

VT12, Barnard Gulf Road 📖 *p. 78* ... ➲ *right 3.8m*–to **Woodstock, VT 05091**: *Post office hours:* Mon-Fri 8:30am-5pm, Sat 9am-12pm; 802-457-1323. A very pretty but rather expensive resort-type town. Shire Riverview Motel (802-457-2211) $98 up, no pets ▪ many restaurants, B&Bs and inns ▪ Bentley's Restaurant: open daily ▪ Grand Union Supermarket: good for long-term resupply ▪ 18-Carrot Natural Food Store ▪ laundromat: open 7 days ▪ bank w/ATM ▪ health clinic ◖ *left 0.2m*–to On the Edge Farm: soda, ice cream, homemade pie, fruit, veggies. Open 7 days Mem day to mid-Oct.

Woodstock Stage Road 📖 *p. 78* ... ➔ *right 1m* (passing the Suicide Six ski area)–to **SOUTH POMFRET, VT 05067**: *Post office hours:* Mon-Fri 8am-1pm and 2pm-4:45pm, Sat 8:30am-11:30am; 802-457-1147; Teago General Store: good for short-term resupply, deli, pasta salads, sandwiches, grinders, picnic tables; open 7 days ▪ library.

Trail to Cloudland Shelter 📖 *p. 79* ... ◖ *left 0.5m*–to the Cloudland Shelter, once an official A.T. shelter but now on private land; owner allows overnight stay in lean-to unless notices say otherwise; water source is small stream you cross before reaching shelter; level areas for tenting around shelter.

WEST HARTFORD, VT 05084 📖 *p. 79* ... *Post office hours:* Mon-Fri 7:30am-11:30am and 1pm-4:45pm; Sat 7:30am-10:15am; 802-295-6293. West Hartford Village Store (good for short-term resupply), deli, breakfast, pizza, burgers, open 7 days. Note that last year, some area residents allowed hikers to tent overnight in their yard for a small fee or free of charge, ask about tenting options at the library or post office.

NORWICH, VT 05055 📖 *p. 80* ... *Post office hours:* Mon-Fri 8:30am-5pm, Sat 9am-noon; 802-649-1608. ◖ *left 0.1m*–to Norwich Inn (802-649-1143): $129 hiker rate, subject to availability; dining room in inn ▪ Dan & Whit's: groceries ▪ banks w/ATM ▪ Baker's Store at King Arthur Flour: bread and treats, 0.4 miles south on US 5.

Purpose of the Appalachian Trail

The ATC Board of Directors has defined the purpose of the Appalachian Trail as this: "The Appalachian Trail experience represents the sum of opportunities that are available for those walking the Appalachian Trail to interact with the wild, scenic, pastoral, cultural, and natural elements of the environment of the Appalachian Trail, unfettered and unimpeded by competing sights or sounds and in as direct and intimate a manner as possible" (*Appalachian Trailway News*, July/August 1997). This official definition carries with it seven ideas that the Board considered integral to the A.T. experience:

▪ Opportunities for observation, contemplation, and exploration of the natural world.
▪ A sense of remoteness and detachment from civilization.
▪ Opportunities to experience solitude, freedom, self-reliance, and self-discovery.
▪ A sense of being on the height of the land.
▪ Opportunities to experience the cultural, historical, and pastoral elements of the Trail and its surrounding countryside.
▪ A feeling of being part of the natural environment.
▪ Opportunities for travel on foot, including opportunities for long-distance hiking.

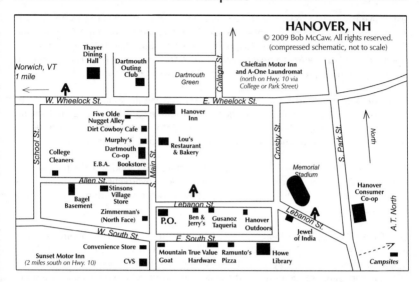

HANOVER, NH
© 2009 Bob McCaw. All rights reserved.
(compressed schematic, not to scale)

HANOVER, NH 03755 🕮 *p. 80 ... Post office hours:* Mon-Fri 8:30am-5pm, Sat 8:30am-noon; for pickup knock at side door until 5:30pm weekdays, until 2:30pm on Sat; 603-643-4544; home of Dartmouth College. **Information**—The Dartmouth Outing Club (603-646-2428): in Robinson Hall on campus, is usually a safe place to drop your pack when you first get to town. A hiker information board is located in the basement, free internet access available. **Important notice!** Please do not sleep or do laundry on Dartmouth property (including D.O.C. and fraternities) unless expressly invited. **Lodging**—Sunset Motor Inn (603-298-8721): weekdays $72S/$81D up (weekends $81S/$91D); no pets allowed; laundry for hikers (available afternoon hours only); located on NH10 in West Lebanon about two miles south of the college (on "Orange" bus route); call to verify vacancy and possible shuttle to motel ▪ Chieftain Motor Inn (603-643-2550): $75S/D mid-week only (discounted price Jun-Aug), laundry, pets $35 extra; located on river, no charge for use of canoes; located on NH10 about two miles north of the college (on "Brown" bus route) ▪ Hanover Inn: $250 per room (up to 4 people), pets $30 extra. *See also*–Norwich Inn, across the river in Vermont, only 1 mile from center of Hanover. **Nearby hostel**—"Tigger's Tree House" Hostel (see Trescott Road entry on next page). **Camping**–several campsites exist near soccer field where A.T. leaves town to the north, within walking distance of town. Please do not camp on the soccer field. **Places to eat** *(all open 7 days)*—Everything But Anchovies ("EBA"): student casual, pizza, several different inexpensive pasta specials from 5pm-9pm *(hint: eat dinner early, specials go fast)* ▪ Five Olde Nugget Alley: burgers, ribs, nightly specials, salads ▪ Lou's Restaurant & Bakery: big country breakfast, home-style meals, soda fountain with milk shakes, full-service bakery ▪ Dirt Cowboy Cafe, coffee shop ▪ Ramunto's Pizza: brick oven Sicilian and NY-style pizzas, highly recommended ▪ Murphy's on the Green: eat-in or take-out, sandwiches ▪ Bagel Basement: fresh bagels every day with flavored cream cheeses, muffins, Green Mountain coffee ▪ Gusanoz, inexpensive Mexican ▪ Jewel of India: East Indian Food ▪ Thayer Hall: the campus dining facility with meals purchased à la carte;

Food Court has deli, grill, salad and soup bar; Home Plate serves low fat and vegetarian food; both open for lunch and dinner only; The Pavilion serves primarily kosher meals. *Groceries*—Hanover Consumer Co-op: good for long-term resupply, natural and bulk food selections ▪ Stinson's Village Store: convenience store, open daily until midnight ▪ Irving convenience store, open 24 hrs. *Stove fuel*—Hanover True-Value (behind post office): Coleman and denatured alcohol by the ounce, open 7 days. *Other services*— A-One Laundromat: coin-operated laundry; 1.5 miles from the college on NH10 (on "Brown" bus route); open 7 days ▪ College Cleaners: offers same-day laundry service Mon-Fri (drop off before 10am, but expensive) ▪ Dartmouth Bookstore ▪ bank w/ATM ▪ theater ▪ Ben & Jerry's ▪ Howe Library with internet. *Outfitters*—Hanover Outdoors, full service, stove fuel ▪ Mountain Goat, full service, stove fuel ▪ Zimmerman's North Face Store, mainly clothing. *In West Lebanon, about 4 miles south on Orange bus line:* EMS (603-298-7716) and L.L. Bean Factory Store (603-298-6975), . **Local buses**– operate hourly, weekdays only, about 6-6. Advance Transit, 802-295-1824, <*www. advancetransit.com*> for routes and schedules ▪ Greyhound service to Boston, tickets and pickup at Hanover Inn ▪ Amtrak service available in nearby White River Junction. *Special event*—Shriner's Parade: featuring clowns, bands, and motorized units, usually held the second Sat in August. *Points of interest*—Hood Museum of Art: on Dartmouth campus, free admission for hikers, open daily.

Trescott Road 📖 *p. 80* ... ➲ *right 0.8m*–to **Etna, NH 03750:** "Tigger's Tree House" (603-643-9213): hostel in private home, please call several days in advance to make sure someone is available (speak to Karen or Ralph) and call from D.O.C. or Etna General Store on arrival; offers tenting on lawn or sleeping space in garage or basement if available; hot shower, laundry with detergent; pets okay, possible work for stay, shuttles to stores, ATM, *etc.*; suggested donation $5, and feel free to buy toilet paper or other supplies for hikers who follow when you get shuttle to the Wal-Mart; one night limit unless sick or injured. ▪ Etna General Store: luncheon special weekdays, grinders, some supplies, Coleman and denatured alcohol by the ounce; open 7 days ▪ Days Inn (603-448-7381): $71 up, 2.5 miles from store.

Etna-Hanover Center Road 📖 *p. 80* ... ➲ *right 0.8m*–to **Etna, NH 03750:** see Trescott Road entry above (both this road and Trescott Road lead into hamlet of Etna)

Lyme-Dorchester Road 📖 *p. 80* ... ☾ *left 1.2m*–to **Lyme Center, NH 03769**: post office only. ☾ *left 3.2m*–to **Lyme, NH 03768**: several inns ▪ restaurant ▪ Lyme Country Store: limited hiker supplies, hot foods, open 7 days ▪ bank w/ATM ▪ hardware store ▪ ATC New England Office (603-795-4935) in the One Lyme Common building.

NH25A 📖 *p. 81* ... ➲ *right 4.5m*–to **Wentworth, NH 03282**: Shawnee's General Store: good for short-term resupply, deli, fruits.

NH25 📖 *p. 81* ... ➲ *right 0.5m*–to **GLENCLIFF, NH 03238**: *Post office hours:* Mon-Fri 7am-10am and 2pm-5pm, Sat 7am-1pm; 603-989-5154; telephone located on the far side of the building next to PO driveway, not visible as you approach from Trail. *Hostel*—Hikers Welcome Hostel (603-989-0040, <*www.hikerswelcome. com*>): across from post office; hostel $15 or campsite $10 includes shower; shower without stay $2.50; laundry $2.50 wash $2.50 dry; hiker foods (Liptons, snacks, sodas, ice cream, pizza, *etc.*); internet access; Coleman and denatured alcohol by the ounce, probable evening shuttle to restaurant and grocery store in Warren; other shuttles by arrangement. ➲ *right 5m*–to **Warren, NH 03279**: Calamity Jane's Restaurant: closes 2pm Mon ▪ Green House Restaurant, open Thur-Mon ▪ Warren Village Market: good for long-term resupply, deli, ATM.

Kinsman Notch, NH112 📖 *p. 82* ... ➲ *right 0.5m*–to the Society for Protection of New Hampshire Forests' Lost River Reservation visitors center, no services, open Mem Day-Oct. ➲ *right 5m*–to the town of North Woodstock, NH (see Franconia Notch below).

White Mountains, White Mountain National Forest 📖 *p. 82* ... home to some of the most delicate and easily damaged ecosystems you will encounter on your trek, so stay within "scree walls" at all times. For safety and enjoyment, take note of the following:
• Adjust your mileage expectations downward, since the terrain in the Whites is some of the most rugged to be encountered anywhere on the A.T.
• Pay attention to the blazes and cairns that mark the A.T. In many parts, the regional trail names are used on signs, so it helps to have Trail maps.
• Carry enough clothing to deal with severe changes in weather conditions, since temperatures can change rapidly (snow can occur any month) and lightning storms are a real danger above treeline.
• Look for posted regulations on camping and fires. Sections in the Whites are designated "Forest Protection Area," which means that you cannot camp closer than 200 feet to trails so marked, closer than ¼ mile to shelters, huts, and tent sites, or closer than ½ mile to a road. Above treeline, camping is permitted only at designated sites, no campfires.

Appalachian Mountain Club 📖 *p. 82* ... AMC (603-466-2721; <*www.outdoors.org*>) operates most of the facilities in the Whites. Fees are charged for overnight use of huts and most campsites/tent sites. Locations at which fees are charged are so noted in the Mileage Index section of this guide, as are full-service dates for huts. There is no fee at Eliza Brook, Trident Col, Gentian Pond, Carlo Col, and Full Goose. Shelters and tent sites are available first come, first served, no reservations. Shelters are very similar to those elsewhere on the A.T. Tent sites have wooden platforms with eyelets for tying off a tent. An $8 overnight fee is charged; caretakers come around in the evening to sign you in. ***Huts***—lodging and two meals (breakfast and dinner) $97 Sun-Fri, $116 Sat, rates about 10% less for AMC members. Lodging consists of a bunk with blankets and pillow provided, inside rest rooms but no showers. Dinner is served promptly at 6pm at all AMC facilities.   Meals are available for overnight guests only; snack foods and drinks may be purchased by non-guests. No pets, smoking prohibited inside, and abuse of alcohol is not tolerated. The huts are very expensive, but it is quite possible to avoid them on your trip through the Whites with a little advance planning. ***Work for Stay***—an option at most huts for the first two thru-hikers (four hikers at Lakes of the Clouds) who request it, involves an hour or two of light chores; check with crew for availability, also a possibility at campsites. ***AMC Shuttle***—(603-466-2727) stops at Pinkham Notch, Crawford Notch, Franconia Notch, other trailheads, fare about $18; operates June 3 - Sept 11, weekends through mid-October.

AMC-Lonesome Lake Hut 📖 *p. 83* ... *On A.T.*–the first AMC hut for northbounders, swimming; fine view across lake; $97 (Sat $116) with meals; full-service Jun 3-Oct 16.

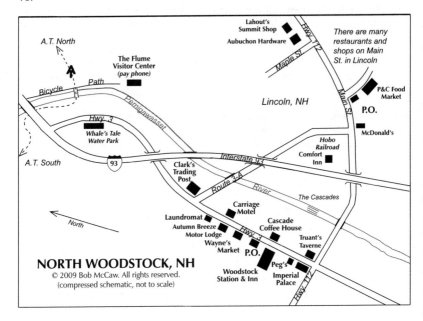

NORTH WOODSTOCK, NH
© 2009 Bob McCaw. All rights reserved.
(compressed schematic, not to scale)

Franconia Notch, Interstate 93/US3 📖 *p. 83* ... A.T. passes under Interstate 93 and US3. ➲ *right 5.8m*–to **NORTH WOODSTOCK, NH 03262**: *Post office hours:* Mon-Fri 9:30am-12:30pm and 1:30pm-4:30pm, Sat 9am-noon; 603-745-8134. ***Lodging***— Autumn Breeze Motor Lodge (603-745-8549) $70S/$80D, $10 per additional person, no pets. ▪ Carriage Motel (603-745-2416): $60S/D (add $4 weekends), $10 each additional person; no pets ▪ Woodstock Inn (603-745-3951): $50 per person double occupancy for shared bath ($63 ppdo for private bath, $15 each additional person); all weekends add $25, prices lower before Jul 1 and are subject to change; no pets. ***Places to eat***—Truant's Taverne ▪ Imperial Palace ▪ Peg's Place: breakfast served all day every day; open 7 days ▪ Landmark Family Restaurant: family-style specials every night ▪ Woodstock Station: casual dining on patio, fine dining inside; hand-crafted brews from on-site traditional brewery; open daily. ***Groceries***—Wayne's Market & Deli, deli with grinders to go; closed Sunday. ***Other services***—bank w/ATM ▪ laundromat: open 7 days ▪ Shuttle Connection (603-745-3140): shuttles to area trailheads, major area cities. From center of N. Woodstock, proceed left 1-2 miles on Main Street/Rt. 112) to **Lincoln, NH 03251**. Lincoln is larger than N. Woodstock, with many restaurants and shops. P&C Food Market: good for long-term resupply; open 7 days ▪ many restaurants ▪ post office, laundromat, and bank ▪ Lahout's Summit Shop (603-745-2882 or 1-800-730-1902): full-service backpacking store with gear and clothing, Coleman and denatured alcohol by the ounce; open 7 days ▪ Comfort Inn ▪ medical clinic.

Franconia Notch Bike Path 📖 *p. 83* ... ➔ *right 0.7m*–(on bike path where the A.T. crosses the Pemigewasset River) to The Flume Visitor Center: cafeteria, public telephone; admission fee to the Flume (a spectacular natural gorge), usually open Jun-mid Oct. ⊂ *left 2.1m*–to Lafayette Place Campground: tent sites $25 (2 people), showers, rest rooms, camp store with limited supplies, lodge with fireplace, swimming at Echo Beach; open mid-May-Oct.

Liberty Spring Tentsite 📖 *p. 83* ... *On A.T.*–with ten large tent platforms, spring across A.T.; caretaker, $8 overnight fee. The summit of Liberty Mountain, 0.6 mile above the tent site on side trail, offers spectacular sunrise and sunset panorama.

Franconia Range 📖 *p. 83* ... mostly above treeline, which is at about 4,000 feet in the Whites. This range is considered by many to be the most scenic section on the entire A.T. Some of the mountains crossed are: Liberty (summit on side trail, 4459'), Little Haystack (4760'), Lincoln (5089'), Lafayette (5249'), Garfield (4488'), South Twin (4902'), and Guyot (4560'). The distances between these peaks will fool your eyes, but your legs won't be fooled.

Mt. Lafayette 📖 *p. 83* ... ⊂ *left 1m*–(down from summit) on Greenleaf Trail to the hut, building visible from summit; $97 (Sat $116) with meals; full-service Jun 3-Oct 16.

AMC-Galehead Hut 📖 *p. 83* ... *On A.T.*–$97 (Sat $116) with meals; open Jun 3-Oct 16.

AMC-Zealand Falls Hut 📖 *p. 84* ... *On A.T.*– near a beautiful, cascading stream with flat rocks and expansive vista; $97 (Sat $116) with meals; full service Jun 3-Oct 16. Self-service outside these dates, bunks $33.

Crawford Notch, US302 📖 *p. 84* ... ⊂ *left 1m*–to Willey House: snack bar; open 7 days, 9am-5pm, mid-May thru mid-Oct. Outside public telephone. ⊂ *left 3.7m*–to Highland Center (603-466-2727): lodge offers basic bunk room $46 per person including breakfast, shared rooms $89, private room with bath $145 up; breakfast and dinner included; dining room serves breakfast and family-style dinner; reservations recommended; lodge open year around; no work for stay. Maildrops accepted, $5 fee. ➔ *right 1.5m*–to Dry River Campground: tent sites $23 (1-2 people), privy, no showers are available. ➔ *right 3m*–to Crawford Notch General Store & Campground (1138 Route 302, Harts Location, NH 03812; 603-374-2779; <www.crawfordnotchcamping.com>): bunkhouse $22 includes shower and towel, cabins $54 up (2 people), tent sites $28 per site (2 people); showers without stay $2; will hold maildrop packages for guests only (address c/o the store); shuttles by arrangement; store (good for medium to long-term resupply), Coleman by the ounce and denatured alcohol; open mid-May-Oct. ***Presidential Range***—The 25-mile section between Crawford Notch and Pinkham Notch is mostly above treeline. Some of the peaks traversed are: Mt. Webster (3910'), Mt. Jackson (4052'), Mt. Pierce (formerly Mt. Clinton, 4310'), Mt. Eisenhower (4761'), Mt. Franklin (5004'), Mt. Washington (6288') and Mt. Madison (5363'). The Presidentials can be breathtaking, but use care when crossing this section in bad weather. Do not hesitate to leave the ridge for cover if the weather takes a sudden turn for the worse, especially if lightning is occurring nearby.

AMC-Mizpah Spring Hut/Nauman Tentsite 📖 *p. 84* ... *On A.T.*–one of the more modern AMC huts in the Whites, solar power system; $97 (Sat $116) with meals; full-service Jun 4-Oct 18. AYCE soup is sometimes available for lunch for about $2, but not every day. Nauman tent site with privy is nearby in the trees; $8 overnight fee. From just beyond here to north of Mt. Madison, a distance of more than twelve miles, the Trail is above treeline and without protection from the elements, so plan carefully.

AMC-Lakes of the Clouds Hut 📖 *p. 85* ... *On A.T.*–called "Lakes of the Crowds" by thru-hikers because of its large size (up to 90 guests can be overwhelming), with easy access to and from the summit of Mt. Washington via the A.T.; $97 (Sat $116) with meals; full-service Jun 3-Sep 11. A small room in the basement, called "The Dungeon," has basic bunk space for six hikers. Thru-hikers can have hut crews radio ahead and reserve a basement bunk space (Jul-Aug only), but no sooner than 48 hours in advance. Cost is $8 per night. Staying in the basement has become a thru-hiker tradition. Dungeon-dwellers may use the rest rooms and other facilities upstairs (but no use of kitchen).

Mt. Washington 📖 *p. 85* ... *On A.T.*–at 6,288 feet, the highest peak in New England and the mountain originally proposed by Benton MacKaye in 1921 as the northern terminus of the A.T. The summit; a New Hampshire state park with weather station that has clocked the highest official surface wind speed ever recorded on Earth (231 mph). *Sherman Adams Summit House*—open daily 8am-8pm, Memorial Day-Columbus Day, with post office, snack bar, backpacker day-use room, and museum, telephones and rest rooms in lobby, weather reports posted just inside the main entrance; no pets permitted in the building. If you have questions or need advice or assistance, a ranger is usually on duty at the desk in the lobby area. *Services*—Snack Bar: pastries, sandwiches, burgers, hot dogs, bagels, and beverages, open daily 9am-6pm • Backpacker Room: for sorting and drying gear only, absolutely no hikers are allowed to stay overnight on the summit for any reason • Attractions: museum, Tip Top House; open daily, small admission fees. *Transportation*—Cog Railway: oldest such railway in the world; $59 round-trip • Mt. Washington Stagecoach: shuttle service $29 per person. *Post office*—Do not use the summit post office as a mail drop location. Your package may be held at the bottom of the mountain, and the post office is not guaranteed to be open on any given day.

Tuckerman Ravine Trail 📖 *p. 85* ... steep four-mile trail from Washington's summit that bypasses the official 13.4-mile Gulfside-Osgood-A.T. route over the northern Presidentials. The blue-blazed trail descends to Pinkham Notch, at mile point 1.7 mile passing a side trail to the right that leads to Hermit Lake Campground with shelter and tent site, caretaker and $10 fee. Space at Hermit Lake must be booked at Pinkham Notch, available first come, first served.

Randolph Mountain Club 📖 *p. 85* ... <www.randolphmountainclub.org> offers Gray Knob and Crag Camp, enclosed lodges similar to AMC huts but below treeline and with a caretaker only (no "croo") and no meals, $12 per night. The Perch has a shelter and four tent platforms, shelter or tent site $7 per night. Water is available at all RMC facilities. Many thru-hikers have enjoyed these RMC facilities as alternatives to the AMC huts located on the ridge.

AMC-Madison Spring Hut 📖 *p.85* ... *On A.T.*–$97 (Sat $116) with meals; open Jun 3-Sep 5 • USFS Valley Way Tent Site: 0.6 mile on Gulfside Trail; platforms, no fee.

Unblazed Trail north of Pinkham Notch 📖 *p.85* ... the trail is unblazed and trail signs can be confusing between the 4000' level of Mt. Madison and the Auto Road. NOBO, go right at the Osgood Tentsite, right at the trail junction "trail south" of Parapet Creek, straight through at the junction "trail south" of Peabody Brook, and left at the Junction beyond the bridge. SOBO, take a sharp right at the junction before Peabody Brook, straight through the junction beyond Peabody Brook, left at the junction beyond Parapet Creek, and left at the Osgood Tent Site.

Pinkham Notch, NH16 📖 *p. 86* ... *On A.T.*–Pinkham Notch Visitor Center (P. O. Box 298, Rt. 16, Gorham, NH 03581; 603-466-2721)—AMC's headquarters in the Whites and a year-round facility with dining room, camp store, public telephone, and pay showers; will hold maildrop packages. Meals can be purchased by non-guests: breakfast $11.50, dinner $22 (reservations not required but it's recommended you get there early, served family-style at 6pm sharp). Deli open 9:30am-4pm, trail lunches to go $9.50 during the summer months. The store sells snacks, drinks, and some hiking items (guidebooks, maps, *etc.*), Coleman fuel by the ounce and denatured alcohol are often available. Coin-operated hot showers are available, get towel and change at the front desk in the main lodge building. Pets are prohibited in all buildings • Joe Dodge Lodge, dormitory-style rooms (4 people per room, you may have to share with strangers) have built-in bunk beds and come with linens, but do not have private bath, $69 with dinner and breakfast (rates off-season and for AMC members a few dollars less). Work for stay not available • Concord Trailways provides daily bus service to and from Boston, get ticket at information desk and catch bus in front of the center. *Camping*—permitted in Pinkham Notch only outside the Cutler River drainage area, campsites must be at least ¼ mile south of the highway, 200 feet off the Trail. ➔ *left 4m*–to Camp Dodge (603-466-9469): home for AMC volunteer trail crews May-Sept, four miles from the Notch. Thru-hikers are invited to join the crews for a half-day of work in exchange for lodging, hot shower, laundromat, and possibly meals; call ahead, don't just show up. *Nearby towns*—Gorham (see listing below) is 11 miles north (left) and is much easier to navigate on foot than the towns south on NH 16. ➔ *right 15m*–to **Intervale, NH 03845**: Limmer Boot Shop (603-356-5378), custom leather hiking boots, renowned throughout New England; Ragged Mountain Equipment (603-356-3042): clothing and gear. ➔ *right 17m*–to **North Conway, NH 03860**: motels, restaurants, supermarket, laundromat • L. L. Bean Factory Store (603-356-2158) • Eastern Mountain Sports (603-356-5433) • International Mountain Equipment (603-356-7013).

Wildcat Mtn Chair Lift: 📖 *p. 86* ... *On A.T.*–Skyride gondola from base camp to summit of Peak E open mid-Jun through mid-Oct, 10am-5pm (last ride up at 4:45pm); $13 round trip; at base deli-style restaurant/cafeteria, coffee & ice cream shop.

AMC-Carter Notch Hut 📖 *p. 86* ... ➔ *right 500ft*–(on Nineteen-Mile Brook Trail) to the main hut building, passing a pond on the way; $97 (Sat $116) with meals; full-service Jun 3-Sep 11; self-service outside these dates, bunks $33.

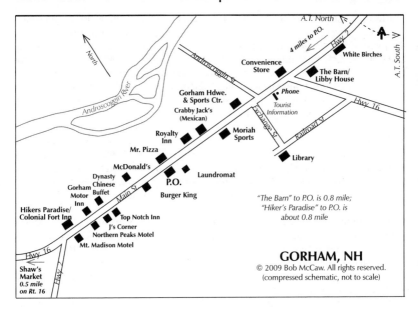

GORHAM, NH
© 2009 Bob McCaw. All rights reserved.
(compressed schematic, not to scale)

US2 📖 *p. 87* ... **☛** *left 3.6m*–to **GORHAM, NH 03581**: *Post office hours:* Mon-Fri 8:30am-5pm, Sat 8:30am-noon; 603-466-2182; services are spread out along US2. ***Hostels***—"The Barn" at Libby House (55 Main St., Gorham, NH 03581; 603-466-2271); mattress bed $20 per person, includes shower with towel, soap, and shampoo; laundry $5; Coleman and denatured alcohol by the ounce; kitchen area available with stove, microwave, and refrigerator; will hold maildrop packages for guests only ($5 charge if you don't stay); shuttles to area trailheads by arrangement; no pets; owned by the Regan family ▪ "Hiker's Paradise" at Colonial Fort Inn (370 Main St., Gorham, NH 03581; 603-466-2732; <*www.hikersparadise.com*>); three separate hostel units, each with beds, linens, bath, and kitchen; bathrooms with tubs and showers; kitchen with stove, refrigerator, cooking utensils, dishes; $20 per person; no pets; regular motel rooms, some with kitchenettes, are available at regular rates; coin-operated laundry for guests only; special hikers' breakfasts in dining room; Coleman and denatured alcohol by the ounce, free shuttles back to A.T. at US2 for guests, shuttles to other area trailheads for a fee; do not send maildrop packages; operated by Bruno and Mary Ann Janicki. ▪ White Birches Inn, 1.8 miles west of A.T. on US2 (603-466-2022): bunks $15 per night, internet, TV, recreation room, pool, laundry, food delivery, pets OK. Tenting available, cabins $49 and up. Will hold maildrop packages from guests, shuttles to town and other destinations available. Hot showers 25 cents. ***Other lodging***—Royalty Inn (603-466-3312), pets in smoking rooms only; Mt. Madison Motel (603-466-3622), pets OK; Top Notch Inn (603-466-5496); several B&Bs. Motel rates vary by season and day of week, typically in the $59-89 range. ***Places to eat***—J's Steak & Seafood ▪ Mr. Pizza: inexpensive Italian meals, pizza; open 7 days ▪ Yokohama Japanese Restaurant ▪ Crabby Jack's Mexican ▪ fast food outlets. ***Groceries***–Shaw's Supermarket: about 1m north, good for long-term resupply, open 7 days. ***Outfitters/stove fuel***—Gorham

---

Hardware & Sports Center (603-466-2312): gear and clothing, shuttles to area trailheads by arrangement, Coleman by the ounce, denatured alcohol; open daily ▪ Moriah Sports (603-466-5050; <*www.moriahsports.com*>): full-service outfitter with backpacking gear and clothing; Coleman and denatured alcohol by the ounce; shuttles to area trailheads by arrangement; open 7 days. *Other services*—laundromat: open 24-hours ▪ bank w/ ATM ▪ Wal-Mart (2m north) ▪ health clinic. *Point of interest*—Railroad Museum. *Nearby town*—Berlin, NH (10 miles north on NH16): Morin Shoe Store (603-752-4810): boot and pack repairs, closed on Sun ▪ bank w/ATM ▪ movie theater.

Mahoosuc Notch 📖 *p. 88* ... *On A.T.*–It is debatable whether this is the "toughest mile on the A.T.," but this jumble of rocks is a unique experience. Go through with a partner if possible, so you will have someone to take your picture when you are squirming under those house-sized boulders. Be extra careful on mossy or muddy patches. This is not the place to have a bad fall. When you hear water below, look for year-round ice.

Grafton Notch, ME26 📖 *p. 89* ... *On A.T.*-parking area with privy. *(1500')* ➲right 4.5m–to Mahoosuc Mountain Lodge (1513 Bear River Rd., Newry, ME 04261; 207-824-2073 <*www.mahoosucmountainlodge.com*>) bunks $35, linen $10 extra, $50 with breakfast, will hold mail drops for guests, Coleman and denatured alcohol by the ounce, rides to and from trail for fee, possible rides to Bethel ➲ *right 17m*–to **Bethel, ME 04217**: a pleasant town near the Sunday River ski area. There are many restaurants and motels in and around Bethel, the following is a partial list near the center of town. *Services*—Chapman Inn (1 Mill Hill Rd., Bethel, ME 04217; 207-824-2657 or 1-877-359-1498): rooms $59S/$69D up; hiker dorm with single or double beds, hot shower, sauna, kitchen facilities for $30 per night with breakfast; laundry $4 per load, pets allowed, will hold maildrop packages, shuttle to and from Trail available at additional cost ▪ Bethel Village Motel (207-824-2989): $60 and up, no pets ▪ Pat's Pizza: menu with six pages of Italian specialties, reasonable prices; open year-round ▪ Sudbury Inn: dinner only, steaks, seafood, pastas ▪ Bethel Foodliner Supermarket: good for long-term resupply, open 7 days ▪ laundromat, open 7 days ▪ True North Adventureware (196 Walkers Mill Rd., Bethel, ME 04217; 207-824-2201; located 1 mile south on Rt. 26): backpacking clothing and gear, boots, Coleman and denatured alcohol by the ounce, will hold maildrop packages; open 7 days ▪ bank w/ATM.

East B Hill Road 📖 *p. 89* ... ➲ *right 8m*–to **ANDOVER, ME 04216**: *Post office hours:* Mon-Fri 8:30am-1:30pm and 2pm-4:30pm, Sat 8:30am-11:30am; 207-392-4571. *Lodging*—Pine Ellis Lodging (20 Pine St., Andover, ME 04216; 207-392-4161; guest phone 207-392-1405 <*www.pineellislodging.com*>): Overnight lodging in home-style family atmosphere. Country home near village, stores, and post office. Shared dorm-style hiker room in house, and hiker bunkhouse, $20 per person. Private rooms $35S/$50D, $10 each extra person. All lodging includes showers, use of kitchen, guest phone, internet, VCR, and cable TV in each room. Hiker box and lender clothes. For fee: laundry facilities on premises, fuel by the ounce. Slack pack and other shuttles arranged (bus station, airport, etc.). Multi-day slackpacking available. Rides back to trail. Free pick-up at East B Hill or South Arm Road trailheads with reservations (call ahead). Happily hosting hikers for 20 years. *Places to eat*—Andover General Store & Diner: pizza, sandwiches, subs, fried chicken, burgers; ATM inside; open daily. *Groceries*—Mills Market: good for long-term resupply; open 7 days ▪ Andover General Store: good for long-term resupply;

ATM in store; open 7 days. **Other services**—outside telephone, UPS pickup station located at Mills Market. **Nearby lodging**—"The Cabin" will no longer provide services as in the past, but prior guests are welcome if someone is home.

South Arm Road 📖 *p. 89* ... spring located 0.3 mile to the right. ➲ *right 9m*–to Andover (see East B Hill Road above). ☾ *left 4.5m*–to South Arm Campground (207-364-5155): tent sites $15 up, limited groceries, showers, laundromat, no credit cards.

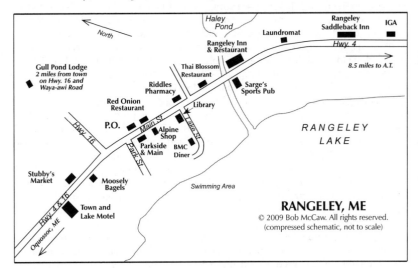

ME4 📖 *p. 90* ... usually an easy hitch in and out until after Labor Day weekend, when tourists disappear from Maine. ☾ *left 9m*–to **RANGELEY, ME 04970**: *Post office hours:* Mon-Fri 9:30am-12:30pm, 1:30pm-4:15pm, Sat 9:30am-noon; 207-864-2233; region once rated the 50th best vacation spot in America by Rand McNally. This may be a dubious honor, but it's a beautiful area. **Hostel**—Gull Pond Lodge (136 Camp Waya-awi Rd., Rangeley, ME 04970; 207-864-5563): $20 per person in hiker bunk room in private home on lake; private room $30S, $50D; kitchen privileges, canoe/kayak, call for pickup from Rangeley; will hold maildrop packages for guests; pets welcome. **Services**–Town and Lake Motel (112 Main St., Rangeley, ME 04970; 207-864-3755) $65S/$85D, pets OK ▪ Rangeley Inn (1-800-666-3687): $84 up, fine dining and tavern ▪ Rangeley Saddleback Inn (207-864-3434; <www.rangeleysaddlebackinn.com>): $90-100S/D, hot tub, pool, restaurant on site, pets $10 extra, will hold maildrop packages, call for possible ride ▪ Red Onion Restaurant: pizza, pasta dishes, sandwiches, burgers; open daily ▪ Parkside & Main Restaurant: reasonable prices, favorite with locals ▪ BMC Diner: breakfast and lunch ▪ Sarge's Pub: bar-type food, pizza, soups ▪ Rangeley IGA Supermarket: good for long-term resupply; open 7 days; about 0.7m from town toward the Trail ▪ laundromat: open 7 days; run by former thru-hiker ▪ Alpine Shop: gear, clothing, Coleman by the ounce; open 7 days ▪ library ▪ banks w/ATM.

Sugarloaf Mtn Trail 📖 *p. 91* ... ➲ *right 0.6m*–to Sugarloaf Summit House, an enclosed building with splendid views. From the nearby summit, at 4237 feet the second highest in Maine, it is possible to see from Mt. Washington all the way to Katahdin ... almost one-sixth the length of the entire Trail! Please note that the Summit House is private property.   Overnight stays are no longer allowed due to lack of sanitary facilities.

ME27 📖 *p. 91* ... ☾ *left 5m*–to **STRATTON, ME 04982**: *Post office hours:* Mon-Fri 8:30am-1pm and 1:30pm-4:15pm, Sat 8:30am-11:30am; 207-246-6461; usually an easy hitch until after the Labor Day weekend. *Services*—White Wolf Inn (Rt. 27 Main St., P. O. Box 590, Stratton, ME 04982; 207-246-2922): $50S/$55D, $10 higher on weekends, pets $5 extra, security deposit required; will hold maildrop packages for guests only; closed Tues ▪ Stratton Motel (162 Main St., P.O. Box 284, Stratton, ME 04982; 207-246-4171, <*www.thestrattonmotel.com*>): hostel with bunkbed $20, private room in motel $45S/$50D. Hiker kitchen and outdoor grill. All lodging comes with shower, linens, free long-distance telephone [in United States], internet access, laundry available $5 per load, free pickup and shuttle back to the A.T.; slack packing; shuttle to area trailheads between Gorham and Katahdin and pickup at major cities by arrangement. Resupply and bounce boxes accepted. ▪ Maine Roadhouse (207-246-2060): on road between Stratton and Rangeley, same owner as Stratton Motel. Bunkhouse $20, private rooms $40 S/D lodging comes with hiker kitchen, outdoor grill, shower, linens, free long-distance telephone [in United States], free laundry, free pickup and shuttle back to the A.T.; slack packing; shuttle to area trailheads between Gorham and Katahdin and pickup at major cities by arrangement. Resupply and bounce boxes accepted.▪ Diamond Corner B&B (207-246-2082): $80 up, no pets, open year-round ▪ White Wolf Restaurant: prime rib, pasta, Wolfburgers, pizza, salad bar; ice-cold Newcastle on tap; usually Fri nite is fish fry night; lunch and dinner Thur-Mon, dinner only Wed, closed Tues ▪ Stratton Diner: diner-style meals, burgers; closed Wed ▪ Fotter's Grocery: good for long-term resupply, fresh fruit, Coleman by the ounce; open 7 days ▪ Northland Cash Supply: limited hiker foods, good for short-term resupply; open daily ▪ laundromat: in basement of apartment building behind the post office, detergent and change available ▪ bank w/ATM. Best place to hitch back to the A.T. is usually across from post office.

Trail to Harrison Camps 📖 *p. 93* ... ➲ *right 0.1m*–to Harrison Camps (207-672-3625): Bed and breakfast for $35S, $30 per person double occupancy; pets on leash at all times; no credit cards. Harrison's features a "lumberjack's" pancake breakfast with 12 pancakes, sausage, eggs, juice, milk, or coffee, all for about $10; rave reviews from many past thru-hikers. Must make reservations night before, it is a short walk from Pierce Pond if you are not staying the night, time of breakfast (usually 7 or 7:30) will be announced when you make reservation. All hikers are welcome whether you stay or not. Potable water available from spigot on side of building and a phone is available for emergency calls.

Kennebec River 📖 *p. 93* ... The Kennebec is very dangerous to ford. A dam upstream releases water automatically on an unpredictable schedule when power generation is needed, and you cannot outrun the water once it starts to rise. An unfortunate section hiker drowned here in 1985. Since then, a ferry service has been in operation during peak hiking season. Catch the ferry (the official A.T. route) where the blazes come down to the river; a signal flag is provided to alert the ferry operator if he is on the opposite side when you arrive. "If you're late, plan to wait!" is the rule, so adjust your plans to arrive during scheduled times. Apoproximate schedule (2010 schedule not available at press time, check local signage for updates): May 22 through July 16, 9am-11am; July 17 through Sept 30, 9am-11am and 2pm-4pm; Oct 1 through Oct 12, 9am-11am. "Off season" service may be availble between May 1 and May 21 and Oct 13 and Oct 31, time and weather permitting. Call 207-672-4879 if you are planning on heading through on those dates (Harrison Camps has a phone). It is strongly recommended that you use the ferry, which is free to hikers during the published dates and hours of operation.

US201 📖 *p. 93* ... A.T. crosses the paved highway, passes through a parking area, and reenters the woods to head northward. ➲ *right 100ft on US201, then left 0.3m on the paved side road to*–**CARATUNK, ME 04925**: *Post office hours:* Mon-Fri 7:30am-11:30am and noon-3:45pm, Sat 7:30am-11:15am; 207-672-3416. ☾ *left 2m on US201*–to Northern Outdoors (1-800-765-7238): room in lodge for $59 per room (for walk-ins only; special thru-hiker rate shown is not for those calling ahead for reservations or for auto-assisted hikers), can have up to 6 people in room; cabin-tents $10 per person, tent sites $8 per person, free shower with or without stay, coin-operated laundry, white water rafting, hot tubs, restaurant; internet access; ATM inside; free shuttle to and from trailhead (times coordinated with ferry service). ➲ *right 1.5m*–to Sterling Inn (207-672-3333): hiker rate $45S (call ahead for reservation), $20 per additional person, will hold mail drop packages, no pets.

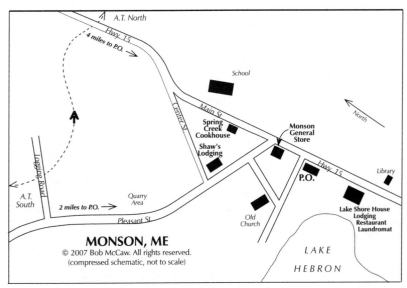

ME15 📖 *p. 94* ... ➲ *right 4.1m*–to **MONSON, ME 04464**: *Post office hours:* Mon-Fri 7:30am-11:30am and 12:30pm-4pm, Sat 7:30am-11am; 207-997-3975; last Trail town for northbounders, first for southbounders; both northbounders and southbounders have reason to celebrate reaching this milestone. Town is small, but businesses here

have adapted to the needs of thru-hikers over many years, so you should be able to find what you need to continue your journey. *Lodging*—Shaw's Lodging (17 Pleasant St., P. O. Box 72, Monson, ME 04464; 207-997-3597; <*www.shawslodging.com*>): bunk room $21.50 per person, private room $32S $54D with linens, shower, and towel (prices include tax); tenting $12 per person includes shower; shower without stay $5; breakfast $6.50 (dinner by request Sun-Tues, $12); camp store offers Coleman and denatured alcohol by the ounce, other fuels, basic backpacking gear and supplies, some backpacking foods. Shuttles available to all locations in Maine by arrangement (can do food drops in the 100-mile wilderness); will hold maildrop packages at no charge for guests ($5 for non-guests); pets allowed in bunkhouse only; no credit cards; open May 15-Oct 15; new hosts are Dawn and Sue ▪ Lakeshore House Lodging, Pub & Laundromat (207-997-7069), cell (207) 343-5033 <*www.lakeshore-house.com*>: open year-round; Rebekah Santagata, owner. Free shuttle to and from Monson trails. Bunks $25, Private $40S/$55D, all include shared bath, living room, dining area with some basic cooking stuff; check-in anytime, check-out anytime; packs out of room by 11 am please; advance reservations taken but not necessary; laundromat open 24 hours ($3 full load W/D); coin-op shower for nonguests; mail drops for anyone to P.O. Box 215, Monson, ME 04464; use of house phone with credit card, kayaks, paddleboats , and water trampoline free for guests; work-for-stay (3 hours of work); shuttle, slackpack, and food-drop arrangements. Well behaved dogs welcome; floating bonfire weekends. *Places to eat*—Spring Creek Cookhouse & BBQ: lunch and dinner, ribs, steaks; hours erratic ▪ Lakeshore House Restaurant & Pub: open Tue-Sat 12-9, Sun 12-8, Thu AYCE tacos, Fri AYCE fish. *Groceries*—Monson General Store: good for long-term resupply, drugstore rack, foot and hair care products, pizza, soup, and sandwiches; open 7 days. *Other services*—Lake Shore House Laundromat: open 7 days, 24 hours; coin-operated showers in laundry $4. *Nearby towns*—Greenville (with Northwoods Outfitters, 207-695-3288), Guilford, and Dover-Foxcroft have supermarkets and banks w/ATMs.

100-Mile Wilderness 📖 *p. 94* ... a 100-mile section through some of the most remote-feeling mountains and forest traversed by the Trail, although not actually as remote as it once was since a number of logging roads have been constructed through this section in recent years. Signs at the Trailhead suggest that you carry a ten-day supply of food, but most thru-hikers make it through in less time. As a northbounder, this is the climax of your odyssey. Consider taking extra time to enjoy this last stretch to the fullest.

Gulf Hagas Trail 📖 *p. 96* ... *On A.T.*–Gulf Hagas has been billed as the "Grand Canyon of the East," a 500 foot deep gorge like nothing else on the Trail. The 5.2 mile loop trail to the left, featuring five major waterfalls, is well worth the extra miles according to many. No overnight camping is permitted in Gulf Hagas. The Gulf Hagas Cut-off Trail, reached at mile point 3.9 on the loop, goes 1 mile to rejoin the A.T. at a point 0.7 mile north of where you left the white blazes to follow the Gulf Hagas Trail.

Mahar Tote Road 📖 *p. 97* ... at the mouth of Nahmakanta Stream on Pemadumcook Lake. ➔ *right 0.9m (use grassy-surfaced Mahar Landing Tote Road 100 yards after a gravel-surfaced logging road)*–to White House Landing Wilderness Camp (207-745-5116): bunkhouse $39 or private room $49 per person, both include AYCE breakfast and shower; camp store with food section (hikers report "enough to get you to Baxter or Monson"), trail supplies, Coleman and denatured alcohol by the ounce; meals available (at breakfast, lunch, dinner hours only); shuttles to Millinocket by arrangement, credit cards (for small fee); open Memorial Day through Oct 15. Use air horn to summon pickup by boat; no pickup after dark.

Abol Bridge 📖 *p. 98* ... *On A.T.*–the "postcard" view of Katahdin as the A.T. crosses the bridge over the West Branch of Penobscot River; use the pedestrian walkway only. *At the north end of the bridge:* Abol Bridge Campground & Campstore: open 7 days, 7am-7pm, May-Nov; public pay-cell telephone available. Store has hiker foods, fuel by the ounce, hot coffee, and the friendly face of owner Linda Belmont. Campground has tent sites for $10, hot coin-op showers for campers only, campground closes end of Sept. *Abol Pines Camping Area*—primitive camping on shore of the West Branch of Penobscot River at Abol Pines Camping Area, $5 per person (self-service pay station); located across the road from Abol Bridge Campstore.

Baxter State Park 📖 *p. 98* ... *On A.T.*–a wildlife sanctuary with 204,733-acres of forest preserve donated by the late Gov. Percival Baxter, with the stipulation that it be maintained as pristine wilderness forever. The park has no paved roads, electricity, showers, stores, or telephones. Overnight stay is permitted only at designated camping areas and by reservation only except for thru-hikers, who have been provided a special registration system for overnight camping at "The Birches" (thru-hiker-only, no family) near Katahdin Stream Campground. Have cash, since no credit cards are accepted for payment of fees anywhere inside park. The park opens for camping on May 15 (the A.T. usually thaws by the end of May allowing access to the summit) and closes for camping on October 15, so thru-hikers should make plans to summit Katahdin no earlier and no later than those dates. *"Baxter thru-hikers"*—a thru-hiker (as defined by Baxter State Park for applying park regulations) is someone who has hiked the A.T. through the 100-Mile Wilderness to enter the park at Abol Bridge. This means that southbounders starting at Baxter, and northbounders who leave the park for overnight stay and return next day by vehicle, do not qualify as thru-hikers under the Baxter definition, day-use rules apply. Southbounders will need to call ahead to reserve overnight camping space in the park. Reservations for regular campground sites can be made over the phone using credit cards 10 days or fewer before the desired arrival date, call the park office at 207-723-5140. Katahdin Stream Campground is unavailable to the public for reservations Fri-Sun during Labor Day weekend. *No dogs allowed in the park*—Your four-legged companion cannot enter Baxter State Park with you, a prohibition to protect the park's wildlife and a regulation vigorously enforced by park rangers, so you should make arrangements for boarding your dog. The nearest boarding option is North Ridge Boarding Kennels (23 Jones Road, Medway, ME 04460; 207-746-9537), $15 per day, open 7 days. *Park Information*—Baxter State Park Headquarters (located outside the park at 64 Balsam Dr., Millinocket, ME 04462; 207-723-5140; <www.baxterstateparkauthority.com>).

Information Board 📖 *p. 98* ... *On A.T.*–where northbounders can sign up for one of twelve overnight camping spaces available to thru-hikers at "The Birches" Campsite. If all spaces for that night are signed for when you arrive, you will need to stay elsewhere. Your best bet is to use the nearby Abol Pines Camping Area. Whatever you do, do not head north with the intention of "stealth camping.". You could get a fine and be escorted out of the park, not the best way to end your hike. Blueberry Ledges Trail (often muddy) leads to the right on blue-blazed trail from here 4.4 miles to "The Birches" Campsite.

Daicey Pond Campground 📖 *p. 99* ... ⊃ *right 0.1m*–(on dirt road) to weather board, ranger station, library, cabins, and the pond; no non-reservation camping. Picture post card view of Katahdin from the dock on the pond.

Katahdin Stream Campground 📖 *p. 99* ... *On A.T.*–with ranger station, sign-in/sign-out clipboard for summiting Katahdin, reservation-only lean-tos, which may be available for walk-ins on weekdays after Labor Day; $18 per lean-to overnight fee (up to two-people); also, an area set aside for thru-hikers only. *"The Birches" Campsite*—a thru-hiker-only campsite with 8 lean-to spaces and four tent-camping spaces, maximum of 12 thru-hikers per night permitted; $9 per person overnight fee, no credit cards. Note that this facility is only for those who signed up for an overnight space at the information board near Abol Bridge; check in at the ranger station here before heading to the campsite. Also, get water from Katahdin Stream here to take to your campsite.

Baxter Peak, Mt. Katahdin 📖 *p. 99* ... *On A.T.*–the name Katahdin means "greatest mountain," and it will be the single biggest climb of your trip, more than 4,000 feet of elevation change to reach the 5,267-foot summit. The ascent will take 3-4 hours, so try to start up no later than 8am. You can leave your spare gear on the enclosed porch at the Katahdin Stream ranger station. A sign-in board is provided for recording the time you start up and route you will follow. You must sign out here when you come down, or at another campground if you take another trail down and thus do not return to Katahdin Stream. Rain or shine, we all wish you Class I companions for your climb, or, if you climb solo, be assured that you will not be alone. Everyone who has ever thru-hiked the Appalachian Trail from Georgia to Maine will be there with you in spirit as you touch the sign. Well done!

Northbounders leaving the park—All motorists leaving the park will be going your way, since there is only one road out of the park and it goes to Millinocket. Ask around at the campground parking area for a ride. Few new 2,000 Milers have trouble getting a ride into town. Services in Millinocket and Medway (including taxi) are listed on the next page, as well as instructions for heading south from Maine.

Southbounders entering the park—Hikers starting at Baxter do not qualify as thru-hikers under the Baxter definition of the term. Therefore, southbounders cannot stay at "The Birches" Campsite for thru-hikers, so you will need to call ahead to reserve overnight camping space in the park before arriving (ask for space at Katahdin Stream Campground). Reservations for regular campground sites can be made over the phone using credit cards 10 or fewer days before the desired date of stay, call the park office at 207-723-5140. If you are being driven to the park by family or friends, see the note on the next page. The park opens officially on May 15 each year but access to the summit via the A.T. usually opens later, so be sure to call the park for information about summit access, weather, and black flies before heading to Maine. See information on Millinocket regarding possible transportation to the park.

Family and friends—If you plan to have family and friends join you in the park for the end/start of your hike, you or they should call the Baxter State Park Headquarters (207-723-5140) well ahead of time to check on vehicle regulations, park visitor/day use entrance fees, and the availability of camping at Katahdin Stream Campground if they want to stay overnight with you inside the park (they cannot stay in the park without reservations). Park personnel are adept at dealing with hikers and helping their families make arrangements. Note that it is often difficult to get last-minute reservations at park campgrounds in late summer (after Labor Day your chances improve).

Services near Baxter State Park—If you or your family and friends need to stay overnight in Millinocket (closest town to Baxter State Park) or nearby Medway before heading home or into the park, here are your options:

Millinocket, ME 04462: *Post office hours:* Mon-Fri 9am-4pm, Sat 9am-11:30am; 207-723-5921. **Lodging**—Appalachian Trail Lodge (33 Penobscot Ave., Millinocket, ME 04462; 207-723-4321 <www.appalachiantraillodge.com>): owners Paul (OleMan) & Jaime (NaviGator) Renaud, $25 bunkroom, private room $35S/$55D, furnished apartment call for rates; parking $1/day; showers for nonguests $3; WiFi, fuel, some hiking supplies; licensed and insured shuttle service to and from bus in Medway, into 100-mile wilderness or Monson, free daily shuttle from Baxter park, Sept 1-Oct 15, between 3pm – 4:30pm. food drops, slackpack in 100-mile wilderness; other shuttles by arrangement; one private room available for hikers with pets; mail drops accepted for guests; credit cards accepted. SOBO special (pickup in Medway, bed in bunkroom, breakfast at AT Cafe', and shuttle to Katahdin Stream, $70pp by reservation. ▪ Pamola Motor Lodge (1-800-575-9746): $59S $69D, jacuzzi, pets OK, continental breakfast; restaurant and lounge in motel ▪ America's Best Value Inn (207-723-9777): Jul-Oct 15 $69S, $10 each additional person, hot tubs, pool, pets $10 ▪ Katahdin Cabins (207-723-6305) special hiker rate $48 up, near town, free use of mountain bikes, pets allowed (call in advance). *Places to eat*—Appalachian Trail Cafe, home cooking (owned by same folks who own the Appalachian Trail Lodge listed above) ▪ Scootic Inn ▪ River Drivers Restaurant, fine dining ▪ McDonald's ▪ House of Pizza. *Other services*—Hannaford's Supermarket and IGA Foodliner, both good for long-term resupply ▪ laundromats; open 7 days ▪ Coleman and denatured alcohol at Katahdin General (hardware) Store. *Taxi*—Town Taxi (207-723-2000) Millinocket to Katahdin Stream, $55. *Festival*—the Trail's End Festival, Sept 11-12, will have food, music, free in-town camping and hiker activities. A great opportunity for an end-of-hike reunion.

Medway, ME 04460: *Post-office hours:* Mon-Fri 7:30am-11:30am, 1pm-4:30pm, Sat 8am-11:30am; 207-746-9949. **Services**—Gateway Inn (207-746-3193): $60 and up, pets allowed; and Katahdin Shadows Motel (207-746-5162) $54S/$59D (possible hiker discount); kitchen, pets allowed, open year-round, will pick up at bus station if you call ahead.

Heading south from Maine—From Millinocket, the nearest public transportation south is on Highway 157 in Medway, near the intersection with Interstate 95. Cyr Bus Line (1-800-244-2335; <www.cyrbustours.com>) has one bus leaving daily for Bangor at 9:30am; fare is $11.50; no pets allowed on bus. You can buy a ticket and catch the bus at Medway Irving Big Stop & Restaurant (207-746-3411). The northbound bus from Bangor leaves the Greyhound station at 6PM.

Important Telephone Numbers

For reporting safety problems—If you need law enforcement or EMS assistance, call the local area 911 service (just dial "911"). For non-emergency safety reports, call the ATC Harpers Ferry Office at ***304-535-6331*** (daytime). Even when you have filed a report with local law enforcement authorities, be sure to file an incident report with ATC, too.

For reporting maintainance problems—The local A.T. clubs are responsible for maintaining of the Trail. The best way for you to report a problem concerning the condition of a Trail section or its facilities is to convey your comments to the ATC regional office responsible for overseeing that section. The regional director will pass your information to the appropriate club for attention, and will check back later to verify that problems have been fixed. Here are the telephone numbers for the regional offices:

Southern: *Springer Mountain to Tennessee-Virginia border* 828-254-3708
Southwest Virginia: *Tennessee-Virginia border to Rockfish Gap* 540-953-3571
Mid-Atlantic: *Rockfish Gap to New York-Connecticut border* 717-258-5771
New England: *New York-Connecticut border to Katahdin* 603-795-4935

For warranty or problems with gear—All major gear manufacturers have toll-free customer service numbers you can call if you have a warranty question or problems with gear during your hike. Here are some of the more frequently needed numbers:

Arcteryx	604-451-7755	Mountainsmith	800-426-4075
Asolo/Lowe Alpine	603-448-8827	North Face	800-447-2333
Big Agnes	877-554-8975	Osprey	970-564-5900
Camp Trails	800-572-8822	Outdoor Research	800-421-2421
Dana Design	888-357-3262	Peak 1/Coleman	800-835-3278
Danner	800-345-0430	Platypus	800-531-9531
Eureka!	800-572-8822	PUR (now Katadyn)	800-755-6701
First Need	800-441-8166	Salomon	800-654-2668
Garmont	800-943-4453	Sierra Designs	800-736-8551
Granite Gear	218-834-6157	Slumberjack	800-233-6283
Gregory	800-477-3420	Sweetwater	800-531-9531
GoLite	888-546-5483	Tarptent (Henry Shires)	650-587-1548
Hi-Tec	800-521-1698	Tecnica	800-258-3897
JanSport	800-426-9227	Thermarest	800-531-9531
Katadyn	800-755-6701	Vasque	800-224-4453
Kelty	866-349-7225	Zzip Stove	800-594-9046
Leki	800-255-9982	***For ordering—***	
Marmot	888-357-3262	Campmor	800-226-7667
Merrell	800-789-8586	EMS	888-463-6367
Mountain Hardwear	800-953-8398	L.L. Bean	800-341-4341
MSR	800-531-9531	REI	800-426-4840

Record telephone number for your local outfitter(s) below:

(   )   _____   (   )   _____
  Area Code   *Area Code*

Post Office Information

The post offices in this listing are the ones most frequently used as maildrop locations by past thru-hikers, according to survey. The number preceding the post-office name indicates how many thru-hikers used that location last year as a maildrop location, as follows: ❶ = 200+, ❷ = 100+, ❸ = 50+, ❹ = special listing.

❶ **Suches, GA 30572**—Mon-Fri 7:30-11:30, 1-4:30, Sat 7:30-11:30;
      3605 Hwy. 60, 706-747-2611

❷ **Helen, GA 30545**—Mon-Fri 9-5, Sat 9-12; 7976 S. Main St., 706-878-2422

❶ **Hiawassee, GA 30546**—Mon-Fri 8:30-5, Sat 8:30-12; 188 N. Main St.,
      706-896-3632

❶ **Franklin, NC 28734**—Mon-Fri 8:30-5, Sat 9-12; 250 Depot St., 828-524-3219

❶ **Fontana Dam, NC 28733**—Mon-Fri 8:30-3, 50 Fontana Rd., 828-498-2315

❷ **Gatlinburg, TN 37738**—Mon-Fri 9-5, Sat 9-11; 1216 E. Parkway, 865-436-3229

❶ **Hot Springs, NC 28743**—Mon-Fri 8:30-11:30, 1-4, Sat 8:30-10:30;
      111 Bridge St., 828-622-3242

❶ **Erwin, TN 37650**—Mon-Fri 8:30-4:45, Sat 10-12; 201 N. Main, 423-743-9422

❷ **Roan Mountain, TN 37687**—Mon-Fri 8-12, 1-4, Sat 7:30-9:30;
      8060 Hwy. 19E, 423-772-3014

❸ **Elk Park, NC 28622**—Mon-Fri 7:30-12, 1:30-4:15, Sat 7:30-11;
      153 Main St., 828-733-5711

❸ **Hampton, TN 37658**—Mon-Fri 7:30-11:30, 12:30-4, Sat 8-10;
      433 Hwy. 321, 423-725-2177

❶ **Damascus, VA 24236**—Mon-Fri 8:30-1, 2-4:30, Sat 9-11;
      211 N. Reynolds St., 276-475-3411

❷ **Troutdale, VA 24378**—Mon-Fri 8:15-12, 1-4:30, Sat 8:15-11:30;
      93 Ripshin Rd., 276-677-3221

❷ **Atkins, VA 24311**—Mon-Fri 9-1, 2:30-4, Sat 9:30-11; 5864 Lee Hwy.,
      276-783-5551

❶ **Bland, VA 24315**—Mon-Fri 8-11:30, 12-4, Sat 9-11; 207 Jackson St.,
      276-688-3751

❶ **Pearisburg, VA 24134**—Mon-Fri 9-4:30, Sat 10-12; will answer knock until
      5:30pm weekdays if anyone working; 206 N. Main St., 540-921-1100

❶ **Catawba, VA 24070**—Mon-Fri 7:30-12, 1-5, Sat 8-10:30;
      4917 Catawba Creek Rd., 540-384-6011

❶ **Daleville, VA 24083**—Mon-Fri 8-5, Sat 8-12; 1492 Roanoke Rd., 540-992-4422

❶ **Troutville, VA 24175**—Mon-Fri 9-12, 1-5, Sat 9-11; 4952 Lee Hwy.,
      540-992-1472

❷ **Big Island, VA 24526**—Mon-Fri 8:30-12:30, 1:30-4:30, Sat 8-10;
      10830 Lee Jackson Hwy., 434-299-5072

❷ **Glasgow, VA 24555**—Mon-Fri 8-11:30, 12:30-4:30, Sat 8:30-10:30;
      805 Blue Ridge Rd., 540-258-2852

❸ **Buena Vista, VA 24416**—Mon-Fri 8:30-4:30; 2071 Forest Ave., 540-261-8959

❸ **Montebello. VA 24464**—Mon-Fri 8-12, 12:30-4:30, Sat 9-12;
      15048 Crabtree Falls Hwy., 540-377-9218

❶ **Waynesboro, VA 22980**—Mon-Fri 9-5; 200 S. Wayne Ave., 540-942-7320

❸ **Elkton, VA 22827**—Mon-Fri 8:30-4:30, Sat 9-11; 102 W. Rockingham St.,
      540-298-7772

❸ **Luray, VA 22835**—Mon-Fri 8:30-4:30; 102 S. Broad St., 540-743-2100

❶ **Front Royal, VA 22630**—Mon-Fri 8:30-5, Sat 8:30-1; 120 E. 3rd, 540-635-7983

❶ **Linden, VA 22642**—Mon-Fri 8-12, 1-5, Sat 8-12; 13734 John Marshall Hwy.,
      540-636-9936

❶ Harpers Ferry, WV 25425—Mon-Fri 8-4, Sat 9-12; 1010 Washington St., 304-535-2479

❷ Boonsboro, MD 21713—Mon-Fri 9-1, 2-5, Sat 9-12; 5 Potomac St., 301-432-6861

❷ Smithsburg, MD 21783—Mon-Fri 8:30-1, 2-4:30, Sat 8:30-12; 43 Grove Lane, 301-824-2828

❷ Cascade, MD 21719—Mon-Fri 8-1, 2-5, Sat 8-12; 25208 Military Rd., 301-241-3403

❶ Blue Ridge Summit, PA 17214—Mon-Fri 8-4, Sat 9-11:30; 14959 Buchanan Trail E., 717-794-2335

❷ Waynesboro, PA 17268—Mon-Fri 8:30-5, Sat 9-12; 118 E. Main St., 717-762-1513

❸ South Mountain, PA 17261—Mon-Fri 8:30-1, 2-4:45, Sat 8:30-11:30; 1044 S. Mountain Rd., 717-749-5833

❶ Boiling Springs, PA 17007—Mon-Fri 8-4:30, Sat 8-12; 301 E. 1st St., 717-258-6668

❶ Duncannon, PA 17020—Mon-Fri 8-4:30, Sat 9-12; 203 N. Market St., 717-834-3332

❶ Port Clinton, PA 19549—Mon-Fri 7:30-12:30, 2-5, Sat 8-11; 8 Broad St., 610-562-3787

❸ Slatington, PA 18080—Mon-Fri 8:30-5, Sat 8:30-12; 605 Main St., 610-767-2182

❶ Palmerton, PA 18071—Mon-Fri 8:30-5, Sat 8:30-12; 128 Delaware Ave., 610-826-2286

❷ Wind Gap, PA 18091—Mon-Fri 8:30-5, Sat 8:30-12, 138 N. Broadway, 610-863-6206

❶ Delaware Water Gap, PA 18327—Mon-Fri 8:30-12, 1-4:45 Sat 8:30-11:30; 12 Shepard Ave., 570-476-0304

❶ Unionville, NY 10988—Mon-Fri 8-11:30, 1-5, Sat 9-12; 1 Main St., 845-726-3535

❸ Glenwood, NJ 07418—Mon-Fri 7:30-5, Sat 10-2; 958 Rt. 517, 973-764-2616

❶ Vernon, NJ 07462—Mon-Fri 8:30-5, Sat 9:30-12:30; 530 Rt. 515, 973-764-9056

❶ Greenwood Lake, NY 10925—Mon-Fri 8-5, Sat 9-12; 123 Windemere Ave., 845-477-7328

❸ Warwick, NY 10990—Mon-Fri 8:30-5, Sat 9-4; 108 Main St., 845-986-0271

❸ Southfields, NY 10975—Mon-Fri 8:30-12, 1-5, Sat 8:30-11:30; 996 Rt. 17, 845-351-2628

❹ Bear Mountain, NY 10911—Mon-Fri 8-10, may extend hours in summer; 30 Service Rd., 845-786-3747; nearby Fort Montgomery preferable

❶ Fort Montgomery, NY 10922—Mon-Fri 8:30-1, 2:30-5, Sat 8:30-12; 130 Firefighters Memorial Drive, 845-446-8459

❸ Poughquag, NY 12570—Mon-Fri 8:30-5, Sat 8:30-12:30; 2546 Rt. 55, 845-724-4763

❷ Pawling, NY 12564—Mon-Fri 8:30-5, Sat 9-12; 10 Broad St., 845-855-2669

❶ Kent, CT 06757—Mon-Fri 8-1, 2-5, Sat 8:30-12:30; 31 Kent Green Blvd., 860-927-3435

❷ Cornwall Bridge, CT 06754—Mon-Fri 8-1, 2-5, Sat 9-12:30; 18A Kent Rd., 860-672-6710

❸ Falls Village, CT 06031—Mon-Fri 8:30-1, 2-5, Sat 8:30-12; 5 Miner St., 860-824-7781

❶ Salisbury, CT 06068—Mon-Fri 8-1, 2-5, Sat 9-12; 22 Main St., 860-435-5072

❷ South Egremont, MA 01258—Mon-Fri 8:15-4, Sat 9-11:30; 64 Main St., 413-528-1571

❷ Great Barrington, MA 01230—Mon-Fri 8:30-4:30, Sat 8:30-12:30; 222 Main St., 413-528-3670

❷ **Tyringham, MA 01264**—Mon-Fri 9-12:30, 4-5:30, Sat 8:30-12:30; 118 Main Rd., 413-243-1225

❶ **Dalton, MA 01227**—Mon-Fri 8:30-4:30, Sat 9-12; 609 Main St., 413-684-0364

❶ **Cheshire, MA 01225**—Mon-Fri 7:30-1, 2-4:30, Sat 8:30-11:30; 214 Church St., 413-743-3184

❶ **Williamstown, MA 01267**—Mon-Fri 8:30-4:30, Sat 9-12; 56 Spring St., 413-458-3707

❷ **North Adams, MA 01247**—Mon-Fri 8:30-4:30, Sat 10-12, 67 Summer St., 413-664-4554

❷ **Bennington, VT 05201**—Mon-Fri 8-5, Sat 9-2 ; 108 Elm St., 802-442-2421

❶ **Manchester Center, VT 05255**—Mon-Fri 8:30-4:30, Sat 9-12; 3452 Richville Rd., 802-362-3070

❷ **Rutland, VT 05701**—Mon-Fri 8-5, Sat 8-12; 173 West St., 802-773-0222

❷ **Killington, VT 05751**—Mon-Fri 8:30-4:30, Sat 8:30-12; 2046 Rt. 4, 802-775-4247

❸ **Woodstock, VT 05091**—Mon-Fri 8:30-5, Sat 9-12; 22 Central St., 802-457-1323

❸ **South Pomfret, VT 05067**—Mon-Fri 8-1, 2-4:45, Sat 8:30-11:30; 2035 Pomfret Rd., 802-457-1147

❷ **West Hartford, VT 05084**—Mon-Fri 7-11:30 and 1-4:45, Sat 7:30-10:15; 4784 Rt. 14, 802-295-6293

❸ **Norwich, VT 05055**—Mon-Fri 8:30-5, Sat 9-12; 293 Main St., 802-649-1608

❶ **Hanover, NH 03755**—Mon-Fri 8:30-5, Sat 8:30-12; 50 S. Main St., 603-643-4544

❶ **Glencliff, NH 03238**—Mon-Fri 7-10, 2-5, Sat 7-1; 1385 Rt. 25, 603-989-5154

❶ **North Woodstock, NH 03262**—Mon-Fri 9:30-12:30, 1:30-4:30, Sat 9-12; 159 Main St., 603-745-8134

❹ **Mt. Washington, NH 03589**—not recommended for sending packages

❶ **Gorham, NH 03581**—Mon-Fri 8:30-5, Sat 8:30-12; 165 Main St., 603-466-2182

❶ **Andover, ME 04216**—Mon-Fri 8:30-1:30, 2-4:30, Sat 8:30-11:30; 6 Church St., 207-392-4571

❶ **Rangeley, ME 04970**—Mon-Fri 9:30-12:30, 1:30-4:15, Sat 9:30-12; 2517 Main St., 207-864-2233

❶ **Stratton, ME 04982**—Mon-Fri 8:30-1, 1:30-4, Sat 8:30-11:30; 95 Main St., 207-246-6461

❶ **Caratunk, ME 04925**—Mon-Fri 7:30-11:30, 12-3:45, Sat 7:30-11:15; 172 Main St., 207-672-3416

❶ **Monson, ME 04464**—Mon-Fri 7:30-11:30, 12:30-4, Sat 7:30-11; 2 Greenville Rd., 207-997-3975

❹ **Millinocket, ME 04462**—Mon-Fri 9-4, Sat 9-11:30; 113 Penobscot Ave., 207-723-5921

IMPORTANT!

Mail sent to post offices in Trail towns should be addressed to: Your Real Name (not a Trail name), c/o General Delivery, City, State, ZIP Code, and the notation "Hold for A.T. Hiker" followed by your expected arrival date on the letter or package. Do not send UPS or FedEx packages to post offices, since by law they cannot accept them. Most post offices ask thru-hikers for some form of photo I.D. (drivers license is acceptable). All post offices will give up to $50 in cash on debit cards only.

Libraries near the Trail

Internet access is available in most small towns at the library. Following is a list of libraries and their hours. Please be considerate of time limitations and other rules. Hours are subject to change; you may wish to call ahead.

Hiawassee, GA (99 S. Berrong St., 706-896-6169), 9-5 MTWF, 10-6 Th.
Franklin, NC (819 Siler Rd., 828-524-3600), 9-8 M-Th, 9-5 F-Sa.
Gatlinburg, TN (207 Cherokee Orchard Rd., 865-436-5588), 10-5 MWThF, 10-8 Tu, 10-1 Sa.
Hot Springs, NC (88 Bridge St., 828-622-3584), 10-7 M, 10-6 Tu, 10-2 W, 10-6 Th, 10-5 F, 10-2 Sa.
Erwin, TN (201 Nolichucky Ave., 423-743-6533), 10-6 M-F, 11-3 Sa
Damascus, VA (temporarily closed)
Bland, VA (697 Main St., 276-688-3737), 9:30-4:30 MWFSa, 9:30-8 TTh
Pearisburg, VA (209 Fort Branch Rd., 540-921-2556) 12-8 M, 12-5 Tu, 9-5 W, 9-8 Th, 9-5 F, 9-1 Sa.
Glasgow, VA (1108 Blue Ridge Road, 540-258-2509) 10-7 M, 10-5:30 Tu-W, 10-7 Th, 10-1 Sa.
Buena Vista, VA (2210 Magnolia Ave., 540-261-2715), 10-5 MTWF, 1-7 Th, 10-1 Sa.
Waynesboro, VA (600 S. Wayne Ave., 540-942-6746) 9-9 M-F, 9-5 Sa.
Elkton, VA (106 N. Terrace Ave., 540-298-2964) 10-5 M-Tu, 2-6 W, 12-5 Th-F
Luray, VA (100 Zerkel St., 540-743-6867) 9:30-5 MWF, 9:30-6 Tu, 9:30-7 Th, 9:30-2 Sa.
Front Royal, VA (538 Villa Ave., 540-635-3153) 10-8 M-Th, 10-5 F-Sa, 1-5 Su.
Harpers Ferry, WV (1515 Polk St., 304-535-2301) 10-5:30 MTuFSa, 10-8 WTh
Boonsboro, MD (401 Potomac St., 301-432-5723) 10-7 M-F, 10-2 Sa
Smiths burg, MD (66 W. Water St., 301-824-7722) 10-7 M-F, 10-2 Sa
Blue Ridge Summit, PA (717-794-2240) 3-8 M-Th, 10-3 Sa
Waynesboro, PA (45 E. Main St., 717-762-3335) 9:30-8 M-Th, 9:30-5 F, 9-4 Sa
Mt. Holly Springs, PA (114 N. Baltimore Ave., 717-486-3688) 10-9 M-Th, 10-6 F, 9-4 Sa
Hamburg, PA (35 N. 3rd St., 610-562-2843) 10-8 M, 12-8 TTh, 10-5 WF, 9-4 Sa
Palmerton, PA (402 Delaware Ave., 610-826-3424) 10-8 M, 10-5 T-F, 9-4 Sa.
Slatington, PA (650 Main St., 610-767-6461) 9-7 MW, 9-3 Tu, 9-5 F, 8-2 Sa
Stroudsburg, PA (1002 N. 9th St., 570-629-5858) 9-9 M-Th, 9-6 F, 9-5 Sa, 1-5 Su
Vernon, NJ (66 Rt. 94, 973-827-8095) 9-5 MWFSa, 9-8:30 TuTh
Greenwood Lake, NY (79 Waterstone Rd., 845-477-8377) 9-5 M, 9-9 T-Th, 9-5 F, 10-4 Sa, 11-3 Su
Warwick, NY (845-986-1047) 9-8 M-Th, 9-5 F-Sa
Highland Falls, NY (298 Main St., 845-446-3113) 10-5 MWThF, 10-7 Tu, 10-2 Sa
Pawling, NY (11 Broad St., 845-855-3444) 10-8 T-Th, 10-4 F-Sa
Wingdale, NY (1797 Rt. 22, 845-832-6605) 10-8 M-F, 10-4 Sa
Kent, CT (32 N. Main St., 860-927-3761) 10-5:30 M-F, 10-4 Sa
Salisbury, CT (38 Main St., 860-435-2838) 10-7 Tu, 10-5 W, 10-7 Th, 10-5 F, 10-4 Sa, 1-4 Su
Great Barrington, MA (231 Main St., 413-528-2403) 10-6 MTuWF, 12-8 Th, 9-1 Sa
Dalton, MA (462 Main St., 413-684-6112) 12-8 M, 10-4 Tu, 12-8 W, 12-5:30 Th, 10-2 Sa
Cheshire, MA (80 Church St., 413-743-4746) 11-4 M, 3-8 Tu, 11-4 W
Williamstown, MA (1095 Main St., 413-458-5369) 10-5:30 MTThF, 10-8 W, 10-4 Sa
North Adams, MA (74 Church St., 413-662-3133) 9-8 MTuTh, 9-5 WF, 9-1 Sa
Bennington, VT (101 Silver St., 802-442-9051) 10-8 MTh, 10-5 TWF, 10-1 Sa

Manchester, VT (48 West Road, 802-362-2607) 10-6 TuTh, 10-8 W, 10-4 FSa
Danby, VT (74 S. Main St., 802-293-5106) limited hours, call ahead
Wallingford, VT (14 S. Main St., 802-446-2685) 10-5 TuThF, 10-8 W, 9-12 Sa
Rutland, VT (10 Court St., 802-773-1860) 9-9 M, 11:30-5:30 Tu, 11:30-9 W, 9-5:30 ThF, 9-5 Sa
South Pomfret, VT (15 Library St., 802-457-2236) 10-6 Tu, 10-8 Th, 10-2 Sa
West Hartford, VT (5133 Rt. 14, 802-295-7992) 12-7 MTuWF, 9-2 Sa
Hanover, NH (13 South St., 603-643-4120) 10-8 M-Th, 10-6 F, 10-5 Sa
Lincoln, NH (22 Church St., 603-745-8159) 12-8 M-F, 10-2 Sa
Gorham, NH (35 Railroad St., 603-466-2525) 10-7 MWF, 10-8 TuTh
Bethel, ME (207-824-2520) 9-1 MSa, 1-5 TuThF, 1-8 W
Andover, ME (46 Church St., 207-392-4841) 1-4:30 TuWSa, 1-8 Th
Rangeley, ME (7 Lake St., 207-864-5529) 10-7 Tu, 10-4:30 W-F, 10-2 Sa
Stratton, ME (88 Main St., 207-246-4401) 10-5 MWF, 1-5 TTh, 9-1 Sa
Monson, ME (Main St., 207-997-3785) 1-5 MWF
Millinocket, ME (5 Maine Ave., 207-723-7020) 9-7 MTh, 1-7 TuW, 1-5 F

Glossary of Trail Terms

Alumni Thru-hiker is a person who has attempted and/or completed a thru-hike.

ATC is the abbreviation for Appalachian Trail Conservancy (formerly Conference), the private organization to which the NPS has delegated day-to-day A.T. management.

AYCE is the abbreviation for "all you can eat."

Blazes are painted, 2-inch by 6-inch, vertical white rectangles that are placed at eye height on trees and other objects, in both directions, to mark the official route of the Trail. Side trails are marked with blue blazes.

Blowdown is a tree or shrub that has fallen across the Trail.

Blue-blazer is a long-distance hiker who substitutes a section of blue-blazed trail for a white-blazed section between two points on the Trail.

Cairn is a heap of stones, set up to look artificial, that serves to mark the Trail route in dense vegetation or above treeline.

Dodgeways are V-shaped stiles through fences, usually at livestock enclosures.

Double blaze refers to two blazes, one placed two inches above the other, at places requiring hiker alertness and usually just before a turn in the Trail. In some areas, the top blaze is offset in the direction of the turn.

End-to-ender is an alternative term for 2,000-Miler.

Flip-flopper is a thru-hiker who begins at one terminus of the Trail, hikes toward the other terminus, then jumps ahead to the other terminus, and hikes back toward the initial terminus to complete his or her thru-hike at the jumping point.

Gear head is a thru-hiker who has hiked over a thousand miles or so and still talks about nothing but gear.

Hike your own hike is the mantra of thru-hiking, and means that you are free to hike the Trail in the way that most satisfies yourself as long as you are acting lawfully, within the scope of the official purpose of the Appalachian Trail *(see page 28)*, cognizant of the traditions of A.T. hiking, and respectful toward all other hikers.

Lean-to is another word for shelter, used primarily in New England.

Long-distance hiker is a somewhat indeterminate term applied to anyone who is hiking more than a few weeks, often used interchangeably with the term thru-hiker.

Maintainer is a volunteer who participates in the organized Trail-maintenance programs of the ATC and its member clubs.

NPS is the abbreviation for National Park Service.

National scenic trail is the official designation for one type of trail protected by the National Scenic Trails System Act of 1968; the A.T. is a national scenic trail.

Power hiker is a hiker who habitually chooses to cover very long distances each day, often hiking late into the evening.

PUDS is shorthand for "pointless ups and downs," referring to the way mountains appear to thru-hikers when the lethargy of long-distance hiking sets in, as it will from time to time; several PUDS in a row are MUDS, "mindless ups and downs."

Purist is a thru-hiker or section hiker who makes it a point to hike every mile of the white-blazed (official) Trail; an "extreme purist" hikes past every white blaze.

Puncheon (aka bog bridge) is a wooden walkway across bogs and marshy areas.

Section hiker is a person attempting to become a 2,000 Miler by doing a series of section hikes over a period of time.

Slabbing is a hiking term that refers to going around a mountain on a moderately graded footpath, as opposed to going straight up and over the mountain.

Slackpacking is a term coined by thru-hikers to describe an unhurried style of thru-hiking (*i.e.,* not taut or tense, slack), but over the years has come to mean simply hiking without a backpack; in recent years the practice has been promoted by lodging owners for commercial and/or social purposes; not usually done by traditional thru-hikers.

Springer fever is the almost uncontrollable urge to be back on the Trail that hits thru-hikers of past years each spring.

Stile is a construction, usually wooden steps or a ladder, that allows easy passage over a fence or other obstacle.

Thru-hike has been defined from the earliest days of the Trail's history as a hike that begins at one terminus of the Trail and continues step by step sequentially and essentially unassisted along the footpath, without the hiker leaving to resume life off the Trail, until the other terminus is reached; can be done south to north or north to south.

Thru-hiker is a person attempting to become a 2,000 Miler by doing a thru-hike.

Tour-hiker is a person who claims to be hiking the entire A.T., but slackpacks day after day, skips sections, and/or takes blue-blazes as a substitute for the official A.T. route; often tries to find a way to beat the system and hike as little as possible; scoffs at the traditions of thru-hiking and thinks "hike your own hike" nullifies the 2000-miler requirements and/or is the only explanation needed to excuse bad conduct/etiquette.

Trail magic is the term used to describe the serendipitous acts of kindness extended to thru-hikers by strangers during their hike; as opposed to pre-planned cookouts and feasts at Trail crossings which should really be called "Trail catering" instead.

2,000 Miler is a person who has hiked the entire distance between termini of the official (white-blazed) A.T., either by thru-hiking or section hiking *(see requirements, p. 4)*.

USFS is the abbreviation for United States Forest Service.

Waterbar is a log or rock barrier that diverts water off the Trail to prevent erosion.

Yogi-ing is the good-natured art of "letting" food be offered cheerfully by strangers without actually asking them directly (If you ask, it's begging!).

Yo-yo-ing is the act of completing one A.T. thru-hike, then immediately turning around to begin another in the opposite direction.

Zero day is a day during which zero miles of the A.T. are hiked, usually a day spent in a Trail town resupplying and resting but can be a day in the woods as well.

Wildflower Guide

This guide lists spring wildflowers commonly seen along the Trail in the South (locations indicated by ✿ in the "Mileage Index" and "Thru-hiker Notes" sections). Flowers are listed by main color, then alphabetically. The brief descriptions are not intended for the serious user, but for the novice. If mistakes are made, so what? As Shakespeare said, "What's in a name? That which we call a rose, by any other name would smell as sweet." Have fun trying to identify wildflowers; above all, simply enjoy seeing them.

BLUE

• *bluets:* four petals, ¼-inch flowers, pale blue with yellow centers; 2-8 inches high.

GREEN

• *jack-in-the-pulpit:* leaf stem 1-3 feet high with three pointed oval leaves, flower on separate stem (a greenish tubelike structure with green to maroonish inside and hood overhanging green to maroon, club-shaped spike).
• *rattlesnake plantain:* greenish-white flowers clustered on downy spike, hairy leaves with white markings, leaves at base; 6-18 inches high.

MAROON

• *red trillium:* three petals, red to maroon with foul smell, also called stinking benjamin.
• *toadshade trillium:* three upright petals, maroon to brownish, three leaves; 4-12 inches high.

ORANGE

• *flame azalea:* flowers orange with reddish veins, trumpetlike; shrub 4-10 feet high.
• *tulip trees:* flowers tuliplike, green and orange; tree grows to 120 feet high.

PINK

• *common wood sorrel:* five petals, pinkish with purplish stripes around star-shaped yellow center, leaves akin to three-leaf clover; 2-6 inches high.
• *eastern redbud tree:* pink flowers in 4-8 clusters, leaves heart-shaped; tree 10-20 feet high.
• *pink lady's-slipper:* nodding pink pouch-like structure with veined lip and purplish-brown twisted side petals; 6-14 inches high.
• *rosebay rhododendron:* white to pink flowers in clusters; shrub 10-20 feet high.
• *spring beauty:* five petals, pink to white with dark pink veins, leaves like blades of grass; 6-12 inches high.

PURPLE

• *birdsfoot violet:* five lavender petals, upper two slanting backward and often darker, leaves on separate stem; 4-10 inches high.
• *common blue violet:* five petals, purple to white, 3-8 inches high.
• *crested dwarf iris:* orchidlike, purple with orange and white crests; 3-5 inches high.
• *dwarf larkspur:* five petals, flower trumpet-shaped, purple or blue with white in center, flowers clustered along stem top, divided leaves on stem; 1-2 feet high.
• *fringed polygala:* three petals, two winglike, rose-purple with fringe at tip, shiny oval leaves; 3-6 inches high.
• *purple rhododendron:* lavender flowers in large clusters; shrub 10-20 feet high.
• *robin's plantain:* violet or lilac with yellow center, 1½-inch rayed flowers, dandelionlike; 6-16 inches high.
• *showy orchis:* purple to pink helmetlike flowers with white spur underneath the helmet, leaves shiny; 5-12 inches high.
• *wild geranium:* five petals, purple to rose, leaves lobed and toothed; 1-3 feet high.

• *fire pink:* five slender notched petals, yellow stamens, hairy leaves; 1-2 feet high.

• *wild columbine:* five red tubular sepals with knobs, yellow cathedral-like petals inside, nodding, leaves fernlike; 1-4 feet high.

WHITE

3 petals—

• *nodding trillium:* solitary flower, white with three backswept petals, nodding from three leaves; 10-18 inches high.

• *painted trillium:* three white petals with reddish-purple stripes; 5-20 inches high.

• *white trillium:* three large ruffed white petals, three leaves atop long stem; 6-20 inches high.

4 petals—

• *flowering dogwood:* four white petals, touch of rust on ends; tree 10-25 feet high.

• *toothwort:* four petals, white to pinkish, ½-inch flowers clustered atop slender stalk, three oval leaves bluntly toothed; 8-15 inches high.

• *wild lily-of-the-valley:* white flowers with four petals in dense spike atop stem; 2-6 inches high; red berries later in year.

5 petals—

• *Confederate violet:* five petals, white version of purple violet (see description above).

• *foamflower:* five petals, white with long stamens, flowers in clusters forming fuzzy cone-shaped spikes, leaves maplelike and hairy; 5-12 inches high.

• *great chickweed:* five deeply cleft petals that look like ten, white flowers ½-inch across, stems sprawling and tangled; 6-16 inches high.

• *sweet white violet:* five petals, white with maroon veins, two upper petals narrow and bent backwards, flower stalks reddish, leaves heart-shaped; 6-10 inches high.

• *trailing arbutus:* five petals, white to light pink, flowers trumpet-shaped, large leathery leaves trailing on ground.

• *wild strawberry:* five rounded white petals around yellow central disk, three oval hairy leaflets; 2-6 inches high.

6 or more petals—

• *dogtooth violet:* white flowers with six upswept petals, mottled leathery leaves at base of stalk; 6-12 inches high, also called "white trout lily."

• *bloodroot:* 8-12 oblong petals, white with golden center, 6-12 inches high; Native Americans used root sap as war paint.

• *white baneberry:* up to 10 spoon-shaped ¼-inch petals, white with hairy stamens, conspicuous purple eye, flowers in ball-shaped cluster on long stem; 1-2 feet high.

• *rue anemone:* two or three ½-inch flowers, 5-10 white petals with reddish stamens, surrounded by whorl of leaves on wiry stem; 2-8 inches high.

flowers in clusters—

• *clintonia:* creamy white bell-shaped flowers clustered atop stem, three shiny oval-shaped leaves at base; 8-16 inches high.

• *false Solomon's seal:* white starlike flowers in dense branching cluster at top of zigzag stem, leaves alternating; 2-3 feet high.

• *mountain laurel:* flowers delicate, white with pink edge in clusters; shrub 10-20 feet high.

• *pearly everlasting:* ½-inch flowers in clusters, pearly white with yellow tuft in center, stem and underside of leaves wooly-white; 1-3 feet high.

• *red elderberry:* creamy-white flowers in clusters; shrub 3-10 feet high.

• *serviceberry:* white flowers in drooping clusters, leaves elliptical and coarsely toothed; tree 30-40 feet high.

• *Virginia waterleaf:* densely clustered bell-shaped flowers, white to purple with long hairlike stamens; 1-3 feet high.

• *white fringed phacelia:* white bell-shaped flowers with fringe on edge of petals, grows in masses resembling patches of snow, 6 inches high.

White (continued)

bell-shaped flowers—

• *Carolina silverbell:* white bell-shaped flowers; shrub 10-30 feet high.

• *hairy Solomon's seal:* greenish-ivory flowers, elongated and bell-shaped hanging on end of arching stem; 1-6 feet high.

miscellaneous shapes—

• *daisy fleabane:* ½-inch daisylike flowers, white to pinkish with yellow central disk, leaves spatula-shaped and clustered at base; 1-5 feet high.

• *Dutchman's breeches:* white with yellowish bottom, waxy flowers with two spurs pointing upward in shape of a "V" carrotlike leaves at base; 5-10 inches high.

• *mayapples:* called "umbrella plants," white cup-shaped flower develops into a pale-colored, up to lemon-sized berry; plant 1-2 feet high.

• *sand myrtle:* white flowers on rocks at Charlies Bunion.

• *squirrel corn:* heart-shaped flowers, white with yellow on bottom, nodding carrotlike leaves around stem; 6-8 inches high, roots have tubers resembling kernels of corn.

• *wood anemone:* solitary ½-inch starlike flower, white with yellowish center on three-leaved stem, leaves divided into three or five leaflets; 4-12 inches high.

• *wood vetch:* ½-inch pea-shaped flowers, white with bluish tip, oval leaves on vinelike stem ending in a curling tendril; a variety of wild pea.

YELLOW

• *buttercup:* five petals, bright yellow with yellow center; 2-3 feet high.

• *cinquefoil:* five rounded yellow petals, toothed leaves in groups of five, crawling runners 6-20 inches long.

• *dandelion:* yellow composite ray flowers atop hollow stalks, seedhead fluffy white, sawtooth leaves clustered at base; 2-18 inches high.

• *downy yellow violet:* five petals, yellow, three lower ones veined with purple, hairy stem; 6-16 inches high.

• *golden ragwort:* 8-15 narrow petals, flowers golden with yellow center in branched cluster; 1-3 feet high.

• *Indian cucumber root:* stem with two whorls of leaves, usually three at top and five below, yellow flowers with six upswept petals, reddish-brown stigma; 1-3 feet high.

• *large-flowered bellwort:* yellow to orange bell-shaped flowers hanging from tips of leafy branches, leaves oval with pointed tips, 1-2 feet high; also called merrybells.

• *rattlesnake weed:* yellow dandelion-like flowers on stalk, maroon-veined spatula-shaped leaves hug ground; 1-2 feet high.

• *trout lily:* nodding orchidlike flowers, yellow with six upswept petals; 4-10 inches high, mostly seen along streams.

• *yellow stargrass:* 6 petals, yellow star-shaped flower at top of long spike stem, leaves lance-shaped and clustered at base; 3-7 inches high.

YELLOWISH-BROWN

• *squawroot:* looks like yellow-brown "pine cones" standing in clusters, small whitish flowers on cone; member of the cancer-root family, a parasite that grows mainly on the roots of weakened oak trees; 3-10 inches high.

Feel free to report wildflower sightings/locations for inclusion in this guide.

Guidelines for Trail Users

General Hiking Guidelines—

☑ Stay on the designated footpath at all times, and avoid taking shortcuts, which cause erosion. In camp, use established paths to the water source and privy. If the trail is muddy, resist the temptation to hike on the edge of the trail -- it just makes the muddy areas bigger.

☑ Pack out everything you carry in.

☑ Wash yourself, your clothes, and your dishes at least 100 feet from any water source. Do not use soap, even the biodegradable kind, in springs and streams, and empty dirty water well away from any water source. Keep your pet out of springs.

☑ Use a privy for solid waste. If no privy is available, dig a cat hole at least 50 feet from the footpath and 200 feet from water sources, and cover everything thoroughly afterwards. Urinate away from the footpath. Do not dispose of feminine hygiene items in privies or the woods. If traveling with a pet, bury its waste as you would your own.

☑ Camp only in designated camping or already-heavily-used areas. Avoid camping in fragile or seldom-used areas, and never camp in restricted areas or on private property. Always restore your campsite to its original condition before leaving.

☑ Use a stove for cooking. Avoid building campfires except at designated campsites. If you do build a fire, use only downed (dead) wood. Afterwards, extinguish thoroughly with water and stir the ashes around with water until they are cool to the touch.

☑ Group travel and overnight camping should be limited to 10 people maximum.

☑ Shelters and lean-tos are available on a first-come first-served basis. If you are first into a shelter, do not occupy all of the space. In bad weather, always try to make room. Don't smoke in the shelter. Pets should remain outside. Refrain from the use of alcohol or illegal drugs. Stay quiet from dusk until dawn.

☑ Sign your real name in Trail registers in case you need to be located in an emergency.

☑ Most hikers carry cell phones nowadays, but please be considerate if using one. Many hikers go to the woods to get away from the distractions of modern life. Keep it turned off, or keep the ringer on silent or vibrate. Use it only out of earshot of other hikers.

☑ Use the Golden Rule and common sense when interacting with townspeople and other hikers.

Acknowledgments

The Thru-hiker's Handbook continues the tradition of A.T. hikers from one year passing along information to a thru-hiker/editor who will make it available to those who hike the following year. Without the help of those who take the trouble to share information, this guide would not be as accurate. I would like to especially thank Chip "Old Goat" Cenci and Karen "Whisperer" Friedrichs for information sent in from the trail, and Jim "Skyline" Austin and Rodney "Rodman" Ketterman for the information provided about the area near Shenandoah National Park. I'd also like to thank a number of people who recommended facilities not in the 2009 *Handbook* and told me of errors I would have been very unlikely to pick up on my own.

Thanks is also extended to the many people who shared information on our *Trailplace. com* website that proved to be useful for this guide. There are just too many of you to list by name here, but your contributions are very much appreciated. As always, thanks is extended to the many members of the various A.T. clubs who provided valuable information about their Trail maintenance sections, to ATC staff members and regional staff, to the staff at Baxter State Park and other state and local parks, to postmasters in Trail towns, and to the owners and managers of the businesses and services listed herein for supplying data used to update the information about services and towns. A special thanks is extended to the Appalachian Trail Conservancy for providing mileage figures from the *A.T. Data Book 2010,* which were used to derive some of the mileage figures in this handbook, so that distances between points will be the same in both books.

THANK YOU ALL!

How to Give Feedback

Users of this guide are requested to give us feedback. We know things change during the year and we want to know about anything you find on the Trail while using this guide that is different from what we provide herein. Your corrections, suggestions, comments, and information for improving the accuracy of the 2010 edition can be sent to *<webmaster@trailplace.com>*.
